THE UNIVERSITIES
OF EUROPE
IN THE MIDDLE AGES

THE

UNIVERSITIES OF EUROPE

IN THE

MIDDLE AGES

BY THE LATE

HASTINGS RASHDALL

DEAN OF CARLISLE

A NEW EDITION IN THREE VOLUMES

EDITED BY

F. M. POWICKE

Regius Professor of Modern History
in the University of Oxford

AND

A. B. EMDEN

Principal of St. Edmund Hall, Oxford

VOLUME II

ITALY–SPAIN–FRANCE–GERMANY–SCOTLAND

ETC.

OXFORD UNIVERSITY PRESS

OXFORD
UNIVERSITY PRESS
AMEN HOUSE, E.C. 4
London Edinburgh Glasgow New York
Toronto Melbourne Capetown Bombay
Calcutta Madras
HUMPHREY MILFORD
PUBLISHER TO THE
UNIVERSITY

First edition 1895
New edition 1936
Reprinted photographically in Great Britain in 1942
by LOWE & BRYDONE, PRINTERS, LONDON, from
sheets of the new edition

CONTENTS OF VOLUME II

CHAPTER VI

THE ITALIAN UNIVERSITIES

CHAPTER VII

THE UNIVERSITIES OF SPAIN AND PORTUGAL

CHAPTER VIII

THE UNIVERSITIES OF FRANCE

CHAPTER IX

THE UNIVERSITIES OF GERMANY, BOHEMIA, AND THE LOW COUNTRIES

CHAPTER X

THE UNIVERSITIES OF POLAND, HUNGARY,
DENMARK, AND SWEDEN

CHAPTER XI

THE UNIVERSITIES OF SCOTLAND

THE MEDIEVAL UNIVERSITIES

CHAPTER VI

THE ITALIAN UNIVERSITIES

[DENIFLE, *Universitäten des Mittelalters, passim,* and see above, vol. i, pp. 88, 89; *Monografie delle Università e degli Istituti superiori* (published by the Ministry of Public Instruction, Rome, 1911–13); Fr. MONTE- FREDINI, *Le più celebri università antiche e moderne;* the bibliography in P. BARSANTI, *Il pubblico insegnamento in Lucca dal secolo xiv alla fine del secolo xviii,* Lucca, 1905; and especially the geographical survey in MANACORDA, *Storia della scuola italiana,* Milan, 1914, ii. 283–337; B. BRUGI, *Per la storia della giurisprudenza e delle università italiane,* Turin, 1915; F. NOVATI, *Storia letteraria d'Italia: Le origini,* continued and completed by A. MONTEVERDI, Milan, 1926, pp. 126–9; P. SILVANI, *Origine in Bologna e sviluppo in Italia dell'istituzione universitaria. Nota storica . . . nel xiv centenario del Digesto,* Bologna, 1933.

For the early schools, &c., A. DRESDNER, *Kultur- und Sittengeschichte des italienischen Geistlichkeit im 10. und 11. Jahrhundert,* Breslau, 1890; G. SALVIOLI, *L'istruzione pubblica in Italia nei secoli viii, ix e x,* ed. 2, Florence, 1912. For the later city-schools see MANACORDA, and, especially, R. DAVID- SOHN, *Geschichte von Florenz,* IV. iii (1927), 113 *sqq.*

No part of the history of medieval universities is more unmanageable by a foreign scholar than the Italian. Denifle laid a massive foundation, but a definitive treatise has yet to be written and can only be written in Italy itself. Moreover, in no other part of the subject is the separation between the history of the *studium generale* and of the educational life which surrounded it, and in which, in Italy at least, it was embedded, so difficult or so lacking in reality. Manacorda, in his stimulating book, has grasped this fact, but the defects of his work, which are more irritating to Italian than to foreign readers, show how hard it is, in the present state of the subject, to give a just and comprehensive survey of medieval Italian education. The juridical distinction between the *studium generale* and other local *studia* or schools was well understood and, with a few exceptions (e.g. Verona), is easily maintained; but, in the intimate civic life which characterized north and central Italy, the educational value of the schools maintained by the communes, or even of those illuminated by great private teachers, was sometimes as great as, or even greater than, that of the universities. The schools of Pisa, Florence, and Ferrara were recognized by the creation of *studia generalia,* the powerful corporation of teachers at Genoa (Manacorda, i. 145) was not, and the epoch-making work of Vittorino da Feltre at Mantua received only a 'paper' acknow- ledgement (below, p. 330), yet no one would maintain that schools of this type stood in anything like the same relation to the Italian *studia generalia* as the cathedral or grammar schools of France and England, or even of Germany, stood to Paris, or Oxford, or Vienna. In one respect, the civilians seem to have acknowledged an equality in status between recognized teachers, whether they were or were not teachers in a univer- sity. The privileges conferred in the Authenticum *Habita* of Frederick I were possessed by students only if they were members of a university

B

CHAP. VI.   (cf. TAMASSIA, *Odofredo*, p. 115 n.), but, if Manacorda is right, they could
convey some immunity to a teacher in the communal school of a small
town (Portovenere, 1260; Cuneo, 1416; see Manacorda. ii. 296, 318;
cf. i. 170, 206).

The co-operation of ecclesiastical, imperial, and civic authority in the
development of higher education, though it finds a parallel later in Germany, had more far-reaching effects upon public life in Italy. Rashdall
probably under-estimated the share of the episcopate and chapters in
university administration, and it was not part of his plan to trace the
influence of the law-schools, whether on papal or imperial behalf, in
Italian political history. We have tried to indicate the extensive literature
on the great importance of the jurists of Bologna in the expression of
imperial policy (see below, under Naples). A fact brought out by Denifle,
but not by Rashdall, is the large share taken by the emperors, especially
Charles IV, in the foundation of the Italian universities. Indeed, apart
from the diploma on behalf of Treviso, granted in 1318 by the anti-king,
Frederick III (*Mon. Germ. Hist.: Constitutiones*, v. 517), the imperial
bulls of Charles IV marked the entry of the emperor as a founder or
patron of universities: Arezzo and Perugia (1355), Siena (1357), Pavia
(1361), Florence (1364), and the 'paper universities' of Cividale (1353)
and Lucca (1369) whose charters begin and end the list (below, pp. 328,
329). See A. VON WRETSCHKO, 'Universitäts-Privilegien der Kaiser aus der
Zeit von 1412–56', in the *Festschrift O. Gierkes zum 70. Geburtstag*,
Weimar, 1911, pp. 793 *sqq.*; and R. SALOMAN in the *Neues Archiv*, xxxvii
(1912), 810–17.

When the history of medieval Italian universities comes to be written
and is definitively brought as a whole into relation with the history of
intellectual life, it will be possible to estimate more truly their literary and
philosophical as well as their legal and scientific contributions. We have
already referred to the importance of the theological *studia* of the various
orders of friars and, in a less degree, of the monastic orders (vol. i, p. 251).
The activity of these schools was part, and a great part, of the theological
life of Europe and deprives the suggestion, based upon the comparatively
late establishment of faculties of theology in the Italian universities, that
the Italians neglected theology, of much of its force. Yet, here also, work
needs to be done upon the study of theology in the universities before
the days of the faculties of theology. Manacorda has emphasized the
later development of the seminaries, which, from the sixteenth century
onwards, took, as distinct ecclesiastical institutions, the place of the short-
lived university faculties.]

Meaning
of *studium
generale*
in the
thirteenth
century.

AT this point it may be desirable, even at the risk of some
repetition, to remind the reader of the vagueness which
long attached to the afterwards definite and highly technical
conception of a *studium generale*. The word originally
meant simply a *studium* which was attended by scholars
from all parts. But as it was only for the study of the higher
subjects that it would be necessary for a student to take a long
journey in quest of adequate instruction, the term naturally
implied likewise a place of higher education and usually a

place where teaching was to be found in one at least of what chap. vi. came to be technically known as the superior faculties, with more or less definite implication of a plurality of teachers therein. Practically in the second half of the twelfth century it was only in a very few great centres—at first indeed, almost exclusively at Paris, Bologna, Salerno, and Oxford—that the highest education in such subjects was attainable. Soon, however, through various causes—intestine feuds at Paris and Bologna, the jealousy and ambition of neighbouring cities, the multiplication of masters in quest of employment, and the like—individual doctors or whole bodies of scholars began to transfer the traditions of the great mother-*studia* to other places. Henceforth it was natural that these places should arrogate to themselves, with more or less success, the rank of *studia generalia*, and, when they ventured to multiply doctors after the fashion of their parents, to claim for them the vague prestige attaching to teachers of the old archetypal schools. Moreover, as the mother-*studia* developed a more and more elaborate and complex organization, this organization was reproduced in the daughter-schools, and the term *studium generale* thus came more and more definitely to denote an organization of a peculiar type. When definite privileges—especially the privilege of dispensation from residence—came to be attached to students and teachers of *studia generalia*, recognition as a *studium* which conveyed these privileges became the most prominent *differentia*, and the way was prepared for that association of the term with a papally or imperially conferred *ius ubique docendi* which has been already sufficiently explained. All that it is necessary to emphasize here is the vague and fluid meaning which the term *studium generale* carried with it at the end of the twelfth and the beginning of the thirteenth centuries.

It is especially in northern Italy that the tendency of a great archetypal university to reproduce itself is exemplified. The number, independence, and rivalry of the cities in this region specially lent itself to the process. And their political autonomy may partially account for a more extended use of the term *studium generale* than is elsewhere observable. It

Small *studia generalia* numerous in Italy.

CHAP. VI. was natural for a city republic which drew students from half a dozen neighbouring cities to style its *studium* general, while it would not occur to the masters of an old cathedral city in France or England to claim such a title for their schools because it drew scholars from a neighbouring duchy or county, though not from foreign countries.[1] Hence in Italy we are obliged to treat as *studia generalia* many schools which were certainly not of more importance than northern *studia* which do not happen to be so described. It is a mere accident that we are obliged to include in our list of universities places like Reggio in Emilia and to exclude schools like Chartres and Laon, Lincoln and Salisbury, even Lyons and Reims, because they are not expressly called *studia generalia* in the twelfth or thirteenth century, and never afterwards acquired the organization and privileges which came to be associated with that term in the fourteenth. Even in Italy itself there may have been towns not expressly so called in any extant document which possessed schools of exactly the same type as those which are.

Claims of Modena.
These remarks may be illustrated by the difficulty of deciding upon the claims of Modena to a place among universities. We have already had occasion to speak of the secession of Pillius from Bologna to Modena[2] some time before 1182.

[1] Yet in a document of 1287 we still read that 'Quatuor Studia generalia ad minus sint in Italia, scilicet in Curia Romana, Bononiae, Paduae et Neapoli' (Renazzi, *Storia dell' Univ. degli Studj di Roma*, i. 30), which shows how dubious was the recognition of many of the *studia* mentioned below.

[2] Above, vol. i, p. 169: for the statement of Pillius, see Sarti, I. i. 84 *sq.* As to the importance of the school, see Tiraboschi, *Storia d. Lett. Ital.* iii. 638 *sq.*, and *Biblioteca Modenese* (Modena, 1781), i. 48 *sq.*; Muratori, *Rev. It. SS.* ix. 771, xv. 560, and *Antiq. Ital. Med. Aev.* iii. 905–6; Sillingardi, *Catalogus omn. Episc. Mutin.*, Modena, 1606, p. 91 (where it appears that Honorius III granted a faculty to absolve scholars for 'iniectio manuum' *c.* 1223); *Monumenti di storia patria della prov. Modenese*, Parma, 1864, Stat. i. Rub. 163. [On the schools and teachers at Modena see Manacorda, ii. 308; the teachers of law in the twelfth and thirteenth centuries may have had some relation with the episcopal school, though some at least were paid by the city authorities. From 1306 Modena had a municipal *studium* of law; see especially T. Sandonnini, *Di un codice del xiv secolo e dell'antico Studio modenese*, Modena, 1906, p. 112. A general study is Vicini, *Profilo storico dell'antico Studio di Modena* (Publicazioni della facoltà giurid. di Modena, x, 1926). See also Denifle, i. 296–8.]

As, however, there is no express evidence that Modena was
ever looked upon as a *studium generale*, it is best not formally
to include it in that category, though it is certain that during
most of the twelfth and the thirteenth centuries[1] there was a
very considerable *studium* of law in the place, for which its
doctors would probably have claimed whatever prerogatives
were enjoyed by such places as have next to be mentioned. It
is often spoken of in the same category as Reggio.[2] There
is, however, no evidence of graduation having taken place
at Modena, which establishes a clear difference between the
position of the school and that of its rival, Reggio. I shall
therefore treat Reggio, and not Modena, as the first of the
spontaneously evolved reproductions of Bologna.

§ 1. REGGIO

TACOLI, *Memorie storiche di Reggio*, Pt. iii, Carpi, 1769. [DENIFLE, i. 294–6.]

AT Reggio, as in so many other older law-schools of Italy,
the special school of law was a development of an ancient
school of rhetoric and grammar in that comprehensive and
quasi-legal sense in which those studies were understood in
the earlier Middle Age. It was here that Anselm the Peri-   Anselm
patetic studied in the first half of the eleventh century under   the Peri-
Sichelmus, a pupil of Drogo.[3]   To the year 1188 belongs a   patetic.
contract between the *podestà* and a certain Jacobus de Mandra
in which the latter undertakes to come to Reggio as a teacher

---

[1] Pillius, in describing his secession, uses the words 'Mutina quae
iuris alumnos semper diligere consuevit' (ap. Sarti, 1888, i. i. 84), but
Savigny's statement that Placentinus taught here earlier in the
twelfth century is due to a confusion with Mantua. Denifle, i.
296.

[2] Odofredus claims the privileges accorded by the civil law to
professors in *Regiae civitates* for
Bolognese professors who teach
'citra Aposam', not otherwise:
'Similiter et liberi eorum et uxores
debent habere immunitatem, non
qui docent leges Regii vel Mutinae:

immo est una proditio' (Dig. L.
xxvii, Tit. 1, ad verb. *Romae*, ap.
Sarti, i. i. 86; the text is very corrupt in the printed edition). [Cf.
Tamassia, *Odofredo*, p. 90.] Accursius likewise denies the privilege of the jurists of Modena and
Reggio, *ad loc.* (ed. Contius, 1576,
c. 258).

[3] 'Itaque tunc temporis apud
Regium ciuitatem magistrum meum
domnum Sichelmum, uestrum di-
scipulum, liberalibus disciplinis a
uobis studiosissime eruditum adii.'
Ep. Anselmi Peripat. ad Drogonem,
ap. Dümmler, *Anselm der Peripatetiker*, Halle, 1872, p. 18.

CHAP. VI,
§ 1.
Possible
Bologna
secession,
1188.

and to bring scholars with him.[1] It is only a conjecture, though a probable one, that the contemplated secession was from Bologna, and it is not certain, though equally probable, that it was ever carried out. It is, however, clear that at the beginning of the following century Modena and Reggio were the most formidable of Bologna's younger rivals. By 1210

Clearly a
studium
generale
in thir-
teenth
century.

Reggio was clearly recognized as a *studium generale* since a canon of Cremona is dispensed from residence to study there[2] —a privilege which could not be claimed except for study at a *studium generale*. A doctoral diploma has been preserved of the year 1276 which testifies to a regular college of doctors, regular examinations by the doctors under the presidency of

Extinction.

the bishop, and a *universitas scholarium*.[3] At the beginning of the fourteenth century, however, seventeen students of law complain that there is no longer a single doctor in the place, and that the salaries are no longer provided by the town; and this petition expressly speaks of the *studium* as having once been general.[4] After this we hear of one or two individual law-teachers here, as there were in almost every considerable Italian town;[5] but the *studium generale* had by this time entirely disappeared.

§ 2. VICENZA (1204)

SAVI, *Memorie antiche e moderne interno alle pubbliche scuole in Vicenza*, Vicenza, 1815. [DENIFLE, i. 298–300.]

Migration
from
Bologna,
1204.

THE University of Vicenza[6] owes its origin to a definite migration of scholars in 1204, and it is practically certain

[1] 'Cum scolaribus causa scolam tenendi et tenebit.' Tacoli, iii. 227.

[2] Denifle, i. 294. [A. Gaudenzi, in his paper 'Sulla cronologia delle opere dei dettatori bolognesi' (*Bullettino dell'Istituto Storico italiano*, xiv. 111), refers to statutes of the *studium* in the communal archives of Reggio, showing a communal organization in 1233.]

[3] Tacoli, iii. 215, 216. [The continuity of the *studium* under a civic organization is illustrated by the regulations of 1242: '*Quod fiat distributio scolarium a strata tam superius quam inferius*. Item statuimus quod fiat distributio scolarium

dominorum magistrorum tam a strata superius quam a strata inferius arbitrio bonorum hominum qui fuerint ad studium ordinandum.' MS. *Consuetudini*, vol. i, Statuti, f. 15ʳ.]

[4] 'Ut antiquitus fieri consuevit et maxime tempore boni status civitatis predicte, imo priusquam generale studium vigere consueverat in civitate predicta.' Tacoli, iii. 225. [5] *Ibid.* iii. 226.

[6] The only earlier trace of a *studium* is the mention of a theologian who taught in connexion with the cathedral in 1184. Savi, p. 12.

that the migration came from Bologna.[1] Its history as a *stu-*
dium generale is a short one; for it seems to have come to an
end in the year 1210,[2] though there was still, as in so many
other Italian towns, an intermittent *studium* of law and of
medicine here.[3] In later times, under the Venetian dominion,
an attempt to get it erected into a *studium generale* by John
XXIII failed, and the fact that such a document was considered necessary suggests, though it does not prove, that it
had ceased to be regarded as a *studium generale* at all.[4] But
during the short period 1204–9 the university appears to have
been a highly prosperous community. The scholars are said
to have actually built or rebuilt the church of S. Vitus, in
which they installed a body of Camaldunensian monks from
the convent at Verona; and in 1209—apparently upon the
departure of the Bolognese students—the patronage of it was
to the order. From the documents relating to this trans-
action it is clear that there were then four rectors and as many
nations or student-universities; while the number of the
doctors, the high position of many of the students, and the Four universities.
distant regions from which they had come testify to the temporary scholastic importance of the place.[5]

---

[1] The evidence for this is the
fact that two of the doctors had
taught at Bologna, taken in connexion with the measures adopted
at this time by the city of Bologna
which point to a secession. See
above, vol. i, p. 169.

[2] 'Huic succedit Bernardus vexil-
lifer papiensis. Sub isto venit stu-
dium scolarium in civitate Vicencie
et duravit usque ad potestariam
Domini Drudi' (i.e. 1204–10).
Maurisius, *Hist.* ap. Muratori, *Rer.
Ital. SS.* (new ed.) VIII. iv. 10.
'Studium generale fuit in civitate
Vicentiae, doctoresque in contrata
Sancti Viti manebant: ubi hodie
apud priorem Sancti Viti apparent
privilegia collati studii.' Antonius
Godi, *Chron.* (*ibid.* VIII. ii. 6).

[3] Some salaries were voted in
1261. Savi, pp. 116, 117. [See

Manacorda, ii. 336, and the authorities there cited, for some later
scholars.]

[4] Savi, pp. 117–19. The petition
contains the words 'cum alias
fuerit studium in civitate Vicentie'.

[5] See the documents in Mit-
tarelli, *Annales Camaldunenses*,
Venice, 1755, iv. 213, and App.,
pp. 260–3. The words relating to
the rectors (in 1205) are 'dilectis
in Christo fratribus magistro Ro-
berto de Anglia, et Guilielmo
Cancelino de Provincia, et Guar-
nerio de Alemannia, et Manfredo
de Cremona, rectoribus pro universitate', &c. In 1206 we have
only 'Mag. Robertus de Anglia et
dominus War. de Alamannia rectores universitatis scolarium in
Vicentina civitate commorantium'.
Among the representatives who

§ 3. AREZZO (? 1215)

[DENIFLE, i. 424–9; R. DAVIDSOHN, *Geschichte von Florenz*, IV. iii (1927), 134–5.]

CHAP. VI, WE have already seen[1] how a law-school was established in
§ 3. Arezzo in 1215 by one of the early seceders from Bologna,
Secession Roffredus of Benevento.[2] Though he could not have re-
from
Bologna, mained in the town long,[3] the *studium* had become by the
1215. middle of the century one of the most important of these
primitive outgrowths of Bologna. One of the earliest Italian
Statutes, codes of university statutes which have come down to us
1255. belongs to Arezzo, and is of the date 1255. Unfortunately
the constitution is totally different from that of the parent
university, on which it consequently throws little light. Here
the rector is elected and the statutes made by the doctors—
now seven in number—of law, medicine, and arts. The university originated in the secession of a master, not in a secession of students: hence the masters seem to have made their
own arrangements, and assumed to themselves the right of
conferring the *licentia ubique regendi*.[4]

The school of Arezzo might no doubt have claimed the
honours of a *studium generale ex consuetudine* while it lasted.
But no trace of its existence can be discovered from the middle
of the thirteenth century[5] till the *studium* was restored by the
immigration of deserters from Bologna, in consequence of an
Imperial Interdict,[6] in 1338. In 1355 a foundation-brief for a *studium*
charter,
1355. cede back the Church in 1209 only
one rector is mentioned—a 'Rector
de Ungaria', which suggests the
possibility of a fifth nation having
arisen.

[1] See above, vol. i, pp. 169, 170.

[2] 'Cum essem Arretii, ibique in
cathedra residerem, post transmi-
grationem Bononiae, ego Rofredus
Beneventanus iuris civilis professor an. Dn. MCCXV,' ap. Sarti
(1888), I. i. 133.

[3] Not after 1218, as appears from
Bulls of Honorius III: see Denifle,
i. 424 note.

[4] It is provided that no one is to
lecture 'nisi sit legitime, et publice,

et in generali conventu examinatus,
et approbatus, et licentiatus, quod
possit in sua scientia ubique regere'.
See the statute in Guazzesi, *Del-
l'antico dominio del vescovo di Arezzo
in Cortona*, Pisa, 1760, pp. 107–8
(reprinted by Savigny, iii, App.).
It should be observed that the
masters of grammar, dialectic, and
medicine seem here to act as a
single college.

[5] Except that provision is made
for the education of citizens by the
town-statutes of 1327. Denifle,
i. 425–6.

[6] 'Suo tempore (i.e. in 1338)
venerunt doctores Arretium ad

generale was obtained from the Emperor Charles IV.[1] All
trace of the revived *studium* is lost after 1373, and a fresh
imperial privilege which was granted in 1456 failed to restore
animation to the defunct university.[2]

§ 4. PADUA (1222)

RICCOBONUS, *De Gymnasio Patavino*, Padua, 1698, &c.; and in Graevius,
Antiq. Italiae, vol. vi, pt. iv; TOMASINUS, *Gymnasium Patavinum*, Udine,
1654; PAPADOPOLUS, *Historia Gymnasii Patavini*, Venice, 1726; J.
FACCIOLATI, *De Gymnasio Patavino Syntagmata XII*, Padua, 1752; and
Fasti Gymnasii Patavini, Padua, 1757; F. M. COLLE, *Storia scientifico-
letteraria dello studio di Padova*, Padua, 1824–5, four volumes (the most
elaborate of these histories); [F. M. COLLE, *Fasti Gymnasii Patavini . . .
vsque ad MDCCCXL perducti a J. Vedoura*, Padua, 1841; Denifle, i.
277–89.] A. GLORIA, *Monumenti della Università di Padova (1222–1318)*,
Venice, 1884, Padua, 1885; the same, *Monumenti della Università di
Padova (1318–1405)*, Padua, 1888; *Monumenti della Università di Padova
raccolti da Andrea Gloria e difesi contro il Padre Enrico Denifle*, Padua,
1888. [The records of examinations and degrees for the years 1406–50
are in C. ZONTA and G. BROTTO, *Acta graduum academicorum gymnasii
Patavini*, Padua, 1922.]

There are also two unimportant pamphlets, GROTTO DEGLI ERRI, *Della
Università di Padova, cenni ed iscrizioni*, Padua, 1841; and DALLE LASTE,
Brano storico postumo di Padova dall'anno MCCCCV al MCCCCXXIII,
Padua, 1844.

Until the discoveries of Denifle, no statutes were known (except the
town-statutes of 1460 referred to below) earlier than the Jurist Statutes
of 1463, printed with additions in 1551 (*Statuta spectabilis et almae Universitatis Iuristarum Patauini Gymnasii*); the *Statuta Dominorum Artistarum Achademiae Patavinae* belong to 1465, with additions of 1496.
[Cf. C. F. FERRARIS, *Il sigillo storico dell'università di Padova*, Padua,
1895, p. 5 note.] The Jurist Statutes of 1331 were printed by Denifle in
Archiv f. Lit.- u. Kirchengesch. d. Mittelalters, vi. 309 *sq.* In spite of the
number of its university historians, much of the history of Padua was
written for the first time by Denifle. Gloria collected some useful documents, but they are edited in a very inconvenient form. He was unwise
enough to enter into an unequal combat with Denifle.

legendum in iure canonico et civili;
et hoc quia non poterant stare
Bononiae, occasione excommunica-
tionis D. Papae, quando expul-
serunt legatum de terra. Habue-
runt salarium cc. florenorum auri.'
Annales Aretini, ap. Muratori, *Rer.
Ital. SS.* xxiv. 878. Cf. above,
vol. i, p. 215.

[1] The brief (ap. Denifle, i. 427)
declares that 'in eadem civitate
longo tempore studium viguerit
iuxta imperialia privilegia que

propter civilium guerrarum dis-
crimina dicuntur deperdita': of
such 'privileges' there is no trace.
By this time the idea that a *studium
generale* must be founded by Pope
or Emperor was so firmly established that, it being known that
Arezzo had once been a *studium
generale*, it was presumed that
there must have been a foundation-
brief.

[2] Guazzesi,' *loc. cit.*, pp. 109,
110.

There is an interesting study by J. A. ANDRICH, *De Natione Anglica et Scota Iuristarum Univ. Patav. ab a. MCCXII ... usque ad MDCCXXXVIII* (Padua, 1892).

[Much work on the University of Padua appeared in 1922, on the occasion of the seventh centenary. The *Archivio veneto-tridentino* issued a double fascicule devoted to the history of the university. This includes a study by B. BRUGI (pp. 1–92): 'L'università dei giuristi in Padova nel cinquecento.' Other publications include G. BROTTO and G. ZONTA, *La facultà teologica dell'università di Padova*, i, Secoli XIV e XV (Padua, 1922), and E. MORPURGO, *Memorie e documenti per la storia della università di Padova*, i (Padua, 1922). The collection of essays, *Omaggio dell'accademia polacca di scienze e lettere all'università di Padova* (Cracow, 1922), contains papers by A. Birkenmajer on Witelo, the thirteenth-century writer on optics (pp. 145–68), and by L. A. Birkenmajer on Copernicus (pp. 177–274) and the University of Padua.

To Andrich's book, noted above, add A. FAVARO, *Atti della nazione germanica di Padova* (Monumenti storici publicati dalla R. Deputazione veneta di storia, xix, 1911), and *Matricula et acta Hungarorum in universitatibus Italiae studentium*, i, Padua, 1264–1864, ed. by A. Veress (Fontes rerum hungaricarum, i, Vienna and Leipzig, 1915).

A. FAVARO, 'Per la storia dello studio di Padova: spigolature da archivi e da biblioteche', in *Nuovo archivio veneto*, n.s. xxxiv (1917), 252–90; the same, 'Lo studio di Padova nei diarii di Marino Sanuto', *ibid.*, n.s. xxxvi (1918), 65–128.]

By far the most important of the daughters of Bologna was the great University of Padua, which early proved a formidable rival of the mother university, and eventually surpassed it in everything but the incommunicable prerogative of greater antiquity. The famous Bologna jurist Martinus, or another of the same name, appears to have taught at Padua some time before the year 1169, when we hear of the election as bishop of Padua of a jurist who was teaching in 'the school of Martinus';[1] but, with the exception of this episode, we find no trace of a *studium generale* till the thirteenth century. The chroniclers say that the *studium* of Bologna was 'transferred to Padua in the year 1222'.[2] It is not improbable that law was taught at Padua at an earlier date, but its history as a *studium generale* begins with this year. We have seen to

---

[1] 'Qui tunc regebat in legibus in domo Martini de Goxo que erat iuxta maiorem ecclesiam Paduanam' (Gloria, *Cod. Dipl. Pad.*, Venice, 1879, pt. i, p. xcviii).

[2] 'MCCXXII . . . Hoc anno translatum fuit studium de Bononia Paduam.' *Regimina Paduae*

ap. Muratori, *Rer. Ital. SS.* (new ed.) viii. i. 305; *Antiq. Ital.* v. 1129. In 1223 Jordan of Saxony preached 'scholaribus apud Paduam' and induced thirty-three of them to enter his order. *Lettres de Jourdain de Saxe*, ed. Bayonne (Paris and Lyons, 1865), pp. 8, 12.

what a pitch the quarrels between the city of Bologna and the chap. vi, § 4. student-universities had been carried by the year 1220;[1] and it is quite possible that the chroniclers' statement is no very gross exaggeration. There may well have been a short period during which Bologna was practically deserted by students. No doubt such a secession cannot have lasted long; but, though a large proportion of the seceders probably returned to Bologna upon the re-establishment of peaceful relations with the town, a large body certainly remained behind. Later historians, anxious as usual to ascribe the origin of a university to some sort of authoritative charter or edict, represent the Emperor Frederick II as the author of the 'transference':[2] but it is certain that whatever attempts the Emperor made to crush the University of Bologna did not begin till 1225,[3] and then were inspired on the one hand by hostility to that city, and on the other by his desire to benefit his own creation at Naples; but not at all by any favour for Padua which was a member of the Lombard League no less than Bologna.

In 1226 we hear of a book, the 'Rhetorica Antiqua' of Buoncompagno, being read in the cathedral 'in the presence of the professors of civil and canon law, and of all the doctors and scholars dwelling at Padua'.[4] It is a singular fact that the next document relating to the new university should be a contract made in 1228 between the representatives of the students and the city of Vercelli for the transference of the *studium*

Contract for migration to Vercelli, 1228.

---

[1] Vol. i, p. 171.

[2] We have an interesting hint as to the reasons for the choice of Padua in Sarti (i. i. 402). The bishop of Padua 'Bononiae degebat' in 1222, and no doubt encouraged the project.

[3] *Corpus Chronicorum Bononiensium*, Muratori, *SS.* (new ed.) XVIII. i. 90; Sigonius, *Histor. Bonon.*, Frankfurt, 1604, p. 100. Cf. E. Winkelmann, *Acta Imperii inedita*, 1885, i. 263: (in A.D. 1227) 'sententias . . . revocamus et specialiter constitutionem factam de studio et studentibus Bononie.'

[4] 'Item datus et in commune deductus fuit Paduae in maiori ecclesia in praesentia domini Alatrini, summi Pontificis capellani, tunc Apostolicae sedis legati, venerabilis Iordani Paduani episcopi, Ciofredi theologi, cancellarii Mediolanensis, professorum iuris canonici et civilis et omnium doctorum et scolarium Paduae commorantium anno domini 1226 ultimo die mensis Martii.' Document in Rockinger, *Ueber die ars dictandi in Italien* (*Sitzungsberichte der bayerischen Akad. zu München*, 1861, p. 135).

to that place. Already the commune of Padua had proved
itself as unaccommodating as that of Bologna : and the emis-
saries of the students had been sent abroad to get better terms
for them elsewhere. Vercelli agreed to make over to the
students 500 of the best houses in the place,[1] and more if
necessary. This fact is one of the best evidences we have as
to the populousness of the early universities. Even now, when
the original single University of Bologna was throwing out
colonies in all directions, we find the possibility contemplated
of a migration from one of them of not less—at a very low
estimate of the average capacity of each house —than 2,500 or
3,000 students. It is provided that the rent of each house
should not exceed 19 *librae papienses*, and should be fixed by
taxors representing university and city. The city further
agrees to lend 10,000 *librae* to scholars at a fixed rate of
interest,[2] to secure a due supply of provisions, and to provide
'competent salaries' for one theologian, three civilians, four
canonists, two doctors of medicine, two dialecticians, and two
grammarians, the masters to be elected by the rectors and to
be compelled to teach gratuitously. The commune further
undertakes to send messengers to announce the establishment of the *studium* in all parts of Italy, to provide two copy-
ists (*exemplatores*) who shall transcribe books for the scholars
at a rate to be fixed by the rectors, and to grant certain immunities from taxation. The civil jurisdiction of the rectors
is recognized, the criminal jurisdiction being reserved to the
town magistrates. On the other hand the rectors and scholars
promise on behalf of 'all the other scholars of their rectorship'
that the whole *studium* of Padua shall come to Vercelli and
there remain for eight years; but there is a cautious proviso
that, if the scholars are not able to execute the contract (as
might easily happen if the Paduan authorities got wind of the
affair), they shall not be bound by its terms.

Migration
did not
destroy the
Paduan
studium.

There has been much controversy concerning the extent
to which this contract actually took effect. On the one hand

---

[1] 'Quingenta hospicia de melioribus, quae erunt in civitate et, si
plura erunt necessaria, plura.'

[2] Savigny's assumption that this
is to pay their debts at Padua is
perhaps too optimistic.

it has been supposed that it remained wholly unexecuted, on the other that the entire *studium* of Padua really was dissolved and transplanted to Vercelli for the eight years specified in the contract. It has now, however, been placed beyond all doubt that a considerable migration of students to Vercelli did take place, but that the *studium* at Padua by no means came to an end in 1228. Both facts are proved by evidence of the same character. The Dominican General, Jordan of Saxony, records the 'conversion' of twenty scholars at Padua in 1229[1]—the year after the contract; while in the same year he mentions the 'conversion' of the rector[2] of the German scholars at Vercelli and of twelve or thirteen masters or bachelors. Nor (as we shall see) did the separate existence of the colony absolutely cease with the expiration of the contract.

The Vercelli contract may be considered the *locus classicus* Early organization. for the condition not only of Padua but indirectly also of Bologna in the first half of the thirteenth century. It is not clear whether there were at Padua three rectors or four: at all events only three of them seem to have taken part in the proceedings. Nor does the head of each 'rectorship' seem necessarily to have been styled rector. We hear of a 'rector' of the French, English, and Normans, a 'proctor' of the Italian scholars, and a 'provincial' of the rectorship of Provençals, Spaniards, and Catalans. But in the university

[1] 'Ubi bene viginti et probi postea intraverunt.' *Lettres*, p. 100. Again about 1232, thirty were converted, several of them masters (*ibid.*, pp. 166, 168). So in a letter from a doctor then teaching at Padua to the Bolognese doctor Petrus Hispanus the latter is invited to come to Padua where 'habebitis multitudinem auditorum, ubi loci viget amoenitas et venalium copia reperitur' (Sarti, I. ii. 364). This letter, referred by Sarti to 1223, could not, according to Denifle (i. 278), have been written before 1228 or 1229. The earliest life of S. Antony of Padua (on the date of which see Denifle's note,

i. 283) speaks of the processions to his tomb in 1231 of 'litteratorum turma scolarium, quorum non mediocri copia uiget civitas Paduana' (*Portugaliae Monumenta SS.*, vol. i, Lisbon, 1856, p. 124); and in the next year, among those who wrote to the Pope to obtain the canonization of the saint was 'favore digna magistrorum atque scolarium universitas tota'. *Ibid.*, p. 125.

[2] 'Studens in iure canonico, Theutonicus, Spirensis canonicus, qui rector erat Theutonicorum scolarium Vercellis.' *Lettres*, p. 114. Cf. *ibid.*, p. 16.

CHAP. VI, which it was proposed to establish at Vercelli there were un-
§ 4. doubtedly to be four rectors, i.e. of the French, the Italians,
the Provençals, and one other. The name of the fourth
rectorship appears to have been left blank in the original
manuscript: in all probability it consisted of Germans.[1]

Decline, Although (as has been said) the Paduan *studium* was not im-
1237-60. mediately extinguished by the Vercelli secession, there can be
no doubt that during the atrocious tyranny of the da Romano
family (1237-60) it was reduced to a very low ebb, and at
Revival, length practically ceased to exist.[2] Its revival dates from the
1260. restoration of freedom in 1260 which was followed by an
exodus of students from Bologna on account of the war
between that city and Forlì, and of the papal interdict on the
Bologna schools. The contract made in 1262 between the
Bologna seceders and the city of Padua survives in a later
statute-book.[3] In the year 1260 the town statutes provide for
the payment of *salaria* to doctors, and make other regulations for the benefit of the *studium*: whereas the statutes of
the preceding year speak only of masters of grammar.[4] At

[1] The original is not extant. In
the first printed copy of it (Zac-
caria, *Iter litterar. per Italiam*,
Venice, 1762, p. 142), there is a
blank after the third 'Rectore'; in
a manuscript copy preserved at
Vercelli, the blank is filled up with
'Theotonicorum'. See Savigny's
note, c. xxi, § 116. It is printed
by Savigny in an Appendix: also
by Gloria, *Mon.* (1222-1318) ii. 5,
and below, Appendix III.

[2] 'Patavium (*sic*), quae nunc
Padua vocatur, in qua multo tempore viguit studium literarum.'
Albertus Magnus, *De natura locorum* in *Opera*, v (Lyons, 1652),
tr. 3, c. 2, p. 286. In 1253 there
is an allusion to a 'notary and
scholar' (Rolandino, ap. Muratori,
Rer. Ital. SS. (new ed.) VIII. i.
101, 108). Gloria has attempted
to show that the university statutes, organization, &c. were preserved uninterruptedly from 1222,

but his case, never a good one, is
rendered hopeless by the discovery
of the statutes mentioned below.
[3] See *Archiv*, vi. 513, cf. Facciolati, *Fasti*, pp. i, vi. In 1262 the
historian Rolandinus recounts his
reading of his chronicle before the
doctors and masters, some of whom
were described as 'doctores in
phisica et sciencia naturali', one
as 'magister in logica', others as
'magistri in grammatica et rhetorica', 'presente eciam societate
laudabili bazallariorum et scol-
larium liberalium arcium'. *Chron.*
xii. 19, ap. Muratori, *Rer. Ital. SS.*
(new ed.) VIII. i. 173.
[4] *Statuti del Comune di Padov*,
ed. Gloria, 1872, pp. 375, 380 (also
printed by Denifle, i. 800). In 1273
the youthful Cervottus Accursius
was hired from Bologna at the
liberal salary of 500 *librae*. Sarti,
I. i. 204. Cf. also Gloria, *Mon.*
(1222-1318), ii. 17 *sq.*

the same time a code of statutes was drawn up.[1] If any earlier
written statutes had ever existed, the very memory of them
had perished: the university made an entirely new start in
1260, and was naturally organized on the later Bologna model
with two universities of *ultramontani* and *citramontani*;
though during the year 1260, and often afterwards, both
rectorships were held by the same person.[2] The licence was
conferred by the bishop, and in 1264 a Bull of Urban IV
sanctioned the practice.[3] In 1346 the university further obtained from Clement VI a confirmation of its prerogatives as
a *studium generale*. But, lest this Bull should be regarded
as in any sense a 'foundation' of the university, it may be well
to add that the preamble recites that there had been a *studium
generale* in the place from time immemorial in all faculties
except theology.[4] The Bull for a *studium generale* in theology
was obtained in 1363 from Urban V.[5]

At the beginning of the fourteenth century (1306) the
numbers were largely increased by a temporary dispersion of

---

[1] See the Preface to the Statutes
of 1331. *Archiv*, vi. 380.

[2] *Ibid.*, p. 399. The rectorships
were permanently united in 1473.
[Between *c.* 1331 and 1463, the
ultramontani and *citramontani* of the
university of jurists had separate
seals; Ferraris, *op. cit.*, p. 9.]

[3] Riccobonus, f. 3; Tomasinus,
p. 9. [For the close connexion between the university and the bishop
and the latter's authority, cf.
Manacorda, i. 216; ii. 312. Cf. the
address in the alibi of Amaury de
Montfort, 17 April 1271: 'Johannes, miseratione divina episcopus
ecclesie Paduane, archipresbyter et
capitulum eiusdem ecclesie, doctores ac scolares universitatis Paduane, prior et conventus fratrum
Predicatorum', &c. (Ch. Bémont,
Simon de Montfort, Paris, 1884,
p. 365.]

[4] See the Bull in Riccobonus,
f. 4; Gloria, *Mon.* (1318–1405), ii.
25; and a confirmation by Eugenius IV in 1439 (Riccobonus, f. 6)

which confers all the privileges of
Paris, Oxford, Bologna, and Salamanca (mentioned in that order).
The jurist Baldus declares that
Padua was a 'Studium generale ex
consuetudine et sic privilegia eum-
dem (*sic*) sunt quae Bononiae ubi
est Studium generale ex consuetudine legitima'. So cited by Colle,
i. 51: but the printed edition
(Frankfurt, 1589, v, cons. 77) has
'privilegia eadem sunt, quae ex
privilegio Lotharii Imperatoris, ut
dicitur'. Baldus adds that the
bishop gave the 'licentia legendi hic
et ubique terrarum'. Cf. Riccobonus, f. 1.

[5] Printed in Gloria, *Mon.* (1318–
1405), ii. 55. [The date is 15 April.
The faculty of theology evolved an
organization slowly, and the convents in which the teaching took
place seem at first to have been
associated with the faculty of arts.
The statutes, now printed by
Brotto and Zonta, were drawn up
in 1424.]

CHAP. VI, the Bologna students in consequence of a legatine interdict
§ 4.   on the city which had expelled the Lambertazzi and the papal
          legate.[1] The troubles of the year 1322 again brought an influx
          of Bologna students who had temporarily seceded to Imola:
          and thither the city of Padua (like Siena and probably other
          Italian cities) sent envoys to negotiate a more permanent
          migration to their university. The treaty drawn up between
          the contracting parties on this occasion has been preserved,
          and makes it plain that the new-comers must have constituted
History of by far the larger part of the Paduan University. Besides con-
statutes. ceding the ordinary university privileges, the city agreed that
          the rectors should be allowed to bear arms (which was at
          present forbidden at Bologna), that scholars should not be
          tortured except in presence of the rectors, that clerks should
          be handed over to the ecclesiastical judge, that salaries should
          be provided for nine doctors of civil and canon law as well as
          for the permanent officials of the *studium*, and lastly that
          the university should henceforth be governed by the Bologna
          statutes.[2] This last provision was found difficult of execution,
          as the seceders had omitted to bring with them a copy of
          their statutes; and the law of the university continued in a
          state of great confusion till the year 1331, when a new code
          was prepared, taken mainly from the then current statutes of
          Bologna, but partly from the older Paduan code.[3] These
          statutes were discovered at Gnesen and published by Denifle.[4]

[1] 'Idem vero legatus (Napuleo
de Ursinis) maximos contra prae-
dictos Bononienses promulgavit
processus, et generali studio et
honoribus et privilegiis pariter
privavit: et fere Scholares universi
cum suis Doctoribus iverunt Paduam.' *Annal. Caesenat.* ap. Muratori, *Rer. It. SS.* xiv. 1127.

[2] The contract is preserved in
the statutes, *Archiv*, vi. 523 *sqq.*

[3] *Ibid.*, pp. 523–34. Another
curious provision is the arrangement that the city should procure
a merchant from Venice to go to
Bologna and fetch the books and
other effects of the students, left
behind them in their hurried flight.

[4] *Ibid.*, pp. 309 *sq.*, 523–6. The
statutes were found in the Chapter
Library of Gnesen by Prof.
Nehring of Breslau. They bear the
date of 1301, but Denifle has shown
that they really belong to 1331.
These statutes reveal with peculiar
clearness the method by which the
student-domination was established. An offending doctor 'pro-
hibeatur publice a legendo, et
scolaribus precipiatur, ne ipsum
audiant in virtute prestiti iura-
menti', and an offending scholar
'proclametur per scolas quod nullus
doctor ipsum in scolis tenere debeat et in eius legere presencia in
virtute prestiti sacramenti' (*ibid.*,

The statutes of 1432 appear in the printed edition of 1551.

CHAP. VI, § 4.

The general resemblance of the Paduan statutes and constitution to those of the parent university will make it unnecessary to give any detailed account of the former. A few points of difference may be noticed. The universities of law were divided into nations more symmetrically than at Bologna.[1] Each university had ten votes, and each vote represented a nation; the Germans alone had two votes.[2] The exclusion of citizens from the universities was maintained as at Bologna:[3] but there was here no counterbalancing monopoly for citizen-professors. On the contrary, citizens are expressly excluded by the statutes from the salaried chairs, though their language shows that the commune had made an attempt to thrust its citizens into them without election by the students. The statutes provide that the salaried doctors should be nominated by the *tractatores studii* who administered the funds provided by the city, but should be formally elected by the students.[4] There was a doctoral college as at Bologna, but here civilians and canonists belonged to the same corporation. At one time the *doctores collegiati* were limited to twelve, the number was afterwards

Constitution compared with Bologna.

p. 486); and this prohibition involved social excommunication: 'qui privatus est ab Universitate, intelligatur esse privatus comodo singulorum' (*ibid.*, p. 491). These statutes are also interesting as showing that there were regular university sermons at the Dominican church here as doubtless in other Italian universities (*ibid.*, p. 479).

[1] *Ibid.*, p. 399.

[2] But there is a trace of another, perhaps older, division of each University into four 'generales' or 'principales nationes' (*ibid.*, pp. 466, 482). Cf. above, vol. i, pp. 154–6.

[3] The *ultramontani* have also a certain superiority; since if the rectors issued contradictory commands, the doctors are to obey the ultramontane rector. *Archiv*, vi. 399.

[4] *Ibid.*, pp. 417–22. The bargains with doctors by the scholars themselves, however, continued: 'ne aliquis rubore alterius consocii sui confusus in promissionibus agravetur, inhibemus singulis scolaribus, ne quis doctori suo in diebus colecte aliquid promittat nec in libro aliquam summam scribat nec publice dare aliquam pecuniam vel alia exenia debeat vel presumat, sed quilibet sine aliqua proclamatione secrete offerat et det suo doctori prout sibi visum fuerit expedire' (*ibid.*, p. 471). The *collecta* must be between twenty and forty *aquilini* (*ibid.*, p. 472).

CHAP. VI, increased to twenty, then to twenty-five, then to thirty. In
§ 4.   1382 all restriction of number was removed.[1]

Medicine   In the earlier portion of our period the university of
and arts. medicine and arts was entirely subordinate to the university
of canon and civil law.[2] Both professors and scholars were
compelled to swear obedience to the statutes of the jurists;
and there was an appeal from the medical rector either to the
ultramontane or citramontane rector of jurists (according to
the nationality of the respondent), or to the *reformator studii*;
and fees were paid upon matriculation or graduation to the
superior university. Such is the state of things confirmed or
established by an agreement of 1360. The agreement itself
probably arose out of some resistance on the part of the
inferior university; and another revolt took place at the end
of the century. At last in 1399, through the mediation of
Francis of Carrara, son of the reigning prince, the jurists
consented to renounce their unnatural supremacy; but the
appeal to the jurist rector was maintained.[3] It should be
added that the relation of the medical university to the
college was here decidedly different from that which obtained
at Bologna. In a documen. of 1393 the college enforces an
oath of obedience to its prior or provost upon all students as
well as upon the professors.[4] In the university of medicine
and arts the rector's jurisdiction extended to all criminal cases
except such as involved mutilation.[5] This university was

[1] Gloria, *Mon.* (1318–1405), ii.
29, 30. The college was now confined to Paduan citizens *or* salaried
professors. Earlier (1303), it would
appear that there were two colleges
(*ibid.*, p. 60).

[2] The artist-rector was also to
receive the hood from one of the
jurist rectors, after receiving authority so to do from the 'cancellarius studii'.

[3] It was on this occasion, by way
of compensation for their loss of
fees, that the prince presented the
university building to the jurists.
Gloria, *Mon.* (1318–1405), ii. 342–
5. See also the document in *Ar-

chiv*, iii. 395 *sq.* The *reformator* at
this time was an ecclesiastical member of the Carrara house. From a
document of 1400 (Gloria, *loc. cit.*,
p. 374) it appears that the *conductiones* were managed by three
tractatores appointed by the commune.

[4] Gloria, *loc. cit.*, pp. 271, 272.
In an earlier document of 1306 the
scholars are enjoined to obey the
prior by the bishop. Gloria, *Mon.*
(1222–1318), i. 145; ii. 63. The
scholars protested, and the bishop
suspended the mandate.

[5] *Stat. Artist.*, f. vi *b*. The jurist
statutes (*Stat. Jur.*, f. 20) simply

divided into seven nations, of which only one was ultra- CHAP. VI,
§ 4.
montane.[1]

In all the universities 'servants and mercenaries' were ex- Disquali-
fication of
poor or
youthful
students.
cluded from a vote, while those who were sent to the uni-
versity by charity (*alienis sumptibus*) were incapable of office.
Boys under thirteen were disfranchised in the artist university, those under fifteen by the jurist statutes.[2]

Padua did not possess a college till 1363, when the *Col-* Colleges.
legium Tornacense was established for six students of law by
a Bolognese citizen, Petrus de Boateriis.[3] The other colleges
founded at Padua up to 1500 were the *Collegium Jacobi de
Arquado* (1390), an endowment for Cypriots in 1393, the
Collegium Pratense or *Ravennense* (1394), the *Scholares
Auximani* (1397), the *Collegium Ridium* (1398), the *Collegium
Curtosii* (1412), the *Collegium Spinelli* (1439), the *Collegium
Engleschi* (1446), and the *Scholares Tarrisiani* (1454). All
these colleges were small, the largest apparently being the
Collegium Pratense with twenty students. As in most other
flourishing Italian universities, the number of colleges
increased largely during the sixteenth and the first half of
the seventeenth centuries; at Padua twenty such foundations
were established between 1512 and 1653.[4]

During the earlier part of its existence the university was Increasing
fame.
dependent for its prosperity upon the troubles of its great
neighbour, Bologna. While actual secessions from Bologna
lasted, it practically took the place of the Bologna *studium*.
In 1274 for instance, during the war with Forlì, the canons
of the Council of Vienne were officially communicated to
Padua.[5] But gradually, with the declining fame of the
Bologna doctors and the incessant disputes with the Bolognese citizens in the first quarter of the fourteenth century,

confer ordinary jurisdiction; but no
doubt at this time the jurist rectors
must have possessed at least as
much power as the medical.

[1] *Stat. Artist.*, f. xiii.
[2] *Stat. Jur.*, ff. 41 a, 45 b; *Stat.
Artist.*, ff. i b, viii b.
[3] Facciolati, *Syntagmata*, p. 120.
[4] *Ibid.*, pp. 124–51; Gloria,

Mon. (1318–1405), ii. 76, 289, 331,
352. As to the endowments not
styled colleges in the above list, it
is not clear, though probable, that
the scholars were obliged to live
together.
[5] Gloria, *Mon.* (1222–1318), ii.
28. Cf. Pez, *Thes. Nov. Anecd.* i,
c. 430.

CHAP. VI, Padua acquired a more independent and permanent reputa-
§ 4.   tion, and eventually rose to the position of the first university
in Italy. Its progress was in no way retarded by the subjection of the city to the dukes of the Carrara family in 1322 or
to the Venetians in 1404. It was from Francis Carrara, in
1399, that the university received for the first time a building
of its own :[1] while the ox-tax and the waggon-tax were assigned
for the payment of the doctors.[2] The Venetian government
likewise adopted the policy of patronizing and encouraging
the university, and largely increased the salaries.[3] Four
Paduan citizens were long allowed to act as *reformatores* or
tutores studii,[4] while the election of professors remained,
nominally at least, in the hands of the students till 1445, and
in the case of some chairs till *circa* 1560.[5] An edict inflicting

[1] Tomasinus, p. 18; *Stat. Jur.*,
f. 162; Muratori, *Rer. Ital. SS.*
xii. 974; and above, p. 18, n. 3. It
was on the invitation of James of
Carrara that Petrarch took up his
abode in Padua as a canon of the
cathedral: but he had no official
connexion with the university,
to whose outlook he was opposed
(cf. above, vol. i, pp. 264–5). It
is noticeable, however, that a chair
of Greek was established before
1465, *Stat. Artist.*, f. xxii. [Padua
flourished greatly as the home of
Averroistic science and medicine
from the days of Peter of Abano
(†1315) till those of Pomponazzo
(†1525). Pico of Mirandola's criticism of the former—'homo con-
gerere plura natus quam digerere'
—illustrates the attitude of the
humanists and has much truth in
it, but it would give a false impres-
sion of the vigour and influence
of the University of Padua in the
fourteenth and fifteenth centuries
if we were to regard it merely as the
home of lost causes. See Michele
Savonarola, *Libellus de magnificis
ornamentis regiae civitatis Paduae*
(Muratori, *SS.* xxiv. 137 *sqq.*),
written about 1445 by the famous
physician, grandfather of the more

famous Girolamo Savonarola; also
Duhem, *Le Système du monde*, iv.
229–305 *passim*. Useful bibliogra-
phy in Ueberweg-Geyer, pp. 613,
614, 618, 786. Cf. L. Thorndike,
*History of Magic and Experimental
Science*, ii. 874–97; and, for
Michele Savonarola, iv. 183 *sqq.*]

[2] Tomasinus, p. 19 *sq.* Hence
no doubt the name of the university building, *Il bo.*

[3] *Ibid.*, p. 18 *sq.*

[4] *Ibid.*, p. 25. It was not till
1517 that a board of three Venetians took their places. *Ibid.*, p. 26.

[5] Riccobonus, f. 8 *b*; Tomasinus,
p. 136; *Stat. Jur.*, ff. 59, 62; *Stat.
Artist.*, f. xx *b*. In 1467 some of
the chairs were assigned to Paduan
citizens and a share in their appointment to the Paduan civic
authorities. The consent of the
Venetian government had, of
course, been required before. *Stat.
Artist.*, f. xxiii *b*. Specimens of the
rotuli containing the names of
the elected professors which were
annually sent to Venice, are given
in Tomasinus, p. 155 *sq.* The appointments to the elective chairs
at the time of the printed jurist
statutes were made by the rector
and *consiliarii* (*loc. cit.*).

a month's imprisonment upon a householder in whose house a student should be found shut up 'to prevent his attending the balloting', suggests a comparison with the most hotly contested of old English parliamentary elections.[1]

Among other honorary privileges, Venice conferred on the rector the right to wear a robe of purple and gold, and, upon resignation of his office, the title of doctor for life with the golden collar of the order of S. Mark.[2] It was under Venetian tutelage that Padua reached the zenith of her glory, becoming in the fifteenth and sixteenth centuries one of the two or three leading universities in Europe. Venetian subjects were forbidden to study elsewhere than at Padua, and eventually a period of study there was required as a qualification for the exercise of public functions at Venice.[3] Padua became in fact the university town or, as Renan has styled it, the 'quartier latin' of Venice: while the tolerance which, under the protection of the great commercial republic, long defied the fury of the Catholic reaction, attracted an exceptional number of students—especially medical students[4]— from England and other Protestant countries, even when the days of medieval cosmopolitanism were elsewhere rapidly passing away.[5]

§ 5. NAPLES (1224)

The fullest special treatment of this university is in G. ORIGLIA, *Istoria dello Studio di Napoli*, Naples, 1753. Cf. also SIGNORELLI, *Vicende della Coltura nelle due Sicilie*, Naples, 1784, ii. 244 *sq.*; iii. 28, &c. Many

---

[1] *Stat. Artist.*, f. xxxiii *a*. (Such episodes are, I believe, not unknown in Scotch rectorial elections at the present day.) From the earlier statutes of 1331 we learn that 'evenit experiencia unum interdum ponere plures ballotas in piside'. *Archiv*, vi. 481.

[2] Conringius, *Diss. Acad.* v, ed. Heumannus, 1739, p. 164.

[3] The first enactment dates from 1468 (*Stat. Jur.*, f. 51 *b*), the second from 1479. Riccobonus, f. 10 *b*.

[4] At an earlier period we find patients coming from long distances to be treated by the Paduan physicians. In 1396 a German

came from Halle to be cured of asthma; after spending nine months under the care of a German M.D. at Padua, he is said to have been cured by Bartholomeus de Mantua. Gloria (1318–1405), ii. 306.

[5] See Andrich, *passim*. There was a considerable number of English and Scotch students here even in the eighteenth century. The English and Scotch nations continued to exist till 1738. According to Itter, *De honor. s. gradibus acad.*, p. 1541, Padua, as early as 1409, was liberal enough to bestow its medical doctorate upon a Jew!

CHAP. VI, documents are printed in HUILLARD-BRÉHOLLES, *Historia Diplomatica*
§ 5. *Frid. II*, Paris, 1852, &c.; and J. C. DEL GIUDICE, *Cod. Diplomatico del regno di Carlo I e II d'Angiò* (Naples, 1863), vol. i, pt. i, 250 *sq.*

[Apart from a collection of studies by F. TORRACA and other writers, *Storia della università di Napoli*, Naples, 1924, which summarizes existing knowledge, no comprehensive history of the university has yet appeared. There are short accounts of the foundation in DENIFLE, i. 452–61; KAUFMANN, i. 324–35; S. D'IRSAY, i. 134–5; cf. also HASKINS, *Studies in Mediaeval Science*, pp. 250–1; the same, *Studies in Mediaeval Culture*, pp. 139–41. Helpful contributions will be found in a rectorial address by E. WINKELMANN, *Ueber die ersten Staatsuniversitäten* (Heidelberg, 1880); H. NIESE, 'Zur Geschichte des geistigen Lebens am Hofe Kaiser Friedrichs II', in the *Historische Zeitschrift*, cviii (1912), especially pp. 520 *sqq.*; K. HAMPE, 'Zur Grundungsgeschichte der Universität Neapol', in the *Sitzungsb. d. Heidelberg. Akad. d. Wissenschaften*, 1924, Abt. x; and especially E. KANTOROWICZ, *Kaiser Friedrich der Zweite*, Erganzungsband (Berlin, 1931), pp. 51–2, 114–26 *passim*, 266–73. Some documents of the Angevin period are printed by G. M. MONTI in the *Archivio storico per le Province Napoletane*, n.s. xix, xx (1933–4), esp. xx. 137–57.

The constitution of Frederick II (1225), in which he deprived Bologna of the *studium* and invited professors and students to come to Naples, was, until 1908, only known through its revocation in 1227 (above, p. 171 n. 5). It was found by A. GAUDENZI and published by him in 1908 in the *Archivio storico italiano*, 5th series, xlii. 352.]

Creation of universities by Pope and Emperor. WE have already seen[1] the important influence which was exercised upon the whole theory of a university, and the mode in which universities could originate, by the efforts of the Empire and the Papacy to call *studia* into being for purposes of policy, and to create by a stroke of the pen that 'generality' which had hitherto been secured only by educational efficiency and widespread appreciation. In these efforts the Empire took the lead. The University of Naples was the first university in Italy which was founded at a definite time by a definite charter, and the first university in any part of Europe to be so founded, with the partial exception of Palencia, which was founded, though not chartered, by the Castilian king Alfonso VIII in 1212–14.

Foundation of Naples, 1224.

Motives of Frederick II. Bologna, though its university was in no sense the creation of the Papacy, was a Guelf city, and the attempt to create a powerful rival to the great Italian law-school originated with the highly cultivated Emperor Frederick II, the friend of learning, the enemy of civic liberty, the mortal enemy of the Papal See. His chief agent in carrying out the scheme was

[1] See above, vol. i, p. 8.

his chancellor, the famous Piero della Vigna.[1] If any precedent were wanted for the assumption by the Emperor of
an ecumenical jurisdiction in matters scholastic, it was supplied by Frederick I's celebrated authentic *Habita*.[2] The
Bull of foundation[3] was issued in 1224, just on the eve of the
outbreak of the great struggle with the revived Lombard
League: and Frederick's Neapolitan and Sicilian subjects
were forbidden henceforth to resort to any other school.
If Frederick's hostility to the north-Italian cities was in a
measure the inspiring motive of the foundation, the war in
which that hostility culminated was the cause of its failure.
By 1239 a 'reformation', which probably meant practically
a new beginning of the *studium*, had become necessary.[4]

'Reforma-
tion', 1239.

[1] [The intentions of Frederick
are expounded in the letter an-
nouncing the foundation (Huillard-Bréholles, *Hist. Diplom.* ii.
450), and especially in the letter to
Bologna, edited by Gaudenzi. In
the latter he insists on the unity
of imperial power, and that those
who resist the statutes of the prince
'divine ordinationi aperte contra-
dicunt'; as the university at
Bologna has attempted to thwart
the new *studium* at Naples,
founded 'ad generale commodum
omnium qui studere voluerint', he
orders all teaching to cease there
within four months under penalty
of *infamia*. The close connexion
between the foundation at Naples
and the imperial court—its policy,
juristic atmosphere, literary forms
and personnel—has been the theme
of many recent studies. For a few
years at any rate, Naples had 'a
place in the history of medieval
thought'. Bologna had hitherto
been the centre from which the
new legal and political tendencies
had come. Piero della Vigna and
the great jurist Roffred of Benevento (who was sent to Naples from
the imperial court, with Peter of
Isernia, to take the lead there) had
studied at Bologna. The Emperor

now hoped to train his jurists,
dictatores, and scholars at Naples.
See especially Niese's article and
the excursuses in Kantorowicz's
volume of notes and discussions
(pp. 266–73); also E. Besta, 'Il
primo secolo della scuola giuridica
napoletana', in *Nuovi studi medie-
vali*, iii. 7–28, and E. M. Meijers,
Juris interpretes saeculi XIII
(Naples, 1924). A good introduction to a criticism of the considerable literature on the wider political
and intellectual movements at
Frederick's court will be found in
Helene Wieruszowski's *Vom Im-
perium zum nationalen Königtum*
(Munich and Berlin, 1933), especially pp. 58–140 *passim*.]

[2] Denifle, i. 454.

[3] The documents are printed in
Huillard-Bréholles, ii. 448–53;
Origlia, i. 77. Cf. Richard of S.
Germano (*Mon. Germ. Hist.: Scrip-
tores*, xix. 344).

[4] See the documents in Huillard-Bréholles, iv. 497 (an invitation addressed to the Bolognese
students), v. 493 *sq.*: Origlia, i.
94 *sq.* Origlia (i. 43), by ascribing
to Frederick's original foundation
documents which belong to this reformation, traces back the origin of
the university to a still earlier period.

CHAP. VI,   All faculties were nominally included in the new university:
§ 5.   but it appears that theology was (as usual in Italy) taught only
by friars, and that no promotions in theology took place by
Second   virtue of the Imperial Bull.[1]   We have already noticed the
failure.   attempt of Conrad IV in 1253 to transfer the *studium* altogether to Salerno: but it is very doubtful whether there was
by this time any *studium* left to transfer.   Denifle thinks that
the Neapolitan *studium* did not outlive its founder,[2] though
during its short spell of life no less a man than S. Thomas
was numbered among its scholars.[3]   The *studium* was a
purely artificial creation, not the outcome of any spontaneous
Second   or genuine educational movement.   Its third lease of life
reforma-   dates from the 'reformation' by King Manfred in 1258–9.[4]
tion,   It was not, however, till the accession of Charles of Anjou
1258–9.   in 1266, when a real reform was carried out with the support
and encouragement of Clement IV,[5] that the university began
to enjoy even a really continuous existence and a modest
prosperity.   Naples, long the only university in southern
Italy, became the university town of a part of Europe which,
after the decline of the medical school at Salerno, played
but little part in the intellectual movements of the Middle

[1] When the Dominicans left
Naples in consequence of the King's
dispute with the Pope in 1234, the
university applied for a theological
teacher to the Benedictines of
Monte Casino. Origlia, i. 102.
But in 1332 John XXII authorizes
the extraordinary graduation of a
friar in theology 'non obstante quod
forsan in eodem studio magistri
promoveri non consueverunt in
facultate iam dicta'. Bull ap.
Denifle, i. 460. The first notice of
a secular D.D. occurs in 1451.
Origlia, i. 248.

[2] Denifle, i. 457. Conrad orders
that the 'studium quod *regebatur*
apud Neapolim, regatur in Salerno'.
Orlando, *Un codice di leggi e di-
plomi Siciliani*, Palermo, 1857,
p. 58.

[3] *Acta Sanctorum*, March, i.
660. [Cf. Grabmann, 'Thomas von

Aquino und Petrus von Hibernia',
in *Philos. Jahrbuch*, 1920, pp. 347–
62, and the literature noted in
Ueberweg-Geyer, p. 744.]

[4] See the documents in Origlia,
i. 104 *sq.*

[5] *Ibid.* i. 131 *sq.*; Giudice, i.
250. Cf. the Bull of Clement IV,
sometimes wrongly ascribed to
Gregory X (see Denifle, i. 459),
printed in Martène and Durand,
Ampliss. Collect. ii. 1274. The
term *universale studium* is here
used for *studium generale*. [In 1272
Charles of Anjou addressed to the
masters and scholars of Paris and
Orleans a glowing description of
the advantages possessed by the
refounded *studium generale* at
Naples; Giudice, i. 252; Fournier,
i, no. 10; an English translation by
D. L. Mackay in *American Historical
Review*, xxxvii (1931–2), 515–16.]

Age. The position and climate of the crowded city must CHAP. VI, § 5. have made it, during a great part of the year, an unsuitable residence for students from any more northern region.

The University of Naples was the creation of despotism Organization: dependence on Crown. and was habitually treated as such.[1] There is no parallel in medieval history for such an absolute subjection of a university, in the minutest as well as the most important matters, to the royal authority. It was placed under the immediate superintendence of the royal chancellor till the time of Ferdinand II (1497), when the King's grand chaplain became governor of the university.[2] In the causes of scholars the jurisdiction belonged to a royal official appointed for the purpose, the *iusticiarius scholarium*; but in civil cases the imperial privilege of trial by the scholar's own master or by the archbishop was respected, and in criminal cases the justice was assisted by three assessors chosen by the scholars —one by the *ultramontani*, one by the Italians, the third by the Neapolitan subjects or *regnicolae*.[3] Whatever corporate life was possible to a university placed in this humiliating position belonged to the professors and scholars together,[4] as at Montpellier and other universities intermediate between the Bologna and the Parisian types. We do not, however, hear of an election of rector or rectors till the fourteenth century.[5] The promotions were carried out under the

---

[1] The only code of statutes printed by Origlia is contained in the royal edict of Charles I in 1278. Origlia, i. 219 (cf. i. 81, 221).

[2] *Ibid.* i. 287.

[3] Document of 1266. Giudice, i. 255; Origlia, i. 81–3, 193 *sq.* [The justiciar can be traced back to Frederick's time; see Kaufmann, i. 334 note. Kaufmann gives a good account of the minute regulation of the university.]

[4] As in other Italian *studia* the doctors of each faculty also formed separate colleges, at least from the time of Joanna II who granted them charters (Origlia, i. 222 *sq.*). The colleges of doctors were confined to Neapolitan subjects and mono-

polized the right of promotion.

[5] In the document of 1291 printed by Origlia (i. 201), he appears to have misunderstood the expression *ad regendum* as an allusion to the rectorship. He speaks of allusions to a rector earlier in the fourteenth century, but the first that appears in his documents is in 1338, when the *rectores studii* are mentioned (p. 182). It is not, however, quite certain that these were elective rectors in the usual sense, and where we hear of 'puncta danda per Vicecancellarios Rectoris studii', the word 'rector' must mean the King's Grand Chancellor, if indeed the text is not corrupt.

CHAP. VI, superintendence of the grand chancellor after examination by
§ 5. the doctors in the presence of the royal court, the doctoral
diploma or licence running in the king's name.[1] On one
occasion, indeed, royal interference was carried to the unprecedented pitch of ordering a re-examination of the whole
staff of regents, when those who failed to satisfy the examiners
were summarily deprived both of degree and salary.[2] The
university was in fact even more completely a mere department of state than the modern university of France. But
a certain measure of freedom was essential to healthy university life: Naples may possibly have been in its later days
a not inefficient educational institution, but it has no place
in the history of medieval thought.[3]

§ 6. VERCELLI (1228)

VALLAURI, *Storia delle Università degli studi del Piemonte*, Turin, 1845,
i. 17 *sq.*; SAULI, *Sulla condizione degli Studi nella Monarchia di Savoia* in
Memorie della r. Academia delle Scienze di Torino, 2nd ser., vi, Turin, 1844;
MANDELLI, *Il Comune di Vercelli nel Medio Evo*, Vercelli, 1857–8, iii.
1–50; BAGGIOLINI, *Lo Studio Generale di Vercelli nel Medio Evo*, Vercelli,
1888; BALLIANO, *Della Università degli studi di Vercelli*, Vercelli, 1868;
G. COGO, *Intorno al trasferimento della Università di Padova a Vercelli*,
Padua, 1892. Mandelli is the most important source for documents.
[DENIFLE, i. 290–4.]

Migration IN dealing with the University of Padua[4] we have already
from   had occasion to examine the provisions of the contract under
Padua,
1228.

[1] Origlia, i. 119 *sq.*, 216 *sq.*,
232 *sq.* In medicine the candidate
disputed with each regent doctor
who sent his *depositio* to the chancellor; afterwards he was again
examined by the King's physicians.
'Et tum examinabitur idem baccalarius per Curiam nostram per
Phisicos nostros qui depositionem
suam referent eidem Cancellario',
loc. cit., p. 220.

[2] Savigny, c. xxi, § 121.

[3] As a note of the progress of the
Greek Renaissance, it is perhaps
worth noticing the appointment of
Constantine Lascaris as rhetor and
professor of Greek, as early as
1405, by Ferdinand I (Origlia, i.
263), but it does not appear what

was his connexion with the university.

[4] See above, p. 11 *sq.* A document in Mandelli (iii. 10) shows
that a doctor of theology was afterwards added to the staff, but this, of
course, does not show that graduation in theology ever took place
here. It is observable that before
1228 (perhaps 1205–8) the commune had ordered the *podestà*
'dare operam ad habendum studium
scholarum' (*leg.* scholarium). *Ibid.*
iii. 14; cf. Balliano, p. 37. [But
Denifle, i. 291, doubts if this document comes from the period before
1228. On the standing of the local
scholars at Vercelli see Tamassia,
Odofredo, p. 115 note.]

which a *studium generale* was established at Vercelli by a CHAP. VI,
large body of students from that university in 1228.[1] The § 6.
testimony of Jordan of Saxony shows that a considerable
body of students with a regular university organization was
actually at Vercelli in the following year:[2] and, even after the
expiration of the eight years for which the contract was made,
it is clear that, though the bulk of the students had no doubt
returned to Padua, some sort of *studium* still maintained a
rather intermittent existence in the place, though it was
probably a *studium* to which nothing but the 'consuetudo'
established during the years of the Paduan secession could
have given any claim to the dignity of a *studium generale*.
About the year 1237, or soon after, the Emperor Frederick II Traces of
sent a doctor of civil law 'to teach your scholars and others subsequent
existence.
who should come from all parts',[3] which seems to suggest
that practically there was no longer any regular law-teaching
in the city. This doctor seems to have attracted students:
since at the beginning of 1238 the Pope threatens the citizens
with the dissolution of their *studium*.[4] An allusion to a
studium sufficiently important to attract a Spanish dignitary
to the place, and to warrant his getting leave of absence for
the purpose, occurs in 1244.[5] There are sparse allusions to

[1] There is no reason to believe
that the cathedral school at Vercelli
was ever anything more than a
cathedral school, but the following
is worthy of reproduction from its
intrinsic interest: 'Volentes prae-
terea statum hospitalis Scotorum
reformare in melius . . . praecipi-
mus quod minister domum emat
vel faciat, secundum quod per
venerabilem patrem Ugonem Ver-
cell. episcopum de consensu Capituli est statutum, in qua comuniter
recipiantur pauperes clerici et alii
indigentes et de hiis quae super-
fuerint annuatim, salva in omnibus
provisione Scotorum et Hiber-
norum et aliorum pauperum, ad
quorum receptionem idem hospi-
tale specialiter noscitur institutum,
misericorditer sustententur.' Statute of cardinal Guala for the

Cathedral of Vercelli (1224), ap.
Mandelli, iii. 13.
[2] He speaks of Germans, Provençals, and Lombards (*Lettres*,
p. 102). One of his biographers, in
speaking of the visit, treats the
studium as a thing of the past:
'nam tunc studium ibi erat'. *Acta
Sanctorum*, Feb., ii. 735. (According to one reading. Cf. Denifle,
i. 293, n. 282.)
[3] 'Pro edocendis vestris scholaribus et aliis undique venturis';
Martène and Durand, *Ampliss.
Coll.* ii, cc. 1141, 1142; Baggiolini,
p. 139.
[4] Denifle, i. 292, 293.
[5] There is a Bull of Innocent IV
(*Reg.* ed. Berger, No. 529) in 1244
which recites that 'M. Velasci,
magister scolarum Astoricensis,
nobis exposuit quod, cum ipse olim

salaria of professors of law up to 1340.[1] The town statutes
of 1341 declare that there is and ought for ever to be a *studium
generale* in Vercelli, and make provision for four civilians,
two decretists, and one doctor of medicine;[2] but there are
no traces of the *studium* after the middle of the fourteenth
century and the newly founded Turin took its place as the
University of Piedmont at the beginning of the next century.

§ 7. THE UNIVERSITY OF THE ROMAN COURT (1244–5)

CARAFA, *De Gymnasio Romano*, Rome, 1751; F. M. RENAZZI, *Storia del-
l'Università degli Studj di Roma*, Rome, 1803–6. Renazzi supersedes
Carafa (who did not distinguish the *studium curiae* from the *studium urbis*),
and has the fullest collection of documents. [DENIFLE, i. 301–10.]

ALONE among the universities of the medieval or of the
modern world the University of the Court of Rome was
migratory, like the ancient law-courts of our own and other
countries, and followed the person of the Supreme Pontiff
when he left Rome for his more agreeable Italian resi-
dences or for a permanent retreat to Avignon. Thus, after
the foundation of a university for the city of Rome in 1303,
there were during the presence of the curia two distinct
universities in the same place, and during the sojourn at
Avignon the *studium curiae* was no less distinct from the
flourishing university of that town.

The University of the Court of Rome was founded by
Innocent IV in 1244 or 1245.[3] It was primarily a university
for civil and canon law, but there was also a theological
faculty, and in the fifteenth century we hear also of degrees
being given in philosophy and medicine.[4] The doctors in the

apud Vercellas insisteret scolasticis
disciplinis', he was persuaded to
enter the order of preachers when
drunk. For traces of the later
existence of the *studium*, see
Mandelli, iii. 24 *sq.*; Baggiolini,
p. 103 *sq.*

[1] Mandelli, iii. 43.
[2] *Ibid.* iii. 41.
[3] Renazzi, i. 30 *sq.* (but not in
full); Denifle, i. 302, supplies the
preamble. Notice that the purpose
of this bull in declaring the *studium*

to be 'general' seems to be primarily
to enable its beneficed students to
avail themselves of the privilege of
dispensation from residence: 'ut
studentes in scolis ipsis . . . talibus
privilegiis omnino, libertatibus, et
immunitatibus sint muniti, quibus
gaudent studentes in scolis, ubi
generale regitur studium, percipi-
entes integre proventus suos ecclesi-
asticos sicut alii.'
[4] Renazzi, i. 51, 255.

theological faculty were as a rule members of religious orders,
mostly Dominicans. A nucleus for the new university was
found in an earlier project of Honorius III, who had founded
the Mastership of the Sacred Palace, an office always held
by a Dominican doctor of theology, who was to give lectures
to the idle courtiers of the papal palace.[1] The more extensive
scheme of Innocent IV was likewise intended to find useful
employment for the crowds of benefice-hunting ecclesiastics,
who, as the Bull observes, 'flocked from all parts of the world
to the apostolic see as unto a mother'.[2] It is particularly
worthy of notice that the civil law received especial encouragement in a school which was the absolute creature of the
holy see, priests habitually receiving dispensations to enable
them to study it in spite of the prohibition of Honorius III—
a sufficient refutation of the idea that the supreme pontiffs
were systematically hostile to that study. Even Honorius III
was no enemy to the civil law as such, though anxious to
promote the study of theology and canon law by the priest-
hood and the religious orders. But the study of civil law soon
became essential to the study of canon law; and the Popes
themselves were usually lawyers rather than theologians.

It is hardly necessary to say that in this *studium* the demo- Constitu-
cratic student-universities never established themselves; it ^{tion.}
was governed (subject to the supreme authority of the Pope)
by the college of doctors. The cardinal chamberlain was
chancellor, and presided over the promotions which were
carried out in the regular way after examination by the doct
of the faculty in the presence of the chancellor.[3]

---

[1] Carafa, i. 135. There is a
history of this office by Catalanus,
De Magistro Sacri Palatii Apostolici,
Rome, 1751). It was held by
Thomas Aquinas [between 1259
and 1268 (Mandonnet in *Xenia
Thomistica*, iii. 9–40)]. At a later
time the master was required, besides lecturing, to exercise a cen-
sorship on sermons to be preached
in the Pope's chapel, and generally
to act as a sort of guardian of the
orthodoxy of the papal household

and as consulting theologian to the
Pope. He was especially to lecture
on theology to the loungers and
attendant clergy waiting for the
cardinals at consistories. Renazzi,
i. 24, 44–5. [According to 'Walter
of Coventry', ed. Stubbs, ii. 198,
Stephen Langton, 'theologiam do-
cebat' at Rome, apparently in the
Curia, in 1206.]

[2] Renazzi, i. 28.

[3] *Ibid*. i. 43, 48, 93, 253, &c.
Cf. *Stat. Fior.*, p. 342.

CHAP. VI,
§ 7.
Papal dis-
pensations
and papal
degrees.

This may be a convenient place to mention that the Pope claimed a right to dispense with the whole or any part of the preliminaries required for the doctorate in any university, and of demanding the admission of the candidate either immediately or after a certain limited period of residence. This right was very frequently exercised in favour of friars at Paris and elsewhere; and, as was natural, with peculiar frequency in the Pope's own university, where the degrees were often conferred merely by Bull without any residence or study whatever. The Council of Constance made an ineffectual attempt to reform this abuse.[1] More rarely we find the Pope commissioning some ecclesiastic to confer a degree with the assistance of a certain number of doctors of any university.[2] But these papal degrees of course carried with them the *ius ubique docendi*: even when the degree was not conferred in a university, the graduate possessed (theoretically) rights in all universities. The degree-giving power possessed at the present day by the archbishop of Canterbury is of course a relic of this papal dispensing power; but in the Middle Ages, with all the abuses connected with degrees, a doctorate which conferred no rights whatever in any university at all would have been scarcely intelligible.

Study of
oriental
lan-
guages.

The University of the Roman Curia was one of the five universities at which the Council of Vienne in 1312 directed that professors of the Greek, Arabic, Chaldee, and Hebrew languages should be maintained.[3] Under the eye of the Pontiff, who had presided at the council, the decree was put into execution at least to a greater extent than was perhaps the case in some of the other universities mentioned. At all events, the professors were appointed and drew their salaries, which is as much as could at times have been said for certain university professors of oriental languages at more recent periods.[4] But the association of the *studium* with Paris, Bologna, Oxford, and Salamanca on this occasion corresponds

---

[1] Renazzi, i. 41; von der Hardt, *Conc. Const.* i. 606, 743. See vol. i, Appendix.

[2] Renazzi, i. 257. The object is here said to be to avoid the ex-

penses involved in taking a degree in a university.

[3] Some manuscripts omit Greek. *Chartul. Univ. Paris.* ii, no. 695.

[4] Renazzi, i. 49; Denifle, i. 307.

rather to the position which the Popes desired their school to
occupy in Italy than to the position which it actually·held.
As it will not again be necessary to say much more about this
somewhat celebrated episode in the history of the universities, it may be well to add that the objects of the measure
were purely missionary and ecclesiastical, not scientific. The
new studies were to promote the conversion of Jews and
Turks in the east, not to promote learning or the better
understanding of the Hebrew scriptures in the west.[1]

§ 8. SIENA (1246, 1357)

There are short notices of the university in GIGLI, *Diario Sanese* (Lucca,
1723), ii. 101, 349. DE ANGELIS, *Discorso storico sull'Università di Siena*,
Siena, 1810 (new edition, 1840), is of no value. CARPELLINI, *Sulla origine
nazionale e populare delle Università di studj di Italia, e particolarmente
della Università di Siena* (Siena, 1861), is an only slightly more substantial
brochure. MORIANI, *Notizie sulla Università di Siena* (Siena, 1873), gives
slight sketches of its history. L. BANCHI has published a most interesting
series of documents dealing with the migration of 1321–2 in *Giornale
Storico degli Archivi Toscani*, v (1861), 237 *sq.*, 309 *sq.* But the most
important authority is DENIFLE (i. 429–52), whose work is here based
upon his own researches in the archives of Siena. Since Denifle two slight
pamphlets have appeared, COLOMBINI, *Cenni storici sulla Università di
Siena* (Siena, 1891); and L. ZDEKAUER, *Sulle origini d. Studio Senese*
(Siena, 1893). [BARDUZZI, *Documenti per la Storia della R. Università di
Siena*, Siena, 1900; the same, *Brevi notizie sulla R. Università di Siena*,
Siena, 1912; R. DAVIDSOHN, 'Documenti del 1240 e 1252 relativi allo
studio senese', in *Bullettino senese di storia patria*, vii (1900), 168 *sqq.*; the
same, *Geschichte von Florenz*, IV. iii (1927), 135–8.]

THE first notice of any kind of school in Siena occurs in 1240,
when we meet with a 'professor of grammar' and a 'master
in the art of medicine'.[2] In 1246, when Frederick II attempted to prevent students from going to Bologna, Siena
took the opportunity afforded by the dissensions in which

---

[1] There are traces of the teaching of Hebrew at Paris up to 1430,
and in this year the faculty of arts
(or at least the French nation) as-
sented to the supplication of 'pro-
fessores quidam Graeci, Hebraei
et Chaldaei' for a *stipendium*.
Bulaeus, v. 393. Cf. *Chartul. Univ.
Paris.* ii, nos. 777, 786, 857. See
also Ch. Jourdain's dissertations in
Excursions hist. et phil. à travers le

moyen âge, pp. 233–45, and above,
vol. i, p. 566 note. In England we
find the Canterbury Convocation in
1320 directing a tax of a farthing
in the pound upon all benefices in
the province for the support of a
converted Jew who is alleged to
have been teaching at Oxford.
Wilkins, *Concilia*, ii. 499.

[2] Denifle, i. 429.

CHAP. VI,
§ 8.

the great university city was involved to hire a doctor of civil law and proclaim the opening of a *studium* by the accustomed method of sending messengers to the neighbouring towns with an announcement of the lectures.[1] In the following year there was a considerable number of doctors in the place. In 1252 Innocent IV granted the 'university of masters and doctors regent at Siena and of their scholars studying in the same' together with their bedels an exemption from certain city taxes, and appointed the bishop as their conservator.[2]

Disputed claim to be *studium generale*.

It is probable that at this time the *studium* would have called itself and been generally recognized as a *studium generale* in the loose and untechnical sense which was then given to the word, and it seems on the whole entitled to be placed alongside of Reggio and Vercelli as one of the spontaneously developed universities of the thirteenth century. There is no reason why it should forfeit this honorary position because it was not permanently able to assert its privilege or to re-establish its position at a later date without making a fresh start and obtaining a papal brief. By 1275 the Bologna immigrants had evidently long since returned, and we find the city adopting a resolution 'upon the having, bringing back, and founding a *studium generale* at Siena'.[3] This combination of terms clearly evidences the fact that in the view of the citizens the place had once been a *studium generale*:[4] with equal clearness it shows that *de facto* no such *studium generale* now existed. But by this time it was becoming less easy than it had been for a university to obtain

---

[1] Denifle, i. pp. 429, 430. [In August 1246, the Emperor's son, Frederick of Antioch, forbade the youth of Siena to go to study in Bologna; Davidsohn, *Gesch. von Florenz*, IV. iii. 135. Davidsohn would date the *studium* from 1240.]

[2] Reg. Vat. quoted by Denifle, *loc. cit.*

[3] 'Super habendo, reducendo et fundando generali studio literarum in civitate Senensi.' Documents ap. Denifle, i. 431. [The revival was due to the Guelfs, though papal

approval was delayed; cf. Davidsohn, *op. cit.*, p. 136.]

[4] It is on this ground that I venture to date Siena from 1246, in spite of the authority of Denifle, who dates it from the Imperial Bull of 1357. See the criticisms of Kaufmann, *Gesch. d. Deutsch. Univ.* i. 376; *Deutsch. Zeit. f. Geschichtswissenschaft*, i. 127. Really such universities occupy a debatable ground between the *studia generalia ex consuetudine* and the universities founded by Bull.

recognition as a *studium generale* by mere prescription.
When a new Italian studium had succeeded in making itself
'general' by merely claiming to be so, it had usually been
because a body of seceders from Bologna had brought with
them something of the fame and prestige of the great *studium
generale par excellence.* The resolution of 1275 suggests the
belief that it lay in the city's power to create a *studium
generale* without invoking the assistance of pope or king.
The necessity of a foundation-Bull was at this time not
sufficiently recognized to prevent the attempt being made;
but it was becoming too well-established for the attempt to
succeed. A few notices of salaried teachers continue to occur,
but there was no real *studium generale* again till 1321. In
that year the city once more opened her gates to a body of
malcontent scholars from Bologna, where a dispute had arisen
with the town.[1] The bulk of the fugitives had temporarily
taken refuge in the little town of Imola, and there the envoys
of Siena succeeded by liberal offers of salaries in attracting
to their city a considerable contingent of the dispersion.[2]
But a reconciliation took place before the close of the year,
and it was not till the next great Bologna exodus of 1338
(when Pisa and Arezzo obtained their foundation-Bulls) that
Siena once more leapt for a moment into the position of a
de facto studium generale.[3]

[1] See above, vol. i, pp. 172–3.

[2] See the accounts and resolutions of the council in Banchi, *loc. cit.*, p. 309 *sq.* In May 1321 the city had to borrow no less than 'summam quatuor millium florenorum de auro, pro expediendis et adimplendis promissionibus per sindicos comunis Senarum rectoribus Universitatis scolarium et ipsis scolaribus'. Banchi, p. 315. [The Sienese archives reveal a rector of the *ultramontani* at this time, and the presence for a year from 1 May 1322 of no less a person than Leopold of Babenberg, previously known only as a student of Bologna. The failure to acquire the 'brevilegia del convento' stood in the way

of the university; see Andrea Dei's chronicle, in Muratori, xx, col. 63, cited by Davidsohn in the additional volume of notes to his *Gesch. von Florenz*, IV. iii. 34, 35.]

[3] In July 1322, however, Dino del Garbo gives a receipt for his salary at Siena at the rate of 100 florins per annum. Banchi, p. 329. [The commentary on the Canon of Avicenna, by this famous physician, who taught at Bologna, Padua, Florence, Siena, and died at Florence in 1327, is of great value for the academic history of Siena, *c.* 1307–27. The decay of the university caused his return to Florence (Davidsohn, pp. 172–3; Notes, p. 35).]

But by this time the necessity of a Bull of erection for a permanent university was established beyond all possibility of doubt. The ancient but somewhat dubious and obsolete pretensions of Siena to the character of a *studium generale* were no longer likely to meet with respect. If the *studium* was to be permanent, if it was to venture to confer degrees, and if these degrees were to be worth anything, such a Bull must be procured. Serious efforts were made to obtain the needful document from the Pope on the occasion of this Bolognese migration; but the attempt failed and the bulk of the masters and scholars no doubt returned to Bologna. After some further failures to obtain the privileges of a *studium generale*, the city at last in 1357 turned in despair to the Imperial Emperor Charles IV, from whom it obtained a Bull which, after declaring that the *studium* had once been flourishing but had now sunk into obscurity, proceeds to confer upon it *de novo* the 'privileges of a *studium generale*'.[1] In 1408 a fresh grant of privileges was obtained from Pope Gregory XII,[2] and it was at this time that the *studium* for the first time entered upon a period of permanent vitality. A little before (1404) a college for thirty poor scholars had been founded by the city, on the basis of an older 'casa della misericordia', known henceforward as the *domus sapientie* or *Sapienza*, which was to live according to the rules of the famous Spanish College at Bologna.[3]

Imperial Bull of 1357.

Sapienza.

A civic university.
The most remarkable feature of this university throughout its history is the closeness of its dependence upon the town.[4] The attempt of the city in 1275 to erect a *studium* by a

---

[1] The whole tone both of the Bull and of the city, in so far as we can judge from the extracts in Denifle (i. 447), negative the supposition that any one whatever *now* supposed Siena to be capable of becoming a *studium generale* without a Bull. A confirmation of imperial privileges was granted by Sigismund in 1433. *Ibid.*, p. 452.

[2] A number of Bulls were granted, one of which, in appoint-

ing the bishop 'cancellarius studii', expressly recognizes the bishop's existing authority under the imperial foundation. *Ibid.*, p. 450.

[3] *Ibid.*, p. 451. [From the time of Charles IV there was a strong German element in Siena (Davidsohn, p. 138).]

[4] It recognized, however, in the amplest way, the rectorial jurisdiction, extending it even to *cives*. Town-statutes of 1338, ap. Denifle, i. 448.

distinct executive or legislative act represents the first attempt CHAP. VI,
§ 8.
of the kind in the history of the Italian city-republics;[1] and
it remains the only instance (except the early secessions from
Bologna) in which the attempt was made without any effort
or apparent intention to apply for a Bull of erection. Writers
eager to gain historical support for the theory of the state's
educational omnipotence have insisted much on the case of
Siena as proving that the medieval conception of a *studium
generale* was simply a *studium* authorized by a sovereign
or independent municipality. If such was the theory to which
the statesmen of Siena attempted to give expression, the
attempt conspicuously failed. Siena was never acknowledged
as a *studium generale* except during the brief periods during
which she welcomed fugitives from Bologna. Many other
Italian universities were, as completely as Siena, the creations
of the free city government, but they never attempted to
dispense with the formality of the papal or imperial Bull.

§ 9. PIACENZA (1248)

Some notices and documents occur in CAMPI, *Hist. Univers. delle cose
eccles. come seculari di Piacenza* (Piacenza, 1651), ii. 187 *sq.*, &c. There are
scattered notices in *Memorie per la Storia Letteraria di Piacenza*, Piacenza,
1789. See also *Annales Placentini*, ap. MURATORI, *Rer. Ital. SS.* xx. 932–41.
[DENIFLE, i. 566–72; A. G. TONONI, 'Gli studi a Piacenza nel medio
evo', in *Strenna Piacentina* (Piacenza, 1890).]

So far the universities which we have considered have been Conver-
sion of
town-
either of spontaneous growth like the great parent University schools
into *studia*
of Bologna, from which most of them may be considered as *generalia*
by Bull.
colonies or outgrowths, or artificial creations of Pope or
Emperor. We now come to a fresh type of university—in
Italy by far the most numerous—the class in which a town-
school, supported by the municipality, obtained the privilege
of a *studium generale* by papal or imperial Bull. The idea
of applying for such a Bull was no doubt suggested by the
precedents of Toulouse, Naples, and the Curia. Schools of
law and arts and often schools of medicine existed—not

---

[1] Putting aside cases where the
city merely negotiated with a secession from some other university. [Cf. L. Zdekauer, *Il constituto*
del comune di Siena dell'anno 1262
(Milan, 1897) especially pp. 410
sqq.]

always continuously, but intermittently—in nearly every important city-republic in northern Italy. Originally, as has been seen, these schools were the private adventure of some doctor who established himself in the town, and supported himself by the fees of his scholars. But even in the second quarter of the thirteenth century the system of state-paid *salaria* began to supersede the voluntary system: and this by itself tended to give a formal and public character to these city schools. The municipalities made contracts with the professor for one, two, or more years. The presence of an eminent lawyer was of value to the town apart from his educational work: and in some of the contracts it was stipulated that the doctor should give legal advice to the government when required as well as instruction to its future magistrates and lawyers. The doctor would of course as a rule have graduated at Bologna or at least at one of those daughter-schools of Bologna at which the Bologna method of graduation had spontaneously established itself; but, while their pupils in the town-schools might learn law, they could not become teachers, or assume in public and professional life the position which was everywhere accorded to the properly accredited doctor of law. So long as a school laboured under these disadvantages, it was not likely to attract students from distant cities, when it was just as easy to go to Bologna or to Padua. Hence the eagerness for those Bulls which, since the assumption of the prerogative of creation by Innocent IV and Frederick II, were recognized as elevating a school at one bound from a *studium particulare* into a *studium generale* with all the substantial privileges and the vague prestige which had gradually become associated with the latter appellation.

The first Italian city to apply for such a Bull was Piacenza. The great jurist Placentinus, best known as the traditional founder of the law-school at Montpellier, was born at Piacenza and taught there in his old age:[1] and there are some

---

[1] [From 1185 to 1189, according to P. de Tourtoulon's chronology, *Vie de Placentin*, i. 119, 121. Placentinus was about 50 in 1185. Cf. below, p. 128.]

other traces of law-teaching in the place from the end of the twelfth century. But the *studium* had no pretensions to being general until a Bull was granted by Innocent IV in 1248,[1] conferring upon the masters and scholars all the privileges of Paris and other *studia generalia*, and bestowing the 'right of promotion' upon the bishop. Little, however, came of the new departure. There is an occasional notice of a doctor of law or medicine teaching at Piacenza,[2] but there is no evidence of the existence of a *de facto studium generale* till the year 1398, when Gian Galeazzo Visconti issued a fresh charter of erection, which he claimed to do by virtue of the imperial power delegated to him as Vicar of the Empire.[3] At this time [a migration from Pavia—generally, but, it would seem, erroneously interpreted as the result of a formal suppression of the university there in favour of the new foundation at Piacenza—gave impetus to the revival.][4]

For a short time we find the usual Italian organization— a university of artists and medical students combined and a university of jurists with their respective rectors[5]—established in Piacenza. Distinguished professors were salaried. Between 1398 and 1402 no less than seventy-two salaried professors (not all simultaneously) are found lecturing in the university—among them Baldus, the most famous jurist of the day.[6] And here we may observe that we have now reached the period at which the progress of humanism may be faintly

[1] The Bull is printed in Campi, ii. 399.

[2] These are collected by Denifle, i. 567, 568.

[3] Gian Galeazzo claims to confer the privilege of Paris, *Padua*, *Bologna* (notice the order), Oxford, Orleans, Montpellier, Pavia, Perugia, 'de nostrae plenitudine potestatis a Caesarea dignitate nobis et nostris successoribus attributa'. Campi, iii. 307. The claim is obviously a usurpation, but the form in which it is made testifies to the general acceptance of the power of creating universities as one of the imperial prerogatives. Denifle (i.

570) considers that the document must have been issued before 1399, the date given by Campi.

[4] [See below, p. 52. Gian Galeazzo's decree, reviving Piacenza, was dated 23 Oct. 1398 and lectures began on 4 Dec. The decree of 1 Jan. 1399 did not thereupon give effect to the decree of the previous October.]

[5] 'In praesentia DD. Rectorum, et caeterorum Doctorum hujus almi studii.' Campi, ii. 190. It would appear that the rectors were here doctors. Cf. *ibid.*, p. 195.

[6] Muratori, *Rer. Ital. SS.* xx. 939, 940.

CHAP. VI,
§ 9.

traced in the altered characters of the academic *curriculum*. Among Gian Galeazzo's professors were not only professors of theology, law (including the notarial art),[1] medicine, philosophy, and grammar, but of astrology, rhetoric, Dante, and Seneca. Yet in spite of this lavish expenditure, the project failed. Gian Galeazzo died in 1402, and his state fell to pieces. Moreover, some risk was always attached to an attempt to establish a university by pure state action when there was no natural flow of students to a town, and when the town was too small to furnish a substantial nucleus by itself. The *studium* had practically, it would seem, collapsed a

Transference to Pavia, 1412.

decade before the year 1412, when it was wisely determined to make the larger Pavia the University of the Milanese, and the subjects of the duchy were forbidden to study elsewhere. But, though not a single lecture was given, the doctoral colleges of Piacenza still went on exercising their university privileges and in fact conducted a profitable traffic in cheap degrees—an abuse of which the Pavians naturally complained, but apparently without effect.[2]

§ 10. ROME (*STUDIUM URBIS*), 1303

For authorities, see above, § 7. [DENIFLE, i. 310–17.]

Foundation.

QUITE distinct from the University of the Curia, though by many writers confounded with it, was the University of the City of Rome, founded by Boniface VIII in 1303.[3] It was a university for all faculties, though practically law and arts were most prominent. In the course of the great Schism

---

[1] As in most Italian universities.

[2] The envoy of Pavia sent in 1471 to the Duke urges 'Privilegium Innocentii IV eis concessum datum fuit docentibus, et sic qui actu docent; cum Privilegium dicat *docentibus et scholaribus* . . .; sed hodie non docent, cum non sit Studium generale literarum.' Muratori, *Rer. Ital. SS.* xx. 932. A *Collegium Jurisconsultorum* and a *Collegium DD. Artium et Medicinae Doctorum* seem, however, to have maintained their ground. Their

statutes are printed in *Statuta Varia Civitatis Placentiae* (Parma, 1860, pp. 467, 559). Those of the college of medicine (though in their present form of the sixteenth century) still contain provisions for graduation, which are absent in the jurist statutes of 1435.

[3] The Bull is printed in Renazzi, i. 258. There is another Bull of John XXII which requires promotions to be made with the consent of the cardinal vicar. *Ibid.*, p. 266.

and the political commotions of that period it was altogether CHAP. VI,
extinguished; Eugenius IV is considered its second founder § 10.
(1431).[1] Under his sanction it was endowed by the Roman
municipality with the proceeds of a wine-tax, and was placed
under a board of *reformatores* or *curatores*. But at no period
of the Middle Ages was this university of much importance
from an educational point of view.

The organization of the *studium* more nearly followed the Constitu-
democratic Italian pattern than was possible in the Univer- tion.
sity of the Sacred Palace. There was a *universitas* and a
rector or rectors,[2] elected by doctors and scholars combined,
who had jurisdiction in civil and minor criminal cases. In
all cases except homicide the scholar had the option of being
tried by his own master, according to the privilege of
Frederick I, or by the cardinal vicar: to whom also belonged
jurisdiction in cases of homicide committed by clerks. Cases
of homicide committed by lay scholars were tried by the
senator.[3] Till the time of Eugenius IV the salaried professors
were elected on the petition of the scholars by a body
described as the 'rectores et syndici Romane fraternitatis',
whom Renazzi supposes to be representatives of the clergy
of the Roman city.[4]

Eventually in the time of Leo X the *studium sacri palatii* United
seems to have been merged in the *studium urbis*, and the one with
Studium
Roman university established in a building since generally Curiae.
known as the *Sapienza*.[5] At this time many distinguished
men were professors in the Roman university, so much so,
indeed, that we are told that the teachers were more numerous
than the scholars.[6]

---

[1] See the Bull in Renazzi, i. 274.
An attempt at restoration by Innocent VII failed. Carafa, i. 167 *sq.*

[2] The Bull of Boniface VIII
speaks of *rectores*, but we never
hear of more than one rector.

[3] Renazzi, i. 275.

[4] *Ibid.* i. 66–7, 261. But the
elections were subject to papal interference, pp. 67, 263.

[5] *Ibid.* i. 55–6. An apparently

quite distinct building was the
Sapienza or *Collegium pauperum
scolarium sapientie Firmane* founded
by cardinal Dominicus de Capra-
nica, bishop of Fermo, in 1455.
Catalanus, *De Eccl. Firmana eius-
que Episcopis*, pp. 254–5.

[6] Leo X declares in 1513 that
'adeo scolarium copia defecit, ut
quandoque plures sint qui legant,
quam qui audiant'. Denifle, i. 315.

§ 11. PERUGIA (1308)

CHAP. VI, V. BINI, *Memorie istoriche della Perugina Università degli studj* (Perugia,
§ 11.   1816), is practically superseded by PADELLETTI, *Contributo alla storia
dello studio di Perugia nei secoli* 14 *e* 15 (Bologna, 1872), which is an edition
of the Statutes of 1457, with an historical introduction, and by the
unusually full and interesting series of documents published by ROSSI,
'Documenti per la storia dell'Università di Perugia' in the *Giornale di
erudizione artistica*, iv–vi (Perugia, 1875–7: also printed separately), and
2nd series, ii, 1883. The series, however, unfortunately stops at the year
1389. [DENIFLE, i. 534–52; O. SCALVANTI, 'Sulle origini della università
di Perugia', in *Annali della R. Università di Perugia: facoltà di giurisprudenza*, 3rd ser., iii (1905); L. TARULLI, 'Documenti per la storia della
medicina in Perugia' (before 1400), in *Bollettino della regia deputazione di
storia patria per l'Umbria* (Perugia, 1922), xxv. See also the statutes of
the city of Perugia in P. SELLA, *Corpus Statutorum*, i.]

Founda-   THROUGHOUT the thirteenth century we find a succession of
tion.   professors hired by the commune of Perugia to teach law
to the sons of its citizens: and in 1276 *nuntii* were dispatched
in the accustomed manner to announce the opening of the
lectures in the neighbouring cities also.[1] By the end of the
century the school had obtained considerable repute, and
this is one of the few cases in which we have positive evidence
of the existence of *universitates scholarium* before the
erection of the school into a *studium generale*.[2] The foundation-Bull was obtained from Clement V in 1308,[3] and it is
significant of the usual connexion in Italy between a *studium
generale* and *universitates scholarium* that the year before, as
a preliminary to obtaining the Bull, the city formally recognized these universities and bestowed upon their rectors 'the
same office and jurisdiction which rectors have in *studia*

---

[1] Rossi, Secoli xiii, nos. 1–4.
(All subsequent references to Rossi
are to Sec. xiv.) [Scalvanti has
attempted to trace a connexion
between the *studium* and the city
school of grammar on the one
hand, and the cathedral school on
the other.]

[2] From documents of 1304
(Rossi, nos. 1, 2) it appears that
steps had already been taken with
a view to the establishment of a
studium generale: in *Brevi annali
della città di Perugia*, edited by

F. Bonaini and others (*Archivio
storico italiano*, xvi, pt. 1 (1850),
p. 59) *sub an.* 1301 we find, 'In
questo millesimo cominciò in
Perugia lo studio generale'.

[3] Denifle, i. 538 n.; Rossi (no.
4) and others wrongly give 1307.
This Bull simply decrees 'ut in
ciuitate predicta sit generale studium illudque ibidem perpetuis
futuris temporibus uigeat in qualibet facultate', without expressly
conferring the 'facultas ubique docendi'.

generalia'.[1] The doctors were elected periodically by the city authorities in conjunction with the rectors. At first, of course, these professors were persons who had already graduated at Bologna or some other 'famous *studium*': and at this transition-period in the development of the medieval ideas about *studia generalia* it was not, it would appear, considered that the mere recognition of the school as a *studium generale* carried with it 'the right of promotion'.[2] If that were so, the only practical benefit which the city had gained by its papal Bull was that terms kept at Perugia could be counted towards graduation at another university, and that its beneficed students might obtain leave of absence from their bishops. In 1318, however, the city succeeded in obtaining a fresh Bull from John XXII authorizing the promotion of doctors in the legal faculties, and in 1321 (when Perugia benefited by the great exodus from Bologna[3]) the privilege was extended to medicine and arts.[4]

In 1362 Nicolas Capocci, cardinal bishop of Tusculum, founded a *Collegium Gregorianum* (afterwards known as the *Sapienza Vecchia*) for forty scholars, of whom six were to study theology.[5] This led to an application for the privileges

[1] Rossi, no. 3.

[2] On 25 Nov. 1317 the subject was brought before a meeting of the *Priores Artium* and the *Camerarii Artium*: 'Cum aliquis sit qui offert dominis prioribus artium et comuni perusij se procuraturum privilegia studij et conventus comuni perusii a domino papa pro mille florenis de auro', &c. (Rossi, no. 27). The Bull was granted on 1 Aug. 1318 (*ibid.*, no. 28). The Bull contains the unusual limitation that no one was to be admitted D.C.L. after less than six years' study or doctor of decrees after less than five, or without having 'read' two books of the civil or canon law respectively as a bachelor.

[3] Above, vol. i, p. 172.

[4] Rossi, no. 33. The dispensation from residence even without the licence of bishop or chapter was conferred in the same year. (No. 36.) [The right of 'promotion' was vested in the bishop, as later at Pisa (1340) and Orvieto (1378); cf. Manacorda, i. 220. In 1304 the city council equalized the stipends of the professors of grammar and logic with those of the professors of law. These masters, described in 1315 as 'in suis scientiis et facultatibus conventati' (Rossi, nos. 9, 37), must, as Manacorda observes (i. 276), have graduated elsewhere.]

[5] Rossi, no. 101. The cardinal gives as a reason for this last provision that 'diebus istis pauci clerici scolares reperiuntur qui sint docti in sacra pagina sciantque populo proponere verbum dei'. For he goes on to remark, 'quod aduocationis officium maxime in partibus

CHAP. VI, of a *studium generale* in this faculty also. The case of Perugia
§ 11. illustrates with great clearness what had been the position of
theological studies in Italy before the erection of academic
faculties of theology in the fourteenth century, and how far—
that is to say, how little—their position was changed by these
papal Bulls. We find here that the students of the new
college were by the founder's statutes to attend the lectures of
the Mendicants. At Perugia, as everywhere else in Italy,
theology had on the whole been abandoned to the Mendicants. Here and there a few secular scholars might be admitted to their lectures.[1] The erection of a *studium generale*
in theology merely gave these students—and also the Mendicant teachers themselves—the opportunity of gaining the
honours of the doctorate in their own schools.

Jacobus de   Soon after the foundation of its university, in 1316, the
Belviso. citizens of Perugia were fortunate enough to secure the
services of Jacobus de Belvisi, one of the most famous
civilians of his age. The university was thus at once placed
(so far as the distinction of a teacher could place it) on a level
with Bologna and Padua, though the city did not succeed
either by threats or bribes in preventing his being enticed
away to Bologna. After five years' teaching, the fame which
the university acquired was permanent. Though its students
do not appear to have been at any time very numerous,[2] the
most famous jurists of the fourteenth century at one time or
other taught at Perugia. The canonist Johannes Andreae,
Bartolus, the most famous of the later medieval civilians, his
pupil, Baldus, and Albericus Gentili, the founder of the
science of international law, are only the most famous of
the distinguished teachers who were attracted to the place by
the exceptional liberality, energy, and discernment of the
Perugian municipality,[3] by whom the whole or most of

Italie danpnationis (*sic*) est anime',
and consequently forbids the study
of the civil law to more than six; the
rest were to study canon law.

[1] [For Bologna, see above, vol. i,
p. 252.]

[2] The Matricula of 1339 contains 12 doctors, 119 scholars in

law, and 23 in medicine. Rossi,
no. 64.

[3] The records contain a series,
probably unique in its complete-
ness, of receipts for salaries and
other documents relating to the
conductiones of professors. Sometimes we find doctors nominated or

the salaried chairs were expressly confined to non-Perugian CHAP. VI,
§ 11.
doctors.

In 1355 the city obtained an imperial Bull of erection in Imperial
Bull of
1355.
addition to the papal charter which it had long possessed.
This unusual step was apparently taken as a kind of advertisement for the university, which had suffered a temporary
depletion in consequence of a recent outburst of the
plague.[1]

The statutes are derived from those of Bologna[2] as regards Statutes
and con-
stitution.
the order and titles of successive paragraphs, but by the
time of the extant edition (1457) they have suffered so much
revision that the matter reproduced *verbatim* from Bologna is
but a small proportion of the whole. The chief constitutional
difference is that at Perugia not only are *ultramontani* and
citramontani now merged in a single university, but the
students of medicine and arts are likewise included in the
same university and placed under the same rector.[3] The
ultramontane nations are France, Germany, and Catalonia;
the citramontane Rome, Tuscany, the March, and the Kingdom of Sicily.[4] The rector's jurisdiction here extends to
minor, but not to serious, criminal cases.[5]

§ 12. TREVISO (1318)

VERCI, *Storia della Marca Trivigiana e Veronese* (Venice, 1786), prints
the town statutes relating to the *studium*. These and some other documents relating to the hiring of professors are now printed in A. MAR-
CHESAN, *L'Università di Treviso* (Treviso, 1892), a history in which a very

elected by the students, but the
appointment was normally vested
in five *sapientes studii* (who were
apparently students) under the
general control of the *Priores Artium.* [The civic statutes of 1342
(in Sella, i. 2771) deal with the
professoriate and the university of
students. The former were to be
foreigners paid by the commune—
fees are forbidden—but the teacher
of *notaria* may be a citizen. In civil
cases the students are to be tried
by three judges elected by themselves according to the 'autentica
avuto sopra questo', i.e. the *Authen-*

ticum 'Habita', of Frederick I.]

[1] Rossi, no. 96.

[2] The resemblance to the earlier
Bologna statutes is much closer
than to the printed Statutes of
1432.

[3] In 1389 the doctors of medicine were allowed to form a
collegium (Rossi, no. 241), but
with the proviso that they were not
to prevent others from practising
in the place.

[4] Padelletti, pp. 64, 65.

[5] 'Levia autem volumus delicta
intelligi, ubicumque arma non in-
tervenerint.' *Ibid.*, p. 61.

few facts are spun out into a book of 314 pages, exclusive of documents. [DENIFLE, i. 461–7; cf. A. MARCHESAN, *Treviso medievale*, Treviso, 1923, chap. xxx; MANACORDA, ii. 330, 331.]

Founda-
tion. IN 1263, four years after the downfall of the da Romano tyranny, the city of Treviso resolved on the re-establishment of a *studium*, from which we may infer the existence of schools at an earlier period. The resolution was carried out, but on a very small scale; since only one doctor of law and one of medicine were hired.[1] In 1314, however, steps were taken for the establishment of a *studium generale*, and no less than twelve professors were elected; but some of the professors whose services the city sought to attract would not accept the salaries offered; and the university had to open with a much smaller and inferior staff to what had been contemplated.[2] It was at first proposed to apply to the Pope for a Bull; but as a matter of fact the foundation-Bull was obtained in 1318 from the imperial claimant, Frederick of Austria (the rival of Lewis of Bavaria), to whom Treviso at that time adhered.[3] But the university always remained insignificant. It is, indeed, doubtful whether it even survived the year of its formal erection. At all events the Venetian conquest of Padua, and the edict of 1407 forbidding Venetian subjects to study anywhere else, must have put an end to a *studium generale* (had such existed) in Treviso, which had formed part of the Venetian territory since 1339.

§ 12 A. VERONA (1339)

[Rashdall included Verona among the paper universities, on the ground that 'there is no evidence of graduation' (see below, Appendix I, p. 328, where the *studium* is discussed. Cf. Denifle, i. 634–5). Others would maintain that Verona was the seat of a university on the grounds that the *studium generale* was formally established and was more or less continuously a centre of organized instruction. Cf. Manacorda, ii. 334–5.]

[1] Verci, ii. 107, 108. Cf. a document of 1271; *ibid.* ii, Doc., p. 135; Marchesan, pp. 317–19. There was some considerable number of students here in 1271.

[2] Verci, vii, Doc., pp. 39, 46, 70, 71, 135, 142. Tacoli, *Mem.*

Stor. d. Reggio, iii. 226; Marchesan, pp. 319–43.

[3] Verci, viii, Doc., pp. 147, 155; Marchesan, p. 343. Cf. Denifle, i. 466, 467. [*Mon. Germ. Hist.: Constitutiones*, v. 517.]

§ 13. PISA (1343)

FABRUCCI, four dissertations in Calogierà, *Raccolta d'Opuscoli scientifici e filologici*, Venice, 1728–57, vols. xxii, xxiii, xxv, xxix; FLAMINIO DAL BORGO, *Dissertazione epistolare sull'origine della Università di Pisa*, Pisa, 1765; FABRONI, *Historia Academiae Pisanae*, Pisa, 1791. The last is the most important and prints the statutes. [DENIFLE, i. 317–21; C. FEDELE, *I documenti pontifici riguardanti l'Università di Pisa* (Pisa, 1908); and *Statuta collegii theologorum almae universitatis pisanae* (Pisa, 1910).]

THE school of Pisa dates from at least the end of the twelfth century.[1] In the thirteenth century its fame was sufficient to attract students from Marseilles;[2] but it did not obtain the privileges of a *studium generale* till 1343, when a Bull was granted by Clement VI, conferring the privileges of 'Bologna, Paris, and other famous *studia generalia*'.[3] The application for this Bull was suggested by a great immigration of students from Bologna, which took place in consequence of the interdict laid on that city by Benedict XII in 1338.[4] The city was no doubt further influenced by rivalry with its enemy Florence, where attempts were being made to found a university. A scheme was proposed, hitherto unusual in Italy though common in Spain, for saddling the expenses of the *studium* upon the ecclesiastical revenues of the diocese.[5] It would, indeed, have been wiser had the Church allowed its revenues to be systematically applied to educational purposes instead of encouraging individual students to study in the universities while holding benefices (often with cure

The early school of law.

Bologna migration in 1338.

Foundation.

---

[1] A 'Nuntius Pisanorum Scholarium' is mentioned in a document of 1194. Fabroni, i. 401. The expression suggests the existence of a *universitas*.

[2] *Ibid.* i. 15.

[3] *Ibid.* i. 404–6. A Bull allowing beneficed clergy to obtain leave of absence to study at Pisa was conferred at the same time. *Ibid.*, pp. 406–8. The foundation was confirmed by Urban V in 1364 (Denifle, i. 320). It should be observed that Bartolus speaks of lecturing 'in Generali Pisano Studio' in 1340, after the Bologna migration, but before the grant of the Bull. Fabroni, i. 49. From a

diploma of 1438 it appears that the 'licences' were then conferred 'Apostolica et Imperiali auctoritate' (*ibid.*, p. 62); but the way in which the opening of the *studium* in 1343 is described (cf. also *ibid.*, p. 403) makes it very improbable that Pisa could have had an imperial charter before the papal Bull, if such a document ever existed. The phrase is possibly a mere piece of Ghibelline sentiment. From Fabrucci, *Raccolta*, &c., xxv, p. x, it would appear that the formula was used in his day.

[4] Fabroni, i. 48. Cf. above, p. 8, n. 6.

[5] *Ibid.*, p. 46.

CHAP. VI, of souls) the duties of which they were unable to perform.
§ 13.   The application was, however, refused by Benedict XII, but
at a much later period we find Sixtus IV consenting to 5,000
ducats being raised by a tax upon the clergy for the support
of the *studium*.[1]

Decline.   For a short time after 1338 the Bologna colony kept the
schools of Pisa full. Even before the foundation-Bull was
granted, the twin universities of *ultramontani* and *citramontani* reproduced themselves in Pisa, even if they did not
exist before the migration.[2] Two of the most eminent jurists
of the century, Bartolus[3] and Baldus, taught here for short
periods. But a combination of misfortunes destroyed the
prosperity of the *studium* a few years after its foundation.
War, famine, and, above all, the Black Death of 1348 dealt
a blow from which it did not recover till the following century. At times the schools seem to have been altogether suspended.[4] The existence of the university again becomes
traceable as the city began to recover from the effects of the
Florentine conquest of 1406. Its second birth, however,
dates from the year 1472, when the restoration of the university was undertaken by Florence. Pisa had to accept
academic prestige as a substitute for departed glory and
Revived by decaying commerce. In 1472 the Florentine University was
Florence
in 1472. dissolved:[5] Pisa assumed the position of the university town
of the conquering state, and soon became one of the leading
universities in Italy, second perhaps to none but Padua. It
was no doubt the policy of Florence, as of Venice in its relations to Padua, to keep up the population of its subject town
in a way which would be politically harmless. A very ample
jurisdiction was allowed to the rector, extending to all civil
cases and all criminal cases short of theft or homicide.[6]

---

[1] Fabroni, i. 481.
[2] A *rector citramontanus* is
mentioned in the year 1340.
Fabroni, i. 60. From *ibid.*, p. 93,
however, it would appear that there
were two rectors, one of the jurists,
the other of the medicals and
artists.
[3] [Bartolus was at Pisa from

1339 to 1343, when he went to
Perugia; Woolf, *Bartolus of Sassoferrato*, pp. 3, 5 and notes.]
[4] Fabrucci, *Raccolta*, &c., xxv,
p. xi *sq.*
[5] See the decree, Fabroni, i. 409.
[6] *Ibid.*, p. 442. It should be
observed that in the course of the
fifteenth century the university of

§ 14. FLORENCE (1349)

The most important authority is GHERARDI, *Statuti della università e* CHAP. VI,
studio Fiorentino (with a 'discorso' by C. MORELLI), Florence, 1881—a § 14.
magnificent edition. There are two articles by RONDONI, 'Ordinamenti
e vicende principali dell'antico studio Fiorentino' in *Archivio Stor. Ital.*
(4th series, xiv, 1884, pp. 45 *sqq.*). PREZZINER, *Storia del pubblico studio e
delle società scientifiche e letterarie di Firenze* (Florence, 1810), deals
chiefly with the careers of the Professors. [DENIFLE, i. 552–66; W.
SCHIFF, *L'università degli studî di Firenzo: notizie storiche*, 1887; and
especially DAVIDSOHN, *Geschichte von Florenz*, iii. 652–4; IV. iii (1927),
142–6, and volume of notes, pp. 37, 38.]

THE reader will probably learn with some surprise the late
origin and comparatively small prosperity of the university
of a city which occupies so high a place in the history of
Italian culture as Florence. While in most of the chief towns
of North Italy we find law-teachers salaried by the commune
throughout the thirteenth century, at Florence we find no
trace of salaried professors even in grammar, arts, and
medicine before 1320.[1] In the following year, when Bologna
was under interdict in consequence of the revolution under
Taddeo Pepoli, an attempt was made to establish a law-school
and to obtain the privileges of a *studium generale*. The main Attempts
body of the seceders from Bologna had established themselves to secure
at Imola. Thither in the accustomed Italian manner envoys Bologna
were dispatched by Florence to bribe away the discontented seceders
professors and their scholars with liberal offers of salaries, in 1321.
privileges, and full respect for the rectorial jurisdiction.[2]

Pisa was temporarily transferred
four times, thrice on account of
plague—in 1478 to Pistoia [see
A. Chiapelli, in *Bollettino storico
pistoiese*, xxxi (1929), 6–23], in 1482
and 1486 to Prato—and again to
Prato in consequence of the revolt
from Florence in 1495. Fabroni,
i. 86 *sq.*

[1] [This statement entirely fails to
do justice to the scholastic vigour of
Florence. Early in the thirteenth
century Florence provided many of
the *dictatores* or stylists of Bologna,
and a hundred years later its arith-
metical schools through their text-
books influenced teaching north of
the Alps. Lay teachers are found

from 1275 and included a married
woman, Clementia, *doctrix puerorum* (1304), who could teach the
rudiments of Latin. The study of
Latin was useful to the merchant
community, and in 1339 there were
four big Latin schools in the city.
See Davidsohn, IV. iii. 113 *sqq.*,
with a valuable commentary on the
famous chapter in Villani (xi. 94).
The *studium generale* had a good
foundation. For the masters of
grammar and medicine appointed in
August and November, 1320, see
ibid., p. 142, and volume of notes,
p. 37.]

[2] *Statuti*, pp. 107–11.

CHAP. VI, Unfortunately the envoys of the republic arrived too late.
§ 14.   The most distinguished professors had already entered into
a contract with Siena, and the bulk of the students followed
them thither.[1] Other professors were secured and law-
Founda- lectures established at Florence. [On 14 May 1321, through
tion of
university. the good offices of King Robert of Naples, a Bull, which
should grant all the privileges of Bologna, was sought from
Pope John XXII.[2] But the effort failed. The *studium* did not
flourish, and nothing is heard of it between 1336 and 1348.
In this year it was revived, and teaching had been resumed
by November. The revival was due] partly no doubt to
jealousy of Pisa, and partly (as was alleged) to a desire to
repair the deficiency of population caused by the great plague
of the preceding year. On 31 May 1349 Clement VI
granted the customary Bull for all faculties.[3] But the same
ill luck which had attended the republic at Imola in 1321
seems to have pursued all its subsequent efforts to make
Florence a leading university. Neither pains nor money were
spared. An annual sum of 2,500 florins was set aside for the
expenses of the *studium*.[4] Conservators were appointed, and
distinguished professors were at times secured, but they
would not stay. At one time Perugia robbed it of Baldus;[5]
at another Bologna enticed away Angelus of Perugia, even
before the completion of the two years during which he was
bound by oath to lecture at Florence.[6] Her own illustrious citizen Petrarch resisted all the importunities by which
Florence tried to entice him away from his canonry at
Padua.[7] Like other republics, too, Florence imitated the
bad example set by the despot Frederick II, and for-

[1] See above, p. 33.

[2] [Davidsohn, pp. 142, 143;
Denifle, i. 554–9. After the tyranny
of Castruccio Castracani and the
departure from Italy of Lewis the
Bavarian, the commune was able to
do rather more for the *studium*; e.g.
Cino da Pistoia was teaching civil
law there in 1334. See Davidsohn,
volume of notes, p. 38; Zaccagnini,
Cino da Pistoia, Pistoia, 1918.]

[3] *Statuti*, p. 116; Matteo Villani,

Chron., lib. i, cap. 8 (ed. Moutier,
Florence, 1825, i. 15). Soon after
the foundation of the *studium* we
learn that the salaries were suspended on account of the expense
to the commune, but they were
resumed in 1357, Villani, lib. vii,
cap. 90 (iii. 325).

[4] *Statuti*, p. 113.
[5] *Ibid.*, p. 302.
[6] *Ibid.*, p. 356 *sq.*
[7] *Ibid.*, pp. 283, 285, 306, 309.

bade its citizens to study elsewhere than in their own university.[1] Like Siena, Florence also obtained a privilege
from Charles IV in 1364,[2] and in 1429 a 'domus sapientiae' for poor scholars was established.[3] Soon afterwards
Martin V sanctioned a tax on ecclesiastical property for
the benefit of the *studium*.[4] All these measures failed of
more than a very moderate degree of success. The university
never attained the position among the *studia* of Europe which
the rank of Florence among Italian cities might have been
expected to secure for it. After the middle of the fifteenth
century the law-school seems to have died out altogether.[5]
For many years together only a few grammar masters received
salaries from the republic. At length in 1472, under the
guidance of Lorenzo dei Medici, the experiment was abandoned, and the separate existence of the university merged in
that of the more successful and prosperous Pisa, which was
now placed under the government of a board of Florentine
officials.[6] The resolution of the signory suggests at least one
reason[7] for the failure of the university—the scarcity and
dearness of houses. It was the very wealth and commercial
prosperity of the city which proved fatal to tne *studium*. Of
course such a consideration would not have prevented
students from coming to Florence had its university ever
achieved any extraordinary academic prestige. But when
hotels were cheap and abundant at Bologna and Padua, what
inducement was there to students to desert those ancient and
famous schools for a dearer residence in the unhistorical
Florentine university? On the other hand at Pisa, as the
document goes on to recite, the declining prosperity of the
place and the departure of its wealthiest inhabitants, had left

[1] *Ibid.*, p. 115.
[2] *Ibid.*, p. 139.
[3] *Ibid.*, pp. 210, 215, 221 *sq.*
[4] *Ibid.*, p. 218.
[5] *Ibid.*, p. 260 *sq.* There are
only one or two isolated elections of
law professors after 1450.
[6] Fabroni, i. 411, 440. We also
hear of a Florentine *Provisor*,
ibid., p. 78. In 1350 Florence had
appointed for its own *studium*,

'octo prudentes viros cives floren-
tinos, populares et guelfos'. *Statuti*, p. 123.
[7] Fabroni, i. 409; *Statuti*, p. 273.
It also remarks that the delights
and attractions of the city proved
unfavourable to study. This would
be likely to be especially the
case with the sons of Florentine
citizens.

CHAP. VI, an abundance of good houses empty. This is not the only
§ 14.   instance in which we find the endowment of the university
         promoted as a means of resuscitating a decaying city.

The uni-   In the old, traditional, professional studies of the medieval
versity and
the Renais- world the University of Florence occupied but a secondary
sance.   position.[1] The plan of this work prevents us from dwelling
         upon the place of Florence in the history of the Renaissance.
         It must suffice to record the bare facts that its university was
         the first to establish a chair of poetry with the especial object
         of providing lectures upon Dante, and that the first occupant
         of that chair was the illustrious Boccaccio (1373–4).[2] Florence
         was also the first university in Europe to provide a professor-
         ship of Greek. In 1360 Leontius Pilatus lectured in Florence
         upon Homer,[3] and in 1396 Manuel Chrysoloras was elected
         to a chair of Greek at a salary of 100 or (according to one
         document) 150 florins, soon afterwards raised to 250 florins,
         a sum far exceeding any salary then paid to a doctor of law
         or medicine in the same university.[4] In 1404 we seem to trace
         a sort of anticipatory breath of the Savonarola spirit in the
         election of the preacher and humanist John Dominic of
         Florence to lecture on the Epistles of S. Paul. It is probable
         that this friar was no mere scholastic *biblicus*, but one who
         would have sought to interpret the real thought of S. Paul to
         his generation. It is not surprising, therefore, to learn that
         his superiors prevented his accepting the offer.[5] Many other
         names of great eminence in the history of humanism occur
         among the professors of the Medicean period, but the uni-

[1] [It may be noted that Florence
was the first university in Italy to
have an effective faculty of theology (1349). Although Perugia
(1308) and Pisa (1343) were earlier
made *studia* with all faculties,
Perugia waited till 1370 and Pisa
till 1367 before obtaining special
Bulls creating a theological faculty.
See Ehrle, *I più antichi statuti*,
pp. lxiv, lxv. On 9 Dec. 1359 the
first doctor of theology was presented with great pomp in the
cathedral; Davidsohn, p. 146.

After 1447 the ceremony took place
in the church of San Salvatore in
the archiepiscopal palace; *ibid.*,
Notes, p. 38.]
[2] *Statuti*, pp. 161, 345.
[3] Prezziner, p. 16; but there is
no trace of any regular appointment to a salary in the documents.
[4] *Statuti*, pp. 365, 370. Cf. p.
376.
[5] *Ibid.*, p. 380. Cf. Quétif and
Echard, *Scriptores Ord. Praed.* i.
864.

versity as such played a smaller part in the humanistic move- CHAP. VI, § 14. ment than might naturally have been expected. Universities, at least in Italy, were above all things places of professional study, and their professors were long the enemies of human- ism. The connexion of some of its representatives with the University of Florence was thus little more than an accident of its history, and just at the brightest period of Florentine literary history, the university disappeared from Florence altogether.[1]

§ 15. PAVIA (1361)

GATTI, *Gymnasii Ticinensis historia et vindiciae a saec. v usque ad finem xv* (Milan, 1704), the character of which is sufficiently indicated by the title. P. SANGIORGIO, *Cenni storici sulle due Università di Pavia e di Milano*, Milan, 1813. [Giacomo PARODI, *Elenchus privilegiorum et actuum publici Ticinensis studii a saeculo nono ad nostra tempora*, (s.l.) 1753.] VOLTA, 'Dei Gradi academici conferiti nello "Studio Generale" di Pavia sotto il dominio Visconteo' in *Archivio Storico Lombardo*, ser. ii, 1890, p. 517 *sq.*, is a valuable article. The *Memorie e documenti per la storia dell'Università di Pavia* (Pavia, 1877, 1878) contain a large collection of mostly very modern documents (with biographies of professors), but add little to the medieval materials. [DENIFLE, i. 572–81; R. MAIOCCHI, *Codice diplomatico dell'università di Pavia*, 3 vols. (I, 1361–1400; II. i. 1401–40; II. ii. 1440–50), Pavia, 1905–15; *Contributi alla storia dell'università di Pavia, pubblicati nell'XI centenario dell'Ateneo*, Pavia, 1925 (by various writers); L. FRANCHI, *Statuti e ordinamenti della Università di Pavia*, 1361–1859, Pavia, 1925; E. NASALLI ROCCA DI CORNELLIANO, *Il trasferimento dello Studio Visconteo di Pavia a Piacenza dal 1398 al 1402*, Milan, 1927 (see C. G. MOR in *Rivista di storia del diritto italiano*, i, 1928, 180–4).

An interesting aspect of Pavian academic history is noticed by E. PICOT, 'Les professeurs et les étudiants de langue française à l'université de Pavia du XIVe au XVIe siècle', in the *Bulletin historique et philologique* (of the Comité des travaux historiques et scientifiques) for 1917, pp. 71–83.]

PAVIA was famous as a school of law before the first dawn of Ancient school of law. the scholastic reputation of Bologna. [The existing university looks back to the famous capitulary of Lothair (825) as the starting-point of the life of Pavia as a centre of learning, and Italian scholars have recently sought to establish the continuity of the schools of Pavia from the early law-school to the establishment of the university.][2] The revival of a law-school

---

[1] [Rashdall added here three paragraphs which will be found below, pp. 59–62.]

[2] [See A. Solmi, 'Sul capitolare di Lotario dell'a. 825 relativo all'ordinamento scolastico in Italia', in *Rendiconti del R. Istituto Lombardo*, lvi (Milan, 1923), fasc. 13,

CHAP. VI,
§ 15.

Founda-
tion of
university.

Vicissi-
tudes.
at Pavia by the commune seems to date from the beginning
of the fourteenth century, when Johannes Andreae includes
it with Bologna, Padua, and Perugia as among the most
famous schools in Italy.[1] Its erection into a *studium generale*
(with the privileges of Paris, Bologna, Oxford, Orleans, and
Montpellier) was obtained from Charles IV in 1361 by its
tyrant Galeazzo II Visconti;[2] and in 1389 a similar foundation-
Bull was granted by Boniface IX (which entirely ignores the
previous imperial Bull), and another conferring the privilege
of dispensation from residence.[3] There was a university of
medicine and arts as well as of law: and Pavia for a time took
a respectable place among Italian *studia*.[4] We have seen that
in 1398 the university was revived at Piacenza, and that the
University of Pavia is generally believed to have been formally
transferred to that city. [Owing to a migration to Piacenza,
which was apparently due to the plague, Pavia was certainly
almost deserted during the next three or four years by the
masters and scholars,[5] and the university again] sank to a very

14; the same, 'La persistenza delle
scuola di Pavia nel media evo fino
alle fundazione dello studio generale, 1024–1361', in *Contributi*, pp.
17–42; the same, on G. Mengozzi,
*Ricerche sull'attività della scuola di
Pavia nell'alto medioevo* (see above,
vol. i, p. 105), in the *Rivista di storia
del diritto italiano*, i (1928), 161–8.]

[1] 'Studia Italie facundissimis et
clarissimis doctoribus floruerunt,
nam hoc Bononiense studium tunc
habuit Ia. Butrigarium in legibus
. . . etiam alia studia sc. Paduanum,
Papien. et Perusinum facundissimis doctoribus claruerunt.' (Ap.
Denifle, i. 577.) Kaufmann (i. 387)
makes Pavia a *studium generale* at
this time (i.e. before 1348) with
somewhat better reason than in the
case of some other of his emenda-
tions of Denifle's list: but a flourishing *studium* was not necessarily
general.

[2] Gatti, p. 129; Sangiorgio, p.
40; *Memorie*, pt. ii, p. 2. [*Statuti*,
p. 3.]

[3] Gatti, p. 139; *Memorie*, pt. ii,
pp. 4, 6. [*Statuti*, pp. 5, 7.]

[4] [The statutes of the university
of arts are lost. Those of the university of jurists (1395) survive in
the Basel archives and were first
published by J. Hürbin, *Die
Statuten der Juristen-Universität
Pavia vom Jahre 1396 (sic)*, Lucerne,
1898; secondly, by Maiocchi, and
lastly by Franchi, *Statuti*, pp. 13–
92. Maiocchi and Franchi both
print the statutes of the colleges of
doctors of law (1395) and of arts and
medicine (1409).]

[5] [Cf. above, p. 37. Mor, in
his criticism of E. Nasalli (see
bibliography above), argues that
Gian Galeazzo's decree of 1 Jan.
1399 'pro felici studio inchoatura'
implies the transformation of the
studium at Piacenza into a ducal
school, and that the transfer of students from Pavia was a similar act of
ducal authority. The solemn acts
of granting the licence continued
to be performed at Pavia.]

low ebb in consequence of the political confusion which CHAP. VI
followed the break-up of Gian Galeazzo's dominions.[1] It had § 15.
no doubt practically ceased to exist by 1412, when its restoration was undertaken by Filippo Maria Visconti, who in that
year succeeded to the duchy of Milan in addition to his
county of Pavia. It is not, however, till about 1421 that the
graduations seem to have became numerous or the university
to have entered upon a period of permanent prosperity.[2]
The edict which Galeazzo Visconti had published in 1361,[3]
forbidding his subjects to study elsewhere than at Pavia, was
renewed. Pavia became the university town of the Milanese,
as Pisa had become the university town of Florence, and
Padua of Venice. But the students of Pavia were by no means
exclusively drawn from the immediate neighbourhood. German students still retained the habit of studying in Italy, and
Pavia is especially mentioned with the more famous Padua
as a university which they frequented.[4] Here, as at Pisa and
elsewhere, commercial and political decline contributed, by
emptying the good houses of the town, to secure academical
success.[5]

§ 16. FERRARA (1391)

BORSETTI, *Historia almi Ferrariae Gymnasii*, Ferrara, 1735; GUARINI, *Ad
Ferr. Gymn. Hist. per F. Borsettum conscriptam Supplementum, &c.*, Bologna,
1740, 1741. Guarini corrects many of Borsetti's uncritical assumptions.
There is an ineffectual *Defensio* by Borsetti (Venice, 1742). The statutes of
the university of arts and medicine are printed by Borsetti, i. 364. EFISIO,
Notizie Storiche sulla Università degli Studi in Ferrara, Ferrara, 1873, is
a very slight affair. [DENIFLE, i. 322–5; A. BOTTONI, *Cinque secoli di
Università a Ferrara*, Bologna, 1892. Much has been written on the
scholars of the fifteenth and sixteenth centuries. See A. SOLERTI, 'Documenti riguardanti lo studio di Ferrara nei sec. XV e XVI', in *Atti e
memorie della deputazione Fer. di storia patria*, iv (1892); and especially
G. SECCO-SUARDO, 'Lo studio di Ferrara a tutto il secolo XV', in the same

---

[1] Denifle (i. 581) declares that
the university at Pavia ceased to
exist in 1404, but the list of rectors
in *Memorie*, pt. i, p. 7, is continued
till 1409.

[2] *Memorie*, pt. ii, p. 9 *sq.*; Volta,
p. 555 *sq.*

[3] Gatti, p. 134; Sangiorgio, p.
42; *Memorie*, pt. ii, p. 3 (renewed

in 1392. *Ibid.*, p. 8).

[4] Aen. Sylvius, *Ep.* 40 (*Opera*,
Basel, 1571, p. 526).

[5] 'Nam ipsa civitas et domus
sunt plerumque vacuae et inhabi-
tatae, et mercatum de pensionibus
domorum habemus pro libito.'
Petrus Azario, *Chron.*, p. 291, ap.
Sangiorgio, p. 41.

CHAP. VI, publication, vi (1894), 27–294; also the works of G. PARDI, *Lo Studio di*
§ 16. *Ferrara nei sec. XV e XVI*, Lucca, 1900, and *Borso d'Este*, Pisa, 1907.]

Founda- THERE were schools in all faculties except theology at Ferrara
tion. at least from about the middle of the thirteenth century, but
the *studium* did not become general till 1391.[1] In that year
the Marquis Albert of Este took the opportunity offered by
a state visit to Boniface IX, as whose vicar he nominally
ruled, on occasion of the papal jubilee, to ask for the privileges
of a *studium generale* in all faculties. A Bull was accordingly
granted[2] conferring the privileges of Bologna and Paris. The
burden of the salaries, however, proved too heavy for the
resources of the town, which three years later petitioned the
Marquis to release it from the obligation.[3] Another unsuccessful attempt was made to renew the *studium* in 1402;[4] but
Revival the real resurrection of the university does not begin till 1430,
in 1430. when the movement for a restoration of the university originated with the city government. A contract was entered
into with the humanist John de Finotis, then teaching at
Bologna, to transfer himself and his pupils to Ferrara,[5] and
in 1436 the still more famous Guarino of Verona, who had
been brought to Ferrara by the Marquis Niccolo d'Este a
few years earlier, was hired; and after the more elaborate
'reformation' of 1442[6] the university rapidly became a
flourishing *studium*, though its celebrity was not of the
Equivocal highest kind. It had the reputation of a place where degrees
reputation. could be had cheaply. Indeed, by the sixteenth century it
had acquired the sobriquet of 'the refuge of the destitute'.[7]

[1] [Miss Helen Briggs has noted
an invitation to Ferrara ('tua noscit
prudentia circumspecta quod Fera-
rie in iuridica facultate studium
reflorescit') in an early thirteenth-
century work on *dictamen*: 'Incipit
sumula dictaminis a magistro Gui-
donis alto stilo', &c. Estensian
Library, Modena, MS. Campori,
n. 26. The work is presumably
by Guido Faba.]

[2] Borsetti, i. 18. The story of
the earlier foundation or transference of the University of Bologna
to Ferrara, accepted by Borsetti,

rests upon no authority. See
Guarini, i. 13. As an illustration
of the received notion as to the
imperial prerogative, it is noticeable that Frederick III in person
conferred the doctorate and its insignia upon a student at Ferrara.
Borsetti, i. 77.

[3] Jacobus de Delayto in Muratori, *Rer. Ital. SS.* xviii. 909.

[4] *Ibid.*, p. 973. Denifle, i. 323 *sq.*

[5] Borsetti, i. 29 *sq.*

[6] *Ibid.*, p. 47 *sq.*

[7] See above, vol. i, p. 226, n. 4.

In 1474 there were no less than twenty-three salaried professors in the faculty of law, and twenty-nine in that of philosophy and medicine.[1] A body of *reformatores*—appointed partly by the duke, partly by the municipality—was entrusted with the general government of the *studium*, including that most important function of academical government, the appointment of professors[2] and the contracts for their salaries. But the constitution closely followed that of Bologna, and the student-ascendancy was fully maintained. The rectors possessed jurisdiction in all civil suits of students, and in minor criminal cases where a scholar was defendant.[3] Among the distinguished scholars of Ferrara were the fifteenth-century humanist Rudolf Agricola (1475–9) and the theologian Cochlaeus;[4] among its most distinguished students the poet Ariosto.[5]

§ 17. TURIN (1405)

PINGONIUS, *Augusta Taurinorum*, Turin, 1577; SAULI, 'Sulla condizione degli studi nella monarchia di Savoia', in *Memorie della R. Academia delle Scienze di Torino*, 2nd ser., vi (1844), 152 *sq.*; T. VALLAURI, *Storia della*

[1] Borsetti, i. 93.

[2] *Ibid.*, pp. 90, 115.

[3] *Ibid.*, p. 406 *sq.* In more serious cases the rector was to ask that a scholar should be amenable to the jurisdiction of the duke in person and of him only. The rector is to aid the defendant in his defence, and a scholar may not be tortured or 'in persona puniri' without his consent.

[4] *Ibid.*, p. 57. The statutes of the college of theologians, though placed by Borsetti in the seventeenth century (*loc. cit.*, p. 62), are interesting: it is worthy of note that the college claims precedence for its dean above the rectors. Guarini, however, gives the date 1467 (i. 23).

[5] Borsetti, i. 130. [More might be said about the importance of Ferrara in the fifteenth century, especially in the time of Guarino (†1460). For example, from the time of the Council of Ferrara, summoned by Pope Eugenius IV in 1438, there was much intercourse between Ferrara and England. Pupils of Guarino visited England, while Englishmen, including William Grey, Robert Fleming, John Phreas or Free, John Tiptoft, John Gunthorpe, studied with Guarino at Ferrara. (See Ludovicus Carbo, funeral oration on Guarino, in Müllner, *Reden und Briefen d. ital. Humanisten*, Vienna, 1899, p. 98.) Some of these came on to Ferrara from Padua, e.g. Grey and Fleming. In 1446 Reginald Chichele, nephew of the Archbishop of Canterbury, was rector of the university; see the letters of King Henry VI, given from the state archives of Modena, in the *State Papers: Venice*, vi, 1580–2. Cf. W. F. Schirmer, *Der englische Frühhumanismus* (Leipzig, 1931) pp. 101–3. The faculty rolls begin about 1450.]

CHAP. VI, *Università degli Studi del Piemonte*, Turin, 1845, 1846; 2nd ed. 1875;
§ 17.   *Cenni storici sulla R. Università di Torino*, Rome, 1873. Of these works
Vallauri's is the most important. Some documents are printed in *Monumenta Historiae Patriae* (Leg. Mun.), i, Turin, 1838.

Founda- THE University of Turin was founded in 1405 by Louis of
tion.   Savoy, Count of Piedmont and Prince of Achaia, with a Bull
from Benedict XIII.[1] The Bull recites that the reason of the
foundation was the war which was then devastating Lombardy and silencing its universities—that is to say, the war
which followed the partial break-up of the Visconti tyranny
upon the death of Gian Galeazzo in 1402. From these
troubles Turin was free, and in that city the unemployed
professors of Pavia and Piacenza were glad to take refuge.
The university obtained a further charter from the Emperor
Sigismund (in which theology was included) in 1412,[2] and
another in the following year from John XXIII,[3] who ι d
by that time been recognized in Piedmont.

Transfer- After the death of the founder in 1418 the university lan-
ence to   guished.[4] It was restored by Amadeo VIII in 1424,[5] but in
Chieri in
1421,   1421 it appears to have been *de facto* transferred to Chieri,
though it was not till 1427, when all efforts to 'reform' the
studium in Turin had failed,[5] that the duke's formal assent
to the change was obtained.[6] At Chieri the university remained till 1434, when the commune became unable or unwilling to pay the *stipendia* with which they had been saddled
and thence by the duke. Accordingly the *studium* was again moved to
to Savi- Savigliano till 1436, when it returned finally to Turin.[7] Upon
gliano,
1434.   its return it received a new charter from the regent Louis, in
Return to the name of the reigning duke Amedeo VIII, in which it is
Turin.

[1] Vallauri, i. 242.
[2] *Ibid.*, p. 243.
[3] *Ibid.*, p. 258.
[4] Sauli, p. 154; Vallauri, i. 52 *sq.*
In 1421 the clergy who had been
taxed for the support of the *studium*
petitioned to be released from the
burden as a *studium* no longer
existed at Turin (Vallauri, i. 259):
while the commune of Chieri
voted salaries. (*Ibid.*, p. 57.)
[5] *Ibid.*, p. 251; *Mon. Hist. Pat.*
(Leg. Mun.), i, c. 478.

[6] Vallauri, i. 261 *sq.* After much
further dispute between the two
cities, the duke in 1429 gave a final
decision for Chieri. (*Ibid.*, p. 269.)
[7] *Ibid.*, pp. 68 *sq.*, 275 *sq.* The
move to Savigliano is usually
ascribed to the plague having
reached Chieri, but Vallauri points
out that this was not till 1435, while
the migration took place in 1434.
A new Bull was granted by Eugenius IV in 1438, and another by
Felix V in 1441. *Ibid.*, pp. 304, 305.

provided that the town shall pay an annual grant of 500 florins CHAP. VI,
towards the expenses of the *studium*, to be defrayed by a § 17.
bridge-toll, while the duke promised 2,000 florins to be raised
by a salt-tax. The university was placed under a body of
reformatores named by the duke. There were to be at least
two canonists, four doctors of civil law, one of law and
medicine combined, and one of theology.[1] A Collegio Grassi
or Sapienza for poor scholars was founded in 1457,[2] and
another college by Sixtus IV in 1482.[3] Turin was never
during our period one of the leading Italian universities, but
many jurists of considerable repute taught in it, and its
reputation steadily increased during the latter half of the
fifteenth century.[4]

§ 18. CATANIA (1444)

AMICO, *Catana illustrata*, pt. ii, Catania, 1741, p. 302 *sq.*; CORDARO
CLARENZA, *Osservazioni sopra la Storia di Catania*, Catania, 1833,
p. 202 *sq.*; AMARI, *Sul diritto che ha l'Archiginnasio di Catania di essere
reconosciuto Università di prima classe*, ed. 2, Catania, 1867. [R. SABBA-
DINI, *Storia documentata della R. Università di Catania*, vol. i, Catania,
1898. (On fifteenth century.) This essay was supplemented and revised
by M. Catalano-Tirrito in 1913.]

IN 1434 a petition was presented to Alfonso the Magnificent, Founda-
King of Aragon and Sicily, on behalf of the senate of Catania tion.
by the Catanian jurist Pietro Rizzari, asking for a *studium
generale* in his native town. The petition was eventually
granted, and in 1444 a Bull for its erection was obtained from
Eugenius IV.[5] The Bull is in a rather unusual form. It gives
the citizens of Catania power to found a *studium generale* in
all faculties (with the peculiar addition 'and other liberal arts,
as well Greek as Latin'), on the model of Bologna, and confers upon it the privileges belonging to *studia generalia* 'by
common law'. The clause relating to Greek letters is probably

---

[1] *Ibid.* i. 289 *sq.*
[2] *Ibid.*, p. 318.
[3] *Ibid.*, p. 325.
[4] Erasmus took his D.D. here in
1506. Sauli, p. 166. [4 Sept. 1506.
The original diploma is preserved
in the University Library at Basel.
See *Opus Epistolarum Des. Erasmi*,

ed. P. S. Allen, i, no. 200, p. 432
and note.]
[5] *Catana illustrata*, p. 304.
Cordaro Clarenza and Amico seem
disposed to connect the university
with the ancient school founded
by Charondas and 'illustrated' by
Stesichorus!

CHAP. VI, duc to the survival of the Greek rite and language in Sicily
§ 18.   and to the attempted fusion of East and West by the recent
Council of Florence, rather than to any renaissance ideas.
There is no express grant of the *ius ubique docendi*. The Bull
was immediately published with a royal edict actually estab-
Endow- lishing the *studium*. The King made a grant of 1,500 ducats
ment.   out of a local tax towards the cost of the *studium*; but the
main part of the expense was borne by the city, in whom
the whole government of the *studium* was vested by the
papal Bull.[1] The Bull also speaks of the intention of the
municipality to found a college or colleges for poor students.
Subse- There seems to be no reason to believe that this last part
quent
history. of the plan was ever carried out. But there can be no doubt
that the university came into actual existence, with Rizzari
as one of its professors,[2] and its continued life is attested by
confirmations of privileges in 1458 and 1494.[3] In 1515 a
royal edict speaks of the 'tenuity of salary, and penury', and
consequent incompetence of the professors at Catania, and
decrees that the *studium* shall be 'reformed' and the salaries
paid in full, 'as they used to be of old time to capable and
sufficient persons, and that lectures shall be read as they
used to be'.[4]

Summary.   Summing up the results of our survey of the Italian universities, we shall find it possible to point out their characteristics with more definiteness and precision than will be the
case with the universities of any other country.

(1.) If the early-extinguished Arezzo and the wholly eccen-
tric or abnormal universities of Naples and of the Roman
Court are put aside, they are all modelled on a single type.
That type is, of course, the University of Bologna. In Italy
alone do we find the university of 'foreign' students in its

[1] *Catana illustrata*, p. 313 *sq.*
[2] Cordaro Clarenza, iii. 204.
[3] Amari, p. 16, who refers to
Coco, *Leges a Ferdinando latae*,
&c., f. x.
[4] *Catana illustrata*, pp. 362, 363.
The edict begins with the preamble

'Cum non paucae pecuniarum
summae a Regno extrahantur, quod
Siculi in aliis mundi partibus studiis
vacare compellantur', which no
doubt supplied one motive for the
multiplication of universities elsewhere.

pure and unqualified form.[1] In most cases the extant statutes are more or less closely copied (often to a large extent verbatim) from those of Bologna; and, where the statutes are not preserved, the same indebtedness may safely be inferred.

(2) The second most important characteristic of the Italian universities—though this is a less distinctive feature than the first—is the prominence of legal studies, to which may be added the hardly less important fact that the second place in the university was everywhere occupied by medicine, to which the study of arts was completely subordinate, while theology at first stands altogether apart from university organization, and afterwards enters into but a slight and formal connexion therewith. The Italian universities were primarily the homes of law and of physical science.

(3) The third most conspicuous characteristic of this group of universities is their municipal character. Wherever their origin is distinctly traceable, all except Bologna are found to be due to the initiative of the city or its ruler, whether acting independently or in concert with a body of seceders from Bologna or one of its elder daughters: while, at least from the end of the thirteenth century, the professors are largely supported by the municipality, and are increasingly subject to civic control and supervision. Though in later times the policy of the free cities was often imitated by a tyrant, the Italian university system may be said to be the outgrowth of civic life.[2] The Neapolitan and Roman universities are of course exceptions, but they form no exception to, and may even have contributed to promote, the close connexion of the universities in Italy with the state.

The statutes of Pisa and Florence[3] supply us with good *Increase of state control.*

---

[1] Even in the most democratic Spanish universities the power of the chancellor constitutes a difference.

[2] [Davidsohn, *Gesch. von Florenz*, IV. iii. 142, stresses the point that the Florentines regarded the erection of a *studium generale* in 1322 as an act of its acquired sovereignty. On the other hand, cf. Rashdall's remarks on Siena, above, p. 32–4. The connexion between the university and the bishop, though it varied in intensity, was always present and should not be overlooked.]

[3] The statutes of Florence are largely copied from those of Bologna. [The three paragraphs which follow in the text have been transposed from the section on Florence, in which they appeared in the first edition of this work.]

CHAP. VI. illustrations of the increasing tendency during the fourteenth and fifteenth centuries to place the universities more and more completely under the control of state boards of *reformatores* or *officiales*. The change was indeed a corollary of the system of state-paid *salaria*. The autonomy of the students was originally founded upon the power of the purse. When that power passed to the state, the real control of the *studium* passed with it. The rector, elected by the students from their own body, is still the superior of the professors; but the professors are now more and more relieved from their humiliating dependence on the students by the subjection of both to the state authorities. At Bologna, as we have seen, a committee of students watched over the conduct of professors, and reported to the rector.[1] At Pisa the bedels were entrusted with the duty of noting the attendance and punctuality of professors, and they reported not to the rector but to the *officiales*.[2] Even where the old system continued, the choice of professors everywhere passed practically if not theoretically to the state.[3]

Fusion of all universities into one.   Another constitutional change of great importance may be traced in the statutes of the fifteenth-century Italian universities. Originally each *universitas* was a perfectly separate and independent guild. At a very early period, however, the four *universitates* of jurists at Bologna, Padua, and elsewhere were reduced to two, and these two became practically amalgamated into one society under the joint headship of two rectors. We have already noticed the difficulty which was experienced, as universities multiplied and the number of rich students at each was proportionately diminished, of finding a sufficient number of residents able and willing to take the

[1] See above, vol. i, p. 197. So as late as 1387 at Florence. *Stat. Fiorent.*, p. 34. Yet earlier (1366) we find the *officiales* secretly taking evidence from the scholars as to whether the doctors observe the regulations of the 'Priores et Vexilliferi justitie et Collegia', *ibid.*, p. 153.

[2] Fabroni, i. 448.

[3] *Stat. Fiorent.*, p. 50: 'Quorum omnium Doctorum et magistrorum electionem, pro meliori et maiori Universitatis nostre commodo et honore, in totum decernimus relinquendam et relinquimus in manibus et prudentia . . . dominorum Officialium et Gubernatorum huius almi Studii.' There were, however, still some minor lectureships left to the students, *ibid.*, p. 51.

rectorship. The fifteenth-century statutes are full of provisions for compelling unwilling candidates to fulfil the office. At Florence, for instance, the rector-elect is required to give security that he will not leave the town before the expiration of his year of office. In the event of refusal, military force is to be invoked and the recusant committed to prison.[1] It thus becomes easy to understand the tendency to limit the number of rectors. Consequently we find that the ultramontane and citramontane rectorships have nearly everywhere been fused into one by the end of the fifteenth century, while frequently, as at Pisa and Florence, there is but one rector of the whole *studium*.[2] This change, facilitated no doubt by the increasing subordination of all the universities to the state, tended to bring the *studia* more into conformity with the Parisian pattern. The separate colleges of doctors and the separate universities of students were alike transformed into mere faculties of a single university.

Another consequence of the altered relation of the universities to the state was the erection of magnificent university buildings or the dedication to university purposes of some palace or public building already existing. We have seen how in the earliest days of Bologna the schools were mere private rooms hired by the professors and paid for by a *collecta* from his students. For congregations or great public functions a convent or church was borrowed. As the expenses of the *studium* came to be more and more transferred from the students to the state, the rent came to be paid by the city governments; but still the buildings were as a rule merely hired. At times more dignified lecture-rooms were obtained by renting rooms in a convent. This was at one time the case for instance at Ferrara and at Pisa.[3] But at the end of the fifteenth century we find a tendency to establish the university—all faculties together—in a handsome building. The

University buildings.

---

[1] 'Alioquin Rector antiquus manu militari compellat, et aliis quibuscumque remediis, si opus fuerit, carceribus mancipando.' *Ibid.*, p. 15.

[2] *Ibid.*, p. 14; Fabroni, i. 93, 440.

[3] Fabrucci, *Raccolta*, xxi. 26. [The University of Florence had no official buildings till 1353, when houses were provided in the Via dello Studio (Davidsohn, *op. cit.* IV. iii. 143, 145; Notes, p. 38).]

university had come to be looked upon as a state institution: it was fitting that it should be as well housed as the municipality itself. Thus at Pisa the corn-exchange was turned into a great university building by Lorenzo dei Medici in 1492. And in the course of the following century a similar transformation took place in all the Italian universities, and to some extent in the Transalpine universities also. At Pisa the same building accommodated a college or *sapienza* for poor students, founded by Lorenzo dei Medici.[1]

(4) All the peculiarities above-mentioned were connected with a fourth—the *comparatively* unecclesiastical character of the Italian universities. Except, of course, the University of the Court of Rome, they were under no further ecclesiastical control than was implied in the papal Bull of erection and in the (wholly formal) conferment of the licence by the archdeacon or the bishop. Where (chiefly during their earlier history) we find papal interference with their internal affairs, the interference is political rather than strictly ecclesiastical. In his relations with the Italian universities the Pope acts rather as one of the rival claimants to Italian sovereignty than as the head of the ecclesiastical order: and here, as in other spheres of Italian life, the prominence of the Papacy in Italy dwarfs the importance of lesser ecclesiastical authorities.[2]

In the next chapter I shall proceed to consider the group of universities which on the whole exhibits the closest approximation to the Italian type—the Universities of the Spanish Peninsula.

[1] Fabroni, i. 63–8.

[2] What distinctly ecclesiastical interference there is arises from the jurisdiction exercised by the Church over all guilds and the oaths by which they were constituted.

CHAPTER VII

THE UNIVERSITIES OF SPAIN AND PORTUGAL[1]

The accounts of the Spanish universities in SCHOTTUS, *Hispaniae Biblio-theca seu de Academiis ac Bibliothecis* (Frankfurt, 1608, i. 28 *sq.*), and in Alfonso GARCÍA MATAMOROS, *De Academiis et doctis viris Hispaniae sive pro asserenda Hispanorum eruditione*, Alcalá, 1553 (in SCHOTTUS, *Hispaniae Illustratae*, Frankfurt, 1603–8, ii. 801 *sq.*), contain very little history; and the three volumes of Antonio GIL Y ZÁRATE, *De la instrucción pública en España* (Madrid, 1855), are almost equally useless. Vicente DE LA FUENTE, *Historia de las universidades, colegios y demás establecimientos de enseñanza en España* (Madrid, 1884–9, 4 vols.), contains valuable documents, and forms (with the most important original researches of Denifle) my chief authority for many of the universities. [Adolfo BONILLA Y SAN MARTÍN's *La vida corporativa de los estudiantes españoles en sus relaciones con la historia de las Universidades* (inaugural lecture for the Session 1914–15, Madrid, 1914), is a polemic mainly based on De la Fuente, but it has the merit of exceptional clarity of exposition, together with notes on the conflict between the humanists and the medieval university system and on the life of the students. The latter is studied in Gustave REYNIER, *La vie universitaire dans l'Ancienne Espagne* (Paris–Toulouse, 1902), and Julio MONREAL, *A estudiar a Salamanca*, in *Cuadros viejos* (Madrid, 1878), with especial reference to the customs of Salamanca in the six-teenth century, for which there is an extensive documentation in plays, novels, &c. As opposed to Alcalá, Salamanca was distinguished for its adherence to tradition, so that these descriptions have an inferential value for the medieval period. The same is true of Aubrey F. G. BELL, *Luis de León* (Oxford, 1925), which, with his monographs on particular scholars published by the Hispanic Society of America, is the best account in English of the Spanish universities at that time. He also publishes an extensive bibliography. A brief account of Spanish education is pub-

---

[1] [This chapter has been revised from material and criticism supplied by Professor W. J. Entwistle. In his additions to the general bibliography Professor Entwistle has called attention to the importance of recent work, especially upon the Renaissance in Spain, and the light which it throws upon the intellectual and social life of the universities—a subject which Rashdall did not touch, partly because he failed to appreciate the connexion between academic movements and new intellectual interests in the later fifteenth and early six-teenth centuries. Moreover, the chronological arrangement tends to obscure the fact that the *medieval* universities were in a sense national. There was one *studium generale* in each kingdom: Palencia-Valladolid in Castile, (subordinated in the combined kingdom to) Salamanca in Leon, Lérida in the county of Barcelona, (superior in the combined kingdom to) Huesca in Aragon, Lisbon-Coimbra in Portugal. We have changed the order in which Valladolid and Salamanca stood in the first edition. The author's notes for his revision of the sections on Valladolid and Salamanca have been incorporated in this edition.]

lished in *España* (Barcelona, 1925, extracted from the *Enciclopedia Espasa*), pp. 1061–90, and bibliography on p. 1507. Monographs on particular universities are indicated under each heading. For all that relates to culture in the kingdom of Aragon the documents of Antoni RUBIÓ Y LLUCH's *Documents per l'historia de la cultura catalana miz-eval* (Barcelona, 2 vols., 1908–21) are indispensable. They do not modify the account of the organization of the *studia* studied in this chapter, but they considerably amplify what was formerly known concerning the relation of the universities and *studia particularia* to the general culture of the country and to the policy of the kings. Particularly notable are the documents relating to theological students both in the seminaries and in foreign universities, along with other documents illustrative of the efforts made by the monarchs to institute theological faculties in the universities.

According to BONILLA the distinguishing mark of the Renaissance system in Spain is the emergence of the privileged college of the type of Sigüenza. Sigüenza and Alcalá in Castile, Saragossa, Palma, and Valencia in Aragon, are Renaissance universities. The primitive establishments are: for Castile, Palencia-Valladolid; for León, Salamanca; for Aragon, Huesca; for Catalonia, Lérida (Lleyda); for Roussillon, Perpignan; for Portugal, Lisbon-Coimbra. Lull's foundations in the island of Majorca and Alfonso X's project of a *studium* at Seville arose from contact with Moslem science. In the latter instance the school had, probably, a special relation to the court of interpreters who created for that king so many of the earliest monuments of Spanish prose; these translators inherited the tradition of the 'school of Toledo', namely, the system by which, in the twelfth and thirteenth centuries, European Latinists who desired to become acquainted with Moslem science found at Toledo, Barcelona, and elsewhere, interpreters to assist them and ecclesiastical patronage to remove financial difficulties. See in addition to the well-known works of JOURDAIN, HAURÉAU, WULF, RENAN, STEINSCHNEIDER, HASKINS, &c.: Marcelino MENÉNDEZ Y PELAYO, *Historia de los heterodoxos españoles*; Adolfo BONILLA Y SAN MARTÍN, *Historia de la filosofía española*; Antoine THOMAS, 'Roger Bacon et les étudiants espagnols', in *Bulletin Hispanique*, vi (1904), 18–28; H. SANCHO, *La enseñanza en el siglo XII*, in *Ciencia Tomista*, xi (1914). For Alcalá and similar foundations in Europe see P. S. ALLEN, 'The Trilingual Colleges of the early sixteenth century', in *Erasmus: Lectures and Wayfaring Sketches* (Oxford, 1934), pp. 138–63.]

General features. THE leading features of the Spanish and Portuguese universities may be summarized as follows:

(1) Their most conspicuous characteristic was their close connexion with the crown. They were created by the sovereigns of the various kingdoms, and many of them long or permanently continued to dispense with any further authorization than was conveyed by royal charters. These *studia generalia* 'respectu regni' are, in any formally recognized shape, peculiar to the Spanish Peninsula. In all the

royal authority was frequently exercised in their government, CHAP. VII. and in some the chancellor was a royal nominee.

(2) In their internal constitution and government they were more or less closely modelled on the Bologna type.

(3) But the last-mentioned fact did not exclude a close connexion also with cathedral or other churches. Some of the universities (especially those of Castile) were distinctly developments—though artificial developments under royal authority—of ancient chapter-schools; and except where (as at Lérida) the chancellor was a royal nominee, the bishop and the capitular master of the schools exercised considerable authority in the *studium*.

(4) In the less ecclesiastical *studia*—especially in Aragon —the cities also took some part in the erection and government of the universities.

(5) The chief sources of endowment were the thirds of the ecclesiastical thirds bestowed on the universities by royal authority with ecclesiastical sanction or impropriations of crown benefices or taxes on ecclesiastical property.

§ 1. PALENCIA (1208–9)

Rafael DE FLORANES ROBLES Y ENCINAS, *Origen de los estudios de Castilla, especialmente los de Valladolid, Palencia y Salamanca*, 1793, reprinted in *Collección de Documentos inéditos para la historia de España*, xx (Madrid, 1852); Clodulfo PELAEZ ORTIZ, *La historia de Palencia y la Universidad Palentina* (Palencia, 1881), a popular sketch. [Pedro FERNANDEZ DE PULGAR, *Teatro clerical apostólico y secular de las iglesias de España* (Madrid, 1679), I. ii. 261–83; *Boletín eclesiástico del obispado de Palencia* (1866), p. 289; A. HUARTE Y ECHENIQUE, 'Los colegios universitarios de Castilla en tiempos del Cardenal Mendoza' (*Boletín de la Real Academia de Bellas Artes y Ciencias históricas de Toledo*, xi, 1929, 37–50).]

THE earliest university which can in any sense be said to have been founded at a definite time by an act of sovereign power is the University of Palencia in Old Castile. The founder was King Alfonso VIII of Castile, and the date 1208–9.[1] We must, however, be careful not to exaggerate

---

[1] 'Eo tempore Rex Adefonsus evocavit magistros theologicos, et aliarum artium liberalium, et Palentiae scholas constituit procurante reverendissimo et nobilissimo viro Tellione eiusdem civitatis Episcopo. Quia ut antiquitas refert, semper ibi viguit scholastica sapientia, viguit et militia'; Lucas Tudensis, *Chronicon Mundi*, apud Schottus, *Hispaniae Illustratae*, iv (Frankfurt,

the difference between the mode in which the university arose at Palencia, and the mode in which the earlier, spontaneously developed universities came into being. On the one hand, there was already an old episcopal school here of considerable importance, presided over by the *magister scholarum* of the cathedral. S. Dominic studied both arts and theology at Palencia about the year 1184.[1] On the other hand, no formal deed of foundation was issued by Alfonso or procured from the Pope. Alfonso's part in the foundation consisted in the invitation of masters from more famous schools, no doubt from Paris and Bologna, to come to Palencia and teach for salaries.[2] Alfonso has, indeed, a better

1608), 109. [The word 'ibi' gave rise to the hypothesis, adopted by Floranes, that the school of Palencia had a much earlier origin. It is corrected by Denifle (i. 474) to 'ubi', which is found in the manuscripts, and this reading is further confirmed by the translation in the *Primera Crónica General*, cap. 1007: 'ca por las escuelas de los saberes mucho enderesca Dios et aprovecha en el fecho de la caualleria del regno do ellas son.' J. Puyol, *Crónica de España, por Lucas, obispo de Tuy*, Madrid, 1926, p. 410, reads 'ibi'. Lucas Tudensis's 'eo tempore' is somewhat vague, but is at all events anterior to the death of Prince Fernando in 1211. Rodericus Toletanus (apud Schottus, *Hisp. Illust.* ii. 128) places this event in the year 1209 (i.e. 1208–9 anno circumcisionis). He connects the *studium* of Palencia with Queen Eleanor's foundation of the monastery of Las Huelgas, and immediately before the rupture of the truce with the Moors in 1209. Against the testimony of the two contemporary chroniclers, Floranes (followed by Denifle) argues (1) that Tello was not bishop of Palencia until 1212, but only bishop-elect, and as such would have no interest

in diocesan improvements, and (2) that he would have had no leisure until after the peace following the battle of Las Navas in 1212. The leisure, however, was that of the truce ending in 1209, and the title of bishop given to Tello Téllež de Meneses by his colleague, Lucas Tudensis, in 1236 is probably not to be taken as legally accurate. Tello attended the Castilian king in 1209 when peace was signed with León, and though he signs himself 'Tellius Palentinus electus', he is in one clause bracketed with another bishop under the plural 'episcopi' (*España Sagrada*, xxxvi, App., p. cxlix).]

[1] 'Missus Palentiam, ut ibi liberalibus informaretur scientiis, quarum studium eo tempore vigebat ibidem; postquam eas, ut sibi videbatur, satis edidicit, relictis iis studiis . . . ad theologiae studium convolavit.' *Vita auctore B. Jordano*, in *Acta Sanctorum*, Aug., i. 546. Another thirteenth-century life of the saint says expressly, 'Palentiam, ubi tunc temporis studium generale florebat' (*ibid.*, p. 388).

[2] Rodericus Toletanus, apud *Hispaniae Illustratae*, ii. 128; the text corrected by Denifle, i. 474.

claim to be considered the first founder of endowed pro- fessorships than the first founder of a university; and the credit for the suggestion of this original step is due to his councillor, Tello, Bishop of Palencia. As yet the idea that a charter from Pope or king was necessary to originate a university, and the idea that such a charter could artificially impart some at least of the prestige of a Paris or Bologna mastership to the graduates of a less distinguished school, were alike undeveloped. Indeed it is not clear that any change took place in the constitution or organization of the old cathedral school in consequence of this enlargement of the scope of its instruction. It is probable that the new masters would introduce the custom of inception and the institution of a magisterial guild which had by this time fairly taken root at Paris, if such an institution had not spontaneously developed itself at Palencia; but on this point we have no evidence. We have no evidence, again, as to whether Palencia degrees at this early period actually obtained any sort of ecumenical recognition; but on the whole it is clear that the *studium* erected or designed by Alfonso VIII was meant to embody the vague ideas then expressed by the term *studium generale*.[1] The teaching was teaching of the kind imparted at Paris, Bologna, and Oxford, and it was intended to attract students from all parts.

It appears that masters of theology, canon law, logic and grammar[2] actually began teaching at Palencia; and that is the only sense in which the university can be said to date from 1208–9. For in 1214 the founder died: and the execution of his design was suspended till the accession of Ferdinand III. In 1220 that monarch asked and obtained from Honorius III leave to use for the payment of masters a fourth part of that third of the ecclesiastical property in the diocese which was in Spain assigned to the maintenance of the

Revivals and extinctions.

---

[1] Denifle calls Palencia the first university in Spain, and groups it among the 'Hochschulen mit kaiserl. oder königl. Stiftbriefen'. In the absence of further evidence than he has produced, this seems to me to require the qualification indicated above.

[2] The grammarian is styled an *auctorista*. Doc. ap. Denifle, i. 475. Cf. below, p. 142, n. 2.

fabrics.[1] At the same time the Pope solemnly took the masters and scholars of Palencia under his protection; but nothing that can be properly called a Bull of foundation was issued, nor was any special privilege conferred on masters licensed at Palencia over and above what would then have been enjoyed by masters licensed in any other cathedral school. The first privilege, as distinct from endowment, conferred upon the masters was derived not, as was usual in later times, from the Holy See, but from the synod of Valladolid, which in 1228 enacted that teachers and scholars of theology at Palencia might claim a dispensation from residence for five years.[2]

Extinction, c. 1250. The brief history of the University of Palencia is, like that of so many of the early Italian *studia*, a mere succession of extinctions and revivals. It still existed in 1243.[3] By 1263 it had disappeared, and a petition was presented to the Pope asking for its revival and the bestowal of the privileges of Paris. A favourable reply was received from Urban IV,[4] but it is not known whether any actual steps were taken towards its resuscitation. At all events it had ceased to exist before the end of the century. Two causes contributed to the failure. I shall frequently have occasion to remark that new and artificially created universities never prospered without endowments of some kind or other, direct or indirect. Palencia was, indeed, endowed with a share in ecclesiastical tithes; but it appears that a tithe-war was raging in Castile at about the time when the university was breathing its last gasp. There can be little doubt that its extinction was in part due to the non-payment of the tithes, in part to the competition of more formidable and more favoured rivals, the *studium generale* of Salamanca, and the privileged though not yet strictly 'general' *studium* of Valladolid. At the revival of

---

[1] See *Reg. Hon. III*, ed. Pressuti, no. 3192, and the Bulls cited by Denifle, i. 475. The concession was granted for five years and renewed in 1225. Denifle, i. 476.

[2] *España Sagrada*, xxxvi. 216.

[3] Rodericus Toletanus, ap. *Hisp. illust.* ii. 128.

[4] Doc. ap. *Colección*, &c., p. 204; *Chartul. Univ. Paris.* i, no. 389. This is, it would appear, the earliest document in which Palencia is expressly called a *studium generale*: 'Erat enim in eadem civitate', . . . scientiarum studium generale', &c.

Palencia in 1220 its second founder Ferdinand III was king of Castile only: but, after the final reunion of the crowns of Castile and León in 1230, the king's favour was at least shared by the Leonese University of Salamanca: while Valladolid actually lay in the diocese of Palencia.

As to the constitution of the university which thus expired there is little information to be had; but from the connexion in which it stood to the cathedral school, from the prominent place of theology among its studies, and from the fact that its original masters were brought from France as well as from Italy, we may infer that the constitution of the university, so far as a university in the strict sense developed itself at all,[1] would have been at least partially influenced by the Parisian model. In the later universities of Spain the constitution may be described as mixed; but on the whole they belong to the Bolognese group rather than to the Parisian.

CHAP. VII, § 1.

Constitution.

§ 2. VALLADOLID[2]

Rafael DE FLORANES, *op. cit.*; DENIFLE; LA FUENTE; Matías SANGRADOR VÍTORES, *Historia de la muy noble y leal ciudad de Valladolid* (Valladolid, 2 vols., 1851–2), i. 186 *sq.*; Mariano ALCOCER MARTÍNEZ, *Historia de la Universidad de Valladolid* (Valladolid, 1918 onwards; seven volumes have appeared, namely, i, *El libro Becerro y los Estatutos*; ii, *Bulas apostólicas y privilegios reales*; iii, *Expedientes de provisiones de cátedras*; iv, *Hacienda universitaria y jurisdicción del Rector*; v, vi, vii, Bio-bibliografías of jurists, theologians and physicians); Juan Ortega y RUBIÓ, *Historia de Valladolid*, and León CORRAL, 'Don Carlos del Moral', in *Boletín de la Sociedad Castellana de Excursiones*, iv (1909), 173; *Estatutos de la insigne universidad real de Valladolid* (Valladolid, 1651). [G. DE ARRIAGA (corrected by M. M. HOYOS), *Historia del Colegio de San Gregorio del Valladolid*, Valladolid, 1928.]

THE School of Valladolid dates from at least the middle of the thirteenth century.[3] And it was in very ancient times

[1] The notion that the University of Palencia was transferred to Salamanca is inconsistent with the dates, and seems to have arisen later from a desire to increase the antiquity of the last-mentioned school.

[2] [Rashdall revised this section; his corrections and additions have been inserted in the text and notes without brackets. The section has been transferred to follow that on

Palencia, and to precede that on Salamanca; for Valladolid seems to have taken over the privileges of Palencia, and was in the same kingdom and diocese, whereas Salamanca was not in Castile, but in Leon.]

[3] But the *studium* could not have been very important earlier than 1228, since a council at Valladolid in that year provides for the restoration of Palencia.

CHAP. VII, something more than a merely local church school. A bishop
§ 2.   who died in 1300 is said to have studied at Salamanca and
Valladolid as if they were *studia* of much the same rank.[1] It
presumably obtained privileges of some kind from the Crown
(though the charters are not preserved) at an early date:
since in 1293 Sancho 'el Bravo', in establishing a *studium
generale*[2] at Alcalá, confers upon it the privileges of Valladolid, and this implies that Valladolid was also at this time
regarded as a *studium generale*. In 1304 it received an endowment of 20,000 maravedis annually from Ferdinand IV,
who expressly styles it an *estudio general*,[3] and alludes to the
rector of the *studium*. In 1312 it possessed a doctor of
decrees,[4] and a bedel in 1323.[5] On the whole there can be
little doubt that Valladolid was held in Spain to be a *studium
generale* by the end of the thirteenth century; and it must
certainly have fulfilled all conditions of the definition

[1] *España Sagrada*, xxi. 109. To
assume (with Floranes, p. 70) that
because the *Siete Partidas* speaks
of *studia generalia* in the plural,
at a time when the *studium* of
Palencia had vanished, Valladolid
and Salamanca must be the universities referred to, is hardly warrant-
able. The provisions of the *Siete
Partidas* are quite general. [Alcocer
Martínez (*op. cit.* i, introd., pp.
x–xv) considers that the description
of the institution at Valladolid as an
estudio general by Fernando IV in
1304 and Sancho IV in 1293 is to
be interpreted in the light of the
Partidas, viz. that a *studium
generale* existed in that city by
virtue of either royal or papal
authority. In the absence of a
charter, he considers that Valladolid
tacitly took over the privileges
conferred on Palencia, when the
Palentine university became mori-
bund after the death of Bishop
Tello in 1246, the privileges being
held valid for the chief *studium* of
the diocese of Palencia. Clement
VI's Bull thus legalized a *de facto*
university. On the other hand, the

legislation of the *Partidas* is sometimes no more than hortatory, and
the practice of Alfonso's immediate
successors was lax. Valladolid appears to have developed through
the failure of the papal resuscitation of Palencia in 1263, and it is
possible that its foundation was
the result of Urban IV's Bull
(above, p. 68).]

[2] 'Estudio de escuelas generales.'
Text in Floranes, p. 75, and La
Fuente, i. 100; also in Alcocer
Martínez, *Bulas Apostólicas*, &c.,
No. 2. So far as I have been able
to ascertain, no *studium generale*
was actually erected at Alcalá at
this time. In 1499 a papal Bull was
granted to the College of San Ildefonso, founded there by Ximenes,
conferring upon it the privileges of
a university, college and university
being fused into one according to
an entirely new plan. See below,
p. 106.

[3] Doc. ap. La Fuente, i. 102.

[4] Doc. ap. Floranes, *Colección*,
p. 81.

[5] Floranes, *loc. cit.*, p. 83.

in the *Siete Partidas*. But since it did not possess the *ius ubique docendi*, it is in 1346 described by Clement VI (from the Roman point of view) as being hitherto a *studium particulare* and is by him erected into a *studium generale* with full ecumenical validity for its degrees.[1] A fourteenth-century jurist would perhaps have described its position up to this date as being a *studium generale respectu regni*. But, as has been already pointed out, the idea of ecumenical validity did not enter into the earlier conception of a *studium generale*. There is therefore no reason, with Denifle,[2] to say that the term 'studium generale' is used in 'an improper sense when applied to such a *studium* as Valladolid'.

The original endowment of Ferdinand IV in 1303 appears subsequently to have been charged upon 'thirds' of Valladolid. In 1380 these particular thirds were transferred to the new monastery of San Benito,[3] and in 1398 other thirds were assigned to the university by King Henry III.[4] At this time there were seven chairs, with the following salaries: canon law, 4,000 maravedis; civil law, 4,000; two vesper or afternoon professorships, apparently one in canon and one in civil law, 200 each; a professorship in the *Decretum*, 3,000; and two in logic, 1,500 each. Clement VI had expressly excluded a faculty of theology, but in spite of this exclusion, Henry III added an endowment of 1,500 maravedis for a chair of theology, as well as 1,000 for a chair of philosophy and 1,500 for one of physics (i.e. medicine). In 1418 a regular faculty of theology was established, no doubt in accordance with the policy of breaking down the theological monopoly of the anti-papal Paris, by Martin V,[5] upon a petition presented by the envoys of the king of Castile and

---

[1] See the Bull (in a confirmation by Clement VII) in *Bulas*, No. 1. It recites that a 'studium, licet particulare, ab antiquo viguit, atque viget', and proceeds in the ordinary terms to enact 'ut in villa Vallisoletana praedicta, perpetuis futuris temporibus generale studium vigeat, in qualibet licita, praeter quam theologica, facultate'.

[2] i. 377.

[3] *Bulas*, No. 6; confirmed by Benedict XIII, *ibid.*, No. 10. A Bull of 1417 speaks of various towns and territories owned by the university; *ibid.*, No. 13.

[4] *Bulas*, &c., No. 21.

[5] *Ibid.*, No. 6.

León at the Council of Constance.[1] In the previous year statutes enacted for Salamanca had been imposed upon Valladolid by Martin V in the face of great opposition from the university.[2]

Constitution. Valladolid was not in the Middle Ages the see of a bishop. The licences were conferred by the abbot of the secular collegiate church of S. Mary, till its erection into a cathedral at the end of the sixteenth century, when the chancellorship of the university passed to the bishop. There were, it would appear, the same ups and downs in the mutual relations of the chancellor and the rector which will be found in Salamanca. In 1488 Pope Innocent VIII conferred a most extensive jurisdiction upon the rector, extending to all manner of causes and all manner of persons, and including complete exemption for all members of the university from all episcopal and archiepiscopal authority. In cases of blood he was to appoint the ordinary official of the secular court of the town as his sub-delegate.[3] In 1489, however, the *scholasticus*, who happened at the time to be the great Cardinal González de Mendoza, archbishop of Toledo, succeeded in getting this jurisdiction transferred to himself; but the Bull was cancelled and the rectorial jurisdiction restored by Alexander VI in 1496.[4]

It may be presumed that throughout the fifteenth century the university continued to be governed by statutes based on those of Salamanca, subject to modifications made from time to time. The Salamanca statutes disclose a constitution which is substantially that of a student-university of the Bologna type, and this constitution is preserved in the Valladolid statutes issued by Charles V.[5] The old student-liberties are, indeed, more strictly preserved in these Spanish sixteenth-century statutes than they were by that time in the majority

[1] *Bulas*, No. 16.

[2] *Ibid.*, Nos. 11, 12. Later in the same year, 1417 (No. 18), Pope Martin cancelled certain statutes of Benedict XIII, but it would appear that these related, not to the whole body of statutes, but to statutes about the collection of the thirds.

[3] *Ibid.*, No. 29.

[4] *Ibid.*, No. 30, reciting *in extenso* the Bull of 1489.

[5] See the *Estatutos*, printed in the work of Alcocer Martínez; especially the preamble and, for the date, pp. lxxxix, cxv.

of the Italian universities themselves. There are, however,
a few departures from the ancient model. The abbot as
chancellor has become incorporated in the university and
takes his position side by side with the rector in university
congregations. Six of the twelve endowed professors (*cathe-drarii*) sit in alternate years as *deputati* with the rector,
chancellor, and eight *consiliarii* (seven elected by the council
of the previous year, and one by the College of Santa Cruz),
to form the executive council or ordinary governing body of
the university. There are four separate colleges of doctors,
one for each faculty; but all the faculties are united by
deputy in a single university. The whole of the ordinary
business of the university is in the hands of this joint body,
but it may not enact new statutes nor alienate the property
of the university, nor use its funds to acquire new property,
nor grant dispensations or 'graces'. The rector has power to
summon a *claustrum* of the whole body of doctors and
scholars.[1] The rector is to be a doctor or master or licenciate,
chosen by lot from among three candidates[2] nominated by
the council: but the councillors, similarly chosen by a mixture
of lot and nomination, were apparently students.[3] Above all,
the election to the salaried chairs was entirely in the hands
of the students and the appointments were for three years
only, whereas in Italy the appointment had almost everywhere
been formally or virtually transferred to the prince or the
city. Every student of the faculty had a vote, provided he had
heard the trial-lectures of all the candidates. This system of
'oppositions' or competitive trial-lectures is established here
as in many other Spanish and French universities.[4] A
bachelor was qualified to stand for a salaried chair, but if

[1] *Ibid.*, pp. xi, xii, xv: 'Deputati ... hii cum Rectore et Chancellario vniuersitatem faciant.' The six *deputati* seem to include the rector, as provision is made for the election of only five.

[2] [High rank was one qualification required for the rectorship: 'quales personae nobiles, vel in dignitate constitutae, siue doctores, seu magistri, aut licenciati, ex illis qui tunc in dicta vniuersitate adfuerint, qui nec religiosi nec uxorati sint, idonei ac sufficientes erunt ad hoc vt vnus eorum in Rectorem prenominatae Vniver-sitatis eligatur.']

[3] *Estatutos*, pp. vi–xiv.

[4] *Ibid.*, pp. xvii, xviii, xxi, xxviii.

CHAP. VII, elected, was required to proceed to the doctorate or master-
§ 2. ship within two years. One remarkable provision, which
seems to be of Spanish origin, may be noticed as a hint to
modern university reformers. After twenty years' service, a
professor was allowed what was known as his 'Jubilee' and
was henceforth permitted to receive his full salary and to
lecture by deputy.[1]

Colleges. The 'greater College of Santa Cruz' was founded by Cardinal González de Mendoza, archbishop of Toledo,[2] in 1484,
and the Dominican College of S. Gregory four years later
by Alonso de Burgos, a Dominican bishop of Cordova,
Cuenca, and Palencia.[3] The surviving 'claustro' of this
college is perhaps the most magnificent collegiate building
in Europe.

§ 3. SALAMANCA (*circa* 1227-8)[4]

In addition to the general works already mentioned: Pedro CHACÓN,
Historia de la universidad de Salamanca, 1569, ed. Antonio VALLADARES DE
SOTOMAYOR, in *Semanario Erudito*, xviii (Madrid, 1788); Jacobus
MIDDENDORPIUS, *Academiarum celebrium universi terrarum orbis libri VIII*,
lib. vii, p. 423 (Cologne, 1602); A. VIDAL Y DÍAZ, *Memoria histórica de la
universidad de Salamanca* (Salamanca, 1869); M. H. DÁVILA, S. RUIZ,
S. D. MADRAZO, *Reseña histórica de la universidad de Salamanca* (Salamanca, 1849); MENDO, *De Jure Academico* (Liège, 1668); Gil GONZÁLEZ
DE ÁVILA, *Historia de las antigüedades de la ciudad de Salamanca* (Salamanca, 1606); id., *Teatro eclesiástico de las iglesias metropolitanas y
catedrales de los reinos de las dos Castillas*, iii. 216 and 265-70 (Madrid,
3 vols., 1650); LA FUENTE, *Historia eclesiástica de España* (Madrid-
Barcelona, 3 vols., 1863-75), the same *La retención de Bulas en España
ante la historia y el derecho*, pp. 4-5 (Madrid, 1865); H. S. DENIFLE,
'Urkunden zur Geschichte der mittelalterlichen Universitäten', in *Archiv
für Litteratur- und Kirchengeschichte*, v (1889), 167-225 ('Die päpstlichen
Documente für die Universität Salamanca'). [Enrique ESPERABÉ ARTEAGA,
Historia de la Universidad de Salamanca (Salamanca, 2 vols., in progress,
1914-17); Modesto FALCÓN, *Salamanca artística y monumental*, 1867;
M. BARCO LÓPEZ Y R. GIRÓN, *Historia de la ciudad de Salamanca*, 1863;
M. VILLAR Y MACÍAS, *Historia de Salamanca* (Salamanca, 3 vols., 1877),
I. iii, cap. i-viii; Bernardo DORADO, *Compendio histórico de la ciudad
de Salamanca* (Salamanca, 1768); Pedro Urbano GONZÁLEZ DE LA CALLE,

---

[1] *Estatutos*, pp. xxxvii-viii.
[2] La Fuente, ii. 21.
[3] *Ibid*. ii. 29.
[4] [Rashdall revised this section
and his notes have been used in
this edition without brackets. The
university authorities lent him

printed copies of the documents,
most of which are published by
Esperabé (see bibliography). He
studied the statutes of Martin V in
a printed text (Salamanca, 1562)
in the university library.]

'Constituciones 1422', in *Revista de Archivos*, xlvi (1925), 217–28 and 345–59 (separately 1927)]; GRAUX, 'L'Université de Salamanque', in *Notices Bibliographiques*, &c. (Paris, 1884), p. 317 *sq.*; DONCEL Y ORDAZ, *La Universidad de Salamanca en el tribunal de la historia* (Salamanca, 1858). [*Particular institutions*: S. Bartolomé (Francisco RUIZ DE VERGARA Y ALAVA, *Historia del Colegio viejo de S. Bartolomé*, 1661, reprinted as Part I of José de ROJAS Y CONTRERAS, Marquis of Alventos, *Historia del colegio viejo de S. Bartolomé*, Madrid, 1766); Convento de S. Estéban (Fr. Justo Cuervo, 1914–15, L. G. Alonso Getino, 1904); S. Agustín (Tomás de Herrera, 1562); Santiago (*Constituciones*, 1586); Pelayo (*Constituciones*, 1627). Cf. J. GÓMEZ CENTURIÓN, 'Jovellanos y los colegios de las órdenes militares en la universidad de Salamanca', in *Boletín de la R. Academia de la historia*, lxiv (1914), 5–42. *Constituciones y Estatutos*: of 1243 in La Fuente and Esperabé; of time of Alfonso X, to be inferred from *Siete Partidas*, partida II, título xxxi, leyes 1–11 (Academy editions, 1807 and 1843), Eng. trans. by S. P. Scott, Chicago, 1931; of 1411 in Denifle, *Urkunden*; of 1422 in *Estatutos*, 1625. Critical prolegomena in P. U. GONZÁLEZ DE LA CALLE, *op. cit.*, and analysis in Esperabé, i. Later statutes and constitutions 1538, 1561–2 (in Esperabé, i), 1595, 1625, &c. Constitutions of S. Bartolomé in ROJAS Y CONTRERAS, *op. cit.*, parte II, lib. ii. A contribution to intellectual history: F. PELSTER, 'Zur Geschichte der Schule von Salamanca', in *Gregorianum*, xii (1931), 303–13. P. U. GONZÁLEZ DE LA CALLE, 'Constituciones y bulas complementarias dadas a la Universidad de Salamanca por el Pontífice Benedicto XIII (Pedro de Luna), in *Universidad*, Zaragoza, viii (1931), 291–320 (with A. Huarte y Echenique); id., 'Latín "universitario"', *Homenaje a Menéndez Pidal*, 1925, i. 795–818. M. DE BARRIO, 'La colación de grados en las antiguas universidades', *Azul*, i (1930), 92–111. Articles on the university during the Renaissance, by A. HUARTE, have appeared in the *Boletín Teresiano*, iv, vi, vii. A. GARCÍA BOIZA, *Intervención de los estudiantes en la Universidad de Salamanca en el siglo XVI*, Salamanca, 1933. J. M. BARTOLOMÉ, *Colegios universitarios de Salamanca*, Madrid, 1911. There are many literary impressions of student life at Salamanca in the Golden Age; probably the most vivid is the play of ROJAS ZORILLA, *Lo que quería ver el marqués de Villena*.]

THE universities of Spain were essentially royal creations: and in this respect they stand alone, with the exception of Naples, among the universities founded before the middle of the fourteenth century. In the same sense in which Palencia was founded by Alfonso VIII of Castile, Salamanca was founded by Alfonso IX of León, at some date before his death in 1230;[1] but there is no reason to assume that a foun-

---

[1] Only masters of theology are mentioned. The text and context of Lucas Tudensis, ap. *Hisp. Illust.* iv. 113, reads: '. . . cuncta quae erant in circuitu de Caceres, scilicet arbores, vineas et segetes ferro et flamma vastavit, et ad propria reversus est. Hic salutari consilio evocavit magistros peritissimos in sacris scripturis: et constituit scholas fieri Salmantiae, et ab illa die magis directa est Victoriae salus in manu eius.' [There were raids on Cáceres in

dation-charter ever existed. Like the earliest foundation of
Palencia, this first attempt to found a university at Salamanca
Re- proved abortive. The second founder of the university was
founded
by Fer- Ferdinand III, the Saint, of Castile, who issued a charter
dinand III,
1243. of privilege in 1243.[1] But the prosperity of the university
dates only from the accession in 1252 of his son, Alfonso X
(the Wise), illustrious alike as astronomer, alchemist, poet,
historian and lawgiver—a worthy patron for a great university.
Charter of The most important privileges of Salamanca were derived
Alfonso X,
1254. from the charter granted by this monarch in 1254.[2] Though
Salamanca owed its character as a *studium generale* or at least
a *studium* of more than local renown to royal liberality, its
schools continued to be constitutionally the schools of the
cathedral, and remained under the jurisdiction of the *scholasticus* or *magister scholarum*,[3] who conferred the licences at
night in the chapel of S. Bárbara in the old cathedral.[4] By
the charter of 1254 the power to imprison and (in the last
resort) to banish scholars is recognized as belonging to the
bishop and the *magister scholarum* jointly.[5] Through all

1218 and 1222, but its capture is
ascribed to the year 1227 (Bal-
lesteros, *Historia de España*, ii.
277)]. La Fuente (*Universidades*,
i. 91) gives the date of Salamanca
as 'about 1215', [apparently by way
of compromise between the impossible '1200' of the inscription in
the university and the death of
Alfonso IX in 1230].

[1] The document (in Spanish) is
preserved in the university archives,
and is printed by La Fuente,
Universidades, i. 89; Esperabé, i.
19. It confirms all privileges conferred by the first founder, as well
as the customs established in his
time; hence the propriety of calling
it 'der eigentliche Stiftbrief der
Universität' (Denifle, i. 480) is
questionable. From the words
'tambien en casas como en las
otras cosas', it may be inferred
that the privileges related chiefly
to the taxation of lodgings, everywhere the earliest subject of uni-

versity legislation. Quarrels between
townsmen and scholars are to be
referred to a commission therein
named, consisting of the Bishop of
Salamanca and other ecclesiastics.
Cf. La Fuente, *loc. cit.*, p. 90.

[2] Printed by La Fuente, *loc.
cit.*, p. 295; Esperabé, i. 22.

[3] The latter title (in Spanish
maestrescuela) appears the usual
one in earlier times; but *scholasticus*
is found in the later documents.
The office can be traced from the
twelfth century. We more rarely
find *cancellarius*. La Fuente, *Hist.
Ecles.* iv. 232; *Universidades*, i. 61.

[4] La Fuente, *Universidades*, i.
178. [After the erection of the new
cathedral in the sixteenth century,
the degree of doctor was conferred
in one of the aisles of the nave
(Esperabé, i. 89).]

[5] [La Fuente, no doubt correctly,
amends 'maestro e escuela' to read
'maestrescuela'.]

later changes the ecclesiastical *scholasticus* held a more important position at Salamanca and most other Spanish universities than the chancellor either at Paris or in Italy. The
cathedral was used for meetings of university congregations;
and some vestiges of the close connexion between the university and the chapter survived into recent times.[1] The use
of the word 'claustro' for a university building and for the
professorial body still testifies to the ancient connexion
between the Spanish universities and the Spanish cathedrals.
By the charter of Alfonso X two conservators—the Dean
of Salamanca and another ecclesiastic—were appointed with
more than the usual powers: since the taxation of lodgings,
elsewhere entrusted to a joint board of scholars and citizens,
was here lodged with the conservators only. It is possible to
trace in the somewhat despotic character of this document the
influence of Frederick II's charter for Naples. There is no
positive proof that as yet an autonomous university, whether
of masters or scholars, existed at all: though at the least there
can be no practical doubt that the former assisted in the
examination for the licence and conducted the inceptions.
The masters are expressly forbidden to make a common seal
without the bishop's consent.

In 1255 Alfonso's regulations were confirmed at his request by
Alexander IV. The Bull, however, is no true Bull of foundation:
it expressly recognizes that the king has already founded a *studium generale* at Salamanca, and does not question his authority
to do so, or profess to improve the status of the *studium*.[2]

In the same year the Pope conferred upon Salamanca (1)
the privilege of exemption from corporate excommunication
without the special authorization of the Holy See;[3] (2) the

---

[1] La Fuente, *Universidades*, i. 86.

[2] 'Apud Salamantinam civitatem
. . . venerabilis fratris nostri . . .
episcopi et dilectorum filiorum
capituli Salamantinorum accedente
consilio et assensu generale studium
statuisti, et ut generale studium a
doctoribus et docendis in posterum
frequentetur, humiliter postulasti a
nobis apostolico id munimine robo-

rari.' *Archiv*, v. 169.

[3] On July 15. *Archiv*, v. 169. It
was repeated in September with an
addition in favour of officers of the
university: 'in universitatem magistrorum vel scolarium seu rectorum
vel procuratorum, aut quemquam
alium pro facto vel occasione Universitatis' (*ibid.*, p. 170). Cf. above,
vol. i, p. 312.

CHAP. VII, right to use a common seal, which had perhaps been refused
§ 3. by the bishop; (3) the right of scholars to get absolution for
assaults on clerks from the master of the schools; (4) the right
of graduates to teach in all *studia generalia* except Paris and
Bologna; (5) leave for priests and beneficed clergy, but not
regulars, to study the civil law.[1] The restriction on the *ius
ubique docendi* was removed in 1333.[2] It is significant, however, of the origin of the Spanish universities that in them,
probably alone among the universities of Christendom,
degrees continued to be conferred in the name of the king
as well as the Pope.[3]

The *Siete*   In the celebrated code or project of a code known as the
Partidas,
1263. *Siete Partidas*, issued by Alfonso the Wise in 1263, a whole
title[4] is devoted to the universities of the kingdom. Its provisions may be said to constitute a sort of educational code—
the first of the kind in modern Europe. It is of peculiar
interest to the university historian because it contains the
first authoritative attempt to define the hitherto vague and
indefinite expression *studium generale*. It formally lays it
down that *studia* are of two kinds—'particular' and 'general'.
The former name may be given to any school in which 'a
master in a town teaches a few scholars'. It may be established by a prelate or a town council.[5] Here we have a mixture of the French and the Italian principles: as indeed in
their actual origin the universities of Spain are developments
under papal or royal authority some of the capitular, others
of the civic schools. In a *studium generale* there must be

---

[1] *Archiv*, v. 170–2.

[2] The previous Bull, though addressed 'Magistro scolarum Sala-
mantino', does not expressly entrust
the power of conferring the 'licentiam ubique docendi' to any definite
person. This technical defect was
set right by the Bull of John XXII
in 1333, which recites that, in consequence of the omission, 'honori
dicti studii multipliciter derogatur'
(*Archiv*, v. 173), and proceeds to
confer the required power without
repeating the restriction.

[3] 'Auctoritate Apostolica et Regia

qua fungor confero tibi gradum',
&c. This formula continued in
use till 1830, when the conferment
of degrees was transferred to the
rector. La Fuente, *Universidades*,
i. 190.

[4] [*Partida*, II, título ii (ed. López,
Madrid, 1843) pp. 352 *sqq*. Cf. S.
d'Irsay, *Hist. des universités*, i.140–3.
On the intervention of King Alfonso
in the redaction of his works consult
A. G. Solalinde's article in *Revista
de Filología Española*, ii (1915),
283–8, &c.]

[5] Tit. xxxi, ley i.

a separate master for each of the seven arts, or at least for grammar, logic, and rhetoric, together with at least one master of laws and one of decrees. Such a *studium* can only be established by the Pope, the Emperor, or the king,[1] and the salaries are to be fixed by the last. The power of the king to create a *studium generale* in the full sense of the word is perhaps something of an innovation. But we must remember that the idea that the degrees of a *studium generale* were necessarily of ecumenical validity is not to be found in the *Siete Partidas*, and was not yet established in Europe generally. When it was established, the jurists very reasonably held that the power of a king only extended to the establishment of a *studium generale respectu regni*. To obtain a universal validity for the degrees of a university, the Bull of pope or emperor or long custom was necessary: and those Spanish universities which had not obtained the *ius ubique docendi* by papal or imperial Bull were not held to have acquired this privilege by custom.[2]

How far the autonomous university organization had established itself before the date of the *Siete Partidas* it is impossible to say. It is, however, fully recognized in the provisions of Alfonso. We may, therefore, be quite certain that rectors were elected from this time, if not earlier.[3] The general principle is laid down that 'colleges and confederacies of many persons'[4] are illegal. The case of masters and scholars in a *studium generale* is declared to be an exception. Masters and scholars are recognized as together forming a *universitas*, which is to elect a rector whom they shall all obey. He is required to suppress feuds and quarrels between scholars and townsmen, or among the scholars themselves,

The rectorship.

[1] Tit. xxxi, ll. i, iii.

[2] See above, vol. i, p. 8 *sq.* The *scholasticus* received the right to confer the *licentia legendi ubique* from Pope John XXII in 1333 (*Archiv*, v. 173).

[3] The rectors are first expressly mentioned in 1301. (See below, p. 82.) According to Chacón (p. 18 n.), *consiliarii* were introduced for the first time by the reform

carried out by Benedict XIII as legate *circa* 1380. [The *cancelarius* and the *consiliarii* are noted as functioning in his letter dated 26 July 1411. The office of *primicerius vel prior doctorum*, the general effect of which was to limit the authority of the rector, was first instituted by this letter.]

[4] 'Ayuntamiento, e Confradias de muchos homes.' Tit. xxxi, l. vi.

and especially to enforce those cardinal but seldom observed rules of medieval university disciplinarians—that scholars should not bear arms or walk abroad at night. He has power to punish offenders; but, if he fails to do so, a scholar is amenable to the king's judges. The last provision applies to criminal cases only. In civil cases the defendant scholar is allowed to appear before the bishop or his own master conformably to the authentic *Habita*, which has also inspired the special protection afforded to scholars travelling to or from their university.[1] At the same time provision is made for the examination of candidates for the licence in the Bologna fashion.[2] Various privileges and exemptions are also conferred upon the masters, particularly upon the masters of civil law, who are styled 'caballeros' and 'señores de leyes'. If a doctor of civil law enters a court of justice, the judge is to rise and to invite him to a seat on the bench, and he has constant access to the king's person. After twenty years' regency, he attains to the rank of a count.[3]

Endowment by Alfonso X. The endowment of the university was provided for by its royal patron, though not on a very munificent scale. A sum of 2,500 maravedis was annually entrusted to the conservators for the payment of professors and the other expenses of the *studium*. In the first foundation by Alfonso IX, theology had (as at Palencia) been a prominent object. But in Spain, as in southern Europe generally, law was driving theology out of fashion. And to the 'Castilian Justinian' the encouragement of legal study was the paramount object. Moreover, it

---

[1] Tit. xxxi, ll. ii, vii. That in the then state of law and society, such protection was needed is clear from the clause of the last-mentioned law which provides that the messengers coming to the scholars shall not be arrested for the debts of their fathers or other fellow-countrymen. At Salamanca the *scholasticus* was probably intended at least to share the power conceded to the bishop. Cf. Chacón, p. 25 n.

[2] 'Decipulo debe ante seer el escolar que quisiere haber honra de maestro: e quando hobiere bien deprendido el saber debe venir ante los mayorales de los estudios que han poder de le otorgar la licencia para esto.' Tit. xxxi, l. ix. The exact relations between the *scholasticus* and the doctors in the examinations are not clear. A characteristic feature of the Spanish inceptions in later times was a university bull-fight given at the expense of the inceptor. La Fuente, i. 173 n.

[3] Tit. xxxi, l. viii.

was the consistent policy of the Popes to preserve the theo- CHAP. VII, § 3.
logical monopoly of Paris. The original staff under Alfonso
consisted of one legist at a salary of 500 maravedis, with a
bachelor as assistant (*bachiller canónigo*), three canonists, i.e.
two decretalists at 500 maravedis each, and one decretist at
300, two masters of logic, two of grammar, and two of physic,
at only 100 each.[1] Here, as in Italy, the doctors of law are
treated as a superior class both in point of salary and position:
the doctor of medicine ranks with the mere M.A. or the still
humbler grammarian. It will be observed that only the more
elementary portion of an arts course, which was alone considered necessary as a basis for legal education, is provided
for. An interesting feature of these provisions is that a
master of the organ is provided.[2] The University of Sala- Music
manca appears to be the first which gave both degrees and ^{degrees.}
practical instruction in music. A master of music was always
included among its professors.[3] We hear nothing of musical
degrees at Paris or in Italy, and at Oxford they do not appear
till the fifteenth century.

In the course of time, however, Sancho IV became Collapse
impatient of paying the small endowment settled on the under Sancho
university by his father. Before the end of the century it IV.
appears that the unpaid professors had struck work: and the
studium was suspended till in 1300 Ferdinand IV bethought
himself of the easier method of endowing the university out
of the thirds of ecclesiastical tithes. These thirds had often,
with or without the papal consent, been appropriated by the

---

[1] La Fuente, i. 295.
[2] Salaries are provided for music
in the Bull of 1313 (La Fuente,
i. 313); and two *magistri in musica*
appear in the *rotulus beneficiandorum* of 1355 cited by Denifle, i.
494. Salamanca produced Bartolomé Ramos de Pareja, who, according to Graux (p. 319), 'passe pour
l'inventeur de la musique moderne'.
[3] The chair survived into the
nineteenth century, its last occupant being 'al célebre Dorjagüe,
quizá el mejor compositor de

música religiosa en España.' La
Fuente, i. 98. Salaries are also
assigned to a *stationarius* and an
apothecarius whom Denifle (i. 483
n.) explains as 'denjenigen, wel-
cher entweder ein Depôt von
Lebensmitteln besitzen oder dafür
sorgen musste, dass an den Lebens-
bedürfnissen für die Studierenden
niemals ein Mangel eintrat.' But I
see no reason why the word should
not have its usual modern and
medieval meaning of a purveyor
of drugs.

CHAP. VII,
§ 3.
Re-
endowed
by Fer-
dinand IV
and Boni-
face VIII
with
thirds.
kings under pretext of the holy war against the Saracens; and in 1301 Boniface VIII authorized the plan of Ferdinand IV for three years.[1] The thirds arising from the diocese of Salamanca were to be consigned to a separate chest in the treasury of the cathedral, the three keys to be kept one by the dean, one by the rectors, and one by the conservators.

The third part of the tithes thus appropriated to educational purposes was (as has been said) the third which properly belonged to the fabrics of the churches. After its withdrawal the churches naturally began to fall into disrepair: by 1310 the condition of the cathedral had become alarming. The thirds were consequently withdrawn from the university by Pope Clement V.[2] The usual strike of professors followed, and the existence of the *studium* was virtually suspended till 1313, when the same pontiff, upon petition of the bishop, restored one-third of the thirds to the professors:[3] and a varying share in these impropriated thirds formed the basis of the endowment of the university down to the latest times.[4]

Endow-
ment of
theological
chairs and
'reform'
by Pedro
de Luna.
The fame of medieval Salamanca was almost entirely that of a school of civil and canon law. After the very earliest days of the university we do not hear of a single doctor of theology till 1355.[5] In 1380, however, the Aragonese Cardinal Pedro de Luna came to Castile as an envoy on behalf of the Avignon claimant to the chair of S. Peter. Salamanca and the Castilian kingdom declared for Clement VII: and an alliance now began between the Avignon papacy and Salamanca which eventually passed into a permanent friendship between the Holy See and the most ultramontane of universities. Pedro de Luna undertook as legate a visitation and 'reformation' of the university, which was completed in 1411 after his accession to the papacy as Benedict XIII. A

---

[1] See the document in an *inspeximus* in *Memorias de D. Fernando IV de Cast.* ii (Madrid, 1860), 267; also in Esperabé, i. 31-3. No mention is here made of the purpose to which the thirds were to be applied.

[2] Denifle, i. 458.

[3] The Bull is printed by La Fuente, *Universidades*, i. 312. Cf. Denifle, i. 490.

[4] The papal Bulls on the subject are noticed by Denifle (i. 490), and the royal edicts are printed by Esperabé. Cf. Vidal y Díaz, p. 27 *sq.*

[5] Denifle, i. 492; and *Archiv*, v. 220.

prominent feature of this 'reform' was the establishment of theological chairs, which were endowed by kings John I and Henry III.[1]

The exclusion of the theological faculty from Salamanca and other *studia* by the earlier popes, especially the Avignon popes before the Schism, was due to a desire to maintain the theological monopoly of Paris. The encouragement of the theological faculty by Benedict XIII and Martin V was no less clearly inspired by antagonism to the Gallican university. From the conciliar epoch the University of Paris became more and more identified with a theology antagonistic to ultramontane claims, and, from the sixteenth century, more and more out of harmony with the prevailing spirit throughout the greater part of Roman Catholic Europe. In Italy itself there was hardly a faculty of theology worthy of the name. In the controversies with Gallicans and with Protestants it was to Salamanca, almost alone among the greater universities of Christendom, that the popes could look for champions of the pure ultramontane faith. At the same time it should be mentioned to the credit of Salamanca that her doctors encouraged the then almost unorthodox designs of Columbus,[2] and that the Copernican system found early acceptance in its lecture-rooms.[3]

Beyond what may be inferred from the *Siete Partidas*, we know nothing of the Salamancan constitution before the date of the statutes promulgated by Benedict XIII in 1411. These statutes, however, presuppose an earlier code issued by Pedro de Luna as legate, and do not enable us to do more than trace the main outlines of the university constitution. We have already seen that that constitution approximates to the Bologna rather than to the Parisian model. It is emphatically a student-university with a rector elected by the students, and a body of *consiliarii* elected by the students of the various

[1] La Fuente, i. 208 *sq.*; Chacón, p. 25 *sq.*; Denifle, i. 492; *Archiv*, v. 208 *sq.* The new statutes were partially confirmed by King John, with the exception of certain provisions about jurisdiction which some regarded as injurious to the royal authority; Esperabé, i. 90–4. [González de la Calle, in *Universidad*, viii (1931); Bell, p. 49.]

[2] La Fuente, ii. 26; Vidal y Díaz, p. 55; Doncel y Ordaz, p. 13 *sq.*

[3] Doncel y Ordaz, p. 9; Graux, p. 319.

nations or dioceses:[1] the doctors form a college of their own, with a *prior* or *primicerius* at its head, though it does not appear that they were actually excluded from votes in congregation as at Bologna.[2] The three other most important modifications of the Bolognese constitution are: (1) the inclusion of all faculties under a single rector (the faculties, with the exception of theology, do not appear even to have separate deans of their own);[3] (2) the existence, apparently, of only one *collegium doctorum*;[4] (3) the extensive powers of the cathedral *scholasticus*, or as he is now called 'Chancellor of the University'. His functions extend considerably beyond the grant of the licence. He has important judicial powers, being recognized as the *iudex ordinarius* of scholars, and his jurisdiction extends both to contracts and to delicts, in addition (it may be presumed) to strictly spiritual causes. The jurisdiction conferred by the *Siete Partidas* upon the rector must now, if not before, have been limited to dealing with offences against the statutes.[5] Besides this the *scholasticus* has several functions of a more directly academical character. The appointment of examiners requires his approval.[6] It is his duty to enforce by ecclesiastical censure the payment of the *salaria* upon the rector and the official immediately charged with that duty and known as the 'administrator of the University', and the appointment to vacant chairs by the rector and *consiliarii*.[7] He is entrusted with one key of the university chest, the remaining four being kept by the rector, another representative of the student-university,

---

[1] The names are not mentioned in 1411. The statutes of Martin V provide for the election of two councillors each by four groups of dioceses, which are not expressly called nations. All lie in the peninsula (including Portugal), but the group at the head of which stands Burgos includes students 'de regnis Aragonie, Navarre vel alia quacunque natione extranea'. *Archiv*, v. 186.   [2] *Ibid*., p. 194.

[3] Cf. La Fuente, i. 274 *sq*. At an earlier period there seems to have been more than one rector.

[4] *Archiv*, v. 194.

[5] *Ibid*., p. 196. The statute only refers to cases where an offending scholar has left the town, but a general jurisdiction is implied *a fortiori*. Royal conservators are also mentioned (p. 186). The apostolic conservators are not named, but the execution of this as well as previous papal statutes is entrusted to the archbishop of Compostela (p. 197).   [6] *Ibid*., p. 199.

[7] *Ibid*., p. 189, 193, cf. p. 181. He conferred bachelors' degrees. Vidal y Díaz, pp. 121, 203.

and two of the senior doctors of law.[1] He has, moreover, a
general power of punishing 'transgressions of oaths and constitutions and other crimes' in the university and of holding
annually 'general and special' inquisitions for their discovery.[2]
In the Salamancan constitution, in short, we see a Bologna
student-university grafted on to an old capitular *studium*
without destroying, though of course it did in a measure
limit, the ancient jurisdiction of the cathedral *scholasticus*.[3]

These provisions[4] of the Avignon Pope were for the most
part confirmed by king John I, but with certain reservations.
The king refused to sanction the increased jurisdiction which
the new statutes conferred on the *scholasticus* over lay
students,[5] and he objected to the powers entrusted to the new
ecclesiastical conservators and to their interference with the
already existing royal conservators.[6] The *scholasticus*, on
being informed of the royal decision, complained that the
royal conservators did not do their duty; whereupon the King
issued an edict to these officials requiring them duly to protect the university and its members,[7] and another addressed
to the *alcalde* and other municipal authorities of Salamanca
requiring them to support the authority of the master of the
schools and to allow him the use of the secular prison for the
confinement of his prisoners.[8]

The statutes of the anti-Pope were not long in force. Soon
after his deposition by the Council of Constance, a new code

[1] *Archiv*, v. 190.

[2] *Ibid*., pp. 195, 196.

[3] At some previous date the university must have obtained exemption from all episcopal and archiepiscopal authority; since in the
Bull of 1411 (*Archiv*, v. 199) its
members are described as 'post
sedem apostolicam immediate sub-
iecti' to the *scholasticus*. The
statutes of Martin V differ only in
detail from those of 1411. They
give the appointment of *scholasticus*
to the 'difinitores negotiorum ipsius
universitatis', who presumably succeeded to the single 'administrator'
of 1411 (*loc. cit*.).

[4] [The four following paragraphs

were written for the revised edition
by Rashdall. Cf. also a note by
J. Puyol on the statutes or constitutions of 1422 in the *Boletin de
la R. Academia de la historia*, xcii
(1928), 23–5; and the articles of
González de la Calle and A. Huarte
y Echenique in the *Revista de
archivos*, xlvi (1925).]

[5] This seems to refer to the
jurisdiction in contracts and delicts.
Archiv, v. 196.

[6] Esperabé, i. 90. The only conservator or 'executor' mentioned in
the papal statutes is the archbishop
of Compostela; *Archiv*, v. 197.

[7] Esperabé, i. 92.

[8] *Ibid*., p. 94.

was issued by Pope Martin V, which was based with some 'changes' upon the provisions of the statutes (no longer extant) made by Pedro de Luna as legate as well as upon those subsequently issued by him as Pope. In these revised statutes[1] it is provided that the rector is to be chosen alternately from León and Castile, and to be admitted to his office by the archbishop of Compostela. There are to be eight *consiliarii*. Appointments to the salaried chairs are to be made by the rector and *consiliarii*; but the senior applicant is always to be chosen unless a majority of the students in the faculty vote for a junior. The rector is to take precedence of the *scholasticus* in congregations; in the graduation ceremonies the precedence is reversed. Some interesting regulations are given for the conduct of examinations and graduations. The candidate for a bachelor's degree might choose a doctor to confer the degree upon him. He was to demand the degree from the doctor sitting in his *cathedra*, which the doctor thereupon would vacate; the bachelor would take his place and deliver a very short harangue or lecture. Before the 'private examination', i.e. for the licence, the candidate is to be presented by the senior doctor to the *scholasticus*, who is to ask him secretly whether he has given or promised anything for the licence. Upon receiving a satisfactory reply, the *scholasticus* is to assign a day *ad recipiendum puncta*, i.e. on which portions of the texts appropriate to the faculty concerned would be assigned. When the day comes the candidate, after hearing a mass of the Holy Ghost in the cathedral, is to present himself, in the cathedral, before the *scholasticus* 'sitting in the midst of the doctors'. The bedel is to hand to each doctor one book of the civil or canon law, as the case may be. Each doctor is to open the book not more than three times, and the candidate is to choose one of the 'titles' or 'matters' from the pages they hit upon; the doctor is to select a chapter or law from this.[2] The candidate is to

---

[1] [Rashdall based what follows upon the printed, but unpublished, text placed at his disposal by the university authorities.]

[2] Such appears to be the mean-ing of the complicated sentence (*Const.* xviii). Salamancan tradition adds that the candidates spent the night before the *examen* in the chapel of S. Bárbara, which still

be given some time for preparation, then to deliver his pro-
bationary lecture before the assembled doctors at a further
meeting in the university chapel in the cathedral. On
the next morning he is to call at the house of the *scholasticus* to hear the decision. As in Italy, this was the real
examination; the subsequent 'public examination', at which
the insignia of the doctorate were delivered, was merely a
formality.

A statute for the theological faculty provides that there
shall be a theological chair in each college which maintained
theological students, in each house of masters, and in the
cathedral. In each Mendicant house the doctor was to be
appointed by the superior of the order, in the other cases by
the *scholasticus* or doctors, until the doctor so appointed has
a bachelor under him who can succeed to the chair, after
which the bachelor succeeded apparently as a matter of
course.

The most important change introduced into the new code
constitutes a very considerable modification of the originally
democratic student-university. Since the general congregations of students had led to undue interruption of studies and
relaxation of discipline, it was provided that the whole business of the university should henceforth be entrusted to a
body of *diffinitores*, consisting of the rector, the *scholasticus*,
and twenty persons selected by the university from student
nobles and holders of dignities (not being under twenty-five
years of age), and ten persons elected by and from the regents
holding salaried chairs. Only if a majority—in important
matters, a two-thirds majority—so determined, could any
matter be laid before congregation. At the same time the
election of the *scholasticus* was entrusted to the new body of
diffinitores. He was to be admitted by the archbishop of
Toledo or by the legate or nuncio of the Apostolic See. It
will be observed that the bishop of Salamanca is now deprived
of all part in the government of the *studium*, which is declared to be subject to the *scholasticus* immediately after the

contains the desks which held their   ideas, a curious way of preparing
books: surely, according to modern   for an examination.

CHAP. VII,
§ 3.

Apostolic See.[1] The right of the *diffinitores* to elect the *scholasticus* was revoked, on the petition of the chapter, by Martin V, but was restored by Eugenius IV. The same pope made the archbishop of Toledo, the bishop of León, and the *scholasticus* conservators of the property and persons of the university.[2]

Women students.

Salamanca is not perhaps precisely the place where one would look for early precedents for the higher education of women. Yet it was from Salamanca that Isabella the Catholic is said to have summoned Doña Beatriz Galindo[3] to teach her Latin long before the Protestant Elizabeth put herself to school under Ascham. The Renaissance may, indeed, be considered to have begun in Spain long before it began in England.

Receives the *Liber Sextus*, 1298.

Recognition by Council of Vienne, 1311.

Numbers.

Salamanca was recognized as one of the great universities of Europe—as the representative university of Spain—by receiving the *Liber Sextus* of Boniface VIII with a special Bull in 1298.[4] Again in 1311–12 the Council of Vienne placed it among the five universities at which professors of the oriental languages were to be established, though at the actual date of the council it was undergoing one of those total eclipses which marked its early history; and we have evidence of the existence of these oriental lectures as late as the fifteenth century.[5] The numbers do not in the fourteenth century appear to have been very large; though by the sixteenth the university had become one of the largest in Europe. A roll sent to Innocent VI in 1355 contains the names of ten masters and licentiates, eighteen bachelors, 179 scholars in law, and 130 in other faculties.[6] All the names are Spanish

---

[1] *Const.* xxxiii. A royal edict of this date speaks of murders having been committed in connexion with the disturbances mentioned above; Esperabé, i. 87.

[2] Papal Bulls preserved in the university registry.

[3] Graux, p. 320. The privileges of a Spanish university—those of Lérida in 1300—are almost the only ones with which I am acquainted, which expressly contemplate married undergraduates.

Villanueva, *Viage Literario*, xvi. 203.

[4] Printed by La Fuente, *Universidades*, i. 299.

[5] At least a 'legens de Ebraica cum aliis duabus linguis sibi ex certo statuto annexis, videlicet Caldea et Arabica' is provided with a salary by the statutes of 1411. *Archiv*, v. 178. Cf. above, p. 30.

[6] In 1602 there were, according to Middendorpius (p. 436), 4,000 students at Salamanca, and there

with the exception of two which are Portuguese. A large CHAP. VII, number of these Salamancan rolls survive. It was 'not for § 3. nothing', as Father Denifle remarks, that the university down to the most recent times has displayed the papal tiara in its arms. An escutcheon bearing Pedro de Luna's arms may still be seen upon the ancient university building which was erected under the auspices of that pontiff, while an inscription in the 'claustro' of the university even describes him as the 'founder and prime restorer of Salamanca'.[1]

The schools of the university were originally erected in 1413–15:[2] the building in its present sumptuous form dates from the days of Ferdinand and Isabella.

Salamanca was late in acquiring colleges. The small Colleges. College of Oviedo is said to have been founded in 1386 by Guterius, bishop of that see, for six poor students in canon law.[3] The earlier and most famous of the 'four greater Colleges'—the Colegio Viejo or Colegio Mayor de San Bartolomé—was founded by Diego de Anaya Maldonado, archbishop of Seville, in 1401 for ten canonists and five theologians, who were first elected in 1417. Its fine buildings still occupy one side of the cathedral square. Its constitution was that of the Italian colleges. It was governed by an annually elected rector and three *consiliarii*; and the statutes are throughout modelled on the plan of a student-university.[4] There was also a Hospital of S. Thomas Aquinas

had formerly been 7,000. The Salamanca matriculation-book of 1552 shows a total of 6,328 persons —an interesting piece of evidence in determining the academical population of the medieval universities. La Fuente, *Universidades*, i. 170. The oath to the rector, in which 'matriculation' consisted, was renewed annually, *loc. cit.* In 1641 Salamanca still boasted 3,908 students; sixty years later there were 2,000; at the beginning of last century 1,000; in 1875, 391. Graux, pp. 330, 332. [Cf. Bell, *Luis de León*, p. 63.] Such has been the fate of the city which, on the

strength of its university, aspired to the title of the Eternal City.

[1] 'Academiae conditor et reparator primarius.' *Archiv*, v. 225; La Fuente, *Universidades*, i. 209.

[2] *Archiv*, v. 203; Esperabé, i. 98.

[3] Vidal y Díaz, p. 300. [According to La Fuente, ii. 89–90, it was founded in 1517.]

[4] See the statutes in the third volume of the elaborate *Historia del col. viejo de S. Bartol.*, Madrid, 1766–70, by Jos. de Rojas y Contreras. As bearing on the usual age for entering on the higher faculties, it is noticeable that the minimum age for admission was

for sick scholars, founded in 1413 on the site of the old Jewish synagogue, and supported by the contributions of the charitable.[1] But it was not till the sixteenth century that colleges began to multiply at Salamanca.[2] Here, however, the colleges remained faithful to their original design, and the old system of regency was superseded by the professorial system, not (as at Paris and Oxford) by collegiate teaching.

SEVILLE[3]

An interesting episode in the history of the Spanish universities is the foundation of a *studium generale* at Seville for the study of Latin and Arabic. The way for such a foundation had been prepared by the missionary efforts of the Dominicans, who from 1250 had assigned certain brethren to study Arabic to qualify themselves for mission-work among the Saracens. Some fifteen years later there were schools for this purpose in Tunis and Murcia. The site of the earliest Dominican School of Arabic is not known: it may have been Seville. Alfonso the Wise—the second founder of

eighteen (*loc. cit.*, p. 20). The students here enjoyed the luxury of separate bedrooms (p. 21). Cursory lectures were given in college (the term *cursare* is used for *legere cursorie*, p. 24), but for ordinary lectures the students went to the public schools. The disciplinary regulations for this self-governing community of students in the higher faculties illustrate the fact that the members of colleges were originally subject to disciplinary regulations as to attendance in hall or chapel, hour of entering, &c., not so much because they were *in statu pupillari* as because they were secular clerks living in community. The statutes confer the privilege of dining in the kitchen instead of the hall in winter (p. 38). Students were to confess twice and communicate once a year (p. 39). A later statute contains the curious provision that for 'atrox percussio, unde exeat sanguis in rationabili quantitate, ipso facto privetur percussor a Collegio' (p. 42). In the code of 1490 (which is in Spanish) occurs the provision that the rector shall not lend the college mule for more than three days without the consent of the *consiliarii* (p. 54).

[1] *Archiv*, v. 204; Esperabé, i. 96. The building survives.

[2] A curious feature of university life at Salamanca was the presence of four colleges of the Spanish military orders. Vidal y Díaz, p. 125. The fine building of the College of Calatrava still remains. One of the four 'greater Colleges'— the College of Santiago or del Arzobispo—is now occupied by the 'College of the Noble Irish', a seminary for Irish priests.

[3] [In addition to the references given in the text, note Antonio Ballasteros y Beretta, *Sevilla en el siglo XIII* (Madrid, 1913), p. 162, and Documents, nos. 67, 109; Joaquín Hazañas y la Rua, *Maese Rodrigo (1444–1509)*, Seville, 1909; A. Berthier, 'Les écoles de langues orientales fondées au XIIIe siècle par les dominicains en Espagne et en Afrique', in *Revue Africaine*, lxxiii (1932), 84–103.]

Salamanca—conceived the design of giving a wider scope to these Arabic studies. Denifle thinks that his motive was in part to facilitate commercial intercourse with the Saracens, but mainly to promote their conversion; and these are certainly the motives expressed in his charter. But a monarch so devoted to astronomical and mathematical studies was probably not uninfluenced by the desire to throw open to the learned of his realm all the wisdom of the Arabians. [The Castilian court was frequently fixed at Seville, and Alfonso's literary plans required a constant supply of orientalists.] La Fuente (i. 130) even conjectures that Arabic was actually meant to include 'astronomy, medicine, and physic', quoting a request of the king to the archbishop and chapter of Seville in 1256 to grant a mosque ('unas mezquitas . . . para morada de los Fisicos que vinieron de allende, e para tenerlos de mas cerca e que ellos fagan la su enseñanza a los que les habemos mandado, que los enseñen con el su gran saber, ca para eso los habemos ende traido'). All that is certain is that in 1254 a charter of privilege was granted very similar to that conferred on Salamanca, and that in 1260 Alexander IV issued a Bull (for a period of three years), in which the new *studium* is recognized as a *studium generale*, and dispensation from residence is granted to its students. Both documents are printed in the *Memorial histórico Español*, i (Madrid, 1851), pp. 54, 163. Whether the school ever existed except on paper, even the diligence of Denifle, to whom (i. 495–9) I am indebted for the above facts, has been unable to discover. [The Bull of Pope Julius II (1505), confirming the foundation of the University of Seville, certifies the lack of any *studium generale* within a range of 230 miles.]

§ 4. LÉRIDA (1300)

The original privileges and statutes are published by VILLANUEVA in the *Viage literario á las iglesias de España*, xvi, Madrid, 1851. Some of the documents are printed by LA FUENTE, i. 300 *sq.* DENIFLE has printed others in the *Archiv für Lit.- u. Kirchengesch. des Mittelalters*, iv. 253 *sq.* [H. FINKE, *Acta Aragonensia* (Berlin and Leipzig, 1908); A. RUBIÓ Y LLUCH, *Documents per l'historia de la cultura catalana miz-eval* (Barcelona, 2 vols., 1908–21); R. ROIG Y REY, 'Noticias relativas a las antiguas universidades de Lérida, Vich, Gerona, y Tarragona', in *Revista crítica de historia y literatura*, 1900, pp. 49–59; Rafael GRAS Y DE ESTEVA, *Catálogo de los privilegios y documentos originales que se conservan en el archivo reservado de la ciudad de Lérida* (Lérida, 1897); Escorial. MS. d–III–3, fol. 89 *sq.* (copies of documents); Anastasi PLEYAN CONDAL, *L'antiga Universitat Ilerdanesa* (Lérida, 1901); Joan LLORENS Y FABREGA, *La universitat de Lleyda* (Lérida, 1901); *España Sagrada*, xliv. 245–54 and 340–60; J. RIUS, 'L'Estudi general de Lleida', in *Criterion*, viii (Barcelona, 1932), 72–90.]

THE zeal for education which, fostered by a spirit of national The first independence, had led to the establishment of three Castilian university for Aragon.

CHAP. VII,
§ 4. universities in the course of the thirteenth century, spread to the neighbouring and rival kingdom of Aragon at the end of the same century.[1] The Spanish universities were above all things national institutions: and befôre the close of our period we shall find every one of the Spanish kingdoms in possession of its own *studium generale*.

Difficulties of classification.   In the great work of Denifle the universities are classified entirely according to their origin, and fall into one or other of three main classes: (1) universities which arose without a charter of foundation; (2) universities founded by papal Bull; (3) universities founded by imperial, royal, or princely edict. There are, however, in point of fact not a few universities which cannot be assigned to one or other of these categories without a very arbitrary procedure. This classification is peculiarly unsatisfactory in the case of Lérida, which is placed by Denifle—rightly perhaps if such a classification is to be adopted at all—in the third of the above classes, but it gives at best a one-sided view of the facts.

Foundation by James II, 1300.   No university, indeed, was more entirely the creation of a monarch's will. The University of Lérida was founded by James II of Aragon in 1300. But the document in which his intention to found a *studium generale* in some town of his realm is first declared is a letter addressed to the reigning pope, asking for apostolical approval for the undertaking. In consequence of this petition a Bull was issued by Boniface VIII conferring upon the university when founded the privileges of Toulouse. The king's actual charter to the university, the seat of which is now fixed at Lérida, declares that it is founded by joint regal and apostolical authority.[2]

[1] The purpose of the foundation of Lérida is thus described by the founder: 'Ut nec potissime nostros fideles et subditos pro investigandis scientiis nationes peregrinas expetere, nec in alienis ipsos oporteat regionibus mendicare'. Villanueva, xvi. 196. [The agitation for a *studium generale* at Lérida dates from the Council of 1229: 'Nos attendentes quod in partibus Hispaniae ex defectu studiorum et literaturae multa et intolerabilia detrimenta animarum proveniunt', cited by J. Tejada y Ramiro, *Colección de Cánones y de todos los concilios de la iglesia española* (Madrid, 1851), iii. 331.]

[2] 'In civitate nostra Ilerdensi studium generale in iure canonico et civili, medicina, philosophia et artibus et aliis approbatis et honestis scientiis quibuscumque, auctoritate Apostolica nobis in hac parte con-

In this procedure it is obvious that a jealous assertion of the royal prerogative is combined with a desire to secure for the new foundation privileges which only an ecumenical authority could bestow. In other respects the charter is clearly based upon the model of Frederick II's foundation-Bull for Naples; in accordance with which precedent another royal edict forbade the teaching of law, medicine, and philosophy in all other places within the king's dominions.[1] This provision brings into relief the real nature of the educational revolution introduced by the foundation of universities. Formerly the schools of any great church might teach all subjects, and authorize qualified persons to become masters in them. In Italy and perhaps parts of Spain the freedom of education was not even limited by the necessity for ecclesiastical authorization. By the foundation of universities 'higher' education was made, either formally (as at Naples and Lérida) or virtually (as in France and England), the monopoly of certain privileged *studia*. At Naples the teaching of grammar only was allowed in other places: at Lérida an explanatory edict exempts logic also from the operation of the royal prohibition. In some points, however, the king of Aragon's legislation was far more wise and liberal than that of the Emperor Frederick II. His original charter[2] exhibits no jealousy either of ecclesiastical authority or of academic liberty. The privileges which it confers are the amplest ever yet bestowed on the first foundation of a university.

Seldom did the actual beginning of a university's existence follow more promptly upon its formal erection. On Michaelmas eve, 1300, the students met and elected as their first rector the then archdeacon of Lérida; and on the same day an elaborate code of statutes was solemnly promulgated. These statutes are of peculiar importance in the constitutional history of universities. They are the earliest detailed code of statutes for a student-university which has come down to us: and, allowance being made for constitutional changes

cessa ac etiam nostra, duximus ordinandum.' Doc. ap. Villanueva, xvi. 200. Degrees were likewise conferred by joint authority of King and Pope; *loc. cit.*, p. 201.

[1] Doc. ap. Villanueva, xvi. 199. Cf. above, p. 23.

[2] Printed by La Fuente, i. 311.

adopted to suit the peculiar circumstances of Lérida, they reveal to us the whole organization and educational system of the University of Bologna on which they are undoubtedly modelled, at a period considerably before the date of the earliest Bologna code now extant. They show us the student-liberties, the student-domination over the professors, already in full operation. Nothing can more strikingly illustrate the extent and the established position of this Bolognese student-ascendancy than the fact of its deliberate adoption (with but few modifications), amid social conditions not a little different from those under which it had grown up, by a Spanish sovereign. It had come to be accepted as an ordinance of nature that law-students should form a self-governing body.

Consti-
tution.
The principal modification introduced into the Bologna constitution is that (in accordance with Neapolitan precedent) a chancellor nominated by the king takes the place of the bishop as the licensing authority. The king, however, as a concession to the connexion generally existing between chapter and schools in Spain, grants that the chancellor shall always be a canon of Lérida.[1] On the other hand the academic jurisdiction of the rector is recognized more fully and un-grudgingly than it was ever recognized by the Bologna muni-cipality. Doctors and students from other parts of the king-dom or from foreign countries[2] are exempted from the jurisdiction of the state courts (if they claimed the exemption)

[1] Villanueva, xvi. 201. He is styled *cancellarius studii*, not (it should be observed) *Universitatis*, *loc. cit.*, p. 214, though being 'de praecipuis officialibus studii, privi-legiis universitatis cancellarius gau-det', *loc. cit.*, p. 219. [In 1318, how-ever, the King styles himself chan-cellor and delegates his authority to the archdeacon of Ribagorza, and similar language is used in 1353. Though the appointment of the *bedellus* lay with the university, the first *bedellus* was appointed by James II. Another royal nomina-tion occurred in 1378, and in 1388 John I protests against the dis-missal of Guillem de Coll by the Pope, declaring that the office 'totaliter profanum est nostrique auctoritate confertur'. See Rubió, ii, Intro., p. lxi, and Doc. 320.]

[2] The university is expressly de-fined as a 'Universitas scolarium forensium, qui non sint de civitate Ilerdae, clerici vel laici in utroque iure studentes', *loc. cit.*, p. 201. But masters and scholars 'cuiuscunque scientiae' must obey the rector (*loc. cit.*, 217). Cf. p. 229, 'Cum te dicas civem Ilerdae, iurare non cogeris universitatis statuta, licet dum in hoc studio fueris, ad eorum ob-servantiam tenearis.' All doctors and bachelors were bound to swear obedience to the rector.

in all civil cases and in all non-capital criminal matters, and CHAP. VII,
§ 4. are allowed to choose between the rectorial tribunal and that of their own master. One other exception is noticeable. A lay student caught in the part of the town specially assigned to students' houses with arms or musical instruments in his hands (the two offences are placed precisely on a level) may be fined by the town officials: a clerical student under similar circumstances is to forfeit the obnoxious weapon or instrument and to be sent to the bishop or rector for correction.[1] The distinction shows how little, in southern Europe, scholarity was held to imply clerkship.

In Aragon the municipalities were at this time more Endowment. powerful than in Castile; and at Lérida it is probable that the municipality had much to do with the foundation of the university. At all events, the endowment was supplied by them, and the *prohombres* of the city were entrusted with the nomination to the salaried chairs—originally two in canon law, two in civil law, one in philosophy, one in medicine, and one in grammar,[2] but they were directed to be guided in their choice by the advice of the rector and *consiliarii*. Whether in consequence of this division of responsibility or otherwise, by the year 1311 the *studium* had come to a dead-lock. In that year, however, the council of the city offered to provide the salaries, on condition that the doctors should be chosen by the bishop and chapter. Eventually the king divided the cost of the *studium* between the municipality and the chapter.[3]

From its revival in 1311 the university seems, but not quite Later history. without interruptions, to have enjoyed a moderate share of prosperity till its gradual evanescence in the course of the fifteenth century.[4] Its fame was chiefly derived from its

[1] *Loc. cit.*, pp. 204, 205.

[2] Villanueva, xvi. 214; *Archiv*, iv. 255 *sq.*

[3] *España Sagrada*, xliv. 351.

[4] The continued existence of the university in the fourteenth and beginning of the fifteenth centuries would seem to follow from the facts mentioned by La Fuente, i. 246, but I can discover nothing as to its later history. [The documents collected by Rubió, who points out the need for a monograph based upon the Lérida archives, illustrate the continuous activity of the university. Thus Pedro IV (1336–87) and John I (1387–95) petitioned the Pope for a theological faculty. Students of theology were frequently compelled to go to Paris or Oxford, a practice which caused difficulties during the Schism.]

school of law; but among the 284 bachelors and scholars whose names appear in a rotulus sent to Benedict XIII in 1394, there are more artists than jurists, and the medical faculty had more prominence here than in most Spanish universities: in 1387–95 John I granted it a privilege already established at Montpellier and elsewhere, i.e. an annual corpse for dissection, with the curious proviso that the criminal assigned for the purpose should be drowned.[1]

S. Mary's College. The oldest college in Spain was situated at Lérida—S. Mary's College founded in 1372 by Domingo Ponz, chanter of Lérida.[2]

§ 5. PERPIGNAN (1350)

This university is one which has been practically disinterred by Denifle (i. 515–19) from manuscripts at Rome and Perpignan, where the statutes of *circa* 1379 are preserved. Its bare existence is recognized by La Fuente, i. 239. The statutes and other documents are now printed by FOURNIER, *Statuts des Universités françaises*, ii (1891), No. 1482 *sq.* [RUBIÓ I LLUCH, *Documents, passim.*]

Project of university in Roussillon. AFTER the annexation of the county of Roussillon to the crown of Aragon in 1344, the victorious King Pedro the Ceremonious—possibly from a desire to gratify his new subjects and promote the fusion of the county with his older dominions—conceived the design of transferring the *studium* from Lérida to some town in Roussillon. In confirming the privileges of Lérida in 1347 he inserts the clause 'so long as the said *studium* shall remain in that City'.[3] The contemplated suspension of the *studium* of Lérida was never carried out; but in 1350 a royal edict[4] was issued erecting a new *Foundation of Perpignan, 1350. studium generale* at Perpignan in all faculties (including theology), inviting doctors and scholars to attend it, promising the usual protection and directing the consuls to provide a students' quarter in the city. The edict declares that there

---

[1] *España Sagrada*, xliv. 354.
[2] The facts about this college are collected by Denifle (i. 505–6) from the Vatican Archives.
[3] Doc. quoted by Denifle, i. 508.
[4] Fournier, ii, No. 1482; [Rubió, i, No. 147: 'Datum Cesarauguste xiii kalendas aprilis anno Domini mccxlix', i.e. Saragossa, 20 Mar. 1350. From Dec. 1350 the year in Aragon was reckoned from Christmas; this document of 20 March was dated under the old system, i.e. 1350 began on 25 Mar., five days later. Cf. Rubió, ii, p. lxvi, n. 2.]

were doctors teaching at Perpignan already: and as the charter is said to be issued at the request of the municipality, it is probable that the university must be regarded (like Huesca and perhaps Lérida) as an expansion of a town-school of law. Little or no effect, however, was produced by the new charter. The university was a failure, and the king (still apparently unfavourable to Lérida) made a more successful attempt to erect a new university at Huesca. The real existence of the University of Perpignan does not begin till the issue of a papal Bull of foundation for all faculties except theology in 1379 by the Avignon Pope Clement VII,[1] whom the university thereafter claims as its founder, at least when supplicating for benefices at the papal court.[2] One of these benefice-rolls (of 1394) contains the names of a rector, four licentiates and twenty-eight bachelors of law, one master of arts, three bachelors of medicine, 137 scholars in law, and 207 in arts—most of them from the dioceses of Elne, Gerona, and Urgel, with a few from more distant regions.[3] A faculty of theology was sanctioned by Nicholas V in 1447.[4]

Bull of Clement VII, 1379.

The original statutes[5] are based upon those of Lérida, but are influenced also by those of Toulouse and contain many original features.[6] The bishop of Elne is chancellor, and approves of the rector-elect in the name of the king. The rectorship is usually held by a bachelor or student, but a doctor (probably not a salaried professor) is occasionally elected. Of the ten *consiliarii* two at least must be bachelors of law, and two members of the faculty of medicine or arts. The salaried chairs are filled by the consuls after consultation with the rector and council.

Constitution.

[1] Fournier, ii, No. 1483. The early royal foundation included theology. [See also Rubió, ii, No. 222. Rubió establishes the names of the first three chancellors.]

[2] Fournier, ii, No. 1487.

[3] *Ibid.* ii, No. 1488.

[4] *Ibid.* ii, No. 1513.

[5] *Ibid.* ii, No. 1485.

[6] A remarkable feature is a specification of the length of time for lectures, which was in winter:

Morning, 3 hours; Tierce, 2 hours; Nones, $1\frac{1}{2}$ hours; Vespers, $2\frac{1}{2}$ 'vel circa'. In summer the hours were shorter. [The *camerarii*, mentioned in these statutes, are described in the regulations of 1412 for the *studium particulare* of Valencia. They acted as tutors, repeated the masters' lectures, held short disputations, and expelled unprofitable students.]

§ 6. HUESCA (1354)

CHAP. VII, In addition to DENIFLE and RUBIÓ I LLUCH, Diego DE AYNSA Y DE
§ 6. YRIARTE, *Fundación, excelencias, grandezas y cosas memorables de la
antiquissima Ciudad de Huesca* (Huesca, 1619), pp. 623–41; and Ramon [DE
HUESCA], *Teatro histórico del regno de Aragón*, vii (Pamplona, 1797),
pp. 214–64 and Appendices V–VIII. [José SANZ DE LARREA, *Libro
ceremonial o lucero*, 1789, in Ricardo del ARCO Y GARAY, 'Memorias de la
universidad de Huesca', in *Colección de documentos para el estudio de la
historia de Aragón*, viii and xi (Saragossa, 1912, 1916). The statutes of
26 March 1470 (in the municipal archives of Huesca) are unpublished.]

The
Roman
school.
HUESCA is the later name of the ancient Osca—the seat of the
celebrated school opened by Sertorius for the instruction of
Spanish youth. But it is of course impossible to establish any
connexion between the school of Sertorius and the later
university. The Saracen occupation by itself forbids the
attempt to bridge over the gulf between the Roman and the
medieval schools.

Founda-
tion by
Pedro IV
in 1354.
In 1354 [Pedro IV issued a charter creating a university at
Huesca in order to serve the needs of his Aragonese subjects.[1]
The intention of James II had been to establish one university at Lérida for all his realms; Pedro, however, discriminat-
ing between his different sovereign titles, considered that
Lérida might serve for the Catalans and Huesca for the
Aragonese. It is in this narrower sense that Paul II's Bull for.
Huesca declares that no other *studium generale* existed in
the kingdom of Aragon. The original document of founda-
tion] is closely copied from the charter of James II for Lérida,
including the prohibition to study elsewhere.[2] Unlike Lérida,
however, Huesca was provided with a theological faculty
from the first. The method adopted for the endowment of
the *studium* was peculiar and suggests an amusing ignorance

[1] Aynsa, p. 624.

[2] [James's prohibition refers to
'dominationis nostre habite vel
habende'. Thus the erection of the
University of Huesca is an infringement of Lérida's monopoly. Paul
II's statement that 'in eodem Regno
Aragonum nullum aliud studium
viget generale' is true in the narrower sense of the word Aragon.
Pedro IV actively fomented theological studies in connexion with
the churches and convents, and he

excepts theology from his prohibition to study elsewhere;] 'praeterquam in Ecclesiis et ordinibus
quibus solitum est legi prefatam
Theologiam'. Doc. ap. Aynsa, p.
624, and La Fuente, i. 317. There
is no mention of papal authorization in Pedro's charter; he claims
to found the *studium generale* entirely *suo iure*, and to bestow the
privileges conferred by the Holy
See on Toulouse, Montpellier, and
Lérida.

of the fundamental axiom of political economy. A tax was CHAP. VII,
§ 6. imposed upon meat sold in the chief market of Huesca. The consequence was that the inhabitants bought their meat in the cheaper market of the Moorish quarter. This mistake was corrected in a subsequent edict which extended the tax to the Saracen market. A heavy contribution was also laid upon the Saracen and Jewish communities. But, in spite of these provisions, the university did not succeed. The competition of Lérida, which, notwithstanding the monopoly clause in the Huesca charter, continued to flourish, was too strong for it. By 1358 it appears that only one bachelor of law was lecturing in the place—a lecture which had been established by the inhabitants themselves long before the foundation of the university.[1] This last circumstance is interesting as showing that the university was in some sense an outgrowth of a town-school of the Italian type. We hear nothing of a chapter school or *maestrescuela*. A privilege of King Martin is the only evidence of the continued existence of the university till the reign of John II, who in 1464 petitioned Pope Paul II in conjunction with the citizens for the renewal of the papal privileges which, it was alleged, had been lost.[2] These, indeed, had never had any real existence, except in so far as the Pope's general permission to the king of Aragon to establish a university in any town of his realm might be held to confer the power of founding Huesca as well as Lérida.[3] A Bull was, however, granted renewing the

Bull of
Paul II,
1464.

---

[1] 'Nec ibi nunc aliquis eorum legit nisi solum iamdictus Dominicus Egidii Davena bacallarius in legibus, quem ad legendum in dicta civitate homines universitatis ipsius (i.e. the town) de novo aduxerunt seu venire fecerunt, prout ante fundacionem ipsius studii homines iamdicti consueverunt tenere unum bacallarium, qui eorum filiis in dicta civitate legebat.' Edict of Pedro IV, printed for the first time by Denifle, i. 511 *sq* (with other documents already printed by Ramon de Huesca).

[2] Bull of Paul II (ap. Aynsa,

p. 625), appointing a commission to inquire into the facts and renew the *studium generale*. It promises the privileges of Toulouse, Lérida, and Bologna. It should be observed that this Bull does not question the right of Pedro to found a *studium generale* solely *regia authoritate*, though it recites that the foundation was 'a sede Apostolica, ut asseritur, approbata et confirmata'

[3] Had Lérida been disestablished, this contention might have held good, but the Pope did not authorize the establishment of *two* universities.

'interrupted' *studium*, and entrusting the right of promotion to the archdeacon.[1] From the year 1473 the university began to be endowed in a more satisfactory way by the impropriation of prebends and other ecclesiastical property,[2] and maintained a substantial though far from glorious existence till it was thrown into the shade by the revival of Saragossa towards the end of the sixteenth century.

[An interesting experiment was made in this university by John I, who in 1394 projected a school of *Lemosin* studies, i.e. for the study of the poetic dialect.[3] His plan took effect in the reign of his successor, Martin I, and is probably the earliest recognition of the modern humanities as a branch of university education.]

§ 7. BARCELONA (1450)

LA FUENTE, *Universidades*, i. 236–40 and 332 *sq.* [Marcelino MENÉNDEZ Y PELAYO, *Antología de poetas líricos castellanos*, xiii. 18–25; CAPMANY, 'Noticia del origen, antigüedad, plan y dotación de la antigua universidad literaria de la ciudad de Barcelona', in *Memorias*, ii, App., p. 29; Dionisio JORBA, *Descripción de las excellencias de la muy insigne ciudad de Barcelona*, ed. 2, fol. 28 *b* (Barcelona, 1589); RUBIÓ I LLUCH, *Documents*; A. DE LA TORRE, *Reseña histórica y guía descriptiva de la Universidad* (de Barcelona), Barcelona, 1929; the same, *Provisión de las cátedras en la Universidad de Barcelona de 1559 a 1596*, Barcelona, 1926.]

THE statutes of the University of Lérida provide for a most imposing array of 'nations', from which representatives were expected by its sanguine founders to flock to the new seat of learning: and it was enacted that the rector should be chosen from each nation in turn. As a matter of fact, however, only two countries availed themselves of the opportunities thus placed within their reach in sufficient numbers for the establishment of academical nations—the Aragonese and the Catalans. Lérida was perhaps selected for the seat of a university as lying in a central position, equally accessible from Aragon and from Catalonia. With this measure of independence the national or provincial aspirations of the king of Aragon's Catalan subjects were content till the year 1430, when the town council of Barcelona founded and endowed

---

[1] The Bull is unpublished. Denifle (i. 514) gives its contents.

[2] Aynsa, p. 630.

[3] [Arco, i. 3.]

a *studium*,[1] for which in 1450 they obtained a royal charter CHAP VII,
§ 7. from Alfonso V and a papal Bull from Nicholas V[2] conferring on it the rights and privileges of a *studium generale* in all faculties. It remained, however, very unimportant till its 'reformation' in the middle of the sixteenth century.[3] Barcelona, like Majorca and Valencia, was a great seat of Lullianist doctrine. [This school appears to have existed from about the year 1303. The Dominicans conducted an important *studium*, which possessed two chairs as early as 1299, according to La Fuente. In 1314 James II contributed 2,000 sous towards the expenses of their institution. A medical university was founded in 1401 under the patronage of Martin I, who approved the appointment of officers, conceded the right to two corpses for anatomical experiments, adjured the masters on no account to abandon the study of medicine, and in September of 1402 petitioned the Pope for the privileges of Montpellier.][4]

§ 8. SARAGOSSA (1474)

La Fuente (i. 248 *sq.*, 340 *sq.*); Jerónimo Borao y Clemente, ' Memoria histórica sobra la universidad literaria de Zaragoza', in *Opúsculos literarios* (Saragossa, 1853). [M. Jiménez Catalán and J. Sinués y Urbiola, *Historia de la Real y Pontificia Universidad de Zaragoza*, 2 vols. (Saragossa, 1922–4); M. Jiménez Catalán, *Memorias para la historia de la Universidad Literaria de Zaragoza. Reseña bio-bibliográfica, 1583–1845*, Saragossa, 1926.]

We have seen that it formed part of the earlier and vaguer conception of a *studium generale* that one at least of the higher faculties should be represented in it. In time,

[1] La Fuente, i. 237.

[2] Printed ap. La Fuente, i. 333 *sq.* The Pope declares that the *studium generale* is to be 'ad instar studii Tholosani', and confers the privileges of that university: the King bestows those of Lérida and Perpignan. The omission of Huesca testifies to the interruption of that university.

[3] [The grammar school at Tarragona, which was instituted by the archbishop and chapter by 1214, was, like that of Barcelona, unable to compete with the privileges of Lérida. This *escola major* became a university, through the endowment of the cardinal-archbishop, Cervantes, in 1572, just as the school at Barcelona was elevated to full university rank in 1559. See S. Capdevila, 'Les antigues institucions escolars de la Tarragona restaurada', in *Estudis Universitaris Catalans*, xii (1927), 68–162.]

[4] La Fuente, i. 147; [Rubió, i. 477, 478, ii. 13: 'collegi de la universitat del studi de medecina de Barchinona.']

CHAP. VII,
§ 8.

however, the idea of ecumenical validity for the degree became the most prominent part of the idea. Hence there was no theoretical objection to the creation of a *studium generale* in arts only; but as a matter of fact, the only instance of such a creation within our period is the University of Saragossa, for which a Bull was granted by Sixtus IV in 1474.[1] The Bull recites that there had existed in the city 'from ancient times' a *studium* in arts, and that the senior master had been styled rector of the *studium*. It proceeds, in accordance with the petition of the chapter and municipality, to create a *studium generale* in arts only, to make the master (*magister maior*) chancellor as well as rector, and to give to the masters and scholars all the privileges of Paris and Lérida.

Bull of Sixtus IV in 1474.

Two years later, in consequence of disputes arising between this glorified head master and the chapter as to the administration of what was no doubt originally a chapter school, it was found expedient to procure another Bull making the archbishop chancellor and the rector vice-chancellor, and giving power to the chancellor, vice-chancellor, and chapter in conjunction to make statutes for the government of the *studium*.[2] The *studium*, however, remained of so little importance that, when in 1541 steps were taken for the erection of a university in the higher faculties, no notice whatever was taken of these earlier Bulls.[3]

Archbishop chancellor, 1476.

§ 9. PALMA (1483)

La Fuente, i. 113–24, 241–5; Juan Dameto, *Historia General de Mallorca*, Palma, 1840–1 (originally published in 1632–50; English trans. 1716–19). [S. Ros, 'La universidad literaria del reino de Mallorca', in *Bolletí de la Societat Arqueològica Lulliana*, xx (1924), 113–16, 129–34.]

Career of Ramon Lull.

It is impossible within the limits of this work to embark on so difficult and obscure a subject as the life and teaching of

---

[1] Printed by La Fuente, i. 340. [According to Borao the cathedral school, with instruction in philosophy and Latin, had flourished since at least 1304: 'inter ceteras regni Aragonum principatum obtinuit', as archbishop García stated in his fourteenth-century constitutions. Its activities are noted by Rubió between 1335 and 1339.

Though recognized by the Bull of 1474, there was no effective university in Saragossa until 1583, owing to the opposition of Huesca.] A *studium generale* 'ex consuetudine' existed at Erfurt in arts only. See below, pp. 246, 247.

[2] Bull printed by La Fuente, i. 344.

[3] *Loc. cit.*, p. 249 *sq.*

Ramon Lull—one of the strangest episodes in the philosophical history of the Middle Ages. Lull acquired fame in two
characters. He was the inventor and propagator of a fantastic
system of logic, including a logical machine which was (like
the *Novum Organum* of Francis Bacon) to 'equal intellects'
and solve all problems. At the same time he was an im-
passioned missionary who spent his life in inciting Pope and
king to found colleges for the study of Arabic and the conversion of the Saracens,[1] and who died a martyr to his own
zeal in the missionary cause. The scientific and the missionary enthusiasm were united by the confidence of its author
that the 'Great Art' must perforce effect the conversion of the
Arabs to the Christian faith. In both characters he left his
mark upon his native Island of Majorca. It was through his
persuasion that James I of Aragon was persuaded to found in
1276 a 'Missionary College of Minorites at Miramar for the
study of Arabic'.[2] This college obtained a Bull of confirma- His
college at
tion from John XXI,[3] and perished before the death of Miramar.
Lull: but in the latter half of the fourteenth century, and
all through the fifteenth, the philosophical, medical, and
scientific doctrines of Lull seem to have been taught at various
places in the island. It is reasonable to suppose that the
studium at Palma traced its origin back to the founder of
the sect; but [the university founded in 1483 by Ferdinand
the Catholic with the privileges of Lérida has no formal connexion with the Lullian schools of Miramar, Monte Randa,
and Montesión. On the other hand, the continuous pre-
eminence of the 'Great Art', from his own day through

[1] The decree of the Council of
Vienne in 1311 for the creation of
Oriental chairs in the great universities is supposed to have been
largely due to his importunity. The
document, which La Fuente calls
'Aprobación de la doctrina de Lulio
por la Universidad de Paris, 1309',
is wrongly described. It is a certifi-
cate of orthodoxy granted by the
bishop's official on the evidence of
certain individual masters, bachelors, and scholars of Paris. [The
literature on Lull is enormous and

unceasing. See Ueberweg-Geyer,
pp. 447–8, 758–9, and E. Allison
Peers, *Ramon Lull* (London, 1929).]

[2] Dameto, iii. 47. The Bull
speaks of the 'Studium Generale
Magistri Raymundi Lulli', but this
must mean only a *studium generale*
for the Franciscan Order (*Studium
Ordinis*).

[3] See the two chapters devoted
to that subject in La Fuente, i.
113 *sq.*, 241 *sq.*, and the documents
in Dameto, iii. 81 *sq.*

CHAP. VII,
§ 9.
Llovet in the fifteenth century and Raimundo Pascual in the eighteenth down to Rosselló, is the distinguishing feature of Majorcan education.[1] Spain also had a national interest in the study of Ramon Lull. He was expounded even in the Renaissance university of Alcalá as late as the youth of Lope de Vega, who complains with justice of his unintelligibility.]

§ 10. SIGÜENZA (1489)

LA FUENTE, *Universidades*, ii. 1–23, and Documents, pp. 525–45. [Toribio MINGUELLA Y ARNEDO, *Historia de la diócesis de Sigüenza y de sus obispos* (Madrid, 1913), III. xvii. 451–86; Eduardo JULIÁ MARTÍNEZ, 'La universidad de Sigüenza y su fundador'; in *Revista de Archivos*, xlvi (1925) and subsequent volumes; Julio DE LA FUENTE, *Reseña histórica del colegio-universidad de San Antonio de Portaceli en Sigüenza* (Madrid, 1877).]

ABOUT the year 1476, Don Juan López de Medina, licentiate in decrees, archdeacon of Almazán in the church of Sigüenza, canon of Toledo and ten other churches, conceived the idea of devoting some portion of his ecclesiastical riches to a foundation of a very peculiar character. Outside the walls of Sigüenza he built a convent to be called the convent of S. Antonio de Portaceli, which he made over to the Franciscans or, in the event of their leaving it, to the 'religious of San Jerónimo'. The occupants of the convent were to be specially devoted to study; and in close connexion with this college-convent three chairs of theology, canon law, and arts were erected, and endowed (by permission of the founder's patron, Cardinal Mendoza, who was bishop of Sigüenza as well as archbishop of Seville), the first two with canonries and the last with a 'portion' in the church of Sigüenza.[2] The chairs were to be filled by secular clerks who had graduated at Sigüenza. It was from the first contemplated that others besides the friars should attend the *studium*: but in 1477 an independent secular college for a rector and twelve scholars (in memory of Christ and His Apostles) with four student-

College annexed, 1477.

---

[1] ['Maioricana siue Lulliana, eo quod ibi Lulli doctrina peculiariter traditur, in urbe Metropoli insulae siue regni Maiorici.' Jacobus Middendorpius, *Academiarum cele-*

brium universi terrarum orbis libri viii (Cologne, 1602), p. 423.]

[2] La Fuente, ii. 1 *sq.*, 525 *sq.* A hospital also formed part of the foundation.

servitors was founded by the archdeacon, and endowed by CHAP. VII,
the annexation of a number of benefices or 'portions'[1] in § 10.
various parochial churches held by him whether in right of
his archdeaconry or otherwise. The patronage was reserved
for the founder and his heirs. It was from the first intended
that the scholars should follow a regular course of a university
character, but it was not until 1489 (after the founder's death) College-
that a Bull was obtained from Innocent VIII, authorizing the university,
1489.
students of the college to receive the degree of bachelor from
the doctors or masters of the *studium* and the degrees of
doctor and licentiate from the bishop as chancellor after
examination by the doctors,[2] and conferring upon them all
the privileges enjoyed by graduates of other universities. A
college and a university were thus fused into one, the rector
of the college (who was assisted by two *consiliarii*) becoming
also rector of the university.[3] The new form of university
thus evolved became the model upon which similar college-
universities were afterwards erected at Alcalá and elsewhere
in Spain.

§ 11. ALCALÁ (1499)

DENIFLE, i. 646–8; LA FUENTE, ii. 66; [E. MELE and A. BONILLA, *Dos
cancioneros españoles* ('Descripción de la vida y trabajos que pasan los
estudiantes de Alcalá'); José CALLEJA, *Bosquejo histórico de los colegios
seculares de la universidad de Alcalá*, 1900; Antonio DE LA TORRE Y DEL
CERRO, 'La Universidad de Alcalá', in *Revista de Archivos*, 3ª época, año
xxi (1909); the same, 'Visitas de cátedras de 1524–25 a 1527–28', in *Homenaje a Menéndez Pidal*, iii (1925), 361–78; the same, ed. Juan DE VALLEJO,
Memorial de la Vida de Fray Francisco Jiménez de Cisneros (Madrid,
1913); Pascual GALINDO Y ROMEO, 'La universidad de Alcalá', in *Revista
de Archivos* (July–Dec. 1918); P. S. ALLEN, in *Erasmus: Lectures and
Wayfaring Sketches* (Oxford, 1934), pp. 140–5]; *Constitutiones insignis
Collegii S. Ildefonsi ac . . . totius almae Complutensis Acad.*, Compluti
[Alcalá], 1560 [first edition, 1510].

IN 1293 Sancho IV of Castile projected the foundation of a
studium generale at Alcalá, and conferred upon it the privileges

---

[1] 'Beneficia simplicia, et praesti-
monia, ac praestimoniales portiones
parochialium ecclesiarum de Pala-
zuelas', &c. *Ibid.*, p. 529.

[2] The Bull is unfortunately not
printed by La Fuente. Its contents are summarized (ii. 16 *sq.*);
Villanueva, ii. 102.

[3] The rector was at first elected
for two years, afterwards for one.
La Fuente, ii. 17. A dispute
soon arose as to the admissibility
of 'new Christians', i.e. converted
Jews or Saracens, which was decided against them in 1497. *Ibid.*,
p. 543.

CHAP. VII,
§ 11.

of Valladolid; but nothing seems to have been done in execution of the scheme. Nothing at all events is heard of any considerable *studium* at Alcalá until 1459, when, on the petition of Alfonso Carrillo, archbishop of Toledo, Pius II granted leave for the establishment of three chairs in arts and grammar by the impropriation of benefices;[1] but, as this Bull does not .expressly create a *studium generale* and no promotions seem to have taken place, the school must rather be looked upon as a *studium particulare privilegiatum* until the year 1499, when a Bull of creation was issued for a university, or rather a college of San Ildefonso, with power to grant degrees, by Alexander VI, on the petition of the famous Ximenes, archbishop of Toledo. The founder of the college declared it to be on the model of the College of S. Bartholomew at Salamanca.[2] The right of promotion was bestowed upon the abbot of the collegiate church of S. Justus and S. Pastor, and the graduates were endowed with the privileges of Valladolid, Salamanca, and the Spanish College at Bologna. By the papal Bull, bachelor's degrees were to be conferred by the professors of the college. The actual inauguration of the college took place in 1508, while the statutes were not published till 1510.[3]

§ 12. VALENCIA (1500)

DENIFLE, i. 643 *sq.*; LA FUENTE, i. 228–35; [Gaspar ESCOLANO, *Décadas de la historia de la insigne y coronada ciudad y reino de Valencia*, 1610–11; *Anotadas y continuadas por* J. B. Perales (Valencia–Madrid, 3 vols., 1878–80); Francisco ORTIZ y FIGUEROLA, *Memorias históricas de la fundación y progresos de la insigne universidad de Valencia* (Madrid, 1730); José TEIXIDOR, 'Antigüedades de Valencia: observaciones críticas', 1767, in Roque CHABÁS, *Monumentos históricos de Valencia y su reino* (Valencia, 1895), ii. 259–62 (Teixidor alludes to his *Estudios antiguos y modernos de Valencia*, in folio); Miguel VELASCO Y SANTOS, *Reseña histórica de la Universidad de Valencia* (Valencia, 1868); Vicente VIVES Y LIERN, *Las casas de los estudios en Valencia* (Valencia, 1902); C. RIBA Y GARCÍA, *El antiguo patrimonio de la universidad de Valencia* (Valencia, 1923); VILLANUEVA, *Viage literario*, ii. 90–124 and App. VII and IX. Constitutions: of 1412 in Villanueva, ii. 186–91; of 1499, *ibid.* ii. 198–212; of 1611, published by Mey at Valencia; A. DE LA TORRE, *Precedentes de la Universidad de Valencia*, 1926.]

---

[1] La Fuente, ii. 556.
[2] *Ibid.* ii. 559. The archbishop's petition (1498) is printed by Ga-

lindo y Romeo. [Note by Rashdall.]
[3] *Ibid.* ii. 66; Denifle, i. 648.

THE history of this *studium* is peculiarly interesting as an indication of the zeal of Spanish municipalities in the cause of education. In 1246 Innocent IV granted a Bull exempting regents in the *studium* which the king of Aragon was intending to erect at Valencia from residence on their benefices.[1] It appears to have been intended to found a *studium generale*, since James I of Aragon proclaimed liberty to teach in arts, medicine, and law at Valencia, and Innocent IV speaks of it as destined to be a *studium* of the highest utility not only to the aforesaid realm, but also to its neighbours; but nothing further appears to have been done till 1374, when the city petitioned the king for a *studium generale*:[2] while on its own responsibility it proceeded to take the modest step of hiring a solitary bachelor of arts to begin teaching in the place. In Spain the right of a council to establish a *studium* (i.e. a *studium particulare*) was not so unquestioned as in Italy, nor the right of the bishop and chapter so well established as in northern France. The bishop excommunicated the *jurats* of the city, and imprisoned the teacher on the ground that the action of the council infringed the monopoly granted by James II to Lérida. He was at length discharged on the strength of the earlier edict of James I: but the opposition of the chapter seems to have thwarted the efforts of the council to establish a more substantial *studium* till 1389, when two jurists, [two doctors of medicine, four notaries, and certain distinguished citizens were commissioned to examine the draft statutes drawn up by Pedro Figuerola, master of arts and medicine]. In 1412 a *studium* of arts with a code of statutes was established by agreement between the council and the chapter.[3] Under the old permission of James I this *studium* might possibly have claimed to be a *studium*

---

[1] *Ibid.* i. 293.
[2] *Ibid.*, p. 320; Villanueva, ii. 105–7.
[3] Villanueva, ii. 167 *sq.* [These Valencian 'Capítols de les Scoles' give an admirably detailed picture of a *studium particulare* in Spain, for which see Bonilla, *La vida corporativa de los estudiantes espa-* *ñoles.* Rubió publishes documents bearing on similar schools in Saragossa, Unicastillo, Teruel, Tarazona, Cervera, Montblanch, Vich, Murviedro, Játiva, Morella, Sueca, Perpignan, Mallorca, Barcelona (all dating from the fourteenth century).]

generale 'respectu regni',[1] though (according to the *Siete Partidas*) a school could not claim this distinction, even if founded by royal authority, unless it included one of the higher faculties; and there is no reason to believe that promotions ever took place here. The *studium* at length obtained a Bull of foundation and privilege from the Valencian Pope, Alexander VI, in A.D. 1500.[2] As an indication of the advance of the Renaissance it may be noted that it was declared to be a *studium* for 'Greek and Latin letters' as well as for the usual faculties.

§ 13. LISBON AND COIMBRA (1290)

Francisco Leitão FERREIRA, *Noticias chronologicas da Universidade de Coimbra* (in *Colecção dos documentos e memorias da Academia Real da Historia Portugueza*, Lisbon, 1729), which unfortunately contains but few documents. These DENIFLE (i. 519–34) largely supplements from the Vatican Archives. (Portuguese translation with notes by RODRIGUES, *A Universidade de Lisboa-Coimbra*, Coimbra, 1892.) An anonymous *Notice Historique de l'Un. de Coïmbre*, Lisbon, 1878. Documents in José Pedro RIBEIRO, *Dissertações chronologicas e criticas*, ii, Lisbon, 1811, and in Francisco BRANDÃO, *Monarchia Lusitana*, Part V, Lisbon, 1752. José Silvestre RIBEIRO deals briefly with Coimbra in *Hist. dos Estabelecimentos scientificos litterarios e artisticos de Portugal* (Lisbon, 1871–93). The *Exposição succinta da organisação actual da Universidade de Coimbra* by the Visconde DE VILLA-MAJOR (Coimbra, 1878), contains an historical introduction, as also does the *Esboço historico-literario da Fac. de Theologia da Univ. de Coimbra*, by Manuel Eduardo DE MOTTA VEIGA (Coimbra, 1872). For copies of the last two books and for some other information, I am indebted to the courtesy of Dr. Viégas, rector in 1891. For other authorities, see Villa-major, *loc. cit.*, pp. 8, 9. There is a *Catalogo dos Pergaminhos do Cartorio da Univ. de Coimbra* (Coimbra, 1880), by Gabriel DE MONTE PEREIRA; the oldest document catalogued is dated 1381. Theophilo BRAGA, *Historia da Universidade de Coimbra*, 4 vols., Lisbon, 1892–1902 (vol. i, 1289–1555). [Antonio DE VASCONCELLOS, *Estabelecimento primitivo da universidade em Coimbra* (Coimbra, 1914), and his article, 'Origem e evolução do fôro académico privativo da antiga universidade de Coimbra' (Coimbra, 1917), an offprint from the *Revista da Universidade de Coimbra*; T. M. Teixeira DE CARVALHO, *A universidade de Coimbra no século XVI* (Coimbra, 1922); H. Teixeira BASTOS, *A vida do estudante de Coimbra* (Coimbra, 1920); J. M. DE ABREU, 'Memórias históricas da Universidade de Coimbra', in *O Instituto* (Coimbra), i, ii; J. DE CARVALHO, 'Instituções escolares', in *História ilustrada da literatura portuguêsa*, i (Lisbon, no date [1930]), 55–62. This work contains many notable photographs of Coimbra.]

THE large number of universities in Spain testifies to the essential distinctness of the Spanish kingdoms which con-

---

[1] It was also from the papal point of view, under the Bull of 1246, a *studium particulare privilegiatum*. [2] La Fuente, i, 347.

tinued to assert their individuality in spite of their rapid
political amalgamation culminating in the Spanish Monarchy
of Charles V. The unity of the kingdom of Portugal from its
first foundation to the present day is proclaimed by the fact
that throughout its history it has possessed (if we except the
Jesuit University of Evora) but one national university.[1] Its
founder was the first Portuguese sovereign who inherited the
whole kingdom of 'Portugal and Algarve', the first Portuguese
monarch great in the arts of peace, the poet-king Diniz.
While, however, the Portuguese university has ever since
maintained a certain historic continuity, it has changed its
local habitation more frequently than any other university in
the world, with the exception of the ever-migratory university of the papal court. Its original seat was at Lisbon. There
are some scanty notices of church schools before the university epoch at Lisbon,[2] but most of them were monastic, and
the most famous of the Portuguese church schools was not at
Lisbon but in the metropolitan city of Braga.[3] The University of Lisbon is one of those which were made, and not
evolved. In 1288 a petition was presented to Nicholas IV by
the abbot of Alcobaça, the prior of Santa Cruz in Coimbra,
and other ecclesiastics praying for the establishment of a
studium generale to be supported by a tax upon the convents
or benefices of the petitioners.[4] In 1290, accordingly, a Bull

[1] Fortunato de S. Bõaventura
(*Hist. da real Abbadia de Alcobaça*,
Lisbon, 1827, p. 55) cites the charter of the abbey of Alcobaça establishing in 1269 a *studium* of
grammar, logic, and theology,
'ad communem utilitatem mona-
chorum nostrorum *et omnium* appe-
tentium incomparabilem scientiae
margaritam': but as the abbot of
Alcobaça is found in 1288 at the head
of the petitioners for a *studium* at
Lisbon, it may be assumed that no
great success attended this interesting—and perhaps unique—attempt
to establish something like a *studium generale* in connexion with
a monastery. [Studies of this sort
appear to have been carried on also

in the monastery of Santa Cruz at
Coimbra, before the arrival of the
university.] J. S. Ribeiro (*Hist.* i.
13) also speaks of the foundation
in 1286 by D. Domingos Jardo,
Bishop of Evora and Lisbon, of a
'College or Seminary' for 'dez
capellães, vinte merceeiros e seis
escholares de latim, grego, theologiae canones'. Evora was founded
in 1558, *loc. cit.*, p. 107.

[2] Motta Veiga, p. 22.

[3] *Mon. Lusit.* v. 524; Motta
Veiga, p. 19.

[4] *Mon. Lusit.* v. 530; Ferreira,
pp. 9, 41; Motta Veiga, p. 22. La
Fuente's claim (i. 69 *sq.*) for Coimbra
as 'the most ancient university' in
the peninsula is quite unfounded.

of privilege was issued.[1] It was not, however, quite in the form of an ordinary Bull of foundation. It recognizes the university as already founded by King Diniz,[2] and recites that an endowment has been already provided by certain monasteries, prelates, and rectors. It sanctions taxation of lodgings in the Paris and Bologna fashion, grants dispensation from residence to masters and students, exempts them from lay jurisdiction, and authorizes the bishop of Lisbon[3] (or *sede vacante* the vicar-capitular) to confer the *ius ubique docendi* in all faculties except theology. But, in spite of royal and papal protection, the citizens of Lisbon soon manifested with exceptional ferocity that hatred for young clerks which was everywhere more or less entertained by medieval citizens. Riots like those which had nearly driven the great French university from the capital proved fatal to the *studium* at Lisbon.

Transferred to Coimbra, 1308–9.
In 1308–9 the university was transferred to Coimbra—a smaller and quieter city, though at that time a royal residence—with fresh papal and royal charters of privilege.[4] The endowment of the university was now provided for by the impropriation of six churches in the king's patronage.[5]

[1] Much is made of the statement that S. Antony of Padua was sent to school at S. Mary's Church, close to which he was born: but it is clear that he was very young at the time, and the statement in the earliest life of the saint ('sacris litteris imbuendum tradunt', ap. *Portugaliae Mon. Hist.* i. 117) probably implies no more than that he was taught to read his Psalter.

[2] 'Sane ad audientiam nostram pervenit, quod procurante charissimo in Christo filio nostro Dionysio Portugal. Rege illustri, cuiuslibet licitae facultatis studia in Civitate Ulixbon. sunt de novo . . . plantata.' [The royal diploma is dated Leiria, 1 Mar. 1290. It places the university under the protection of S. Vincent, the patron saint of Lisbon, and guarantees the personal safety of the scholars. See A. de Vasconcellos, 'Um documento precioso', in *Revista da Universidade de Coimbra*, i; it is transcribed and reproduced in the *Historia ilustrada da literatura portuguêsa*, i. 60–1.]

[3] The see became an archbishopric in 1394.

[4] Ferreira, p. 94; *Mon. Lusit.* v. 531; Motta Veiga, p. 241. The petition to the Pope explains the cause. Extracts are given from this and other documents by Denifle, i. 524.

[5] *Reg. Clem. V*, Rome, 1885, No. 2666. Ferreira (p. 110) prints an edict of 1323, distributing salaries —600 livras for law, 500 for decretals, 200 for physics, 200 for grammar, 100 for logic, 65 for music. Braga (i. 112) misreads '75' for '65'. The money was provided by the 'commendadores' of Soure and Pombal. Other impropriations followed (*ibid.*, p. 115).

The shade and retirement of Coimbra proved, it would CHAP. VII, seem, even less favourable to academic prosperity than the § 13. turmoil and strife of Lisbon. In 1338 a petition was presented Back to Lisbon, to the king for the re-transference to Lisbon of the university 1338–9. which Diniz had declared to be 'ineradicably' planted at Coimbra—a change which was carried out in that or the following year.[1] But, whether owing to a renewal of the old Return to hostilities or otherwise, the year 1355 saw the restless univer- Coimbra, 1355. sity re-established at Coimbra. This migration seems to have been more fatal than the former. A petition presented to the anti-pope Clement VII in 1377 informs his Holiness that there was no longer any *studium generale* existing in Portu- gal.[2] It appears, however, that in that year the university was University formally re-established in Lisbon,[3] though it was not till 1380 transferred to Lisbon that a regular foundation-bull of the ordinary type was issued, again, taking no account of the previous existence of a university 1377. either at Coimbra or Lisbon, and conferring the *ius ubique docendi*. At Lisbon it remained, with a greater degree of prosperity than it had enjoyed at any former period, till the year 1537, when—this time against its will—it was transferred Final once more to Coimbra in the interests of study and morality.[4] return to Coimbra, At Coimbra, in spite of the modern tendency to educational 1537. centralization, the university still remains.[5]

In the earlier days of the university theology had been Theo- taught, as in other university towns where there was no logical faculty, theological faculty, in the convents. We first hear of a doctor 1411. of theology (who must have graduated elsewhere) teaching at Coimbra at the beginning of the fifteenth century: and a

---

[1] Ferreira, p. 140 *sq.*

[2] It also speaks of the former *studium* in Lisbon as having been only a *studium particulare*. Either the old charters were forgotten or the assertion must mean that the *studium* never *de facto* came up to the standard implied by the ex- pression *studium generale*. This and the documents next alluded to are unpublished, but extracts are given by Denifle, i. 531. There has been much uncertainty and con- fusion about these changes in previous writers.

[3] Braga, i. 120.

[4] *Ibid.*, p. 450 *sq.* A charter for the transference to Coimbra was issued in 1443 by the Infante Don Pedro, but came to nothing. *Ibid.*, p. 144.

[5] [Although since 1911 sister universities have existed in Lisbon and Oporto, the prestige remains with Coimbra.]

regular faculty of theology was founded and endowed with impropriations in 1411.[1]

Constitu-
tion.
The royal charter of privilege issued in 1309 and the very short statutes apparently made at the same time are sufficient to show that the constitution must have been a student-constitution on the Bologna model. The influence of Alfonso the Wise and his Salamancan charter is plainly discernible. How many universities or nations then existed is not known, but there was certainly a plurality of rectors,[2] and the statutes enforced attendance at congregation and obedience to the rectors in other ways—particularly in case of a cessation.[3] The prominence of this feature is noteworthy: it is hardly too much to say that universities were in their origin societies for enforcing student-rights by the threat of cessation or migration. The royal charter confers all the usual scholastic privileges. It recognizes the jurisdiction of the bishop and master of the schools over the scholars, but without derogation to the Bologna right of trial by the scholar's own master.[4] Houses were to be taxed, not as usual by two scholars and two citizens, but by two scholars and two members of the royal council.

Royal in-
terference.
The exercise of the royal prerogative in the government of the university—a characteristic feature throughout the Penin-

---

[1] Denifle, i. 533. [A chair of theology was founded in 1411, endowed by Prince Henry (the 'Navigator') in 1438 and by his will in 1460, and confirmed by the Pope in 1472. Manuel I founded a second chair.]

[2] After the return to Lisbon in 1377, there is only one rector. Ferreira, p. 202.

[3] 'Statuimus, ut Doctores et Magistri obediant Rectoribus in licitis et honestis, ut cessent a legendo, si et quando ex aliqua causa rationabili per eosdem, sive ex parte ipsorum, eis fuerit demandatum, habita tamen prius deliberatione cum Oficialibus, et facta promulgatione in Congregatione generali.' J. P. Ribeiro, ii. 241. A later royal statute, dated 1471, is given in J. P. Ribeiro, ii. 265.

It shows that the chairs were still elective.

[4] 'Episcopum vel eius Vicarium, seu Magistrum scholarum, si hoc noscatur ad suum officium pertinere. Per hoc tamen legi dicenti quod Magistri in suos scholares ius dicere valeant non intendimus derogare.' (Mon. Lusit. v. 532; Motta Veiga, p. 34.) Scholars are protected from the secular courts, 'nisi forte in homicidio, vel vulnerum illatione, seu furto, vel rapina, aut mulierum raptu, vel falsae monetae fabricatione fuerint comprehensi'. (Ibid.) The influence of Salamanca is still more plainly discernible in the royal decree of 1323 apportioning the salaries. It provides for a chair of music. Ferreira, p. 114: cf. above, p. 81, n. 2.

sula—was peculiarly marked in Portugal. From the middle CHAP. VII, § 13.
of the fifteenth century the appointment of professors rested
with the 'protector' of the university, who was usually either
a royal prince or the king himself.[1] Eventually the university
was deprived of the power of making statutes for itself, and
even of the management of its own property.[2] Until the end
of the monarchy the king was protector of the university.[3] A
college for ten scholars in grammar and arts and four servants College of Diogo Alfonso, 1447.
was founded by the will of Doctor Diogo Alfonso de Màn-
gancha in 1447,[4] but the college system never attained any
considerable development in Portugal.

Coimbra still retains perhaps more of the appearance and Medieval traditions of Coimbra.
atmosphere of the old medieval university town than any city
of continental Europe. There, almost alone in Europe outside
the British Isles, students of all faculties may be seen parading
the streets in academical costume. Their dress is, indeed,
much more obviously the descendant of the old 'clerical habit'
of the medieval student than the scanty gown of the Oxford
commoner.[5] In its theological faculty too there would seem

[1] The illustrious Henry the Navigator was the first protector elected by the university in 1418. Braga, i. 135; Villa-major, p. 31. In addition to the endowment of a chair of theology he founded a university building in 1431. Braga, i. 130, 160. As to his school of *mathematica*, *nautica*, and *geographia*, founded at Sagres in 1419, see Braga, i. 135, 160.

[2] This last step was taken in 1414. Braga, i. 133.

[3] The appointments to chairs in the University of Coimbra are still made after a public competitive lecture, as in the Middle Ages. *Notice Historique*, p. 150. Another curious survival is the degree of *Baccalarius formatus* (*loc. cit.*, p. 100). The system of examination by *puncta* is still in vogue at Coimbra, and the examinations are still preceded by the mass of the Holy Ghost. [1895.]

[4] Braga, i. 140 *sq.*; [Monte

Pereira, p. 16: 'collegio para 10 estudantes pobres nas suas casas a S. Jorga, e 4 servidores.']

[5] A statute of 1321 required doctors, licentiates, and bachelors to wear gowns reaching to the heels, undergraduates' gowns reaching to the middle of the thigh. At the present day 'the Coimbra man wears a gown not unlike the Johnian gown at Cambridge: he has no cap; but the *gorro*, which was originally the begging-pouch (?), and which he carries in his hand, serves to cover his head when the sun is very powerful'. *Handbook for Travellers in Portugal* (London: John Murray, 1875), p. 99. The robes of Coimbra doctors vary with the faculty. D.D.s wear white; doctors of law, red; of medicine, yellow; of arts, blue. These colours, according to the *Notice Historique* (p. 35), date from the medieval period. The same writer describes the costume of the undergraduate

to have lingered a more important and (so far as Catholic
Europe is concerned) still rarer survival of the Middle Ages—
some faint tradition of the old antagonism to Roman auto-
cracy of which the secular university schools of theology were
so long the depositaries.[1]

as consisting 'd'une soutane, d'un manteau et d'un bonnet de drap noir' (p. 173).

[1] 'The whole tone of theological teaching at Coimbra is very much opposed to ultramontane tenets, and several of the text-books employed are in the Roman Index.' Murray's *Handbook*, p. 100. But one at least of these books seems to have been abandoned in 1845. See Motta Veiga, p. 278. Opposition to ultramontane Salamanca may possibly explain the phenomenon, or more probably hostility to the Jesuits, who dominated education in Portugal down to 1772. [1895.]

CHAPTER VIII

THE UNIVERSITIES OF FRANCE

Short accounts of the French universities may be found in old books such as LIMNAEUS, *Notitia Regni Franciae*, Strasbourg, 1655, i. 392 *sq.*, and PIGANIOL, *Description de la France*, Paris, 1753. RIANCEY, *Histoire de l'instruction publique et de la liberté de l'enseignement en France*, Paris, 1844, Ludwig HAHN, *Das Unterrichtswesen in Frankreich mit einer Geschichte der Pariser Universität*, Breslau, 1848, and THÉRY, *Histoire de l'éducation en France depuis le Ve siècle jusqu'à nos jours*, Paris, 1858, touch on our subject but do not enter in any detail into the organization of the university system. No work of any importance on the subject as a whole had appeared till the publication of vol. iii (no other vol. published) of Marcel FOURNIER's *Histoire de la Science du Droit en France* (Paris, 1892), which is devoted to *Les Universités françaises et l'enseignement du Droit en France au Moyen-Âge* (dealing in detail with Orleans, Angers, Toulouse, Montpellier, and Avignon). Though M. Fournier's method is somewhat dry and involves much repetition, the volume is not unimportant, at least from the special point of view indicated by the title of the larger work of which it forms part. I am under great obligations to the same writer's work, *Les Statuts et Privilèges des Universités françaises depuis leur fondation jusqu'en 1789*, 3 vols., Paris, 1890–2—a most valuable collection of documents, edited without much annotation, with too much haste, and with insufficient acknowledgements to Denifle. It was severely criticized by DENIFLE in a pamphlet, *Les Universités françaises au Moyen-Âge*, Paris, 1892, where a few omitted documents are printed. For minor magazine articles and pamphlets on the various universities, often dealing hardly at all with the medieval period, the reader may be referred to the ample bibliographies in both of M. Fournier's books. [Cf. P. VIOLLET, *Hist. des institutions politiques et administratives de la France*, ii (Paris, 1898), 367–73; S. D'IRSAY, *Histoire des universités*, i. 110–38 *passim*, 209–13.]

WRITERS who divide universities into two sharply con- trasted groups—the universities of masters and the universities of students—have usually assigned the French universities other than Paris, with few exceptions, to the latter class. That the older French *studia*, even those so near Paris as Orleans or Angers, were little influenced, either in their original constitution or in their subsequent development, by the example of that university, is undoubtedly true. They cannot, however, with any propriety be regarded as imitations of Bologna. In their original form they represent on the whole a distinct type of university organization: the oldest of them must be numbered among the universities which grew and were not made. In their subsequent development they were

CHAP. VIII. no doubt powerfully influenced by the Bologna model; some of them did eventually become on the whole universities of students rather than universities of masters, but still (as we shall see) they were student-universities of a very modified type. In so far as this transformation was due to the influence of Bologna, that influence finds its most natural explanation in the fact that they were mainly universities of law. In the south of France there was the same demand for law that there was in Italy; while even in parts of France that were governed by customs not of directly Roman origin, an education in Roman law was the ordinary preparation for the career of the secular as well as of the ecclesiastical lawyer, and the exclusion of civil law from Paris created a demand for law-teaching even in the immediate neighbourhood of the great northern university. There were parts of France no doubt which sent students in equal numbers to scholastic Paris and to the legal universities of Orleans, Angers, and Montpellier. Often of course the same individual studied in both. Still it is worth remarking how large a proportion of the students of Paris came from the north and east of Europe: the names of the Parisian nations are a sufficient attestation of the fact. Of the law universities, on the other hand, a large proportion were situated in the south of France; and even Orleans and Angers —though both on the northern bank of the Loire—drew the majority of their students from France south of the Loire, that is to say, from the most romanized part of France, the region whose social and political condition most resembled the original home of the great law revival of the twelfth century. This is particularly the case with the university which, on the whole, has the best claim to the first place in a chronological list of the French universities other than Paris.

§ 1. MONTPELLIER

The older authorities are: STROBELBERGERUS, *Historia Monspeliensis*, Nuremberg, 1625. [RIOLAN], *Curieuses Recherches sur les Escholes en Médecine de Paris et Montpellier*, Paris, 1651. C. D'AIGREFEUILLE, *Histoire de la ville de Montpellier*, Montpellier, 1737. J. ASTRUC, *Mémoires pour servir à l'histoire de la Faculté de Médecine de Montpellier*, Paris, 1767. PRUNELLE, *Fragmens pour servir à l'histoire des progrès de la Médecine dans l'Université de Montpellier*, An. 9. Many other CHAP. VIII, historical pamphlets were evoked in the seventeenth century by the § 1. exclusion of Montpellier doctors from practice in Paris which led to an acrimonious controversy. PRIMEROSE, *Academia Monspeliensis*, Oxford, 1631, contains no history.

The most elaborate work on the history of the university has been done by A. GERMAIN in his *Histoire de la Commune de Montpellier*, 3 vols., Montpellier, 1851 (new ed., 1879: I have used the first edition), and in a number of monographs of which the most important are *L'École de Droit de Montpellier*, 1877; *La Méd. arabe et la Méd. grecque à Montpellier*, 1879; *L'École de Médecine à Montpellier*, 1880; *Les Maîtres de Chirurgie de Montpellier*, 1886; *Le Cérémonial de l'Université de Médecine de Montpellier*, 1879; *Du Principe démocratique dans les anciennes Écoles de Montpellier*, 1881; *La Faculté des Arts et l'ancien Collège de Montpellier*, 1882; *La Faculté de Théologie de Montpellier*, 1883. These and many other articles more or less relating to the university appeared originally in the *Mémoires de la Société archéologique de Montpellier*, 1860–81.

Germain's earlier works were largely superseded, as collections of documents, by the magnificent *Cartulaire de l'Université de Montpellier* (vol. i, Montpellier, 1890 [vol. ii, 1912]); to which he contributed an introduction on the history of the university. Germain is one of the best and most readable university historians, though not always quite trustworthy as to academical technicalities. Astruc is the most important of the older writers, though of the superstitious order, seeking to make Montpellier older than Salerno. Mlle GUIRAUD has produced elaborate histories of the Colleges of St. Bénoit and Mende in *Les Fondations du Pape Urbain V à Montpellier*, Montpellier, 1889–91. I have also consulted J. CASTELNAU, 'Notices sur la vie et les ouvrages de Placentin' in *Mém. de la Soc. archéol. de Montpellier*, 1840 (i. 480), and THOMAS, *Le Collège de Pézenas* (*ibid.* iii. 730). See also the books on medical history mentioned above, vol. i, p. 75, to which may be added MONTEIL, *La Médecine en France*, ed. Pileur, Paris 1874, and articles by BOYER in *Montpellier Médical*, 1882.

[A. GERMAIN, 'Étude sur l'origine de l'université de Montpellier', in C. DE VIC and J. J. VAISSETE, *Histoire générale de Languedoc*, ed. Privat, vii (Toulouse, 1879); F. FABRÈGE, *L'Université de Montpellier*, Montpellier, 1911 (from the *Histoire de Maguelone*); C. FLAHAUT, A. JOUBIN, and E. C. BABUT, *Conférences sur l'histoire de Montpellier*, Montpellier, 1912.

The history of the university is bound up with the history of medicine and allied studies in Salerno and in Arabic and Jewish circles in Spain and southern France. Cf. S. KAHN, *Les Écoles juives et la faculté de médecine de Montpellier*, Montpellier, 1890; SUDHOFF, 'Salerno, Montpellier und Paris um 1200', in *Archiv für die Geschichte der Medizin*, xx, 1928. The important study, prefixed by J. CALMETTE to the second volume of the *Cartulaire* (1912), which has as its sub-title, 'Inventaires des archives anciennes de la Faculté de médecine et supplément au tome i du Cartulaire (1181–1400)' is concerned with post-medieval times. There is a good introduction to the subject in S. D'IRSAY, i. 110–20.

M. CHAILLAN, *Registre de comptes pour le collège papal saint Benoît et Germain à Montpellier, 1368–70*, Paris, 1916.]

Montpellier but slightly connected with France.

IN 1204 Montpellier lost even feudal dependence upon France, which was not restored until it passed under the immediate sovereignty of the French kings in 1349.[1] Not only was this independence retained much longer by Montpellier than by the neighbouring dependencies of the French Crown, but the Pyrenees were not then the boundary-line that they have since become. The Spanish saints reverenced in the diocese of Montpellier still testify to a Visigothic origin,[2] and during the Moorish occupation of Spain the Spanish element in its population was increased by large numbers of fugitives from the Peninsula.[3] Throughout our period the Mediterranean, that great highway of the ancient world, brought Montpellier and the neighbouring towns into closer connexion with Aragon, and even with Italy, than with northern France and its capital.

Its political position. The once distinct towns of Montpellier and Montpelliéret, which have now coalesced into the present town of Montpellier, were situated on the opposite sides of the hill from which the latter name is taken. Both were once feudally dependent upon the bishop of the older see-town of Maguelone; but in the tenth century Montpellier passed, as a fief held of the bishop, to the Guillem family, who were themselves vassals of the counts of Melgeuil. From the beginning of the thirteenth century these Guillems became closely connected by marriage, by alliance in war, and by feudal dependence with the kings of Aragon. On the other hand, Montpellier was no less closely connected with the Papacy. In 1085 Count Peter of Melgeuil submitted to the feudal suzerainty of Gregory VII, whose successor appointed the bishop of Maguelone his perpetual vicar or representative. The Guillems, too, all through their history, were characterized by a romantic and passionate loyalty to the Holy See. They were a family of crusaders; and were among the most ardent champions of the Popes against Frederick II. Their sympathies were clerical and ultramontane to the core. One scion

---

[1] [In 1293 Philip the Fair acquired the suzerainty by exchange from the Bishop of Maguelone, but the French kings, as the bishop's successors, continued to hold Montpellier of the kings of Majorca, the younger branch of the house of Aragon, until 1349, when the direct or full lordship was bought by Philip VI.]

[2] Germain, *Commune*, i, p. ix.

[3] Astruc, p. 5.

after another of the family ended his days in a monastery.
The town itself was no less profoundly ecclesiastical in spirit:
Montpellier was a 'Catholic centre in the midst of the
Albigensian country'.[1] Under these circumstances it - is
natural to find that at least one important modification was
introduced into the Bologna constitution when it was imitated
by the legal university at Montpellier. From first to last the
university was more closely dependent upon the bishop than
was the case even at Paris or in England.[2]

I. *The University of Medicine.*

The earliest fame of the schools of Montpellier was not
legal but medical. The first notice of a medical school at
Montpellier takes us back to 1137, when Adalbert, afterwards
archbishop of Mainz, is said to have studied here after having
gone through a course of arts at Paris.[3] In the days of John
of Salisbury it stood almost on a level with the school of
Salerno. In enumerating the careers open to Parisian students
when weary of grammar and dialectic, he says, 'Others went
to Salerno or Montpellier and became clients of the physicians.'[4] And the fame of Montpellier increased while that of
Salerno decreased.

*Early
notices of
the
medical
school.*

---

[1] Germain, *loc. cit.*, i, p. lxiii.

[2] The ecclesiastical character of
the university itself is less marked.
The tonsure is only enforced in the
case of clerks beneficed or in holy
orders and religious. *Cartulaire*, i.
181; Fournier, ii, No. 882. We find
the chancellor may be a 'clericus
coniugatus, in minoribus ordinibus
constitutus', *Cartulaire*, i. 249;
Fournier, ii, No. 924.

[3] Anselm of Mainz or Havel-
berg, *Vita Adalberti*, in Jaffé,
Bibliotheca rerum Germanicarum,
iii. 592; cf. Caesarius of Heister-
bach, *Dialogus miraculorum*, vii. 24,
ed. Strange, ii. 34 (1221–2). S.
Bernard (*Ep.* 307 in *Patrol. lat.*
clxxxii. 512) speaks of the archbishop of Lyons going to Montpellier to be cured, where 'cum

medicis expendit et quod habebat,
et quod non habebat'.

[4] 'Alii autem, suum in philosophia intuentes defectum, Salernum uel ad Montem Pessulanum
profecti, facti sunt clientuli medicorum, et repente, quales fuerant
philosophi, tales in momento
medici eruperunt. Fallacibus enim
referti experimentis in breui
redeunt, sedulo exercentes quod
didicerunt. Hipocratem ostentant
aut Galienum; verba proferunt
inaudita, ad omnia suos loquuntur
afforismos, et mentes humanas,
uelut afflatas tonitruis, sic per-
cellunt nominibus inauditis. Cre-
duntur omnia posse, quia omnia
iactitant, omnia pollicentur.' *Meta-
logicon*, i. 4, ed. Webb, p. 13. John
of Salisbury's estimate of the

CHAP. VIII,   The origin of this school is wrapped in obscurity. It may
§ 1.   have been an offshoot from Salerno. On the other hand, those
Its origin.   who are fond of seeing 'Saracenic' influence at work in all the
intellectual movements of the Middle Ages may here indulge
their *penchant* with some plausibility. The origin of the town
is traditionally connected with the destruction of the older
city of Maguelone, and of the Saracenic power on the shores
of the Mediterranean, by Charles Martel in 737, when the
fugitives are said to have taken refuge at Montpellier; and
there was a considerable Arabic as well as Jewish population
in the town as late as the thirteenth century,[1] while many of
the original inhabitants were Spaniards who had long resided
among the Moors.[2] It is possible that some tradition of
medical science or skill may thus have survived the downfall
of the Saracenic Empire, and may have accounted for the
direction here taken by the general revival of the European
mind in the twelfth century. Or again, somewhat less im-
probably, the new impulse may be ascribed more directly to
contact with the flourishing Jewish and Arabic schools of
Spain in the twelfth century, or with the Jewish schools of

medicos of his time is curiously
like Molière's view of their seventeenth-century brethren. To the
twelfth century also belong the
lines (from a poem on Becket):

'Vicit Cantuaria Montem Pes-
    sulanum
Victa (et) Salernia iactant se in
    vanum.'

In du Méril, *Poésies Populaires Lat.
du moyen-âge*, Paris, 1847, p. 91.
Cf. also Matthew Paris, *Chron.
Maj.*, ed. Luard, v. 453–4, 647
(1254–7). Extracts from the letters
of a Montpellier student at the end
of the twelfth century are printed
in the *Cartulaire*, i. 700; Fournier,
ii, No. 880. Giles of Corbeil
(*c.* 1198) tells of a certain Renaudus

'Qui Pessulani pridem vetus in-
    cola montis
In medicinali doctor celeber-
    rimus arte
Iura monarchiae tenuit',

who afterwards turned monk and
attended the poor *gratis*. Leyser,
Hist. Poet. Med. Aevi, p. 574. [Cf.
Neckam, *De naturis rerum*, ii. 123,
174 (ed. T. Wright, London,
1863).]

[1] Germain, i, p. lxiv *sq.*
[2] They were attracted by the
privileges offered by Lewis the
Pious, Jourdain, *Recherches*, p. 91;
[F. Soldevila, *Història de Catalunya*,
i. 30–49 (Barcelona, 1934), gives a
good summary of the relations between the county of Barcelona and
the south of France in the ninth
century. The Arabic and Jewish
influence upon the social life of the
Midi is brilliantly defended and
illustrated by Mr. Christopher
Dawson in his essay, 'The Origins
of the Romantic Tradition', reprinted, from the *Criterion* for
January 1932, in his *Mediaeval
Religion and other essays* (London,
1934), pp. 121–54.]

medicine at Arles and Narbonne.[1] The names of the three nations into which the legal university was divided—Provence, Burgundy, Catalonia[2]—are a sufficient indication of the districts from which Montpellier drew its students. At the same time the markedly ecclesiastical character of the school forms an objection to the theory that the earliest Montpellier medicine was immediately derived from Jewish or Arabic sources. But whatever be the exact origin of the school, we cannot be wrong in connecting the prominence of medicine at Montpellier with the comparatively advanced state of material civilization in the rich and prosperous commercial cities in the countries bordering upon the Mediterranean. The study of medicine prospered at Montpellier from the same causes which ensured its prosperity in Italy. Before the days of mechanism, medicine was the one branch of speculative knowledge which had a distinct commercial value.[3]

[1] This is the view of Germain, i, p. lxx, and was apparently the tradition current at Montpellier in the time of Strobelbergerus. Prunelle traces the origin of the school to the Arabs and Jews combined (p. 15). It is worthy of note, as a datum for further investigation, that there was a large settlement of Greeks at Marseilles during the ninth, tenth, and eleventh centuries. Jourdain, *Recherches*, p. 45. Marseilles also carried on an extensive commerce with the Saracens of Spain. *Ibid.*, p. 92. The Jewish traveller, Benjamin of Tudela (ed. Asher, i. 33), says that Christian and Mahometan merchants from all parts were to be seen at Montpellier (1174).

[2] *Cartulaire*, i. 319; Fournier, ii, No. 947.

[3] [We have omitted here some comments and notes in which Rashdall sought to show that Arabic medicine came late to Montpellier and that until the fifteenth century 'Galen predominated over Avicenna'. This argument is now out of date in view of

later investigation into the literature and medieval methods of teaching: see above, vol. i, pp. 75, 86, on Salerno. Salerno certainly influenced the development of Montpellier, especially after *c.* 1170, but translations from the Arabic into Latin by Jewish scholars had been made in the cities of the south of France in the twelfth century (S. d'Irsay, i. 113 and the authorities there mentioned). The *Canon* of Avicenna was translated, probably by Gerard of Cremona, at the end of the century. The difference between Salerno and Montpellier may be summarized as follows: although the *ars medicinae* or body of prescribed medical texts, due to the work of Constantinus Africanus, was largely composed of translations from the Arabic, Salerno was not in such direct touch with Arabic learning as Montpellier was. For example, it was one of the centres of direct translation from the Greek and has a place in the early transmission in Greco-Latin of some of the works of Aristotle (A.

Not only the medical school but its organization in university form was much more ancient than the university of
jurists. The two universities were always quite distinct from
each other and from the university of arts. The constitution
of the university of medicine is not, so far as we know,
directly derived from any earlier model. A proclamation of
Guillem VIII, lord of Montpellier, in 1181, allowing all who
will freely to teach medicine at Montpellier suggests that at
present neither masters nor bishop possessed—or at least
possessed undisputedly—the right of granting or refusing
the *licentia docendi*,[1] if its language does not positively exclude
the existence of a magisterial society. At all events the masters

Birkenmayer, *Le Rôle joué par les médecins et les naturalistes dans la reception d'Aristote*, Warsaw, 1930, pp. 4, 5). On the other hand, the closer relations with Arabic medicine which existed from *c.* 1200 at Montpellier were important, not so much in affecting the alleged balance between Galen and Avicenna, as in the encouragement of medicine as a *luminare maius* among the sciences (cf. the Statutes of 1239, *Cartulaire*, i, No. 4, cited by S. d'Irsay, i. 119 note) and not only as a practical art. Hence the development of a separate university of medicine.]

[1] Guillem promises 'quod ego de cetero . . . non dabo concessionem seu prerogativam aliquam alicui persone, quod unus solus tantummodo legat, seu scolas regat in Montepessulano in facultate fisice discipline. . . . Et ideo mando, volo, laudo atque concedo in perpetuum, quod omnes homines quicumque sint, vel undecumque sint, sine aliqua interpellatione regant scolas de fisica in Montepessulano'. *Cartulaire*, i. 179, No. 1; Fournier, ii, No. 879. James I of Aragon in 1272 forbade Jews or Christians to practise medicine at Montpellier who had not been duly examined and licensed. *Cartulaire*, i. 202;

Fournier, ii, No. 896. This *licentia practicandi* was distinct from the doctoral licence. *Cartulaire*, i. 195, 217; Fournier, ii, Nos. 891, 909. [Gaines Post, in his paper, 'Alexander III, the *licentia docendi* and the rise of the Universities' (*Haskins Anniversary Essays*, Boston, 1929, pp. 266–8), strongly emphasizes the point made by Rashdall and draws a contrast between the policy of the Pope and the 'far more liberal policy' of William VIII. But the absence of any reference to the licence to teach does not prove that no tests or qualifications were required. William undertook to grant no monopoly, and it seems more likely that he was falling into line with Alexander's injunctions of 1170–2 and 1179 that nobody 'docere quemquam, qui sit idoneus, petita licentia interdicat' (cf. *Chartul. Univ. Paris.* i, Introduction, Nos. 4, 12). S. d'Irsay's note (i. 118 note) on the subject is misleading. It suggests that the Pope had ordered free grant of the licence at Montpellier in 1171, but the Bull which he quotes from the *Histoire de Maguelone* is the well-known letter to the archbishop of Reims about the schools at Châlons-sur-Marne (Jaffé-Löwenfeld, No. 12096; *Patrol. Lat.* cc. 840).]

soon began to imitate the guild-system already established at Bologna and Paris and probably at Salerno, while the bishop claimed that authority over the schools which was everywhere enjoyed by the Church north of the Alps. The ceremonies of graduation were more probably borrowed from Bologna than from Paris, if indeed the medical university of Montpellier does not represent an almost independent application of the guild-principle to scholastic organization. The first allusion to the existence of a university of medicine occurs in 1220, when the statutes which speak of a 'universitas medicorum tam doctorum quam discipulorum'[1] were confirmed by the cardinal legate Conrad.[2] By these statutes it was provided, apparently for the first time, that the bishop should appoint a chancellor to preside over the university. The chancellor was to be nominated by the bishop together with three masters—the senior among them and two others named by him and the bishop.[3]

The Montpellier chancellorship offers the nearest parallel that any continental university presents to the chancellorship

---

[1] The phrase was often used at Paris and other universities ruled by the masters. The statutes make it plain that all power was with the masters; the code is conceived entirely in their interest. The fact that a master-university was established rather than a student-university may possibly be due in part to the precedent of Salerno; but we know too little of the organization of Salerno to say whether it exerted any influence upon Montpellier. The system of examinations and graduation-ceremonies resembled in the main those of Bologna. At inception the doctor was girt with a golden cincture in addition to the other *insignia*. (Fournier, ii, No. 1194.) It is worth noting that a S. Andrews doctor of medicine still wears the cincture.

[2] *Cartulaire*, i. 180; Fournier, ii, No. 882. They were confirmed in 1239 by another legate (*Cartulaire*, i. 185; Fournier, ii, No. 884); and in 1240 we find the masters appoint-

ing arbitrators to interpret or modify these statutes. It seems that this is the first attempt at legislation on the part of the society itself, and we hear of no more statutes made in this way till 1313. *Cartulaire*, i. 186, 229; Fournier, ii, Nos. 885, 914. Fournier (*Hist*. iii. 353) speaks of the statutes as 'en partie extraits de ceux de Salerne de 1231'. The traces of indebtedness seem to me extremely slight.

[3] 'Episcopus Magalonensis, adiuncto sibi antiquiore magistro, et postea aliis duobus eis adiunctis magistris discretioribus et laudabilioribus, iuxta testimonium extrinsecus et secundum conscientiam propriam, eligat cum predictis sibi adiunctis unum de magistris, sive sit de illis tribus sive de aliis, qui iustitiam exhibeat magistris et scholaribus, vel aliis contra magistros vel scolares agentibus, querimonia apud eum deposita.' *Cartulaire*, i. 181; Fournier, ii, No. 882.

CHAP. VIII,
§ 1.

of Oxford, established in like manner by legatine authority only six years before.[1] The powers of the chancellorship were, however, much more limited than those attached, even at its first institution, to that office in the English universities. The chancellor of Montpellier resembled the chancellors of Oxford and Cambridge in being the presiding officer of the university as well as the representative of the bishop, and also in the absence of connexion with any capitular body. But at Montpellier the chancellor's jurisdiction was purely civil. Maguelone was nearer to Montpellier than Lincoln to Oxford, or even Ely to Cambridge. Here the bishop always reserved to himself the criminal and spiritual jurisdiction over masters and scholars, an appellate civil jurisdiction, and also the right of conferring the licence. Even in the absence of the bishop, he was represented not by the chancellor but by his ordinary official. All statutes required the episcopal confirmation. It was not till the fourteenth century that the masters obtained any legal control over the bishop and the examiners of his choice in the admission to the licence and doctorate. Indeed, in 1289, we hear of the bishop imprisoning examiners who refused to pass a candidate until they withdrew their objections. These arbitrary proceedings led to an appeal to the Holy See,[2] and at length, in 1309, a Bull of Clement V required the assent of a two-thirds majority of the masters of the faculty for the conferment of the licence, and by another Bull of the same date the concurrence of a two-thirds majority was likewise made necessary for the election of the chancellor.[3]

The proctors.

Nor does the parallelism with Oxford end with the chancellorship. As at Oxford, the masters are more directly represented by two proctors, the office circulating among

[1] See below, vol. iii, p. 37.

[2] *Cartulaire*, i. 209, 213; Fournier, ii, Nos. 902, 904. [The Bull of Nicholas IV, dated 1 Oct. 1289, and printed from copies in the *Cartulaire*, i. 209–10, has been re-edited from the original in the supplement added to the second volume of the *Cartulaire* (ii. 855–6, cf. p. cxliv)].

[3] *Cartulaire*, i. 222; Fournier, ii, Nos. 911, 912. At times, however, we find the Pope 'reserving' the chancellorship to himself. *Cartulaire*, i. 250, 254; Fournier, ii, Nos. 925, 926. Each master could license his own bachelor and present him to the rector. *Cartulaire*, i. 187; Fournier, ii, No. 885.

them. The functions of these proctors were primarily finan- CHAP.VIII,
cial,[1] as originally were those of the proctors of Paris and § 1.
Oxford: but the existence of a dean in the medical faculty at The dean.
Montpellier, who was always the senior doctor and ranked
next to the chancellor, restricted the functions of the proctors
to this their original department.[2] There was also a third The
proctor appointed by the students, and after 1533 two *con-* student-proctor
siliarii, one of whom was a bachelor, the other a student.[3] and *consiliarii*.

The earlier statutes appear to be made by the masters and Restricted
to contemplate no limit to their authority: but by 1340 the powers of the
democratic spirit seems to have so far spread from the legal student-congrega-
to the medical university that any alteration of the statutes tion.
which affected the students now requires their consent as
well as that of the masters.[4] The rights of the students do not,
however, appear to have been in practice very extensive. It
was only twice a year that the chancellor summoned an assembly of the entire university of masters and scholars[5] in the
church of S. Firmin, when the students conferred with the
doctors as to the arrangement of a lecture-list for the ensuing
session, and an opportunity was afforded for the general
ventilation of student-grievances. We find the students at
these assemblies petitioning that lectures should be given on

[1] *Cartulaire*, i. 341, 343; Fournier, ii, No. 947 *quater*. The senior
master is entrusted with certain
functions by the legate in 1220,
though the name *decanus* does not
appear.

[2] Another parallel with Oxford is
the use of the Oxford term 'cetus
magistrorum' which I have rarely
noticed except at Montpellier and
Oxford. *Cartulaire*, i. 229; Fournier, ii, No. 914.

[3] Germain, *École de Méd.*, p. 26;
Cartulaire, i. 68. The student
proctorship was suppressed in 1550,
but the *consiliarii* still retained the
right of petition and remonstrance
against the irregularities of the
doctors. The *consiliarii*, who at
this time were actually appointed
by the doctors from among the
students, were abolished in consequence of a revolutionary movement among the students in 1753.
From other evidence, however, it
would appear that they were selected by lot from among the
bachelors.

[4] *Cartulaire*, i. 367; Fournier, ii,
No. 947 *quater*. At the same time
all previous statutes are quashed,
even though 'de voluntate Magistrorum et Scholarium, *coniunctim vel
separatim*', which points to previous collisions between the rival
powers.

[5] The earliest record of such a
meeting is in 1332 'de quadam cam-
pana facienda, emenda et ponenda'.
Cartulaire, i. 287; Fournier, ii, No.
940. It was perhaps for purposes
of extraordinary taxation such as
this that the consent of the students
was considered necessary.

such and such a book.[1] The student-proctor was moreover
at any time at liberty to remonstrate with a doctor negligent
in the performance of his duty, or otherwise infringing upon
the rights of the students.[2] But, if their demands were neglected, the university of students had no power to fine or
suspend a doctor after the summary fashion in vogue at
Bologna: they could only carry their complaint to the college
of doctors or to the superior ecclesiastical authorities. This
Montpellier system of consultation and co-operation between
teachers and students in the arrangement of lectures constitutes one of the few pieces of medieval student-autonomy
which might possibly be imitated with advantage by the
modern university reformer.

Require-
ments for
degrees.

The period of study required for the bachelorship in
medicine was fixed in 1340 at twenty-four months of actual
attendance at lectures.[3] Ordinary lectures ceased at Easter;
it was customary for bachelors and the senior students to
spend the whole of the summer in practice, often at a distance
from Montpellier.[4] Indeed, before taking the degree of
bachelor in medicine a student had to go a round of visits to
the sick accompanied by his own doctor, under whose supervision he apparently experimented upon the patients.[5] The
doctor's degree was obtainable in five years by masters of
arts, in six years by other candidates.[6] [By the statutes
of 1239 no scholar could practise independently, on pain of

[1] Germain, *École de Méd.*, p.
80 *sq.*

[2] An illustration may be taken
from the extant *Liber procuratoris
studiosorum*: 'Anno   Domini
XV^cXXVIII^o, et die IX^a novem-
bris, conquerentibus studentibus
medicine doctores ob malitiam non
legere, ego viceprocurator cum
consiliariis ad eos accessi simul cum
notario et testibus, quos rogavi ut
legerent, ut tenentur, alioquin,
prout penes me habetur, apud
superiorem querimoniam facerem;
qui responderunt ut continetur in
archivis notarii.' Germain, *École
de Méd.*, p. 31. So in 1579 the 'Consiliarii, studiosorum nomine, con-

questi sunt apud R. D. doctores,
quod R. D. Saporta illos omnes
vocasset asinos'. *Ibid.*, p. 38.

[3] *Cartulaire*, i. 351; Fournier, ii,
No. 947 *quater*.

[4] *Cartulaire*, i. 70, 617: Fournier, ii, No. 1025.

[5] See the statute limiting the
number of students who might ac-
company the candidate to six. *Cartulaire*, i. 716; Fournier, ii, No.
1057.

[6] According to the earlier statute
of 1309. *Cartulaire*, i. 220; Fournier, ii, No. 910. A college statute
allows nine years for the whole
course. *Cartulaire*, i. 618; Fournier, ii, No. 1025.

excommunication, unless he had been examined and received
letters of authorization from the bishop and his examiners.[1]

In 1309 Pope Clement V, by the advice of his Montpellier
physicians, Arnald of Villanova and others, prescribed the
following as the books which candidates for the licence must
possess—Galen, *De complexionibus*, *De malicia complexionis
diverse*, *De simplici medicina*, *De morbo et accidente*, *De crisi
et criticis diebus*, *De ingenio sanitatis*, together with either the
books of Avicenna or those of Razes, Constantinus Africanus,
and Isaac, with commentaries thereon. He must further have
'read' as a bachelor three books, one with and one without
comments, selected from the following list—the *Tegni* of
Galen, the *Prognostics* and *Aphorisms* of Hippocrates, the *De
regimine acutorum* of Johannicius, the *liber febrium* of Isaac,
the *Antidotarium*, the *De morbo et accidente* of Galen, and the
De ingenio sanitatis of the same writer.[2]

It may be well to add the list of books appointed as subjects
for lectures in 1340, arranged in courses, each of which was
to be taken by one doctor:

(1) *Primus Canonis* (Avicenna).

(2) *Liber de morbo et accidente* (Galen) and [*de*] *differentiis
febrium* (Galen).

(3) *Liber de crisi et criticis diebus* and *de malicia complexionis
diverse* (Galen).

(4) *Liber de simplicibus medicinis* and *de complexionibus*
(Galen).

(5) *Liber de iuvamentis membrorum* and *de interioribus* (Galen.)

(6) *Liber Amphorismi* (Hippocrates) with *de regimine acutorum* (Hippocrates) or *de prognosticis*.

(7) *Liber de ingenio* (*sanitatis*) and *ad Glauconem* (Galen).

(8) *Quartus Canonis* (Avicenna), 'quoad duas primas seu
cum Iohannicio de pulsibus et urinis Theophili'.

(9) *Tegni* (Galen) with *de prognosticis* and *de regimine
acutorum*.

(10) *Liber de regimine sanitatis* and *de virtutibus naturalibus*
(Bartholomew the Englishman).

[1] [The prohibition was enforced
by King James I of Aragon, over-
lord of Montpellier in 1272; *Car-* *tulaire*, i. 202.]

[2] *Cartulaire*, i. 220; Fournier, ii,
No. 910.

Upon these books there were always to be lectures; if the number of doctors sufficed, there might be lectures on other parts of the canon, other books of Galen, or the *de febribus* and *de dietis universalibus* of the Jew Isaac.[1]

II. *The University of Law.*

The law-school of Placentinus.

The law-school of Montpellier traces its origin to Placentinus, one of the most distinguished of the jurists of the second generation from Irnerius.[2] After teaching at Bologna and at Mantua, he was driven about the year 1166 to seek an asylum at Montpellier by the jealousy of less distinguished colleagues. The memory of Placentinus was ever kept alive at Montpellier. The university of law in after days chose S. Eulalia, the saint commemorated on the day of his death, for its patroness: the mace of the bedel was tipped with her image, and down to the days of the Revolution the Hall of the faculty bore the inscription *Aula Placentinea*.[3] But it is impossible to trace a complete continuity between the school founded by Placentinus and the later university. Bassianus[4] is the only

---

[1] *Cartulaire*, i. 347, 348. Fournier's transcript (No. 947) is defective.

[2] Placentinus was born about 1135. His first work, *De actionum varietatibus* (ed. Pescatori, 1897, and L. Wahrmund in *Quellen zur Geschichte des römisch-kanonischen Processes*, iv, part 3), was written at Mantua. He tells us how at Montpellier it occurred to him 'tyronibus legum introductiones ad libros iuris maiores componere, Institutionum summas conficere'. See the passage quoted by M. Castelnau in *Mém. de la Soc. archéol. de Montpellier*, i. 481 (Savigny has mistakenly altered the text and sense). Roffredus of Benevento tells us that 'dominus Henricus (de Baila) qui erat in contraria opinione de nocte assalivit dominum P. et sic timore illius recessit de Bononia et ivit apud Montempessulanum'. [This, according to P. de Tourtoulon, *Pla-*

centin, i, *La Vie, les œuvres* (Paris, 1896), p. 121, was between 1166 and 1170, when Placentinus was between thirty and thirty-five years of age. He returned to Italy in 1183, and came back to Montpellier in 1189. He died on 12 Feb. 1192 (*ibid.*, p. 67)]. M. Fournier declines to believe 'que Placentin vint à Montpellier sans être assuré de trouver un élève' (*Hist.* iii. 350). Would it not be possible at this rate to prove that no school ever had a beginning? The already existing school of medicine would be much more likely to suggest Montpellier than its fame as a 'centre . . . d'études juridiques qui se rattachaient à l'étude du Talmud'.

[3] Germain, i, p. lxxiii.

[4] Not, as Germain (iii. 9), Azo. The true reading of the gloss on which Germain depended is 'Baz', not 'Az'. See Denifle's note (i. 344). [Johannes Bassianus taught

important jurist who is supposed to have taught here between the time of Placentinus and the third decade of the thirteenth century. It was, it would seem, about the year 1230 that doctors and students of law began to multiply at Montpellier —partly, perhaps, on account of the difficulties with the city at Bologna.[1] The bishop immediately claimed the same control over the conferment of licences in canon and civil law which he had always enjoyed in medicine: he procured a royal brief enforcing his claims, and authorizing him to demand of graduates an oath of obedience to his see.[2] In 1268, however, King James of Aragon put in a claim to bestow a licence without the consent of the bishop, and actually granted such a licence to one Guillaume Séguier. The bishop excommunicated Séguier; and there was an appeal to Rome. It is certain that at this time there was a fully organized college of doctors in law and a body of statutes made by the bishop and doctors. Clement IV ingeniously put a stop to the quarrel without sanctioning the royal pretensions by making the intruder a doctor at Rome.[3] In 1285 a legatine decree established the

CHAP. VIII, § 1.

Rise of university, c. 1230.

'in Provincia', but there is no certainty that he was at Montpellier, which is not in Provence. As Tourtoulon shows (pp. 95–100), Placentinus was the only civilian known to have brought the traditions of Bologna to Montpellier in the twelfth century. Johannes, as he is usually called, was a younger contemporary, who, with Azo and other disciples, put an end to the authority of Martinus, to whose school Placentinus belonged. See especially E. M. Meijers, 'Sommes, lectures et commentaires (1100–1250)', in *Atti del Congresso Internazionale di diritto romano* (Rome, 1934), i. 460 *sqq.*]

[1] In 1268 Clement IV says to the king of Aragon: 'Constat enim Magalonensem episcopum a longissimis retro temporibus dedisse licentiam in aliis Facultatibus . . . et si non consuevit in ista (*sc.* Iuris Civilis) quia nec etiam petebatur,

nec petendi erat occasio, ubi nec studentium vel discentium numerus exigebat.' *Cartulaire*, i. 201; Fournier, ii, No. 894. But licences were certainly granted in 1230, though it is clear that graduations had been very exceptional.

[2] *Cartulaire*, i. 184; Fournier, ii, No. 883.

[3] *Cartulaire*, i. 199–202; Fournier, ii, Nos. 894, 895. [On the significance of this Bull as a statement for the ecclesiastical control of universities, see Manacorda, *Storia della scuola italiana*, i. 196 *sqq.*] Séguier had been unable to graduate at Bologna 'propter dissensionem inter . . . archidiaconum Bononie . . . et scolares inibi studentes'. He afterwards committed a murder, but the consuls acquitted him 'quod est sexagenarius et fame probate'. Fournier, ii, No. 1215.

CHAP.VIII, rights of the bishop,[1] and in 1289 Nicholas IV formally or-
§ 1.   dained the creation of a *studium generale* at Montpellier and
conferred upon its doctors the *ius ubique docendi*.[2] Although
this Bull is expressed in the ordinary terms of a Bull of foundation, there can be no doubt that the *studium* had long been
treated as 'general' both by custom and by express Apostolic
recognition.[3] It is true, however, that Montpellier had only
recently become important as a school of law: and the recognition of its degrees may have been less decisive and universal
in this faculty than it was in medicine;[4] though it must be
remembered after all that it was a dispute between the legal
university and the bishop which led to the issue of the Bull.

Constitu-   We have no precise information as to the organization of
tion of the jurist the law-university before the year 1339. It is pretty evident
university. that the bishop at first attempted to govern the *studium* on
much the same lines as those upon which the university of
medicine had always been ruled. In 1292, for instance, he
refused to seal some projected statutes presented to him by
the doctors on the ground that he was shortly coming to
Montpellier and would then confer with them about the
matter.[5] But the students, many of whom from time to time
would, no doubt, have studied at Bologna, in time began to
raise the cry of student-right against both bishop and masters.
In 1320 there is a proclamation of the bishop against 'secret
conventicles and congregations', 'confederations and colliga-
tions' of the students, and against hostile risings of the

[1] *Cartulaire*, i. 208; Fournier, ii,
No. 900. It is provided that those
licensed 'officium magisterii libere
valeant ubilibet infra legationis
nostre terminos exercere'.

[2] *Cartulaire*, i. 210; Fournier, ii,
No. 903.

[3] Denifle (i. 352-3) says that
possibly it had not the *ius ubique
docendi* in law till 1289, and that
there were no promotions in law
till that date, though he admits that
it was considered 'general' in both
faculties before 1289.

[4] This is more than we can lay
down with absolute certainty. In

1256 the Pope had spoken of the
'studium, quod ibi *sollempniter*
regitur' (*Cartulaire*, i. 194; Fournier, ii, No. 889), and the Bull of
1289 expressly erects a *studium
generale* in medicine and arts as
well as in law; hence its terms can
no more be used to show that it was
not a *studium generale* in law than
in medicine. If the argument is
good for anything, it will prove that
there was no *studium generale* before this, even in medicine.

[5] *Cartulaire*, i. 216; Fournier, ii,
No. 905.

'scholars of one province against the scholars of another'.[1]
It seems as if the scholars were in the act of forming themselves into nations or student-universities independently of the bishop or the doctors. It is to be observed that only a year before the Pope had quashed a statute recently made by the rector and university,[2] and this is the first allusion to the rectorate. At last, by the year 1339, the triangular quarrel between the bishop, the college of doctors,[3] and the rector and university of students had led, as such quarrels were wont to lead, to cessations, excommunications, and appeals to Rome. The mutual rights of the parties were now adjusted by statutes framed on the model of those of Bologna, by the cardinal legate Bertrand di Diaux. The constitution which results from these statutes (the earliest which we possess for the jurist university)[4] is a student-university of a very modified type—modified by the inclusion of the doctors in the guild and by a tolerably jealous assertion of the episcopal supremacy over the *studium*. In its main outlines these statutes no doubt represent the *de facto* constitution of the *studium* before their enactment.

The rector is to be elected from among the doctors by the outgoing rector and councillors: he is to be confirmed by the

---

[1] *Cartulaire*, i. 247; Fournier, ii, No. 923.

[2] *Cartulaire*, i. 239; Fournier, ii, No. 922. The statute required candidates for the licence to pay a certain sum to each doctor unless he performed his 'solemne principium' within a certain time. It was no doubt objected to by the bishop; but it was clearly in the interest of the doctors.

[3] For another subject of contention, see *Cartulaire*, i. 236; Fournier, ii, No. 918.

[4] *Cartulaire*, i. 296 *sq.*; Fournier, ii, No. 947. Fournier (*Hist.* ii. 417) discusses elaborately, but not very satisfactorily, the relation between the *collegium doctorum utriusque iuris* (headed by their prior) and the *facultates* of canon and civil law.

It is clear that there was a close and limited college of regent doctors (to whom were no doubt reserved the rights of a 'faculty of promotion'): but they did not enjoy the same monopoly of ordinary lectures as at Angers and Orleans. The exact extent of their privileges must be left doubtful. I see no reason for calling into existence (with Fournier, *Hist.* iii. 418) a prior of each faculty (canon and civil law) in addition to the prior of the joint college. In 1341 the bishop attempted to give the *insignia* to a doctor as well as to license him (*Cartulaire*, i. 399–400; Fournier, ii, No. 958). The sequel is not known: but the later practice certainly was for this to be done by a doctor.

bishop, who is required to grant the confirmation as a matter of course; but the rector is to swear obedience to the bishop, and his power of decreeing a cessation without the consent of the bishop is limited to a period of eight days. The doctors are only enjoined to swear before the rector to give their lectures according to the statutes, but do not take a general oath of obedience to the rector and university as at Bologna. There are to be twelve *consiliarii*, one elected from the chapter of Maguelone, one from the town—that is, presumably the students who were natives of the town—the rest 'according to nations and provinces of nations, as hitherto observed'. These nations were (as has been mentioned) Provence, Burgundy, and Catalonia: the rector being elected from each nation in turn.[1] The councillors were in practice usually licentiates or bachelors. In this university, as in many others of the same type, it is curiously difficult to determine with what authority the power of statute-making ultimately rested. It is clear enough that the ordinary governing body of the university was the rector and his councillors, and the statutes were promulgated by the rector with the consent of the council. But sometimes the 'advice' of the doctors is also mentioned, and sometimes also that of many nobles and other 'notable persons'. Occasionally these persons formally claim to be the 'major and saner' part of the whole university; but it is clear that, if the whole body of students was ever summoned and allowed to exercise any real voice in legislation, this was an exceptional rather than an ordinary method of procedure. It must be remembered that even in the University of Bologna itself statute-making was an affair of very rare occurrence, and even the statutes were made only by the nominees of the students, not by the students themselves. Finally, it must be observed that at Montpellier, even after the students had obtained the constitution of 1339, important statutes still seem to require the consent of the bishop.[2]

[1] *Cartulaire*, i. 319; Fournier, ii, No. 947.

[2] Fournier, ii, Nos. 1081, 1111 *sq.* The appointment of a master of the ceremonies (*preceptor ceremonia-rum*) in 1491, to marshal processions, &c., is a feature which I have not noticed elsewhere. *Ibid.*, No. 1195.

The statutes contain nothing about the jurisdiction in cases of scholars, which remained with the bishop.[1] Throughout the history of Montpellier the relations between citizens and students were somewhat exceptionally strained; but we must forbear to enter into the details of such quarrels. The great subject of contention was the right claimed by the students to import wine into the town in spite of the protective system which excluded all wine except that grown on the land of citizens.[2]

III. *The University of Theology.*

The regular orders made a practice of establishing their *studium generale* or chief school of theology for the province in the towns where there was a secular university, even where there was no secular faculty of theology. A college was founded for the Carthusian monks of Valmagne by James I in 1263.[3] And round this nucleus it would seem that something like a *studium* of theology grew up,[4] though it is certain that there was no graduation in theology or *ius ubique docendi*[5] till the Bull of Martin V in 1421, which created a *studium generale* in theology with the bishop as chancellor. Its students remained members of the legal university; its

[1] *Cartulaire*, i. 403. Afterwards in 1351 the royal *iudex parvi sigilli* was made guardian or conservator of privileges, with a certain jurisdiction including the taxation of houses which had for many years been taken away from the ordinary taxors (*ibid.*, pp. 424, 430, 482; Fournier, ii, Nos. 976, 980). A special body of 'guardians' for the medical university was appointed in 1395 (*Cartulaire*, i. 670). There is no mention of conservators apostolic till the time of Martin V (1421). Fournier, ii, No. 1089.

[2] *Cartulaire*, i. 332; Fournier, ii, No. 947, &c.

[3] *Cartulaire*, i. 197 *sq.*; Fournier, ii, Nos. 892, 893.

[4] King John of France in 1351 granted to the bedels of the 'societas' of theological masters the right of carrying silver staves like the bedels of the other faculties. *Cartulaire*, i. 428.

[5] The Bull of 1289 does not mention theology; yet a Bull of 1364 for the College of S. Ruf speaks of Montpellier as a 'studium generale' in theology as well as canon law, and the students were certainly to graduate in theology (*Cartulaire*, i. 464 *sq.*; Fournier, ii, No. 992). But the Bull may mean a 'studium generale' of the order, and monastic students educated elsewhere often graduated at Paris. Or the college may have been founded in anticipation of a *studium generale* in theology, for which the city petitioned, *circa* 1365, *Cartulaire*, i. 474; Fournier, ii, No. 994. Cf. Denifle, i. 348; Germain, iii. 63.

CHAP.VIII, masters formed a college with a dean of their own.[1] It is
§ 1. just worth noticing that regulars were not at Montpellier, as
in most universities, excluded from the rectorate. In the
declining days of the school the monastic colleges formed too
large an element in the university to be ignored. There were
not too many students at Montpellier as well off as a Benedictine prior.[2]

IV. *The University of Arts.*

Arts held the subordinate position which they had everywhere in the law *studia*, but there was a regular university
of 'doctors and students in Arts' at least as early as 1242,
the date of an extant code of statutes.[3] These statutes, like
all very early statutes, are extremely short and simple; but
they are sufficient to exhibit one or two very striking constitutional peculiarities. The statutes are not made by the
masters, but imposed upon them by the authority of the
bishop. There is no trace of a student-university, except
that after the dean, who is the head of the faculty, there is
mentioned a 'rector of the said university'. This rector is a
master, and it is improbable that he was elected by the students. After the French annexation, the school of arts was
placed under the more direct control of the consuls, and the
single regent of logic and grammar received a municipal
salary. The faculty, though it continued to give degrees,
became really—as in many other French provincial universities—little more than a grammar-school.[4]

Colleges.   The colleges at Montpellier were: (1) the College of Valmagne, already mentioned (1263); (2) the College of Brescia
or Pézenas, founded in 1360 by Bernard Trigard, bishop of

[1] Fournier, ii, Nos. 1092, 1112.
At the same time the Pope conferred the 'ius non trahi extra'
(*ibid.*, No. 1095) and many other
privileges.

[2] *Ibid.* ii, No. 1081.

[3] *Cartulaire*, i. 190. [An interesting passage in the *Summa* of
Placentinus, 'si dicamus: hic est
magister Petrus, litteratorie scien-
tie preceptorem designamus. Si

dicimus: hic est Petrus magister,
aliquando cerdonem, aliquando
locorum turpium purgatorem si-
gnificamus', possibly suggests the
presence of masters of arts at
Montpellier in the late twelfth
century. See Tourtoulon, *op. cit.*
i. 93, and note.]

[4] Faucillon in *Revue Archéol. de
Montpellier*, iv. 248; Fournier, ii,
No. 1197.

Brescia;[1] (3) the College of S. Ruf, founded in 1364 by Cardinal Angelico Grimouard, brother of Urban V, for eighteen canons regular of the Monastery of S. Ruf at Valence;[2] (4) a Benedictine House, partly monastery, partly college, and known as the College of S. Benedict, founded in 1368 by the Benedictine Pope Urban V (who had been a Montpellier student), and dependent upon the abbey of S. Victor at Marseilles;[3] (5) the College of Mende or des Douze-Médecins, also founded by Urban V in 1369 out of Church property, for the benefit of his native diocese of Mende—perhaps the first purely medical college in Europe;[4] (6) the college founded by Michael Boel, physician, for medicine, in 1421;[5] (7) the College of Gironne or Aragon or du Vergier, partly legal and partly medical, founded in 1460-8 by Jehan Brugère, master of medicine, and Jehann du Vergier, president of the Parlement of Languedoc.[6] Besides there were, of course, as in most university towns, the convent-colleges of the four great mendicant orders.

We have seen that in the twelfth century Montpellier was already one of the great *studia* of Europe—all but on a level with Paris, Bologna, and Salerno. This position it retained till about the middle of the fourteenth century. The growing influence of the Arabic medicine, with its astrological and alchemistic absurdities, may represent a real retrogression in medical science:[7] but it in no way diminished the fame of

Medical fame.

---

[1] Fournier, ii, No. 1067.

[2] *Cartulaire*, i. 464, 495; Fournier, ii, Nos. 992, 1006, 1218.

[3] *Cartulaire*, i. 492; Fournier, ii, No. 1004.

[4] *Cartulaire*, i. 551; Fournier, ii, No. 1010. The statutes (*Cartulaire*, i. 609 *sq.*; Fournier, ii, No. 1025) are the only college statutes I have noticed which prescribe minimum hours of study, i.e. lectures for three 'horas magistrales', one or more 'horas licentiatorum seu bacallariorum', and three hours' private study before supper. The rector was the senior student and held office for three years.

[5] Fournier, ii, No. 1088. The document is simply a bequest. Nothing seems to be known as to its actual execution.

[6] *Ibid.* ii, Nos. 1167, 1169, 1170. The College of Gironne has sometimes been mistakenly made a distinct college from the College du Vergier. The statutes are remarkable as giving the patron absolute authority over the college and its administration.

[7] Prunelle, p. 20 *sq.* Ramon Lull was a pupil of Arnald of Villanova, whose medicine was highly alchemistic (*ibid.*, p. 38). Sometimes the Montpellier physi-

Montpellier. Rather its fame was enhanced by the decline of the 'Civitas Hippocratica'. No medieval physicians stood higher than Arnald of Villanova, Bernard de Gordon,[1] and the other Montpellier doctors of this period; and, on the other hand, it was just at the moment when the Arabic influence became predominant that a new era in the history of surgery was introduced by the Montpellier physician Gui de Chauliac:[2] here the men of the later Middle Ages unquestionably advanced beyond the Arabs and the Jews, with whom the superstitious horror of mutilating a corpse forbade much progress in anatomy or surgery.[3] The statutes of 1340 provide for at least one 'anatomy' in two years.[4] The results even of the scanty opportunities for anatomical study thus afforded were by no means contemptible. It is said that operations were successfully performed in medieval Montpellier which were unknown to surgical practice at the beginning of the last century, and cures effected of diseases then regarded as incurable.[5] It should be added, as an illustration of the

cian descended lower than alchemy. Gerson has occasion to denounce a Montpellier physician who recommended a talisman for kidney disease. Astruc, pp. 91, 212. [Later writers have taken a more favourable view of 'neo-Arabic' medicine; cf. C. Singer, *From Magic to Science* (London, 1918), pp. 94-6, and S. d'Irsay, i. 163.]

[1] Known as the author of the *Lilium Medicinae*, printed at Frankfurt in 1617, Venice 1496, and elsewhere.

[2] Author of a treatise on anatomy styled *Inventorium seu Collectorium in parte Chirurgicali scientiae Medicinae*, published in 1367. Aigrefeuille (1737), ii. 346. Cf. Prunelle, p. 43 *sq*. This same physician, so really eminent in surgery, accounted for the plague of 1348 by a conjunction of Saturn, Jupiter, and Mars (Germain, iii. 119). The fact that surgery was practised by physicians shows the superior position of the art as compared with the

position it held at Paris. The surgeons were not, however, usually physicians. By an edict of Charles VI in 1399 the practice of surgery is forbidden without the licence of the consuls granted after examination by the *magistri iurati*. *Cartulaire*, i. 682; Fournier, ii, No. 1055.

[3] [Cf. above, vol. i, pp. 243-6.]

[4] *Cartulaire*, i. 344; Fournier, ii, No. 947 *quater*. In 1376 increased to one a year. (*Cartulaire*, i. 569; Fournier, ii, No. 1020.)

[5] Prunelle's treatise contains a number of details of great interest. He (p. 43) says of Gui de Chauliac that he 'pratiquoit la plupart des opérations qui sont encore en usage. Celles de la cataracte, de la taille lui étoient familières. Ce fut lui qui releva la méthode de Celse', &c. Among the diseases, since regarded as incurable, which Gui treated successfully are cancerous tumours, which he is said to have cured by means of arsenic. *Ibid*., p. 44.

influence of the works of the ancient physicians upon medical CHAP. VIII, § I.
progress, that most of the operations or remedies adopted by
Gui de Chauliac appear to have been known to the ancients
and adopted by him from their writings.

After the middle of the fourteenth century a rapid decline Decline of Montpellier.
is discernible in the position of Montpellier. In 1362 the
university of law complains bitterly to its *alumnus* on the papal
throne, Urban V, that whereas it once possessed 1,000 students there were now scarcely 100.[1] The colleges founded by
Urban V and other acts of patronage seem to have produced
a slight revival. The roll of petitioners for benefices dispatched to Clement VII in 1378 still shows the names of some
380 graduates and students in law, but the medical roll contains only fifty-six names.[2] Of course, the roll only contains
the names of ecclesiastics, who in the case of the medical
students would hardly be a large majority. About 1390, however, we find the university complaining bitterly of its
diminishing numbers.[3] Many causes may be assigned. The
French annexation, the consequent estrangement from Spain,
the growth of rival universities at Perpignan and elsewhere,
may have had some effect.[4] But it is more important to

---

[1] *Cartulaire*, i. 450 *sq.*
[2] *Ibid.* i. 578 *sq.*
[3] About 1390 (*Cartulaire*, i. 649; Fournier, ii, No. 1060) the medical students petition the consuls and royal councillors against the masters, who have nearly ruined the university by their 'exhigua diligentia et effrenata cupiditas obcecantis avaricie', and the promotion of 'appothacharios et barbitunsores ignaros'. How low the university had sunk in the fifteenth century may be gathered from the ruinous condition of the Collège des Douze-Médecins in 1422, when we find a student describing himself as 'unicus collegiatus honorabilis collegii dominorum (*leg.* duodecim) medicorum'. Fournier, ii, No. 1100; Guiraud, *Le Collège des Douze Médecins*, p. 24. The rebuilding of the college in 1494

(Guiraud, p. 27) is a sign of life in the university.

[4] I see no reason whatever for ascribing the decline of the university with Fournier (*Hist.* iii 389) to 'le pouvoir trop absolu de l'autorité ecclésiastique'. For (1) this power was not greater, but on the whole less, in the second half of our period than in the first, and (2) this power was not greater at Montpellier than in some universities, e.g. Angers and Orleans, which continued flourishing. Equally little ground is there for attributing it (with Germain) to the hostility of the consuls. It must be remembered that the fifteenth century was a period of decadence in the universities generally, though not equally so everywhere. I do not see any evidence that the Pope nominated professors here (*Hist.* iii. 486).

CHAP. VIII,
§ 1.

notice that the system of *salaria* was never introduced at Montpellier till the close of our period, which must have made it difficult for the university to compete with better-endowed institutions. Nor did the restriction of the ordinary lectures to a small number of specially-appointed professors answer the purposes of an endowment as in some other French universities. As a school of law the fame of the university disappears after the fourteenth century. But the importance of its medical school was by no means at an end. The Renaissance introduced a period of revived activity; and this revival was powerfully stimulated, under the influence of their Montpellier physicians, by Charles VIII and Louis XII. The latter in 1498 made an annual grant of 500 *livres* to the *studium*, 400 of which were to be devoted to providing salaries of 100 *livres* per annum for four doctors.[1] Sooner or later the old system of an unlimited number of unendowed regents everywhere broke down. When it was not supplanted by endowment, university teaching was superseded (as at Paris and Oxford) by the college system.

Continuance of medical fame of Montpellier.

The influence of the Renaissance was as much felt in the schools of medicine as in those of theology and arts. In 1537 a new era is marked by the announcement of a course of lectures upon Hippocrates in the original Greek by the illustrious Rabelais,[2] and from this time the Greek influence again becomes predominant at Montpellier, though lectures on the Arabic physicians occasionally make their appearance upon the lecture-lists up to 1607.[3] In the seventeenth century

---

[1] Fournier, *Hist.* iii. 400; *Statuts*, ii, No. 1209. Among other favours granted by Charles VIII was a prohibition to the Master Chirurgeons in Montpellier in 1486 to make new 'Masters in Chirurgery' unless they had been examined and approved by the chancellor or dean and one doctor named by the faculty (Fournier, ii, No. 1186).

[2] 'D. Franciscus Rabelaesus pro suo ordinario elegit librum prognosticorum Hippocratis quem Graece interpretatus est.' *Liber*

Lectionum, ap. Germain, *La Méd. Arabe*, p. 15.

[3] Germain, *École de Méd.*, pp. 93, 94. The Arabic authors were, however, struck out of the 'books required for the Schools' on the petition of the students in 1567. (*Ibid.*, p. 75.) How faithful the school remained to the Greek tradition may be inferred from the fact that in 1673 a doctor was required on pain of suspension to cease teaching a doctrine contrary to that of Hippocrates, Aristotle, and

Montpellier still continued to be a formidable rival to Paris,[1] and to attract students from distant countries. Our own Sir Thomas Browne studied at Montpellier as well as at Padua and at Leyden. The constitution of the university, with all its ecclesiasticism and medievalism, survived with few changes till the Revolution: and even at the present day a tradition of the extinct university seems to place the 'Faculty of Montpellier' at the head of the French provincial schools of medicine.

§ 2. ORLEANS[2]

Le Maire, *Histoire et Antiquitez de la Ville et Duché d'Orléans* (Orléans, 1645), p. 332 *sq.*, traces the university back to the Druids, but prints a few documents. S. Goyon, *Histoire de l'église et diocèse, ville, et université d'Orléans* (Orleans, Paris, 1647 *sqq.*), contains scattered notices. [A. Gollnitz, *Ulysses belgico-gallicus*, Lyons, 1631, pp. 225–352]. The principal modern work is J.-E. Bimbenet, *Histoire de l'Université de lois d'Orléans*, Orleans, 1853; also 'Les Écoliers de la nation de Picardie et de Champagne à l'Univ. d'Orléans', in *Mém. de la soc. arch. de l'Orléanais*, xx (1885); and 'Chronique historique extraite des Registres des Écoliers allemands', in *Mémoires de la soc. d'agriculture, sciences, &c.*, *d'Orléans*, 1874. Loiseleur has an article on 'Les Privilèges de l'Université de lois d'Orléans', in *Mémoires de la société archéologique de l'Orléanais*, xxii (1889). A most interesting account of the earlier schools of rhetoric and grammar is given by Léopold Delisle in the *Annuaire-Bulletin de la Soc. de l'Hist. de France*, vii (1869), 139–54.

See also Mlle A. de Foulques de Villaret in *Mémoires de la soc. archéologique de l'Orléanais*, xiv (1875). A few documents were published by Thurot in *Bibliothèque de l'École des Chartes*, xxxii (1871), 379 *sq.* But all collections of documents are now superseded by Fournier's collection. Fournier has also a monograph on 'La Nation allemande à l'Université d'Orléans', in *Nouv. Rev. Hist. de droit*, 1888. [E. Jarry, 'Les écoles de l'université d'Orléans, leur topographie', in *Mémoires de la société archéologique de l'Orléanais*, xxxv (1919), 45 *sqq.*, and separately, (cf. L. Auvray in *Bibliothèque de l'école des chartes*, lxxxii, 1921, 375–7); E. M. Meijers, 'De Universiteit van Orleans in de XIIIe eeuw', in *Tijdschrift voor rechtsgeschiedenis*, Leiden (1921), 168 *sqq.*, 443 *sqq.*; (1922), 460 *sqq.* This is a very important study on the history of the study of civil law in Europe, notably on the relations between the Italian and northern schools.

Galen. The medical teaching continued to consist chiefly in lectures upon the Greek texts till the eighteenth century, when they take a subordinate place. (*Ibid.*, p. 100.)

[1] Especially during the short period at the beginning of the seventeenth century, when Montpellier was Protestant. At this time the law-school revived under Pacius and other eminent teachers. Casaubon was here from 1596 to 1599.

[2] [Mrs. Dorothy Mackay Quynn has kindly helped us in the revision of this section.]

CHAP. VIII,
§ 2.

The university records, used imperfectly by Bimbenet and Fournier, have now been classified. They form series D of the archives of Loiret at Orleans, and are described in the *Inventoire sommaire des archives departmentales: Loiret*, Orleans, 1917. The most important material is the records of the German nation. The records of the Scottish nation are in the Vatican (Regina 405) and of the French nation at Wolfenbüttel (Cod. 78).

Several articles not noticed by Rashdall, and others which have appeared since 1895, will be found in the *Mémoires de la société archéologique de l'Orléanais.*]

For the school of rhetoric and the battle with Paris over the ancient classics see L. J. PAETOW, *The Arts Course at Mediaeval Universities* (University of Illinois studies, Urbana, 1910), and the same, ' "La Bataille des VII ars" of Henri d'Andeli' (*Memoirs of the University of California*, iv. 1914; reprinted in *Two Mediaeval Satires on the University of Paris*, Berkeley, California, 1927); C. H. HASKINS, *Studies in Mediaeval Culture*, Oxford, 1929 (ch. i, and pp. 190–2), and the literature there noted; cf. E. FARAL, *Les arts poétiques du XIIe et du XIIIe siècle*, Paris, 1923, and E. K. RAND, 'The Classics in the Thirteenth Century' in *Speculum*, iv (1929), 249–69.]

The ancient law-school of Orleans.

WE have already seen that in the earlier Middle Ages some instruction in law everywhere entered into the ordinary curriculum of the schools as a branch of the 'liberal arts'. In the ninth century this was the case as much in France as in Italy. But both in Italy and in France there were one or two schools at which the teaching of law gradually attained an exceptional prominence, and the teachers of law eventually became a distinct body under the title of masters of law. The position which was held in Italy by the school of Pavia, and afterwards by that of Bologna, was occupied in France by the schools of Lyons and Orleans. With Lyons, since in the Middle Ages it never rose to full university rank, we are not concerned. Of the legal fame of Orleans we have an interesting illustration in the account of a suit between the great monasteries of Fleury and S. Denis which took place about the year 830.[1] The case was heard by the bishop of Orleans and the count Donatus of Melun as royal judges: but, since the dispute related to church property, the proceedings had to be governed by Roman law, with which the royal judges were unfamiliar. They therefore adjourned the case to Orleans,

---

[1] A still earlier instance is cited by Fitting from Mabillon, *Acta sanctorum ordinis S. Bened.* (Venice, 1733), saec. i, p. 144, where S. Lifardus, a native of Orleans, is described as 'in causarum temporalium legibus discretor praecipuus'.

where they could have the assistance of 'masters' or 'doctors CHAP. VIII, § 2. of the laws'.[1]

Respecting this ancient law-school, we have little more The Brachy-logus. direct evidence till the thirteenth century; though, according to Fitting, its existence and importance at the end of the eleventh and the beginning of the twelfth centuries are attested by the production of the compilation known as the *Brachylogus*, which he believes to have been composed in that place. The same writer also gives reasons for believing that in the earliest period the law-teaching of Orleans was based on the West-Gothic *Breviarium*, and that it was not till a later period that the older law texts were introduced into the school.[2]

In the twelfth century, however, we hear most of the fame The classical school of the twelfth century. of Orleans as a school of grammar, rhetoric, and classical literature, subjects we must remember at that time more closely connected with legal studies than was the case in the later universities.[3] At the school of Orleans were educated the classical commentators,[4] the professional letter-writers,[5] and the versifiers of the twelfth century. Orleans seems to have escaped almost wholly the dialectical frenzy of the age: here, and here almost alone after the decline of Chartres, there lingered down to at least the middle of the thirteenth century the classical traditions of the age of Bernard and John of

[1] 'Visum est missis dominicis placitum Aurelianis mutare. Venientes itaque ad condictum locum legum magistri et iudices utraque ex parte acerrime decertabant. Enimvero namque aderant legum doctores tam ex Aurelianensi quam ex Vastinensi provincia.' *Mon. Germ.: Scriptores*, xv. 490.

[2] *Die Rechtsschule zu Bologna*, pp. 46–8, 67, but cf. above, vol. i, p. 104.

[3] This seems to me to be forgotten by Denifle when he denies all connexion between the law-university of the thirteenth century and the ancient classical schools. I am glad to find my view supported by Fournier, *Hist.* iii. 5 *sq.* It may just be worth mentioning as suggesting the continuity of the law-school that a 'magister scholarum Aurelianensium' is one of the papal delegates for the decision of a dispute between the Bishop of Paris and the Abbot of Ste Geneviève in 1201. *Patrol. Lat.* ccxiv. 1188.

[4] Several commentaries on Lucan's *Pharsalia* and on the amatory works of Ovid emanated from the school of Orleans. Delisle, p. 144.

[5] All the secretaries of Popes Alexander III and Lucius III were educated here; *loc. cit.*, p. 153. 'Dictamen' is spoken of almost as the name of a distinct faculty at Orleans. A master of the school is styled 'magister in dictamine'; *loc. cit.*, p. 156. Cf. above, vol. i, p. 109 *sq.*

Salisbury. A versifier of the time of Innocent III still places
Orleans, as the school of letters, on a level with Salerno the
school of medicine, Bologna the school of law, and Paris the
school of logic:[1] while in the *Battle of the Seven Arts*, a French
poem of the same period, grammar is personified as the lady
of Orleans, as logic is the lady of Paris.[2] This school of
grammar, however, appears to have dwindled into insignifi-
cance before A.D. 1300, though even in the second half of the
thirteenth century the clerks of Orleans still retained a repute
for scholarship in the somewhat degenerate form of a skill in
the art of capping verses.[3]

The law-
school of
the thir-
teenth
century.
In the thirteenth century Orleans began a new life as a
school of civil and canon law. Though there is no reason
(with Denifle) to negative all continuity between the thirteenth-century school of law and the twelfth-century schools
of grammar and *dictamen*, or to deny that law may have
continued to be studied at Orleans throughout the earlier
period,[4] it is probable that the revival of the school was due

---

[1] 'In morbis sanat medici virtute
Salernum
Aegros. In causis Bononia legi-
bus armat
Nudos. Parisius dispensat in
artibus illos
Panes unde cibat robustos.
Aurelianis
Educat in armis autorum lacte
tenellos.'—*Loc. cit.*, pp.
143–4.

[2] The poem is printed by Jubinal
in his edition of Rutebeuf, Paris, iii
(1875), 325 *sq.* [and, more recently,
by Paetow (see bibliographical note
above, p. 140)]. Three lines of the
poem are worth quoting on account
of the light they throw upon the rare
word with which they conclude:
'Car Logique, qui toz jors tence,
Claime les auctors auctoriaus
Et les clercs d'Orliens *glomeriaus*.'
Cf. below, chap. xii, § 8. Most of
the Latin poets are mentioned in
this composition, but few of the
prose writers (Seneca is an exception), which shows that the classical

culture of Orleans was far behind
the level attained by Chartres in
the preceding century. Even the
most unintelligent study of the
Latin Aristotle was better than that
of the silver-age poets who ab-
sorbed the energies of the scholars
of Orleans. Cf. also a passage, cited
by M. Gatien-Arnoult in the
*Mémoires de l'Acad. des Sciences de
Toulouse*, 1857, p. 208, from the
discourse of Helinandus at the opening of the University of Toulouse:
'Ecce quaerunt clerici, Parisiis artes
liberales, Aurelianis auctores, Bononiae codices, Salerni pyxides, Toleit
daemones, et nusquam mores.' Cf.
also du Méril, *Poésies pop. du Moyen
Âge*, pp. 151, 152.

[3] Delisle, *loc. cit.*, p. 147. [There
is an enthusiastic letter from an
English student at Orleans in Brit.
Mus. Royal MS. 12 D 11.]

[4] Fitting (*Die Rechtsschule zu
Bologna*, p. 47) insists much upon
the assertion of Clement V in 1309
that the *studium* of law 'lauda-

to external influences, and was connected with the prohibition CHAP.VIII, of the civil law at Paris by the Bull of Honorius III in 1219.[1] § 2.
It is not, however, till 1235 that we have direct evidence of a distinct law-school at Orleans; though we know that it was one of the places in which the masters and scholars of Paris took refuge during the dispersion of 1229.[2] In 1235 Gregory IX,[3] in reply to an inquiry from the bishop, rules that the prohibition of his predecessor was confined to Paris; at Orleans the bishop might freely allow its study, except to certain beneficed ecclesiastics, to whom it was forbidden by another Bull of Honorius III. That no question was raised at an earlier period is explained by the fact that a new bishop had just mounted the episcopal throne who felt a scruple as to the legitimacy of the encouragement which his predecessor had probably given to the exiled civilians of Paris. The prohibition of the civil law was highly injurious to a scientific study even of the canon law in the French capital: and as a school of law Orleans began almost from its foundation to surpass the fame of Paris.[4] From this time at least it may be considered a *studium generale ex consuetudine*; and it remained throughout the Middle Ages the greatest law-university of France. Thomas Aquinas, indeed, places it on a level with the three great *studia generalia*—Paris, Bologna, Salerno.[5] It is a curious fact that some of the

biliter viguerit ab antiquo' (cf. Denifle, i. 258); but he hardly allows for the shortness of the medieval memory or the exuberant rhetoric of medieval scribes.

[1] So Denifle, i. 259. Le Maire (p. 374) makes Bouchard d'Avesne study and profess civil law at Orleans *circa* A.D. 1180, but cites no authorities.

[2] See above, vol. i, p. 336.

[3] *Chartul. Univ. Paris.* i, No. 106; Fournier, i, No. 2. At the same time the Pope granted a faculty to the bishop to absolve for assaults on clerks. Fournier, i, No. 3.

[4] In 1286 a bishop of Amiens speaks of 'Aurelianenses peritiores in iure quam Parisienses et magis

intelligentes'. Fournier, i, No. 1287. [See Meijers, *op. cit.*, for the civilians connected with Orleans, who served the French crown in various ways throughout the thirteenth century; also for the lives and writings of the chief teachers at Orleans—Simon of Paris, a doctor of Bologna, John of Monchy, Pietro Peregrossi, the pupil of Odofredus (above, vol. i, p. 218, n. 3), the great James (*Jacobus*) of Révigny, the pupil of John of Monchy, Peter of Belleperche, and others. Cf. Tourtoulon, *Les Œuvres de Jacques de Révigny* (1899).]

[5] 'Bononia in actoribus, Aurelianis in legibus.' *De Virt. et Vit.*, cap. ult.

CHAP. VIII,
§ 2.

Orleans professors are said to have been in the habit of partially employing the vulgar tongue in their lectures.[1]

The *scholasticus.*

I hope hereafter to show that the origin of the university of Oxford must be sought in a scholastic migration similar to that which probably originated the importance of Orleans. I shall then have occasion to point out how decisive were the effects upon the constitutional development of that university of the circumstance that Oxford was not the see of a bishop. Had it been so, the head of the chapter schools would certainly have claimed a jurisdiction over the newly established schools of the Parisian settlers: the development of an independent university would probably have been delayed, and its constitution would certainly have been profoundly modified.[2] At all events, this is exactly what happened at Orleans. The *scholasticus* of the cathedral, already accustomed to grant licences to the masters of grammar, at once claimed over the masters of law all the authority which was asserted, and something more than was permanently retained, by the chancellor of Paris. The emancipation of the masters from the capitular yoke was here very slow. The masters no doubt from the first formed a *universitas* of the vague and indeterminate character which had grown up at Paris towards the end of the twelfth century. We have tolerably clear evidence of the existence of such a *universitas* at the middle of the thirteenth century.[3] It is not quite certain whether there was any

Growth of a university.

---

[1] 'Fuerunt (ut dicitur) Aurelianenses lectores, qui partim latinum, partim gallicum in cathedra loquebantur.' Joh. Faber (a Montpellier jurist of the fourteenth century) ap. Savigny, c. xlviii. An extract is given by Savigny (c. lvi) from an Italian jurist in a language 'half Latin, half Italian', but he appears to have employed this dialect only in the moral digressions which he introduced into his lectures.

[2] [For this view and some criticisms on it, see below, vol. iii, pp. 11–30 and notes.]

[3] When the Pastoreaux invaded Orleans (*c.* 1251), one of them was killed by a student, and a serious riot ensued, since the citizens took the side of the heretics. Matthew Paris concludes: 'Novum quippe et absurdum fuit, ut laicus, immo plebeius, spreta auctoritate pontificali, in publico tam audacter et in tali civitate, ubi viguit scolarium universitas, praedicaret . . . Exturbata est igitur tota universitas, et compertum est circiter viginti quinque clericos, absque laesis et diversimode dampnificatis, miserabiliter occubuisse.' *Chron. Mai.* (ed. Luard), v. 250. The writer's whole tone implies the importance of the school and the large numbers of the

rector; it is more probable that the doctors had no head except the *scholasticus*. At all events the right of the university to elect a rector was a matter of dispute as late as 1270–80.[1] And when the doctors attempted to arrogate to themselves the powers of a really independent corporation, and to make statutes for the government of the schools, we find their claim disputed by the bishop. The first written statute of which we have any record was made between 1288 and 1296 for the purpose of limiting the number of 'ordinary' lecturers. It fixed the staff of the university as follows: two doctors in decrees, three in decretals, and five in civil law. The statute is enacted by the *scholasticus* after deliberation with the doctors and the chapter, and with the consent of the bishop.[2] At

students. The expression 'scolarium universitas' probably points to a formal guild, though it does not prove it. Another contemporary account speaks of the 'congregationem clericorum que ibi iamdiu resederat'. Fournier, i, No. 8. An earlier brawl (in 1236) testifies to the presence of 'scolares iuvenes illustrissimi et genere praeclari' (Matt. Paris, *Hist. Mai.* iii. 371; Fournier, i, No. 4). Other documents are published by Doinel, *Hugues de Bouteiller et le massacre des clercs à Orléans en 1236* (Orleans, 1887), which show that Denifle's attempted correction of the date to 1241–2 (i. 260) is mistaken. [Cf. the *Morale Scolarium* of John of Garland, c. xiv, with Paetow's note; *Two Mediaeval Satires*, pp. 166, 221.]

[1] 'Lex ista allegatur cotidie ad hoc, quod universitas potest facere et eligere iudicem, licet electus alias nullam habeat iurisdictionem, unde privatus consensus non facit iudicem eum, qui non est alias iudex. Hoc est verum, nisi sint privilegiati collegiati, unde scolares Parisienses, qui habent Universitatem, possunt sibi eligere rectorem. Sed nos, qui sumus hic Aurelianis, singuli ut singuli non possumus hoc facere.

Itaque bonum esset adire, ut impetraretur, nam collegium illicitum est, si non fuerit a superiore approbatum ut ff. *Quod cuiusc. univ.* l. I. Dico colligunt hic, quod qui habet curam collegii vel rectoriam, est iudex singulorum de collegio seu de universitate et lex ista hoc dicit. Sed quod universitas eligat eum, certe lex ista hoc non dicit nec lex alia.' This is an extract from the *Lecturae* of the Orleans professor, Jacques de Révigny. (Fournier, i, No. 11.) The date is not certain. Note the contrast between this French view of the law of corporations and that of Italian jurists. See above, vol. i, pp. 151 *sq.*, 300 *sq.* [and the discussion by Gaines Post, mentioned above, vol. i, p. 298. Meijers, *op. cit.* i. 479, ii. 477, cites the criticism of Pierre de la Chapelle on the effect of the statute described in the text. The bishop of Orleans was Pierre de Mornay. See Meijers also for a discussion of the life and work of Jacques de Révigny].

[2] 'Prefatus scolasticus ad quem eiusdem studii gubernatio et dispositio ab antiquo approbata et hactenus pacifice observata consuetudine pertinet . . . habito super hiis tam cum doctoribus tunc in studio

the beginning of the following century, however, a new bishop wanted the doctors to admit a sixth civilian, and, upon the refusal of the university, threatened to add four or five more to the number at his own pleasure. An appeal to Rome followed; then the bishop by his own authority allowed the intruded doctor to lecture, and, to stop the progress of the appeal, forbade the doctors to hold congregations without his special leave. The upshot of the affair was that a few years later (1306) a series of Bulls were procured from Clement V (once a student of Orleans), which recognized a university after the manner of the University of Toulouse,[1] and conferred upon the doctors some of the rights hitherto monopolized by the *scholasticus*—the right of making statutes for certain definite purposes, the right of electing a rector, and all the privileges of the University of Toulouse. The prison of the *scholasticus* was abolished, and his jurisdiction transferred to the bishop. Provision was also made for the taxation of houses.[2] Although the Bull seems to confer power only on the masters, the practice of Toulouse was that the students should enjoy at least a nominal participation in the government of the *studium*. Accordingly we find the statutes enacted by the rector, the doctors, and the proctors of the ten nations, the latter being students and elected by students.[3] It is probable (though not certain) that this student-organization had existed in some form or other from a much earlier period.[4]

Bulls of Clement V, 1306.

Quarrel with the town, 1309. The masters and scholars had hitherto lived in Orleans without any special university privileges whether papal or

predicto legentibus, quam cum capitulo ecclesie diligenti tractatu, de ipsorum consensu et voluntate, interveniente insuper auctoritate tua, qui tunc Aurelianensi ecclesie presidebat . . . duxit . . . statuendum.' Fournier, i, No. 17. (Bull of 1301.)

[1] 'Habeant Universitatem et collegium regendum et gubernandum ad modum Universitatis et Collegii generalis studii Tholosani.' Fournier, i, No. 19.

[2] *Ibid.* i, Nos. 18–22. The limitation of the chairs to five ap-

pears to have been maintained, since bachelors from other universities swore 'quod iuxta statutum apostolicum doctorum iuris civilis numerum quinarium observabit'. Bimbenet, p. 204.

[3] Fournier, i, No. 22.

[4] It is noticeable that at Toulouse, according to the constitution, there were also, in 1311, ten *consiliarii*, sometimes styled *procuratores*, but of these four were masters. There were no nations at Toulouse. See below, p. 169.

royal; and the reader will by this time have seen too much
of the invidious character and working of these privileges to
be surprised at their introduction being resented by the
townsfolk, however necessary they may have been to protect
the students from as bad or worse oppression at their hands.
When in 1309 the masters and scholars had assembled to hear
a certain papal Bull read in the Dominican convent,[1] the
assembly was dispersed by a violent irruption of burghers,
who significantly reminded them of a great massacre of clerks
by the Pastoreaux fifty-nine years ago[2] and declared that they
would never be at peace with the gownsmen until they renounced their privileges.[3] In 1312, after three years of confusion, Philip IV—who was just completing his subjugation
of the Papacy, of the Templars, of the archbishop of Lyons,
of the clergy throughout his realm—declared in favour of the
town. The masters and scholars were forbidden to exercise
their papal privileges, to hold congregations, to elect a rector,
to demand oaths, or assume any other rights of an independent corporation. Both the *universitas* and the nations
were suppressed. Only the masters might meet at the summons of their dean to make necessary regulations for the
most strictly scholastic purposes.[4]

[1] The Bull read was probably
No. 25. The fact that the university congregations met in the
Dominican convent appears to be
Bimbenet's only authority for supposing that the schools were held
here also. Of course, his theory
(p. 306) that the university grew
out of the convent schools is quite
contrary to all analogy and probability. Afterwards the usual meet-
ing-place for congregations was
the university chapel in the church
of Notre-Dame de Bonne-Nou-
velle. [The very beautiful building
traditionally known as the *Salle
des theses*, which was probably the
library of the old university, is now
used by the Société archéologique
de l'Orléanais. The *Grandes Écoles*,
one of several buildings used for
lectures, was destroyed in 1824.

See Jarry, *op. cit.*]

[2] The text has LXIX. Either
this must be a distinct episode from
that mentioned above (p. 144, n. 3),
or more probably LXIX is a mistake for LIX or LXI. As to the
date of the incident itself, Fournier
appears to be wrong in giving 1310.
See Denifle, i. 260, n. 161.

[3] Fournier, i, Nos. 27–31.

[4] *Ibid.* i, Nos. 36–40. The ordinance (No. 37) is instructive as
an account of the clear distinction which it draws between the
studium generale and the *universitas*. 'Universitatem huiusmodi
que causam huic prestabat scan-
dalo, nec fuerat auctoritate nostra
subnixa, tolli decrevimus . . .
Ceterum . . . studium generale
presertim iuris canonici et civilis,
dante Deo, perpetuum ibidem esse

CHAP. VIII, § 2.

By way of adding insult to injury, the king attempted to compensate the scholars for the loss of their university rights by handing them over to the protection or surveillance of the bailiff and provost of Orleans, the latter being made conservator of such privileges as the king chose to recognize.[1] After a few more years of discontent and agitation the scholars determined to resort to a remedy which seldom failed to extract reasonable terms from the enemies of scholastic liberty. A little before Easter 1316 the whole body bound themselves by an oath to leave the town if their demands were not acceded to before the ensuing festival. The threat was executed, and the masters and scholars decamped in a body to Nevers,[2] which then lay in Burgundian territory. Pope John XXII (an *alumnus* of Orleans) interposed on behalf of the exiled scholars, and Philip V was at last driven to accept his mediation. The compromise which he suggested—the limitation which it imposed upon the privileges of scholars—shows exactly where the shoe which the burghers of the university town were required to wear pinched most intolerably. By the Pope's mediation it was arranged that the university should never interfere as a corporation in disputes between a private citizen and an individual scholar.[3] If the criminous

Migration to Nevers, 1316.

Compromise.

volumus, hoc salvo quod theologie magistri nullatenus creentur ibidem, ne detrahatur privilegiis romane sedis studio Parisiensi concessis . . . Congregationes generales, que necdum vagandi, sed frequenter scandali materiam prestare solent, inhibemus eisdem.' It is observable that Orleans is spoken of as a 'studium liberalium artium, precipue iuris', &c., but there is no trace of any organized *studium* except in law after the decay of the old schools of rhetoric.

[1] Fournier, i, Nos. 35, 37, 41.

[2] *Ibid.*, No. 47. The consent of the town of Nevers was only obtained by a renunciation of most of the university privileges. It will be noticed how different the feeling of northern towns, who regarded scholars as 'clerks', was to the wel-

come generally accorded to migrating students by the Italian cities. The settlement at Nevers ended in a riot, in which the citizens pitched the doctors' *cathedrae* into the river to float back to Orleans, 'clamantes alta voce, "Ecce studium portamus in ripperia Ligerris submergendum, et postmodo de scolariis (*sic*) simili modo faciemus!"' *Ibid.*, No. 53. Cf. No. 71, which gives the fines imposed by the Parlement of Paris on fifty-seven offenders. There are two articles on this secession to Nevers, one by Duminy in the *Bulletin de la Soc. nivernaise des Sciences et Lettres*, xi (1883), 358, the other by Bimbenet in *Mém. de la Soc. d'Agricult., Sciences et Arts d'Orléans*, 1877, p. 5.

[3] 'Universitas, rector, doctores aut scolares illius de factis singu-

scholar was still allowed almost total impunity through his exemption from the jurisdiction of the lay tribunals, the town magistrates were at all events freed from the necessity of allowing their fellow-citizens, guilty or innocent, to be imprisoned or heavily fined at the bidding of the academical authorities for fear of a 'suspension of lectures', or an eventual dispersion.[1] The terms were accepted by the town and enforced by a royal edict in 1320: after which the scholars returned to Orleans. It is from this time that the most flourishing period in the history of the university begins. The *rotulus beneficiandorum* presented to Benedict XIII in 1394 contains the names of ninety-five resident licentiates in one or both laws,[2] and in all 844 students, of whom 551 were resident. This may be conjectured to represent an academic population of not less than 800 or 1,000; though it is, of course, impossible to estimate precisely the proportion of enrolled to unenrolled. Probably the expectants of ecclesiastical benefices would prove a majority.

The constitution of the university exhibits a remarkable compromise between the rival types of Paris and Bologna. We have seen that before the papal Bull of incorporation the *scholasticus* of Orleans, like the chancellor of Oxford, occupied a double position as the bishop's representative and at the same time head of the magisterial guild. After the final establishment of a rectorship, the *scholasticus* recedes into the

---

lorum scolarium et doctorum universitatis nomine se nullatenus intromittant' (Fournier, i, No. 55). The privilege was the more invidious since private individuals were not allowed to appear in the courts by a legal representative (*ibid.*). All scholars are here assumed to be clerks, but a doubt arises as to the fiscal immunities of married scholars (*Ibid.*, No. 199).

[1] *Ibid.* i, Nos. 58–68.

[2] *Ibid.* iii, No. 1891. Fournier (*Hist.* iii. 41) seems to assume that the 844 represents the total number of students. But (1) it is doubtful whether every clerk, how-ever young, would have put down his name; (2) it is certain that there must have been law-students who could not hold, and did not want, a benefice. Considering the large proportion of students elsewhere who did not proceed so far as the licence, 230 licentiates, of whom ninety-five were residents, must represent more than 551 residents. Note that the numbers were not swollen, as in many universities, by boy-students in arts and in grammar. (Fournier afterwards disclaimed the above interpretation of his words.)

CHAP.VIII, position of the Parisian chancellor, and the rector becomes
§ 2.   head of the university proper. From this time the ordinary
affairs of the university were administered by a college consisting of the doctors ordinary and the ten proctors of the
student-nations. These nations were France, Germany,
Lorraine, Burgundy, Champagne, Picardy, Normandy,
Touraine, Aquitaine, and Scotland.[1] The rector was elected
by the nations, but was often, if not usually, a doctor. The
occasions on which the whole university of doctors and
students are summoned appear, however, to have gradually
increased in frequency:[2] and in 1389 a dispute between the
students and doctors led to a more exact determination of the
relations between the college and the university by the Parlement of Paris. The university was not to be summoned till
the matter had been discussed in the college, but a majority
of the proctors could insist on a general congregation. On the
other hand, the college could not disburse more than twenty
solidi in a single rectorship without consulting the nations.
The proctors were to be licentiates, or at least bachelors,
wherever possible.[3] Later changes slightly increased the
power of the students.[4]

[1] The names are collected from various documents. All appear in Fournier, iii, No. 1891, except Germany, one proctor being mentioned without the name of his nation. In 1400 the nation of France was divided into five provinces (Fournier, i, Nos. 238, 239), afterwards styled *Parqueta*. Here, as in Italy, the German nation enjoyed mysterious privileges, i.e. of taking the licentiate's and bachelor's degrees by accumulation after five years, while others took five years for the bachelorship and five more for the doctorate. *Ibid.*, Nos. 154, 344.

[2] *Ibid.* i, No. 155, contains the first allusion to such general congregations. A statute of the German nation (No. 192) for-bidding its proctor to consent to the expenditure of more than forty *solidi* 'inconsultis eis' perhaps indi-cates the powers by which the stu-dents managed to acquire a direct instead of a representative share in the government of the university. A Bull of 1388 allows a licentiate or bachelor to be rector. (Denifle, *Les Univ. françaises*, p. 51.)

[3] Fournier, i, No. 216.

[4] In 1406 three proctors were given the power to demand a general congregation (*ibid.*, No. 251). The reform of Charles VII in 1447 (No. 294) (1) disfranchised students 'in primo volumine audi-tionis existentes', (2) recognized an intermediate *collegium solenne* at which all doctors, licentiates and persons summoned by the rector attended besides the *collegium ordinarium*. The *procurator gene-ralis* (registrar, treasurer, and syndic in one), becomes an increas-

After the decay of the literary schools in the thirteenth
century, no regular faculty of arts manifests its existence in
the Orleans documents, nor any other faculty except that of
law.[1] Hardly any university of such high repute[2] remained,
as appears to have been the case at Orleans, without a single
endowed college for poor students.[3] On the other hand, we
find that there were *hospicia* for students presided over by
doctors, bachelors, or students, who in the middle of the
fifteenth century are required to maintain quite as much
discipline over their *socii* as was exercised by the principals
of Parisian or Oxonian halls.[4]

§ 3. ANGERS

Pocquet DE LIVONNIÈRE, *Privilèges de l'Université d'Angers*, 1709 and
1736. DUBOYS, *Privilèges des Professeurs de Droit*, Angers, 1745. RAN-
GEARD, *Histoire de l'Université d'Angers*, éd. Lemarchand, Angers, 1872,
is one of the best, most learned, and most critical of the older university
histories, containing many documents. (Rangeard lived 1692–1726.)
DE LENS, *L'Université de l'Anjou*, i, Angers, 1880, continues Rangeard
(who stops at 1428) and adds a few documents; also 'La Faculté de
Théologie de l'Université d'Angers' (*Revue de l'Anjou*, 1879). PORT,
Statuts des quatre Facultés de l'Université d'Angers, 1406–98, Angers,
1878; also 'La Bibliothèque de l'Université d'Angers' (*Revue de l'Anjou*,
1867).

ANGERS was an ancient cathedral school which gradually
developed into a university. But here, as in many other cases,
the development was not entirely spontaneous and indepen-

ingly important official, and was
evidently present at meetings of the
college, but it does not appear that
he had a vote.

[1] In 1446 we find *grammatici*
allowed to enjoy the university
privileges (Fournier, i, No. 290);
and in 1447 (No. 294) there is a
provision against 'acquiring time'
in arts at the same time as law, but
this may refer to residence kept in
other universities. [There is a
reference to 'doctores regentes in
artibus' in 1512: archives of Loiret,
D 4 f. 9. It may be noticed here
that the University of Orleans had
a reputation for the study of the
occult. The magician in Chaucer's
Franklin's Tale was a clerk of Or-

leans, and there are other instances;
see G. L. Kittredge, *Witchcraft in
Old and New England* (Cambridge,
Mass., 1929), pp. 50, 187, and the
references there given.]
[2] Among the *alumni* of later days
are mentioned Reuchlin, Calvin,
Beza [Charles Perrault], and du
Cange.
[3] [An additional indication that
law-students were well to do and
that the study was profitable.]
[4] 'Doctores, licentiatos et bacha-
larios et alios quoscumque scolares
ad suam pensionem tenentes, quod
eos moribus et doctrina diligenter
instruant', &c. Fournier, i, No.
294. Cf. the *paedagogi* at Angers.
below, p. 159.

CHAP. VIII, dent. It owed its position as a *studium generale* to an immi-
§ 3.   gration from one of the two great archetypal *studia*: and its
institutions were moulded more or less in conformity with the
models already established at Paris and Bologna.

The old   The cathedral school of Angers was in the first half of the
cathedral
school. eleventh century taught by two successive pupils of the
celebrated Fulbert of Chartres:[1] at the end of the eleventh
and beginning of the twelfth century it attained considerable
reputation under two successive *scholastici*, Marbodus, afterwards bishop of Rennes, and Ulger, afterwards bishop of
Angers. The mythical accounts of the origin of the university
seek to connect it with the names of these two prelates, the
former of whom is even alleged to have procured a foundation-
Bull from Rome.[2] The later statutes represent Ulger as the
founder of a benefaction for the bedels.[3] Assuming that the
fact and the date are correct, we cannot feel sure that the
bedels meant were originally the bedels of the schools, and

[1] During the episcopate of Hu-
bert of Vendôme (1010–47). The
masters were Sigo, afterwards
abbot of S. Florent, and Hilduin,
afterwards abbot of S. Nicholas,
near Angers. De Lens, i. 8.

[2] [M. Manitius, *Geschichte der
lateinischen Literatur des Mittelalters*, iii (Munich, 1931), 719 *sqq.*,
898–900.] Cf. De Lens, i. 9;
Rangeard, i. 10 *sq.* Marbodus became chancellor and *scholasticus* in
1069, bishop of Rennes in 1096,
and died 1123: Ulger became
bishop of Angers in 1125. A
'magister divinorum librorum' is
mentioned by Abelard as teaching
an extreme and heretical realism
'in pago Andegavensi' (*ante* 1120),
Opp. ed. Cousin, ii. 84. De Lens
makes Berengar teach at Angers *c.*
1089, not as *scholasticus* but as *gram-
maticus*, a fact which he declares
to be established by an ancient
obituary of the cathedral, *loc. cit.*
(cf. Rangeard, i. 17, 18). If the document, of which a notarial certifi-
cate is given in Rangeard, ii. 158, be
genuine, it would show that the

College of S. Maurice was established in connexion with the Chapel
of S. Mary for the instruction (or
rather support) of the clerks and
chaplains of the church of S.
Maurice in 1032; but this is rather
early for endowed colleges. The
'scholastria' was endowed in 1077.
Document in Rangeard, ii. 159.
[Josèphe Chartrou, *L'Anjou de
1109 à 1151*, Paris, n.d., has some
pages on the episcopal school of
Angers, pp. 215–22.]

[3] 'Quiquidem bidelli illa die, durante tempore licentie, debent ad
unam comestionem recipi in parva
aula dicti palatii; et quisquis sit
claviger seu custos eiusdem debet
eis de bonis episcopi Andevagensis
pro tempore ministrare panem et
vinum et alia cibaria eisdem necessaria; que predicta bone memorie domínus Ulgerius, quondam
Andevagensis episcopus, eisdem
contulit et donavit, et predicta
fieri perpetuo voluit et precepit.'
Statute of 1373 in Rangeard, ii.
223; Fournier, i, No. 396.

the whole story has a very apocryphal aspect; but there is no reason to deny (as Denifle seems rather disposed to do) all continuity between the old cathedral school and the later university. We know, indeed, nothing of the special subjects for which Angers obtained its scholastic fame under Marbodus and Ulger; but the early connexion with the celebrated canonist, Fulbert of Chartres, may be held to indicate a probability that law was included under its curriculum. After the time of Ulger, however, we have no positive knowledge of the schools of Angers until the year 1229, when the great Parisian dispersion compelled many—perhaps the main contingent of the fugitive students—to seek a home in Angers beyond the direct control of the French king. As, however, this migration fails to account for the special predominance of law at Angers, it seems highly probable that the prohibition of the civil law at Paris in 1219 had already led to the transference of some civilians from Paris to Angers. At all events it is to this prohibition that Angers, more even than Orleans, owed its prosperity. Angers was *par excellence* the school of *civil* law. It is doubtful, indeed, whether promotions in any other faculty than civil or canon law ever took place here[1] before 1432. Though Angers never possessed in medieval times the same scientific importance as the school of Orleans, it was hardly less famous as the school of practical lawyers, especially during the fifteenth century, and in the sixteenth surpassed it as a seat of the great legal Renaissance.[2]

Angers is reckoned by Denifle among the universities which grew up 'ohne Stiftbriefe': and from the fact that no less than seven doctors are found teaching here at one time in the course of the thirteenth century, it is practically certain

---

[1] There were, of course, schools of grammar and logic. In 1298 there were such schools at the collegiate church of S. Peter, and the dean had the right 'duos pueros et duos *baccalarios* duntaxat ponere et instituere in choro ecclesie Sancti Petri predicti' (Rangeard, ii. 187; Fournier, i, No. 370). The use of the word *baccalareus* may naturally suggest that promotions already took place in arts, but according to Rangeard (i. 324) the term was then applied to the younger ecclesiastics of a church without reference to their academical status. See above, vol. i, p. 207, n. 2.

[2] Fournier, *Hist*. iii. 206, 207.

CHAP. VIII, that regular graduations must have taken place.[1] By a curious
§ 3.   accident we find the *studium*, just at the time of the Parisian
immigration, expressly described by a contemporary writer
[*c.* 1250] as a *studium particulare*,[2] while Matthew Paris no
less distinctly implies its generality,[3] though it is not till 1337
that it is officially recognized as such.[4] We see the school in
the act of passing from a 'particular' to a 'general' *studium*.
It is one of the very few undoubted *studia generalia* that
never obtained either a papal Bull of foundation or express
recognition of its *ius ubique docendi*. It was not till 1364 that it
received a charter from Charles V conferring upon it all the
privileges of the University of Orleans and appointing the sene-

---

[1] The *Questiones Andegavis disputate* in Bibl. Nat. Cod. Lat. 11724 (Denifle, i. 271). The MS. belongs to the second half of the century.

[2] 'Annum millenum Domini,
   centum bis et annos,
Vigintique novem, semita solis
   agit,
Sanguine Parisius studium dissolvitur: orbe
In toto sentit praelia sacra Syon.
Andegavis studium quod particulare cohaeret
Illud dissolvunt proxima bella novum.'
John of Garland, *De triumphis ecclesiae*, ed. T. Wright (Roxburghe Club, London, 1856), p. 99. [As J. C. Russell has pointed out, in 'An ephemeral University at Angers (1229–1234)' in *Colorado College Publication*, No. 148 (1927), p. 48, the last line of this passage refers to the capture of Angers by Louis IX in 1234; cf. the annals of Dunstable in *Annales Monastici*, iii. 117: 'qui paulo post pro guerra dispersi sunt.' There is, therefore, no proof of continuity, but rather a suggestion of a break, between the scholars of the dispersion and the later masters at Angers.]

[3] 'Recedentes itaque clerici generaliter universi contulerunt se ad maiores civitates regionum diversarum. Quorum tamen maxima pars civitatem Andegavensium metropolitanam ad doctrinam elegit universalem' (Matt. Paris. *Chron. Mai.* (ed. Luard), iii. 168: see above, vol. i, p. 336). 'Universalem' is, of course, equivalent to 'generalem'. In the following year the Pope writes 'magistris et scholaribus Parisius et Andegavi commorantibus' (Fournier, i, No. 362). The first express notice of the teaching of the civil law occurs in 1242 in a letter from Otto de Fontana, 'iuris civilis professor docens Andegavi' (Rangeard, ii. 178; Fournier, i, No. 363). But there is perhaps a slight presumption that there was a *studium* of law within the province when the provincial synod of Tours in 1236 required a period of legal study for officials and advocates in the ecclesiastical courts (Mansi, *Concilia*, xxiii. 412).

[4] In an episcopal ordinance (Fournier, i, No. 378), 'Statum honorabilem et antiquum Andegavensis studii generalis . . . in quo tot boni viri ducum, comitum et aliorum principum et baronum fratres, filii et nepotes et alto sanguine derivati retroactis temporibus studuerunt.'

schal of Anjou and provost of Angers conservators.[1] But by this time it had long been treated both by kings and popes as completely on a level with the formally constituted *studia generalia*.[2]

The constitution of Angers is in the main strikingly parallel to that of Orleans. There is no evidence to show which of them was the more ancient, but the total dissimilarity between the original constitution of these two universities and those of the greater universities—Paris and Bologna—is the best evidence of their antiquity. Such a constitution could not well have grown up after the first half of the thirteenth century. In Angers and Orleans we have in fact a survival of that primitive and imperfect university organization out of which Paris began to emerge early in the thirteenth century and Oxford (as we shall see) some thirty years later:[3] and Angers retained this primitive simplicity longer even than Orleans. As late as 1350 the *scholasticus* or 'maistre-escoles' is still the sole head of the university. He is himself a regent doctor of the school and the head of the college of doctors. Statutes of some kind are already in existence, but so little authority has the college acquired—so little has it emerged from the merely customary stage of its existence—that a licentiate is found attempting, with the approval of the *scholasticus* but in defiance of the college and its regulations, to incept under a doctor who is not and never has been a regent doctor at Angers.[4] The result is an appeal to the

Constitution.

The scholasticus head of the university.

---

[1] Rangeard, ii. 210; Fournier, i, No. 388.

[2] Fournier, i, Nos. 375–84. The first *rotulus beneficiandorum* mentioned by Fournier is in 1342 (No. 379): the first general permission to enjoy the fruits of benefices while residing in the *studium* is dated 1363 (No. 387; Rangeard, ii. 208). It received the *ius non trahi extra* from Gregory XI in 1371 (No. 394).

[3] It is worth noticing that many of the Parisian settlers of 1229 were Englishmen. It seems to be implied that the five Englishmen mentioned by Matthew Paris went to Angers. Some of these are alleged

to have afterwards studied at Oxford, where the chancellor's position was very closely parallel to that of the *scholasticus* at Angers (Matt. Paris. *loc. cit.*; Rangeard, i. 136).

[4] 'Ad nostri devenit notitiam quod venerabilis vir magister Garnerius de Cepeaux actu tunc non regens, neque rexerat in dicto studio ordinarie, intendebat et iactavit se in dicto studio venerabilem virum magistrum Laurentium Beaulamère [?] creare in doctorem in legibus; et quod ipse magister Laurentius intendebat incipere sub eodem', &c. (Rangeard, ii. 200; Fournier, i, No. 381).

CHAP. VIII,
§ 3.

bishop, of whose authority over the *studium* there is no question. The earliest extant statutes are of some twenty years
later and enable us to complete our picture. Under the
scholasticus is a dean of the college of doctors who exercises,
concurrently with the *scholasticus*, a judicial authority over
masters and scholars, and acts as treasurer of the college.
There is no rector of the university. The power of making
statutes is thus lodged entirely with the *scholasticus* and the
doctors. Indeed, the doctors themselves seem only just
emerging from that original state of absolute bondage to the
scholasticus from which the masters of Paris had emancipated
themselves more than a century and a half before: the statutes
of 1373 are made by the *scholasticus* 'with the consent' of the
doctors. There are, indeed, as at Orleans, certain nations of
students—probably dating from the thirteenth century[1]—
side by side with the college of doctors, but neither the university of students nor its constituent nations or their proctors
are recognized by the magisterial college as sharing the supreme legislative power, though their statutes do recognize
the authority of the proctors over the students.[2] The nations
are still the mere student-clubs or guilds which the Bologna
universities themselves must have been in their origin towards
the close of the twelfth century.

The
nations.

It was inevitable that the students should grow impatient
of the yoke which the students of most other law universities
had thrown off. The first quarrel between the students on
the one hand and the *scholasticus* and doctors on the other

Assertion
of student-
rights.

---

[1] The number is usually given as
ten, and the names as the same as at
Orleans, except that Brittany takes
the place of Germany: but there
seems to be no express mention of
them before 1373, and then there is
nothing to fix the number at ten
(Fournier, *Hist.* iii. 161–2) except
the statement of Rangeard (i. 259).
The ordinances issued in 1279
by Charles I, king of Sicily and
count of Anjou, as to interest,
regrating, &c. at the request of the
burghers and 'des escolliers demeu-

rans à Angiers', make it probable
that some kind of student-organization existed at that time. Rangeard,
ii. 180; Fournier, i, No. 365.

[2] 'Item quod scholares infra
mensem (Fournier reads 'menses';
if so, the number must have
dropped out) a tempore sui primi
adventus teneantur iurare statuta
dicti studii observare: quod iuramentum teneantur prestare pro-
curatori sue nationis.' Rangeard,
ii. 226; Fournier, i, No. 396.

arose in 1389, when 283 students—'the major and the saner
part' as they styled themselves—appealed to the Parlement
for a redress of grievances. By this time it was customary for
the students to be summoned on important occasions to
general congregations, and the students contend that the
scholasticus was bound to decide by a majority of votes. It
appears, however, that he sometimes disregarded the views
of the majority or refused to 'conclude' at all: and the doctors
still claim that they are really the university.[1] Initiation and
administration clearly rested with the doctoral college, though
there were rare occasions on which the proctors of the nations
were summoned to confer with the doctors.[2] The result of
this rebellion was that the students acquired the modest right
of electing a representative to assist at the audit of the university accounts.[3] It is probable, indeed, that it was the necessity
of getting the students' consent for taxation on such occasions
as the sending of a roll to Avignon that originally compelled
the doctors to summon general congregations, and that here,
as so often both in universities and in states, the power of the
purse ultimately carried with it legislative supremacy. At all
events it was the administration of the *collecta* raised for
sending a roll to the Pope in 1395 which led to a renewed
rebellion. The students again brought their grievances before
the Parlement and petitioned for a constitution like that of
other universities.[4]

The report of the commissioners of Parlement was favour- Reform
able to the demands of the students, and the upshot of the of 1398.
affair was that in 1398 the university was reorganized on the
model of Orleans and a new code of statutes drawn up. The
scholasticus and the doctors, however, retained a rather more
favourable position than at Orleans. There was a rector, but
it was provided that the doctors should hold the office by

[1] Fournier, i, No. 414.
[2] 'Disoit outre ledict maistre-
escolle que il et les docteurs régents
ordinairement en ladicte Université
seuls et pour le tout font Université
et collège sans les escolliers, car ils
ont arche, séel et profession et
signes de l'Université, de corps et

de collège': while the students are
spoken of as 'eux qui n'ont corps
ne collège, arche, séle, ne aucun
signe de Université'. *Ibid.* i, No.
425.
[3] *Ibid.*, Nos. 417, 418.
[4] *Ibid.*, Nos. 422–7.

CHAP. VIII, rotation. The *scholasticus* was allowed precedence over the
§ 3. rector in scholastic acts, though not on other occasions. The
ordinary administration was entrusted to the college of doctors and proctors presided over by the rector, to which was
here added the procurator-general of the university. Three
proctors might demand a general congregation, which is now
definitively recognized as the governing body of the university.[1] In 1410, whatever their previous number, there are six
nations only and the sixth is spoken of as a new creation.
Their names supply interesting evidence as to the regions
from which the university drew its students. They are, (1)
Anjou (including the adjoining diocese of Tours), (2) Brittany,
(3) Maine, (4) Normandy, (5) Aquitaine (including the
'provinces' of Bourges, Bordeaux, Narbonne, Toulouse,
Auch), and (6) France.[2] At the same time the constitution

Demo-
cratic
changes.
is still further modified in a democratic direction. The rector
is to be chosen exclusively from the licentiates by electors
named by the nations: doctors are ineligible as electors.
Moreover, it is provided that in the council or congregation
the doctors shall have no votes in matters affecting themselves
and their college. The superiority of the rector to the
scholasticus is now for the first time proclaimed, respect being
paid to the interests of the then occupant of the office.[3] The
scholasticus has ceased to be the head of the university, and
he is henceforth limited to the conferment of the licence, like
the chancellor of other universities.[4]

---

[1] *Ibid.*, Nos. 430–7; Rangeard,
ii. 232. Yet it is worth noticing that
the nations seem to have no means
except social excommunication to
compel a new scholar to join their
body. Cf. the statute of the nation
of Maine in 1419: 'Noviter
venientes . . . si iuramenta prelibata
noluerunt . . . facere, presentes in
artibus scolasticis ipsos non socia-
bunt, ymo ipsum iuramentum
prestare recusantes, ut prefertur,
quantum poterunt evitabunt, nec
eos conviviando associabunt.' Fournier, i, No. 465.

[2] 'Sexta erit natio Franciae, quae

de novo certis de causis virtute
commissionis nostrae per nos con-
stituta est, et habet sub se provin-
cias Lugdunensem, Senonensem et
Remensem' (Rangeard, ii. 240); but
the historian tells us (i. 385) 'Elle
subsistoit cependant avant leur (the
commissioners') arrivée à Angers,
mais sans avoir encore une forme
aussi régulière.' As to the date, see
Fournier, i, No. 449, note.

[3] Rangeard, ii. 244; Fournier, i,
Nos. 448, 449. The former wrongly ascribes these statutes to 1400.

[4] He appears at first to have retained the right of making bach-

As the sixteenth century approaches we find here as else- where a reaction in favour of magisterial authority. The statutes drawn up by the commissioners of the Parlement of Paris in 1494 enact that in future no one shall have a vote in the congregation of the university or of any of its nations who is below the degree of master of arts or bachelor in one of the superior faculties.[1] It is interesting to notice that by this time the pedagogy-system had spread from the faculty of arts to that of law. There were, it appears, a class of young students in law known as *Iustiniani*, who lived in the houses kept by *paedagogi*, by whom they were prepared for the study of law without necessarily attending any of the regular univer- sity regents or professors. Law students presumably went direct to the study of law without any preparatory training in arts. It was not till 1432 that regular faculties of theology, medicine, and arts, under their respective deans, were estab- lished at Angers under a Bull of Eugenius IV; the students were, however, united in the same university with the students of canon and civil law. The licence in arts was conferred by the dean of the collegiate church of S. John the Baptist.[2]

elors. But after 1435 he took no part either in the inceptions or the conferment of the baccalaureate. De Lens, i. 22.

[1] Fournier, i, No. 492. It is, however, provided that when pos- sible the proctors shall consult their nations (in which students still had votes) beforehand on matters to be brought before general congrega- tions. It may be noticed that Sun- day is contemplated as a usual day for meetings of the nations. In the same year it was ordered by the Parlement that the senior licentiate of each nation in turn should be rector of the university, and the senior bachelor of each nation proctor, to avoid 'les grands meur- tres et battures, et autres grands scandales et perdition de temps', involved in rectorial elections. It appears that five or six scholars in the one nation of Maine, besides others, had been 'tuez, mutilez, et

battuz' within the last few years (*ibid.*, Nos. 495, 496). Promotion by seniority was, however, found to involve 'graviora mala et damna prioribus', and was abolished the next year (*ibid.*, No. 499).

[2] Fournier, i, Nos. 472, 474, 488. There is a stray allusion to 'au- diendo . . . in iure canonico vel *in theologia*' in 1317 (Fournier, i, No. 374). This may refer to the schools of the Dominicans, who in 1405 were admitted to the privileges of the university (Rangeard, ii. 271; Fournier, i, No. 442). The Bull of Eugenius IV grants the right of graduation but not expressly the *ius ubique docendi*. The members of the faculty of arts were not ad- missible to offices of the university till 1494 (Fournier, i, Nos. 491, 494); and then a long conflict be- tween the faculties began, which extends beyond our period.

CHAP. VIII,
§ 3.
Number of
chairs.

The mode of graduation and the regulations of the *studium* are for the most part similar to those of the University of Orleans. Here also the full rights of regency (i.e. the right of giving ordinary lectures) were confined to a small, limited, and probably co-opting college of doctors. The statutes of 1373 provide for three or four doctors of law, two or three in the *Decretals*, and two in the *Decretum*.[1] In 1494 the number of regents in law was reduced to six—four in civil and two in canon law.[2]

Colleges.

The Collège de Fougères for four scholars of law was founded by Guillaume de Fougères in 1361;[3] the Collège de la Fromagerie for four scholars in 1408;[4] the Collège de Bueil for a principal, chaplain, and six scholars in 1424.[5]

Numbers.

A roll of the year 1378 gives the names of 14 doctors, 5 licentiates, 73 nobles, 286 bachelors, and 188 students.[6] From the large proportion of bachelors to simple students, it is probable that a large number of the latter did not send in their names.

§ 4. TOULOUSE (1229, 1233)

There is no complete history of the University of Toulouse. A few documents and notices occur in DE LAFAILLE, *Annales de la Ville de Toulouse*, 1687. There is a clear sketch of the history of the university in a succession of articles by GATIEN-ARNOULT in *Mém. de l'Acad. des sciences, inscriptions et belles-lettres de Toulouse*, xlviii–liii, 1877–82; also 'Trois maîtres de Théologie à l'Université de Toulouse', in *Revue de Toulouse, ibid.*, 1866. But the most important work on the subject is contained in the new edition of C. DE VIC and J. J. VAISSETTE, *Histoire de Languedoc*, vii, viii, published by Privat, Toulouse, 1879, with a full collection of documents and *études* by E. and A. MOLINIER. There are also articles by RODIÈRE, 'Recherches sur l'enseignement du droit à Toulouse', in *Recueil de l'Acad. de législation de Toulouse*, ix (where the statutes of 1314 were printed for the first time), x, xii, xv (1860–6); and by DU BOURG,

[1] Rangeard, ii. 216; Fournier, i, No. 396. Afterwards we hear of a regent 'pour la nation d'Anjou' (*ibid.*, No. 439). There are traces of a connexion between a regent and a particular nation at Orleans also.

[2] Fournier, i, No. 492. At this time they enjoyed 'salaria . . . de erario publico totius nostre Universitatis' (*ibid.*, No. 498).

[3] Rangeard, ii. 205; Fournier, i, No. 385.

[4] Rangeard, ii. 273; Fournier, i, No. 447. It is noticeable that the deed of foundation contemplates the admission of pensioners. The college was under the supervision of the college of the university.

[5] Rangeard, ii. 307; Fournier, i, No. 467.

[6] *Ibid.* iii, No. 1897.

'Épisode des luttes de l'Un. et du capitole de Toulouse' in *Mém. de l'Acad.* CHAP.VIII,
de Toulouse, 1889. SAINT-CHARLES has published a series of articles on • § 4·
the various colleges in the *Mém. de l'Acad. de Toulouse*, 1883–6.

[René GADAVE, *Les Documents sur l'histoire de l'Université de Toulouse
et spécialement de sa Faculté de Droit civil et canonique* (1229–1789)
(Bibl. Méridionale publiée sous les auspices de l'université de Toulouse,
xiii, Toulouse, 1910); M. SALTET, 'L'ancienne université de Toulouse',
in *Bulletin de littérature ecclésiastique* (Toulouse), vii (1915–16), 50–65;
E. J. BARBUT, *Les chroniques de la Faculté de médecine de Toulouse*, i,
Toulouse, 1905; A. THOMAS, 'Lettres closes de Charles VI et de Charles VII
adressées à l'université de Toulouse', in *Annales du Midi*, 1915–16,
pp. 176–91; F. PUGET, 'L'Université de Toulouse au xive et au xve siècle',
ibid., 1930, 345–81.]

THE foundation of the University of Toulouse is an event of very considerable importance in the history of the medieval university-system. It exercised a marked influence over the development of the university idea in the medieval mind. It was, indeed, the first university (with the partial exception of Palencia) that can properly be said to have been founded at all. A very peculiar combination of circumstances suggested to the Pope the idea of reproducing artificially in the city of Toulouse the institution or system of institutions which had spontaneously developed themselves at Paris and Oxford. And this precedent in turn suggested the notion that the Pope could 'found' other *studia generalia* at the request of a ruler or a city, in the same way as he had founded Toulouse for his own special purposes; and from that notion it was but a step to the development of the theory that a *studium generale* could only be founded by the Pope or his rival in the government of the medieval world-state, the Holy Roman Emperor.[1]

Toulouse the first university founded by papal Bull.

It would lead us too far away from our subject to dwell in any detail upon that momentous crisis in the history of medieval Europe which is constituted by the Albigensian

Origination in the triumph of the Church over the Albigensian heresy.

[1] [It is perhaps worth while to remind the reader that this theory is not inconsistent with the view, as characteristic of medieval as of ancient thought, that it was an obligation upon a prince to establish or encourage places of learning (*studia*). S. Thomas Aquinas said, 'ordinare de studio pertinet ad eum qui praeest reipublicae' (*Contra impugnantes religionem*, c. 3). See the observations and evidence drawn from German foundation charters, &c., in F. von Bezold, *Aus Mittelalter und Renaissance*, pp. 229 sqq. But the establishment of a *studium generale* required papal confirmation.]

movement and its tragical sequel, the Albigensian crusade. In that movement, at once religious and intellectual, born of the freedom, the brightness, the 'lay spirit' engendered of prosperous commerce and a sunny city life, we seem to trace the dawn both of a healthier Renaissance and a more joyous Reformation. In the suppression of all that Languedocian and Provençal freedom, civil, religious, intellectual, by the assembled chivalry and the assembled ruffianism of Europe, we see anticipated the hardly less ferocious if less earnest counter-reformation of the sixteenth and seventeenth centuries—the S. Bartholomew, the Dragonnades, the Jesuit-domination. The place that was occupied in the counter-reformation by the Jesuit colleges was taken in the thirteenth century by the Dominicans, but to some extent also by the University of Toulouse; which was, indeed, largely in the hands of that order. The university was intended as a sort of spiritual garrison in the heart of the conquered land of heresy.

Intended as a spiritual garrison of Languedoc.   Toulouse was the very focus of the religious and intellectual fermentation which had at length broken forth in the Albigensian heresy: at Toulouse therefore it was determined to establish a great school which should be specially devoted to the maintenance of the catholic faith and the extirpation of heresy. In the north of France, where culture was more theological and more ecclesiastical than it was in the south, the intellectualism of the age was on the whole of a far less bold and destructive character than in the south of France with its educated laity, its sceptical troubadours, and its peculiarly indolent and ignorant clergy: it was determined, therefore, to build up a seminary of ecclesiastical learning upon the ruins of the vernacular and secular culture of Languedoc. It was, indeed, recognized that even among the clerks of Paris the spirit of inquiry and bold speculation had made great advances: at Toulouse the danger was to be averted by a careful choice of teachers. The theological faculty was in the hands of the friars; and an abbot was sent to Paris to select masters for the other faculties.[1]

[1] Elias of Guarni, abbot of Grandselve. Gatien-Arnoult, *Mémoires*, 1857, p. 206.

The idea of sending Parisian theologians to extirpate heresy in Languedoc seems to have originated with that great patron of the rising universities, Honorius III;[1] and some theological lectures were actually started. In the mind of his successor, Gregory IX, the project grew and ripened into the conception of a completely equipped *studium* of the Parisian type. On Maundy Thursday, 1229, before the great door of Notre Dame at Paris, the final treaty was signed between the conquered count Raymond of Toulouse and his orthodox conqueror, Louis IX. By an article of that treaty it was provided that for ten years Raymond should pay salaries amounting altogether to 400 marks per annum divided among fourteen professors; there were to be four masters of theology with fifty marks, two decretists with thirty, six artists with twenty,[2] two grammarians with ten. The moment was most auspicious for the success of the new enterprise. The University of Paris had just decreed a dispersion in consequence of the great dispute with the burghers. There was therefore no difficulty about attracting unemployed professors to Toulouse; and Parisian scholars would naturally follow the Parisian masters. The lectures started before the year was out. At least the grammarian, John of Garland, was there by the close of the year;[3] though the chief theological teacher, the Dominican

CHAP. VIII, § 4.

Germ of the university in lectures founded by Honorius III.

The Treaty of Paris, April 1229.

Favoured by the Parisian dispersion.

---

[1] In 1217 Honorius III had written to invite Parisian masters to come to Toulouse to apply themselves 'lectioni, predicationi et exhortationi' (Fournier, i, No. 502). [It should be added that the first house of the Dominican order was at Toulouse, and that S. Dominic set out from there to seek papal confirmation for his order (1215–17). According to the Dominican scholar and historian, Nicholas Trivet (*Annales*, edit. T. Hog, London, 1845, p. 224), Alexander of Stavensby, later bishop of Coventry and Lichfield, was *lector* in theology at Toulouse—'cum aliquando Tholose in theologia regeret'. As Alexander was in Rome at the latest by 1223 and returned to Eng-

land in 1224, he must have taught in the earliest days of the order at Toulouse, just as another secular, Robert Grosseteste, taught in the Franciscan priory at Oxford. In fact, he was probably one of the theologians of Paris invited by Honorius III in 1217. See, for Alexander, M. Gibbs and E. Lang, *Bishops and Reform*, Oxford, 1934, pp. 29, 30, where, however, his teaching in Toulouse is dated earlier.]

[2] Fournier, i, No. 505. [Teulet, *Layettes de Trésor des Chartes*, ii, No. 1992, p. 147.]

[3] [See Paetow's introduction to his edition of John of Garland's *Morale Scolarium* (Berkeley, California, 1927), pp. 89–92. Rashdall's

CHAP. VIII,
§ 4.
The
circular
pro-
gramme. Roland of Cremona, did not arrive till the next.[1] Soon after the opening of the schools a sort of prospectus or advertisement of the university written, probably by John of Garland, in the name of the masters and scholars of Toulouse, and addressed to their scholastic brethren throughout Europe, describes in glowing terms the advantages offered by the new institution.[2] It is a noteworthy indication of the spirit which governed the educational policy of the Popes that, so far from any attempt being made to suppress the new Aristotelian science, it is specially mentioned as one of the attractions of the *studium*, that the works of Natural Philosophy (which had been forbidden at Paris) were to be taught freely at Toulouse.[3] It was the teachers rather than the books that had been suspected at Paris. Dominican influences were paramount in the establishment of the schools of Toulouse; and the policy of the order was to direct education, not to suppress it. They believed in reason, though in reason supplemented by force. John of Garland[4]

remark, in the first edition, that John was 'afterwards one of Roger Bacon's instructors in Paris' was due to a misunderstanding of a passage in the *Opera inedita* (i. 453) which refers to a meeting in Paris about 1245 (Paetow, p. 95). On the other hand it is probable that John of London, the master who taught John of Garland at Oxford, was also Bacon's teacher (*ibid.*, p. 84).]

[1] Denifle, i. 327; see above, vol. i, p. 377, n. 1. John of Garland has left a poem, *De triumphis ecclesiae* (ed. Wright, London, 1856, pp. 92–105), in which the establishment and decay of the university are vividly described. As authorities for the subsequent narrative, I may refer generally to this poem, to the ghastly account of the suppression of heresy in Toulouse during these years in the *Chronicon* by one of the Toulouse Dominicans, Guillelmus Pelissus (ed. Molinier, Anicii [Puy], 1880), and to the accounts derived

mainly from these authorities by M. Gatien-Arnoult and Denifle.

[2] [Inserted at the end of the fifth book of the *De triumphis* (ed. Wright, pp. 96–8, and reprinted by Fournier, i, No. 504, and in the *Chartul. Univ. Paris.* i, No. 72). No other copy has been found, and Paetow regards the document as a 'rhetorical exercise', written by John of Garland himself, and not as a manifesto which was actually circulated; *op. cit.*, pp. 90–1.]

[3] 'Libros naturales, qui fuerant Parisiis prohibiti, potuerunt illic audire qui volunt nature sinum medullitus perscrutari.' It is not quite certain, as is assumed by M. Gatien-Arnoult, that the prohibition was still in force at Paris. See above, vol. i, p. 357. Though nothing has been said in the treaty about the teaching of music, one of the attractions held forth is that 'organiste populares aures melliti gutturis organo demulcent'.

[4] *Loc. cit.*, p. 92.

has neatly expressed the attitude of the Dominican inquisitor-
doctor in the line:

> Pravos extirpat et doctor et ignis et ensis.

I have dwelt on the constitutional importance of the foundation of Toulouse by papal Bull. The issue of a formal Bull of
erection was, however, a mere after-thought. Originally the Failure of
the first
founda-
tion.
schools set up in Toulouse by the papal legate differed in no
respect from the schools established by voluntary migrations
from the old *studia generalia* at Padua or Vercelli, at Orleans
or Cambridge, except in the fact that their teachers were
salaried. At first the schools were no doubt more or less filled
by some of the voluntary exiles from Paris; but, as soon as the
troubles at Paris were at an end, the old university naturally
asserted its superior prestige; and then difficulties of a different kind arose at Toulouse. The count would not pay the
stipulated salaries: the consuls of Toulouse, in spite of the
crusade, retained sufficient spirit to offer a scarcely veiled
resistance to the wholesale burnings of the Dominican in-
quisitors; and the university, in which the Dominican doctors
occupied so prominent a position, was naturally involved in
the dispute. The *studium* gradually melted away.[1] The issue
of a charter bestowing on the masters and scholars of Toulouse all the privileges enjoyed by their brethren of Paris,
and artificially ensuring for the Toulouse promotions the
prestige which had been gradually and spontaneously accorded to those of the great self-developed *studia generalia*,
was one of the expedients adopted by the Pope to secure the
success of his scheme for extinguishing the remains of the
great spiritual rebellion which, though damped, was still
smouldering in the capital of Languedoc. The Bull[2] con- Papal Bull
conferring
ius ubique
docendi,
1233.
ferring on the graduates of Toulouse the *ius ubique docendi*,[3]
the dispensation from residence, the right to have rents taxed

---

[1] 'Florentis studii paulatim turba
    recedit;
  Haec ego qui scribo cuncta
    recedo prius.'
      (*De triumphis*, p. 105.)
[2] Fournier, i, No. 506. Yet from
the first the *studium* was to be

a 'studium solemne', i.e. *generale*
(*De triumphis*, p. 92).
  [3] 'Ut quicumque magister ibi
examinatus et approbatus fuerit in
qualibet facultate, ubique sine alia
examinacione regendi liberam habeat potestatem.'

CHAP. VIII,
§ 4.

Second
collapse.

by a joint board of clerks and laymen, the immunity from the secular courts, and in general all the privileges enjoyed by the masters of Paris was issued in 1233. At first, however, the expedient failed to produce the desired effect; for in 1235 the consuls waxed bold enough to expel the most prominent Dominicans, and the salaries were still unpaid.

Revival,
1239.

Excommunication at length reduced the count to obedience. In 1236 the black terror was re-established, and the fires were rekindled in Toulouse. By 1239 we learn that the salaries had been duly paid: the opposition of the consuls was suppressed;[1] and a further and more ample charter of privilege conferring in detail all the liberties and privileges recently bestowed upon Paris was issued by Innocent IV in 1245.[2] By this Bull it was directed that the *scholasticus* of the cathedral, who from the first had no doubt presided over the promotions, should be called chancellor.

Bull of
1245.

Theo-
logical
faculty,
1360.

From the letter to the scholars of Christendom it appears that all the faculties were represented at Toulouse from its earliest days: Toulouse was one of the very few universities wherein this was the case. In the faculty of theology, however, a peculiar sanctity still attached to the degrees of Paris; and the permission to create doctors of theology, though apparently involved in the terms of the Bulls granted by Gregory IX and Innocent IV, was rarely if ever acted upon. At all events in 1335 we find Benedict XII addressing a Bull

[1] Pelissus, p. 31 *sq.*; Fournier, i, Nos. 510–16. The university was clearly in working order in 1243, since a college was founded in that year. See below, p. 172. We hear nothing of any salaries in later times, but it is clear that the ordinary chairs were limited in number. In 1441 we find a doctor selling his place and 'auditorium' to a successor, whom he undertakes to present to the university for the appointment (Fournier, i, No. 821). In 1470 the Parlement of Toulouse declared that 'les recteur et docteurs régens de la dicte Université vendoient communément et ont

vendu et délivré au plus offrant et dernier enchérisseur les chaires et régences des ditz facultés . . . et comme choses estans au commerce des hommes' (*ibid.*, No. 858), and forbade the practice.

[2] *Hist. de Lang.* viii, c. 1184; Fournier, i, No. 523. [Berger, *Registres d'Innocent IV*, i. 230 b. This is an enactment for Toulouse of Gregory IX's Bull *Parens scientiarum*. It may be doubted if all the provisions were pertinent to Toulouse. For example, the chancellor is not otherwise found before the third quarter of the century.]

to the chancellor in which a recent graduation in theology at Toulouse is treated as an unauthorized usurpation and the practice forbidden for the future.[1] In 1360, however, the university petitioned Innocent VI, himself an *alumnus* of Toulouse, for the express authorization of graduations in theology. One of the grounds alleged in support of the petition is interesting to the English reader; it is noticed that in England, though a smaller country than France, there were two *studia generalia* in theology.[2] Oxford and Cambridge had been, indeed, till very recently the only universities in the world besides Paris ·hat possessed faculties of theology with an unquestioned right of promotion. The earlier policy of the Popes had been to respect the Parisian monopoly. It was the Toulouse Pope, Innocent VI, who first infringed this monopoly by issuing a Bull, authorizing the conferment of theological degrees at Toulouse, in 1360;[3] and a regular theological faculty was henceforth organized: but theology still continued practically in the hands of the regular orders. Throughout the Schism Toulouse, the child of the Papacy, showed herself worthy of her parentage and justified her foundation by steady devotion to the curialist cause and sturdy resistance to the Gallicanism of Paris and the other universities.[4] The university was, however, mainly, like all the universities of France, except Paris and the medical school of Montpellier, a university of law. As such it occupied in the south of France, especially after the decline of the law faculty of Montpellier in the middle of the thirteenth century, the position which was occupied by Orleans in the north. In southern Europe generally it was for legal education— the indispensable qualification of the growing profession of

Prominence of law.

[1] *Chartul. Univ. Paris.* ii, Nos. 993, 994; Fournier, iii, Nos. 1902, 1903.

[2] 'In regno Anglie, quod modica insula respectu regni Francie existit, duo sunt generalia studia in facultate predicta' (Fournier, i, No. 640).

[3] *Hist. de Languedoc*, vii, notes c. 551; Fournier, i, No. 641. This Bull makes it plain that there was

a regular and organized teaching faculty of theology in the town already. Degrees in theology were sometimes conferred at an earlier date by special papal Bull (Fournier, i, Nos. 605, 606).

[4] Bulaeus, iv. 755; v. 4 *sq.*, 120 *sq.* Cf. Fournier, i, No. 760, note. See also an art. by Astre in *Mém de l'Ac. des Sciences de T.*, 1869.

secular lawyers as well as the safest road to preferment in the Church—that the demand was keenest. The institution of the Parlement of Languedoc in 1273[1] no doubt gave an impulse to the legal studies of the university and accounts for the prosperity which soon after this period began for the first time to attend the university. In many of the French provincial capitals we shall find the establishment of a university looked upon as the natural sequel to the establishment of a Parlement. At this time Toulouse produced several jurists of considerable political and historical and even some scientific importance. According to some writers, these included the three advocates whom Philip IV chose to plead his cause against the bishop of Pamiers, that is to say, in reality against the Pope himself, at the court of Boniface VIII—Pierre Flotte, Guillaume de Nogaret, Pierre de Belleperche.[2] The university, in spite of its papal origin, gave in its adhesion to the king's appeal to a general council.[3] It was the French schools of civil law which formed the great jurists and judges to whose political theories and judicial activity the French monarchy and the French state owed so much in their struggles against ecclesiastical domination; and among these schools Toulouse was second in importance only perhaps to Orleans.

Constitu-
tion. The constitution of Toulouse exhibits an attempt to combine some features of the Parisian constitution with the recognition in a very attenuated form of student-rights in the jurist faculty only: like the Solonian constitution approved by Aristotle, it allowed to the democratic element τὴν ἀναγκαιοτάτην δύναμιν. The general congregation would appear to be composed of the students in law and the pro-

---

[1] Rodière, *Recueil*, ix. 253. The Roman law prevailed in all dominions of the counts of Toulouse. It may be more than a coincidence that Accursius taught in Toulouse in this very year (*ibid.*, p. 254).

[2] See Gatien-Arnoult, *Mém. de l'Ac. des Sci. de T.*, 1881, p. 2 *sq.* [In spite of much investigation, the early careers of these men are still obscure. Pierre Flotte came from the Auvergne and studied at Montpellier, if not at Toulouse. Nogaret was a teacher of law at Montpellier and came from the neighbourhood of Toulouse. Pierre de Belleperche was one of the glories of Orleans (cf. above, p. 143, n.).]

[3] Fournier, i, No. 537.

fessors of all faculties—including the *lectores* in theology
(whether doctors or not) and the masters of grammar.[1] The
rector must be a master, but is elected by the students:[2] he
is taken from each of the four faculties in turn, and in practice
is chosen by rotation in order of seniority. The students
formally enact the statutes, but their direct share in the
government is an almost nominal one. The ordinary administration of the university is in the hands of a body composed
of the rector and the *consiliarii* or (as they were sometimes
styled) proctors. The *consiliarii* are chosen by the students,
but four are to be masters (one in each faculty);[3] two are
bachelors of law and only two simple students in the last-
named faculty. To these elected councillors one was added
by the bishop and one by the chancellor, while the whole of
the *lectores* in theology (whether doctors or not) sat with
them.[4] This body was known as the *concilium rectoris*.

In 1313 this constitution was modified by the admission of

[1] The statutes of 1311, 1313,
and 1314 are given in *Histoire de
Languedoc*, vii, notes, c. 447 sq.,
c. 462 sq., c. 478 sq.; and in Fournier,
i, Nos. 543, 544, 545. Canon law
and civil law count as separate
faculties. Grammar is always
treated as a distinct faculty,
though scholars of the faculty were
often children under ten. At the
latter age they were required to
swear obedience to the rector. In
1311 there was evidently no regular faculty of medicine. 'Medici'
seem contemplated in 1314.

[2] 'De concilio et assensu magistrorum in theologia, vel ipsis non
existentibus, de concilio et assensu
lectorum et doctorum, magistrorum
et procuratorum, bacalariorum et
scolarium vel majoris partis eorum-
dem' (Stat. of 1313, c. 5). The
exact effect of this statute is doubtful, but the share of the students
was probably meant to be nominal.
It is not clear whether students of
logic and grammar had votes—
probably not. Nor do the artists
appear to have had any congrega-

tions of their own. In 1480 the
scholars appoint a syndic to take
legal proceedings against the regents (Fournier, i, No. 860).

[3] i.e. canon law, civil law, logic,
grammar. There are some earlier
traces of medical study at Toulouse,
but the first document in which
masters of medicine appear in the
university Council is dated 1423
(*ibid.* i, No. 796).

[4] The statutes of 1314 are
enacted by the doctors 'de consilio
et assensu et de voluntate etiam et
assensu totius universitatis studii'.
The statutes of 1311 speak of
consiliarii, those of 1313 of *procuratores*. The doctors (without
the *consiliarii*) had, it appears, the
power of making 'ordinances'
about lectures and other small
matters. In 1470 the Parlement
ordered that the two bachelor-
councillors should be collegiate
students, the other two non-
collegiate, and should be elected by
the regents (*ibid.* i, No. 858). It is
quite probable that this had long
been the actual practice.

CHAP.VIII, the doctors and masters of all faculties and of the syndic.
§ 4.   The nominated councillors seem to disappear, but the
bachelors and the students retain their four proctors. It is
doubtful whether after this date the students were ever really
assembled for any purpose except the election of rector and
proctors. Certainly we find statutes enacted by the council
without consulting the students and published in an assembly
to which, besides the council, certain prelates and the priors
of the four principal colleges were summoned: these give
their adhesion to the statutes, but there is no indication of
the students as a body being invited to any effective kind of
co-operation. While within the university the lion's share
of influence[1] decidedly belonged to the masters, the legislative
powers of the university were in the earlier days of the
studium much restricted by the large prerogatives still reserved to the bishop, whose consent was required for all but
the most trivial acts of congregation,[2] and later by the frequent interference of papal legates. The chancellor, too, had
more power than in most universities which possessed a
rector. He presided over the rectorial elections, received an
oath of obedience from candidates for the bachelor's degree,
and conferred that degree himself. Though the elected rector
gradually gained in importance upon the chancellor and became the working head of the university, the latter retained
to the last his right of precedence.[3] Jurisdiction over scholars
was divided between the diocesan (or his official), the apostolical conservator, and the seneschal of Toulouse, who as royal

[1] Fournier, i, Nos. 764, 765, 766.
In No. 779 we find, however, a
large body of bachelors and scholars
'maiorem et saniorem partem Universitatis predicte . . . facientes'
professing to appoint syndics or
legal representatives of the university.
[2] Thus in 1311 the licence of the
bishop is required for any acts of
congregation except the expenditure upon 'lights and other pious
uses' of sums not exceeding sixty
pounds of Tours, while the *inter-
dictio* or 'cessation of lectures',

except 'per modicum tempus', is
also reserved to him or to his
official, though this restriction had
disappeared before 1426. See
ibid. i, No. 800, note.
[3] In 1430, however, they were to
march side by side where possible.
As illustrating the position of the
chancellor, it is interesting to notice
that it is stipulated that he shall be
styled 'Cancellarius Tholosanus' or
'in ecclesia Tholosana', never 'Universitatis Tholosane' (*Hist. de
Lang.* vii, notes, c. 604; Fournier, i,
No. 774).

conservator, occupied much the same position as the provost CHAP. VIII, at Paris.[1] § 4.

A roll presented to Clement VII in 1378 enables us to Numbers. furnish a tolerable estimate of the numbers of the *studium*. It contains, of course, only the names of ecclesiastics, but here these would probably be a large majority. As the mere grammarians are included, whose title to preferment cannot have been great even if we suppose the youngest boys to be excluded, we may take it that the list includes at least the whole body of students who were prepared to take orders if a benefice could be secured. The list contains the names of five regent doctors of theology (all regulars), six of canon law, two of civil law, one of arts and two of grammar, four non-regent doctors, 29 licentiates of various faculties, 154 bachelors of decrees, 62 bachelors of civil law, 401 scholars of decrees, 130 scholars of civil law, 47 bachelors of arts, 246 scholars of arts, and 295 grammarians. The total number of licentiates, bachelors, and scholars was 1,384.[2] In the year 1335 a contemporary chronicler speaks of 3,000 students.[3] By putting the two statements together it is made tolerably clear that the total number of students in the fourteenth century cannot have fallen far short of 1,500 and (allowing for the usual medieval exaggeration) cannot have much exceeded 2,000.[4]

[1] Fournier represents the bishop as 'ceding part of his jurisdiction' to the consuls in 1269 (Nos. 526, 527); but he authorizes nothing but the arrest of scholars for immediate surrender to ecclesiastical custody. This power was usually exercised, even where the rights of the clergy were most respected, without special ecclesiastical approval. It involved no *jurisdiction* over clerks; till a man was arrested it could not be ascertained whether he was a clerk or not. Even the canon law did not require the lay authority to let a criminous clerk taken red-handed run away before their eyes. In 1292 Philippe le Bel had to restrain the capitouls from imprisoning or torturing scholars or flinging them into the Garonne by night. Later there is no doubt about the episcopal jurisdiction over clerks, but there remained much dispute as to the justice of lay scholars which is claimed by the Pope for the archbishop (Fournier, i, Nos. 561, 563 *sq.*; Denifle, *Les Univ. franç.*, p. 63). It will be noted that the *scholasticus* or chancellor had no jurisdiction in the strict sense.

[2] Fournier, i, No. 697.

[3] *Ibid.* i, No. 575.

[4] As Molinier and M. Fournier seem puzzled by the expression *bancarii* or *banquarii* in the Toulouse statutes, it may be well to explain that they are evidently the

In the early days of the university we find Innocent IV giving general directions that poor scholars should be received into the hospitals for poor folk in the outskirts of the city.[1] Toulouse afterwards became peculiarly rich in colleges, some of them of considerable size and endowment. The first, named after its founder, Vidal Gautier of Toulouse, dates from 1243.[2] The Cistercians of Grandselve established a college for their order in 1286.[3] The Collège de Verdale, for two chaplains and ten scholars, was founded in 1337 by Arnaud de Verdale, a doctor of both laws, and afterwards bishop of Maguelone.[4] In 1358 the Toulouse Pope, Innocent VI, richly endowed and privileged the college of S. Martial, which provided for ten civilians, ten canonists, and four chaplains.[5] The other colleges founded before 1500 were: (1) The Collège de Bolbonne (for monks of the abbey of that name), 1286–90; (2) the Collège de Montlezun, founded by the brothers Bertrand and Peter Montlezun in 1319; (3) the Collège de Bérenger, before 1341, by a citizen of that name; (5) the Collège de Narbonne, in 1341, by Galbert, Archbishop of Arles; (5) the Collège de Périgord or de S. Front, founded by Cardinal Talleyrand de Périgord about the year 1360; (6) the Collège de Maguelone, founded by the will of Audouin Aubert, Cardinal Bishop of Ostia in 1363 (for Arts); (7) the Collège de S. Raymond, before 1373, probably much earlier; (8) the Collège de Ste Catherine or de Pampeluna, by Pierre de Montirac, Cardinal of Pampeluna about 1378; (9) the Collège de Mirepoix, by a bishop of that see, in 1415; (10) the Collège de Foix in 1440 by the Cardinal de Foix.[6]

private bedels of the doctors, probably so-called from their looking after the benches (*banchi*) of the schools. [See Fournier, ii, p. 60.]

[1] *Hist. de Languedoc*, viii, c. 1188; Fournier, i, No. 520.

[2] *Hist. de Languedoc*, viii, c. 1110; Fournier, i, No. 517.

[3] *Ibid.* i, No. 529.

[4] *Ibid.* i, Nos. 593, 597.

[5] *Ibid.*, Nos. 613–22, 624–39, &c.

[6] The names and dates are collected from the documents in Four-

nier. Besides these, there were many hospitals and churches which maintained scholars (*ibid.* i, No. 640). A College 'de l'Estude' is mentioned in 1406 (*ibid.* iii, No. 1913). For indications of college teaching see a document of 1486 (*ibid.*, No. 866). Most of these colleges lasted till the Revolution. Part of the Collège de Foix now forms the Convent of the Compassion; a description and picture may be seen in *Mém. de l'Acad. de*

These colleges were of an even more distinctly ecclesiastical CHAP. VIII, type than those of Paris. Most of them were under the §4. government not of a single head but of two chaplains. At the College of St. Martial, where there were four chaplains, two of them served as 'priors' in alternate years. It is interesting to notice, however, that the dual control was not a success and was abandoned at this college in 1380.[1] A similar change is shown in all later college statutes at Toulouse. The colleges of Toulouse seem to have been peculiarly well endowed, and we hear complaints that their bursaries were enjoyed by rich and well-beneficed persons.[2] As an interesting anticipation of a later mode of scholastic encouragement, it may be noticed that the town of Albi frequently made grants to enable poor students to study at Toulouse.[3]

§ 5. AVIGNON (1303)

The chief special authority is LAVAL, *Cartulaire de l'Université d'Avignon* (*1303–1791*), i, Avignon, 1884; but this small collection of documents is largely supplemented by Fournier. Laval has also written an *Histoire de la Faculté de Médecine d'Avignon*, Avignon, 1884, which is chiefly on the post-medieval period. There is also a slight dissertation by ÉCOIFFIER, *Recherches historiques sur la Faculté de Médecine d'Avignon*, Montpellier,

T. for 1885. The Collège de Périgord is now the Diocesan Seminary (*ibid.*, 1886). There is no reason with Fournier (i, No. 530) to assume that there was a 'Collège de Moissac' because certain monks were sent from that abbey to study at Toulouse. There is no actual documentary evidence of a 'Collège de Bolbonne', though Fournier (*ibid.*, No. 531) says there is no doubt of its existence. The Collège Bérenger (*ibid.*, No. 594) was very probably founded by one of the capitouls condemned for the affair of Aimery Bérenger in 1331. See below, chap. xiv. One of the capitouls bore the same name as the victim.

[1] Fournier, i, Nos. 617, 700. There was, from the first, a proviso that the college may elect others as priors. At the Colleges of Verdale and Narbonne the two chaplains

are perpetual *gubernatores* or *provisores* (*ibid.*, Nos. 593, 595).

[2] An elaborate account of the revenues of these colleges is given in the pleadings of the City of Toulouse against their claims to exemption from contributions in respect of their houses and estates, the repair of the walls, and other civil purposes in *circa* 1406. It is alleged that they are often filled by 'plusieurs hommes grandement bénéficiés qui des revenues de bénéffices, et les autres des biens de leurs parens et amys, se pourroyent bien soutenir et nourrir oudit estude' (*ibid.* iii, No. 1913, p. 588). It is also alleged that 'les escolliers desdiz collèges, quant il leur plaist, se marient et sont gens lais'.

[3] Jolibois, *Inventaire des Archives municipales d'Albi*, Pref. p. 53 (cited by Fournier, *Hist.* iii. 276).

1877. To these may be added BARDINET's academic dissertation, *Universitatis Avenionensis historica adumbratio*, Limoges, 1880, and FOURNIER, 'Une corporation d'étudiants à Avignon en 1441' (*Nouvelle Rev. hist. de droit. franç.*, 1887).

[J. MARCHAND, *La Faculté des arts de l'université d'Avignon; notice historique, accompagnée des statuts inédits de cette faculté*, 59 pages, Paris, 1897.]

An ancient school of law. A SCHOOL of law existed at Avignon before its erection into a *studium generale*.[1] There were apparently doctors of law teaching here in 1263.[2] In 1298 Charles II, King of Naples and Count of Provence, issued an edict taking the scholars of Avignon under his special protection, and ordaining that in future 'the students and readers as well in decrees as in laws shall be declared and licensed' by the prince's chancellor of Provence or his deputies.[3] It is difficult to decide from this somewhat ambiguous document whether it was proposed that graduations in law should take place by virtue of it alone and without any further papal or imperial authority. If such was his intention, he was no doubt imitating the constitution of his predecessor's university at Naples, which was likewise under the government of the royal chancellor.[4] But at all events there is no claim to the *ius ubique docendi*, and no evidence that any promotions ever actually took place. It is, however, clear that a 'university of doctors and scholars' was organized before the year 1302,[5] when the same count confers further privileges upon the university, and in particular accedes to their request to be allowed to elect

[1] Fournier (*Hist.* iii. 572; *Statuts*, ii, No. 1236) mentions the provision made in 1227 by the cardinal legate Romanus for the teaching of theology at Avignon (as at Toulouse, above, p. 166), and the support of twelve poor scholars, but nothing may have been done in the execution of this provision: there is no trace of a *studium generale*, nor did it have any influence upon the eventual development of a university.

[2] *Ibid.* ii, No. 1239.

[3] *Ibid.*, No. 1241. This document was unknown to Denifle. A document of 1297 (*ibid.*, No. 1240)

shows almost certainly that there was no university in the place—at least no medical faculty—since the examination of *medici* was entrusted to the 'Officiales civitatis'.

[4] See above, p. 25.

[5] When Fournier (*Hist.* iii. 577, 603) objects to Denifle treating Avignon as a university founded by papal Bull, he seems to forget that a *universitas* does not necessarily make a *studium generale*. There is no evidence that the *studium* at Avignon was regarded as, or even pretended to be, general before the Bull.

a 'merchant' (or banker) from whom they might borrow CHAP. VIII,
money in spite of a recent edict against usury.[1] We know, § 5.
however, little or nothing as to the organization of the Bull of
Boniface
studium until its erection into a *studium generale* by a Bull of VIII,
1303.
Boniface VIII[2] in 1303, with a charter of privilege from the
count.[3]

As in all the older universities of this group, the authority Constitu-
of the bishop over the *studium* was originally supreme. Under tion.
the bishop, the doctors possessed the chief power. The first
statutes were issued by Bishop Bertrand Aymin in 1303[4] 'by
the advice and assent of the doctors'; and by these statutes
the doctors were authorized annually to elect a *primicerius*[5]
as the immediate head of the university, whose office, though
less important, was closely parallel to the chancellorship of
the Montpellier university of medicine. The title was no
doubt borrowed from that of an official who in some cathedrals discharged the functions of a chancellor. The bishop
reserved to himself the conferment of the licence, and at first
the appointment of the ordinary doctors, who formed a college which practically monopolized the government of the
studium. Eventually, however, this body seems to have co-
opted its own members.[6] The university long remained

---

[1] 'Universitas hominum civitatis Avenionensis, cetusque doctorum studii venerabilis ibidem ... ostenso quod doctoribus et scholaribus, ipsis presertim exteris et remotis ibi studentibus . . . inedia et defectus frequenter emergunt ... suppliciter postulaverunt.' Fournier, ii, No. 1242.

[2] *Cartulaire*, p. 1; Fournier, ii, No. 1244.

[3] *Cartulaire*, p. 9; Fournier, ii, No. 1243.

[4] *Ibid.*, No. 1245.

[5] The title, which appears as a university office only here, and (later) at Aix and at Valence, is a very ancient one. We hear of a 'Primicerius Scholae Forensium Civitatis Ravennatis' (Marini, *Papiri*, No. 110). There is a title

in the Decretals of Gregory IX (lib. I, tit. xxv, c. 1), *de officio Primicerii*, from which it appears that in some churches the *primicerius* performed the duties of chancellor or *magister scolarum*: while the *primicerius* of the *scola cantorum* at Rome appears in a deed of 949, printed in *Il regesto Sublacense* (ed. Allodi and Levi, Rome, 1885), docs. 112, 113, and in a decretal of Alexander III (Sarti, I, i, p. xvii).

[6] The claim is made in the stat-utes framed by the *primicerius* and college in 1376 (Fournier, ii, No. 1256). In 1439 the bishop is ex-pressly styled chancellor (*ibid.*, No. 1326). It is clearly a mistake to say (writes Fournier) that 'la remise des *insignia doctoralia* . . . les

CHAP. VIII,
§ 5.

almost exclusively a university of law. The statutes of 1303 mention doctors of medicine and arts, though it is very doubtful whether the first of these faculties had any substantive and continuous existence[1] till the time of Innocent VIII, and the faculty of arts probably existed chiefly in the form of grammar schools. A faculty of theology was created by John XXIII in 1413.

Student-right movements.

As at Angers and Orleans in the second half of the fourteenth century the students of Avignon are found in rebellion and asserting their right to elect a rector and to participate in the government of the *studium*, like their more favoured brethren south of the Alps. But at Avignon, where ecclesiastical influence was supreme,[2] the democratic movement met with a very different fate. Urban V in 1367 and Gregory XI in 1376[3] issued Bulls against these rebellious students who wanted to have a rector, in which they uncompromisingly maintained the rights of the *primicerius* and the doctors. In

faisait docteurs et membres du *collegium doctorum*' (*Hist.* iii. 613). This may have been so at first when the college was open to all resident doctors, but when it became (if it was not always) a close corporation, there must have been doctors outside it, and the tradition of *insignia* was here as elsewhere part of the ceremony of taking the doctor's degree. See the doctoral diplomas in Fournier, *passim*.

[1] We hear of doctors of medicine in 1371 and of artists in the roll of 1394; but in 1458 the university petitions the Pope for a faculty of medicine and arts (Fournier, ii, Nos. 1254, 1270, 1357). For the result see below, p. 177; but in 1491 we again hear 'quod nulli erant regentes in medicina' (Laval, *Fac. de Méd.*, p. 29). In this year the faculty made a real beginning. Its previous failure was perhaps due to the large number of Jewish practitioners in the place (*ibid.*, p. 8).

[2] It is instructive to contrast the fate of the student-movement at Avignon with that of the similar movement at Angers. The triumph of the students was there secured by the lay judges of the Parlement, themselves very probably educated in law-universities: the *scholasticus* did his best to get the case transferred to the ecclesiastical courts. Rangeard, i. 379; above, p. 157.

[3] *Cartulaire*, pp. 18, 24; Fournier, ii, Nos. 1249, 1257. The first Bull recites: 'Cum . . . inter dilectos filios doctores et scolares studii Avinionensis ex eo questio sit exorta quod doctores per unum ex eis primicerium appellatum, secundum antiquam consuetudinem dicti studii, scolares vero prefati per unum ex ipsis appellandum rectorem et per ipsos eligendum, sicut fit in nonnullis aliis studiis, asserunt debere regi studium prelibatum; nos . . . mandamus quathenus antiquam consuetudinem dicti studii super hoc facias inviolabiliter observari.' The old constitution is still upheld in the statutes issued by the bishop with the consent of the doctors in 1407. Fournier, ii, No. 1279.

1393 the students were again in rebellion, and bound themselves by an oath not to go to the schools of the reigning doctoral oligarchy until their demands were granted. Again, it would seem, the rebellion was crushed, since we find two cardinal legates dispensing the scholars from the obligation of their contumacious oath.[1] It was not till 1459 that the students at last obtained from Pius II some scant recognition of what were everywhere else in southern Europe regarded as the natural and indefeasible rights of the civilians and canonists. And then the partial success of the students (if such it was) would seem to have been largely due to the *hauteur* with which the proud doctors of law had given the cold shoulder not only to the doctors of the inferior faculties of medicine and arts but even to their rightful superiors, the doctors of theology. The pontiff had heard with indignation that 'lay polygamous jurists' had presumed to take precedence of masters of theology, and to monopolize for themselves and the *primicerius* the whole authority in the university. These pretensions are peremptorily rejected. It is declared that all the four faculties shall form a single university. The office of *primicerius* is abolished and the university placed under the immediate headship of the bishop as chancellor. Under the bishop there is to be a rector elected by the council of the university, to which all academical power—except the elective vote—is to be entrusted. The rector is himself to be at least a master of arts or a bachelor in any other faculty, and is to be chosen from the faculties in rotation. The council consists of all the regents, together with representatives of each faculty, of whom one is to be a non-regent doctor, one a licentiate, one a bachelor, and two 'nobles or other scholars'. The constitution was thus a somewhat less democratic reproduction of that of Orleans or Angers, the faculties being here, moreover, substituted for the nations. The number of regents who were apparently to be salaried is henceforth fixed at fourteen—five

[1] *Cartulaire*, p. 32; Fournier, ii, No. 1268. It is amusing to notice that the oath included the obligation 'minime per vos vel alium directe vel indirecte relaxationem, vel super illis dispensationem, vel absolutionem peteretis'. But alas! it was as easy to get dispensed from the anti-dispensation clause as from any other.

in theology (at least four of them Mendicants), two in decrees, three in decretals, three in civil law, two in medicine, and four in arts.[1] It is, however, extremely doubtful whether this Bull ever obtained any real execution at Avignon. Long after its date, we still hear of the *primicerius*. It seems probable that the constitution of the university remained entirely unaltered.[2]

Fluctuations of prosperity.   In spite of the want of student-liberties, and (what is perhaps more remarkable) in spite of the absence of *salaria*,[3] the University of Avignon became a very prosperous *studium* towards the end of the fourteenth century, after it had recovered from the desolation wrought in Avignon by the plague of 1361.[4] In the days of the Avignon Papacy the students of Avignon naturally had advantages in connexion with their benefice-roll which were not enjoyed by students of more distant universities; and it is not surprising to find that Avignon was particularly popular with aristocratic students. A benefice-roll of 1394 contains the names of eighteen doctors of one or both laws, forty nobles, fifty-three licentiates and 359 bachelors of law, 467 students in law, and 127 artists and grammarians.[5] At this time the professors were entirely supported by their fees, which their supremacy in the academic constitution enabled them to fix at a somewhat high rate.

Removal of papal court.   After the removal of the papal court from Avignon the university gradually declined. In 1478 we are told that the *studium* had been emptied by the refusal of the doctors to lecture without salaries, which the city declined to give. Its continued existence and even some revival of prosperity were, however, secured partly by a succession of munificent college-builders and still more by the papal patronage which the connexion of Avignon with the see of S. Peter enabled it to

[1] *Cartulaire*, pp. 91–103; Fournier, ii, No. 1362. (The total is given as 18.)

[2] See *Cartulaire*, pp. 105, 109, 141, and Fournier (*Hist.* iii. 593, note), who cites the *Liber Computorum Universitatis* for 1463 relating to payments for the mission to Rome 'tempore quo agebatur de suppressione primiceriatus officii dicte universitatis et nova creatione rectoris in eadem'.

[3] Fournier, iii, No. 1950.

[4] Denifle, i. 361; Fournier, ii, No. 1248.

[5] *Ibid.*, No. 1270.

secure. Its greatest patron was the Cardinal Giuliano della
Rovere, nephew of Sixtus IV, and afterwards Pope as Julius
II, who became bishop of Avignon in 1474, in the following
year archbishop of the same see, and in 1476 papal legate.[1]
Through his influence Sixtus IV was induced to bestow, in
addition to a peculiarly bounteous shower of privileges, an
annual grant of 600 ducats for the payment of eight doctors
of law. The payment was at first, in 1475, charged upon the
papal taxes and court-dues of the city.[2] Shortly afterwards,
however, a new and very curious expedient was adopted. The
Pope annexed to the university certain secular courts in the
surrounding district, and authorized it to appoint the judges
and appropriate to itself the resultant fees and fines.[3] Sixtus
IV also bestowed upon the Collège du Roure the papal
library at Avignon.[4]

The jurisdiction over scholars was, it would appear, less Jurisdiction.
wholly reserved to the ecclesiastical courts than might have
been expected in so ecclesiastical a city. The clerical scholars
at least must, of course, have been subject to the bishop's court
in criminal and personal suits; but we find no special exemption in favour of scholars as such from the tribunals of the
city magistrates. Conservators apostolic were not appointed
till 1413.[5]

In 1379 a College of S. Martial (or rather a college- Colleges.
monastery for twelve choir-brethren and twelve students)
was founded for monks of Cluny;[6] the College of Annecy by

---

[1] Fournier, iii, No. 1950. In this
year the city resolved to invite extraneous doctors to lecture without
salary.

[2] *Cartulaire*, p. 109; Fournier, ii,
No. 1366.

[3] *Cartulaire*, p. 119; Fournier,
ii, No. 1378. From the frequent
confirmations, it is clear that the
measure encountered opposition.

[4] *Ibid.*, No. 1383. [Cf. L. H.
Labande, 'Les Manuscrits de la
bibliothèque d'Avignon provenant
de la librairie des papes du XIVᵉ
siècle', in *Bulletin historique*, 1894,
145–60.]

[5] Fournier, ii, Nos. 1281, 1283,
1289 (*Cartulaire*, p. 50); *Hist.* iii.
641. Fournier is certainly wrong in
supposing (as he seems to do) that
the *conservatorium* of 1413 conveyed a general jurisdiction over
students. The conservators apostolic, here as at Paris (above, vol. i,
pp. 342, 418) and elsewhere, only
punished breaches of university
privilege and heard causes which
but for the *ius non trahi extra* would
be heard at a distance from the
place.

[6] Fournier, ii, Nos. 1260–4.

Cardinal de Brogny in 1424;[1] the College of S. Michel by Jean Isnard, doctor of laws, in 1453.[2] In 1471 the Orphanage of Jujon was made into a college—known as the College of Jujon or Dijon—for the Abbey of Montmajour.[3] In 1476 the College of S. Pierre or du Roure was founded for thirty-six students in law by the Cardinal Giuliano della Rovere, Archbishop of Avignon, already mentioned as a great patron and restorer of the university;[4] in 1491–4 the College of Notre-Dame de la Pitié[5] by the Dominican Barthélemy de Riquetis, doctor of theology (this was really two distinct colleges, one for twelve secular priests, the other for twenty-four Dominican novices); in 1496 the College of Senanque or S. Bernard by Jean Cazaleti, Abbot of Senanque, for Cistercian monks;[6] and in 1500 the Collège de la Croix by Guillaume Ricci.

The Confraternity of S. Sebastian. But perhaps the most interesting institution connected with this university remains to be mentioned. The statutes of many universities contain allusions to student-clubs or societies of various kinds for the purpose of electing a captain or abbot or chancellor of their own. Wherever the masters were in power these confederations, whether permanent or temporary, were put down with a strong hand. In other cases, as we have seen, the university was itself a student-club or embraced within it national organizations composed of students. Avignon is the only instance in which we have before us the statutes of a student-club which was recognized as a lawful society by the authorities, but yet formed no part of the official organization of the university. It would seem that the students, baulked in their efforts to elect a rector and get the government of the *studium* into their own hands like the students of other law-universities, had formed an independent society of their own which eventually secured for itself a cer-

---

[1] Fournier, ii, No. 1295 *sq.* [A number of documents relating to the foundation of this college, also known as the 'Magnum Collegium Sabaudiae', will be found in a volume, partly printed, partly in manuscript, relating to a lawsuit at Rome in 1646–8. This collection is now in the Bodleian Library.]

[2] *Ibid.*, Nos. 1349, 1351, 1354, 1355.

[3] *Ibid.*, Nos. 1364, 1365.

[4] *Ibid.*, Nos. 1368, 1372, note.

[5] *Ibid.*, No. 1399.

[6] *Ibid.*, No. 1409.

tain legal authority and privilege. In 1441 over 200 students of Avignon (probably at this time the whole body of law-students or nearly so) formed themselves into a Guild or Con-fraternity of S. Sebastian for the promotion of exactly the same religious and social ends which were aimed at by other confraternities—the peaceable adjustment of quarrels, the promotion of mutual harmony and good fellowship, the cele-bration of a weekly mass, the care of sick members and the performance of funeral rites. The confraternity was governed by a prior and twelve councillors. Membership of the guild was nominally a matter of voluntary consent, though the statutes provide for practical compulsion in the shape of organized bullying or 'boycotting': the well-known work-man's device of hiding an offending comrade's tools here assumed the form of 'subtracting' his books. It is curious to find Popes and legates giving their solemn sanction to a society which enforced its decrees by acts of private robbery. Though never forming part of the university organization, the prior and council were treated by the university authori-ties as the recognized representatives of the students. As such we find them negotiating on equal terms with the *primicerius* and doctors, while their prior receives papal privileges and acts as visitor of an important college.[1]

There was another and very similar institution at Avignon to which it would be difficult to find an exact parallel in any other university—a guild or 'confraternity' of doctors to which all new doctors were required to belong, though it appears it might also be joined by scholars, and its benefits, if not its membership, extended also to the doctors' wives. As to what those benefits were we have no information except that they included the attendance of the officers of the con-fraternity with torches at their funerals.[2]

Confra-ternity of doctors.

---

[1] See the statute and other docu-ments in Fournier, *Une corp. d'étu-diants &c.*, afterwards reprinted in his *Statuts*, ii, Nos. 1332, 1344, 1345, 1363, 1380, 1382, 1411. As to the somewhat similar but less formal society, in the College of Annecy, see below, vol. iii, p. 383.

[2] 'Tenebuntur dicti baiuli cum brandonis dicte confratrie associare funus ipsius defuncti ad ecclesiasti-cam sepulturam.' Fournier, ii, No. 1342 (*c.* 1450–80).

§ 6. CAHORS (1332)

CHAP. VIII, CRUCIUS (La Croix), *Acta et series episcoporum Cadurcensium*, Cahors,
§ 6.   1617. *Statuta Academiae Cadurcensis*, Toulouse (no date). M.-J. BAUDEL,
Discours prononcé à la distribution des prix du Lycée de Cahors (no date or
place); and *Notice historique sur l'Université de Cahors*, Cahors, 1876.
M.-J. BAUDEL and J. MALINOWSKI, *Histoire de l'Université de Cahors*,
Cahors, 1876. The last is the only important work and reprints the
statutes, but as a collection of documents it is superseded by Fournier.
Cf. LACOSTE, *Hist. Gén. de la Province de Quercy*, Cahors, 1833–5.

Founda-
tion, 1332.
THE University of Cahors was erected on the basis of an old
cathedral school, where licences had from an early period
been granted more or less after the manner of regular graduations, though without the *ius ubique docendi*, by the *scholasticus*
of the cathedral.[1] The Bull of foundation was granted by
John XXII, who was a native of Cahors, in 1332, on the
petition of the consuls of the city.[2] Among other Bulls afterwards conferred by the same pontiff was an almost verbal
reproduction of the celebrated *Parens Scientiarum* of Paris.[3]
The constitution given to the university was that of the
neighbouring University of Toulouse.[4] Professorial chairs
or *regentiae* were filled up at first by the chancellor alone,
afterwards by the chancellor, rector, and regents.[5]

[1] 'Quodque, sicut accepimus di-
lectus filius Petrus Andree qui nunc
est scholasticus ipsius Ecclesie
Caturcensis et eius predecessores
scholastici eiusdem Ecclesie qui
fuerunt pro tempore consueverunt
hactenus in Civitate Caturcensi
scolas conferre, et ibi legere volen-
tibus legendi, licentiam impartiri,
bidellos creare,' &c. (Fournier, ii,
No. 1424). This Bull, like its Parisian prototype, gave the power of
imprisoning scholars to the bishop
only, but appears to recognize the
chancellor's spiritual jurisdiction.

[2] Fournier, ii, No. 1422. A later
Bull (*ibid.*, No. 1424) declares the
scholastria to be henceforth a *can-
cellaria*. It is instructive to notice
that, though the original Bull of
foundation does not expressly confer the *ius ubique docendi*, this later
Bull assumes that the chancellor
already possesses the power of con-

ferring it since the *studium* had
become 'general'. Another bull of
the same year, however (No. 1425),
excepts Paris from the *ius ubique docendi*. The *scholasticus* was,
it would appear, styled *capiscol*
(Baudel, *Discours*, p. 3). In 1368
Edward the Black Prince, as Duke
of Aquitaine, confirmed the privileges of this university, including
the *ius non trahi extra* (Fournier, ii,
No. 1433), and made his seneschal
conservator.

[3] See above, vol. i, p. 339.

[4] 'Item quod pecunia que de col-
lectis faciendis pro negotiis universitatis et pro banchiis, vel aliis,
nomine universitatis . . . deponatur
penes aliquem bonum virum per
Rectorem et Cancellarium ac con-
siliarios studii eligendum.' Fournier, ii, No. 1425.

[5] *Ibid.*, No. 1428; *Statuta*, p. 24.

A benefice-roll of 1343 contains the names of twelve professors in all faculties;[1] but by 1371 the founder of a college
for 'grammar and logic' at Cahors speaks of the *studium* as
'attenuated and, as it were, annihilated on account of the wars
prevailing in those parts'.[2] In the preceding year the duke of
Anjou had assigned a small pension for the maintenance of
four doctors of law and two of arts for eight years, but this
does not seem to have been continued.[3] A benefice-roll of
1378 contains fifty-eight names: in 1380 there are only
twenty-seven, in 1394 ninety-eight.[4] Another attempt to
resuscitate the collapsed *studium* was made in 1452 by Charles
VII,[5] but the university seems to have been chiefly kept alive
by means of its three colleges. These were: the Collèges
(1) de Pélegry (1358), founded by Raymond de Pélegry,
canon of London and dean of a collegiate church in the
diocese of Cahors;[6] (2) de Rodez, for logic and grammar and
afterwards law (1371), by Bernard de Rodez, Archbishop of
Naples;[7] (3) de S. Michel (1473), by Jean Rubey, Archdeacon
of Tornes.[8]

§ 7. GRENOBLE (1339)

VALBONNAIS, *Hist. du Dauphiné* (ii, Geneva, 1721), prints some documents. Cf. NADAL, *Hist. de l'Un. de Valence*, p. 64 *sq.* Fournier adds a
few documents. BERRIAT-SAINT-PRIX, 'Hist. de l'ancienne Université de
Grenoble' (*Revue du Dauphiné*, v, Grenoble, 1839).

THE University of Grenoble was founded by a Bull of Benedict XII, granted at the request of Humbert II, count of the
Viennois, in 1339 for all faculties except theology;[9] a separate

---

[1] Fournier, ii, No. 1429.
[2] *Ibid.*, No. 1441.
[3] *Ibid.*, No. 1437 *sq.*
[4] *Ibid.*, Nos. 1443, 1445, 1450.
[5] Denifle, i. 364.
[6] Fournier, ii, Nos. 1430, 1447.
Cahors formed part of the duchy of
Aquitaine, and was then in English
hands. The foundation was extended by Hugh de Pélegry,
treasurer of Lichfield, and papal
collector in England (*ibid.*, Nos.
1431, 1444; Denifle, *Les Univ.
franç.*, p. 89). Among the executors

of the first founder's will are the
'burgenses Londonienses'.
[7] Fournier, ii, Nos. 1441, 1461.
[8] *Ibid.*, No. 1473.
[9] *Ibid.*, No. 1546. The founder's
privilege of the same year is printed
in Valbonnais, ii. 412; Fournier,
ii, No. 1548. It contains a curious
provision that *martineti* (metal
forges) shall be removed three
leagues from Grenoble, 'cum sint
vorago nemorum et lignorum'.
This was, of course, for the benefit
of poor students in winter evenings.

CHAP. VIII,
§ 7.

Bull granted later in the same year gave the right of promotion to the bishop with the *ius ubique docendi*.[1] Grenoble was badly placed for the seat of a university, since Dauphiné lay in the debatable territory between the Empire and the French monarchy. There is just enough evidence to show that the *studium* actually came into existence;[2] but it was never prosperous, and had clearly disappeared before the foundation of Valence in 1452.[3] It was restored in 1543[4] by Francis of Bourbon, Count of S. Pol, on the petition of the town council. In 1565, however, it was suppressed and incorporated with the University of Valence by an edict of Charles IX.[5]

§ 8. ORANGE (1365)

Institutio, privilegia, statuta, &c., Universitatis civitatis Arausionis, Orange, 1718. MILLET, *Notice sur l'Université d'Orange,* Avignon, 1878.

Origin of
studium.

A *STUDIUM* of law and grammar existed at Orange from the second half of the thirteenth century. In 1268 we find an agreement between the bishop and the two princes of Orange, uncle and nephew, who both bore the name of Raymond de Baux. In this document the bishop waives the objections which he had apparently raised to the setting up of a *studium* by the secular power. Further regulations for its government are to be made by the archbishop of Arles.[6]

Foundation, 1365.

In 1365 the school obtained a highly peculiar and exceptional privilege from Pope Urban V.[7] This Bull recognized the *studium*, and ordained that study at Orange should entitle students to take degrees in other universities but not at Orange itself. The document is interesting as throwing light upon the true *differentia* of a *studium generale*, which has been sometimes mistakenly supposed to consist in the mere posses-

---

[1] Fournier, ii, No. 1549.
[2] Berryat-Saint-Prix, pp. 92, 93.
[3] See below, p. 201.
[4] Valbonnais, ii. 413.
[5] In 1343 the university presented a most singular 'roll' to Clement VI. It is presented exclusively for one master of arts, so poor that 'lapides et morterium, ob sue vite sustentationem, in nostro opere deportavit'. While endea-

vouring to present his supplication to His Holiness he had been atrociously wounded by the Pope's satellites, and his petition pitched into the Rhône. Wanted: a benefice 'cum cura vel sine cura' in the diocese of Elne (Fournier, ii, No. 1553). In 1345 the dauphin salaries a bachelor of laws (*ibid.*, No. 1554).
[6] Fournier, ii, No. 1541.
[7] *Ibid.*, No. 1542.

sion of papal privileges. Orange became henceforth a privi- CHAP.VIII,
leged *studium particulare*: it was not a *studium generale* § 8.
because it had no right of promotion or *ius ubique docendi*.
But later in the very same year Orange found means of
obtaining from another source full university privileges,
which had been denied by the Pope. Orange belonged to the
kingdom of Arles and therefore to the Empire; and when in
June, 1365, Charles IV came to Arles to be crowned, the *Ius ubique*
prince of Orange and the syndic of the town obtained from *docendi,*
him a Bull which recognizes the *studium* as already existing, 1365.
and confers upon it the privileges of a *studium generale* in
all faculties, though theology is not specially named.[1] The
licence was to be conferred by the provost of the town with
the assistance (in the infancy of the *studium*) of the rector of
the university. In the next year we hear of the university as
having been totally extinguished by a papal interdict, but
recently 'reformed by papal favour'[2]—a statement not easy
to interpret. The Bull of Charles IV was afterwards in 1379
confirmed by the Avignon Pope Clement VII.[3]

After these two Bulls it is st.ange to find Sixtus IV in 1475 Suppres-
issuing a Bull against those who took degrees at 'Orange and sion, 1475.
other places where there was no *studium generale*'. Either
the privileges conferred by the Bulls were considered to be
dependent upon the *de facto* continuance of instruction of the
studium generale type (which is in itself probable), or the
papal chancery had received its information from a partial
source. The Bull, it appears, was granted in favour of the
rival University of Avignon.[4] An edict of Charles VIII in
1485 throws some light upon the state of things which had
called for the papal interposition. There was, it appears, a
single master, one Honorat Picquet, who really only taught
grammar, but called himself a master of medicine. He was in
the habit, it would appear, of constituting himself rector of the
university for the purpose of conferring degrees in all faculties
upon 'vagabond, ribald, unprofitable, and ignorant scholars'

[1] *Institutio*, &c., p. 1; Fournier,   [4] Laval, *Cartulaire de l'Univ.*
ii, No. 1543.   *d'Avignon*, pp. 114–18; Fournier, ii,
[2] Denifle, *Les Univ. franç.*, p. 94.   No. 1367.
[3] Fournier, ii, No. 1545.

CHAP. VIII, who had been refused degrees elsewhere.[1] At the request of
§ 8.   the University of Montpellier the promotions at Orange were
           forbidden in future, but the university managed to escape
Obscure   absolute extinction. Its ignoble existence can just be traced
survival. into the eighteenth century. When the traveller Gollnitz
           visited Grenoble in the seventeenth century, there was a joke
           current in the place to the effect that the three persons who
           were necessary to constitute a college or corporation were
           supplied at Orange by the rector, the secretary, and the
           bedel.[2]

§ 9. AIX (1409)

HENRICY, *Notice sur l'ancienne Université d'Aix*, Aix, 1826. F. CHAVER-
NAC, *Hist. de l'Université d'Aix*, Aix, 1889; a not uninteresting but very
uncritical production. The statutes (1420–40) were first printed by
B. BLACAS, *Almae Aquarum Sextiarum universitatis vetera et nova statuta,
constitutiones et consuetudines*, Aix, 1667. Cf. also PITTON, *Histoire de la
Ville d'Aix*, Aix, 1666. [F. BELIN, *Histoire de l'ancienne Université de
Provence*, Paris, 1892. G. FLEURY and A. DUMAS, *Sources de l'histoire de
l'ancienne Université d'Aix*, Aix-en-Provence, 1923.]

Possible   AIX was the capital of *Gallia Narbonensis secunda*, the earliest
connexion home and the last refuge of Roman civilization in Gaul, styled
with the
old Roman by the elder Pliny 'another Rome in another Italy'.[3] The old
town-   Roman schools and the culture which they fostered lingered
school.   here as long as they lingered anywhere; and a somewhat de-
           generate classicism certainly survived in Provence long after
           it was extinct in Italy itself. It is even barely possible that the
           cathedral school of Aix, which attained some importance
           both before and after the eleventh-century revival of letters,
           may have originally had some connexion with the old Roman
           town-schools: such a conjecture might be supported by the
           very unusual circumstance that the syndics of the town had
           a share in the appointment of the *scholasticus* who presided
           over the cathedral schools.[4] The minute and circumstantial

---

[1] Fournier, ii, No. 1184.

[2] *Ulysses Belgico-Gallicus* (Leiden, 1655), p. 422.

[3] 'Ut Roma altera alterā in Italia
iure appellari mereretur.' *Hist.
Nat.* liv. 3, c 4.

[4] Chavernac, p. 32, calls him
scholarius, but if this form is found

it must be only a parallel form of
scholasticus. Besides this official
there was here a *theologus* and
a *capiscol* or *caput chori* or *scholae*
(master of the school of music);
all these were provided with prebends.

account given by Chavernac of the 'University' of Aix
before the date of the papal Bull is, however, so mixed up
with historical delusions and so entirely unsupported by
original authorities that it is almost impossible to extract
from it any trustworthy facts as to the condition of the schools
here in the twelfth and thirteenth centuries. It appears to
be made up by the aid of the convenient assumptions which
we have seen to be responsible for so many pages of university history. The first of these is the assumption that every
place where professors taught was a university; the second,
that wherever a doctor or professor of law is mentioned in
a deed relating to a particular town, he must have graduated
and taught in that town; the third that writers of the sixteenth
and seventeenth century can be trusted when they apply the
technicalities of the university system to the early state of
schools in which they are interested without producing contemporary evidence. It does seem, however, possible to A solitary
disengage from this jumble of confused and uncritical erudi- case of
graduation the fact that at some time before 1303 the jurist Jacobus tion,
de Belvisio, afterwards the master of Bartolus, received at c. 1303.
Aix the degree of doctor in civil law from Peter of Ferrières,
afterwards archbishop of Arles,[1] himself a distinguished
jurist.

So far it might seem that Aix has as good a right to be But no
styled a *studium generale* as Orleans or Montpellier before *studium generale.*

---

[1] 'Ad preces reverendi patris et
domini mei, D. Petri de Ferrariis,
iuris utriusque professoris . . . qui
me doctoratus honore, in Aula
Regis, civitatis Aquensis, ipsiusque
praesentia, decorauit.' Jacobus de
Bellovisu, *Aurea Practica Criminalis*
(Cologne, 1580, pp. 1, 2). This
must presumably have been before
the elevation of Peter to the see
of Noyon in 1302. He was archbishop of Arles from 1303 to 1307.
[Though Bartolus often refers to
him it is doubtful if Belvisio was
one of his masters; Woolf, *Bartolus
of Sassoferrato*, Cambridge, 1913,
p. 2 note.] Pitton (p. 597) adds that
Durandus (author of the *Rationale*,

† 1296) took the degree of doctor of
law at Aix, but without mentioning
any authority. [Pitton is not confirmed by other writers on Durandus, who is believed to have studied
at Bologna and Modena (*Hist. litt.
de la France*, xx. 412; F. von
Schulte, *Die Geschichte der Quellen
und Literatur des canonischen Rechts*,
ii. 144–5). It is easy to confuse the
various canonists of this name; for
example, Gatien-Arnoult includes
the younger Durandus in his list
of canonists of Toulouse, con-
founding him with yet a third
member of the family. See Paul
Viollet in *Hist. litt. de la France*,
xxxv. 4, 5.]

CHAP. VIII, the issue of the papal Bulls conferring on them the *ius ubique*
§ 9.   *docendi*. But the very words in which this solitary instance
of graduation at Aix is recorded are sufficient to show the
exceptional character of the occurrence. It was 'in the king's
court and in the king's presence' that Jacobus de Belvisio
received the doctorate. The king was probably Charles,
King of Naples and Count of Provence. And one is tempted
to conjecture that this graduation was an incident in the
great struggle of the age between spiritual and temporal
sovereignty—an attempt to place the secular power on a level
with the Papacy in the conferment of exceptional degrees. If
the reference be too vague to warrant such an inference, the
evidence is certainly insufficient to enable us to pronounce
that Aix was ever regarded as a *studium generale* before the
date of its papal Bull.[1] At all events, by the fifteenth century,
the claims of the place to that dignity had ceased to be sufficiently recognized to satisfy students, and measures were
Bull of taken by the aediles for procuring a papal Bull. On their
Alexander
V, 1409. petition, Louis II, King of Jerusalem and Sicily, Count of
Provence, who was also the founder of the Parlement at Aix,
took advantage of his journey to Italy in 1409, on the crusade
against Ladislaus of Naples, to urge the claims of his capital
upon Alexander V, the newly elected Pope of the Council of
Pisa.[2] An adherent of such importance as the count of
Provence, and zealous enough to tender his homage to the
pontiff in person, was not likely to make so innocent a
petition in vain. The Bull now issued recognizes the fact
that 'certain masters in theology' were actually teaching in
Aix. It does not, however, recognize the existing *studium* as
an actual *studium generale*, but proceeds to create one for
all faculties with the privileges of Paris and Toulouse.

Constitu-   The count's letters patent were issued in 1413, after his
tion.

[1] 'Adiicimus quod dictum generale studium, in eadem civitate, in
sacra theologia, necnon in canonico
et civili iure et in quibuscunque licitis facultatibus huius modi vigeat'
(Chavernac, pp. 84, 85; Fournier,
iii, No. 1577). The Bull recognizes

the existence of 'nonnulli magistri
in sacra pagina atque plerique do-
tores et scholares in iure canonico
et civili', but creates the *studium
generale* for the first time.
[2] Chavernac, pp. 81–4.

return to Provence. They compelled all Provençal students
to study at Aix only.[1] No chancellor had been named in the
papal Bull. The then archbishop was now made first chancellor of the university for life; but it was provided that upon
his death the chancellor should henceforth be freely elected
by the rector, masters, and licentiates[2]—a very exceptional
arrangement to which there is no exact parallel in any other
French university. The nearest approach to it is at Montpellier. The constitution, however, differed from that of the
medical university of Montpellier in having a rector (sometimes styled *primicerius*, as at Avignon) as well as a chancellor;
while at Montpellier, moreover, the chancellor did not confer
degrees. The rector was to be a 'simple student', who nevertheless possessed an apparently unlimited civil and criminal
jurisdiction in all cases wherein one party was a doctor or
scholar of the university, subject to the provision that a
defendant dissatisfied with the rector's decision might demand the 'adjunction' of a *doctor legens*.[3] The *consiliarii*,
elected annually by their predecessors, were eleven in number;[4] one was to be a canon of Aix, two theologians but not
doctors, one a representative of the medical faculty (likewise
not a doctor), one a master of arts, and the others elected by
the three nations, which were styled (as at Montpellier)
Burgundian, Provençal, Catalan.[5] The constitution was entirely that of a student-university; the 'college of doctors'
had here no great authority except in the conferment of
degrees.[6]

[1] Fournier, iii, No. 1578.
[2] *Ibid.*, Nos. 1581, 1582.
[3] The clause runs as follows: 'nisi
supplicaretur a dicti domini rectoris
sententia, aut peteret adiunctum,
videlicet unum doctorem legentem,
prout infra, opponendo contra
dictam sententiam iniquitatem aut
nullitatem.' *Ibid.*, No. 1582.
[4] At the university mass every
Sunday blessed bread was distributed to all members of the
university, the councillors receiving
extra portions, and the rector twice
as much as a councillor.
[5] 'De regentibus scholas in civitate.' *Ibid.*
[6] There seems to be a limited
number of ordinary chairs, but
leave to erect a new chair is vested
with the rector, not with the doctors
(*ibid.*, § 52).

§ 10. DÔLE (1422)

Labbey DE BILLY, *Histoire de l'Université du Comté de Bourgogne*, Paris (no date). H. BEAUNE et J. D'ARBAUMONT, *Les Universités de Franche-Comté, Gray, Dôle, Besançon*, Dijon, 1870. [J. GAUTHIER, *L'Université de Besançon*, Besançon, 1900.]

Abortive attempts. As early as the year 1287, when it was the exception rather than the rule for a small principality to have a university of its own, the idea of establishing a university of all faculties in the county of Burgundy (Franche-Comté) was conceived by count Otto IV. A charter erecting a *studium generale* at Gray was issued in that year;[1] and in 1291 a Bull was actually granted by Nicholas IV;[2] but we learn from the later foundation-Bull of Dôle that the university never actually came into being.[3] The wars in which the count was engaged, the temporary annexation of Burgundy to the French crown by the marriage of Otto's daughter Jeanne to the second son of Philip the Fair (afterwards Philip V of France), and the great fires which reduced the town of Gray to ashes three times in the course of the fourteenth century are quite sufficient to account for the non-realization of the project. When the academical aspirations of Franche-Comté were revived, the quieter Dôle, the seat of the count's Parlement, was preferred to the busy commercial town of Gray as the site of its university though the latter made strenuous efforts to obtain the coveted honour for itself.[4]

Foundation in 1422. A Bull for the erection of a university at Dôle was granted by Martin V in 1422 on the petition of Philip the Good, duke of Burgundy.[5] The Bull is expressed in a rather unusual form. It is addressed to the archbishop of Besançon, and authorizes him, if the 'said place is more apt and fit than the place of Gray in the said diocese', in which a university was formerly

---

[1] Beaune et d'Arbaumont, pp. 1, 2; Fournier, ii, Nos. 1567, 1568.

[2] *Ibid.* i, No. 1566.

[3] 'Locus de Grayaco dicte diœcesis in quo olim felicis recordationis Nicolaus, papa quartus, predecessor noster, per suas literas studium generale nondum tamen inibi incœptum vigere et esse concessit.' Bull for Dôle in Beaune,

pp. xiii, 3. The Bull is also printed by Denifle, *Archiv f. Lit. u. Kirchengesch.* iv. 248; and by Fournier, iii, No. 1611.

[4] Beaune, pp. xx, xxi, 14.

[5] *Ibid.*, p. 3; Fournier, iii, No. 1611. A Bull of the preceding month directing an inquisition into the expediency of such an erection is lost. (*Ibid.*, No. 1610.)

erected, to establish a *studium generale* at Dôle, and to confer
upon it the privileges of other universities. The *studium* is
declared to be for all faculties, but the right of promotion
is limited by the exclusion of theology. The archbishop is
made chancellor. In 1423, ducal letters patent decreed the
establishment of a university, confirming the grant of 9,693
livres voted by the estates of Burgundy for procuring the
Bull, erecting buildings, and paying professors. Exemptions
from taxation and other privileges were conferred, the duke's
bailiff at Dôle created conservator, and an endowment
granted.[1] The right of graduation in theology was bestowed
by a Bull of Eugenius IV in 1437.[2]

The constitution of the university was a modified demo-
cracy of a somewhat new type, followed by several of the later
French universities.[3] The rector was to be a licentiate,
master of arts, or bachelor of law, and must not be a native of
Dôle. He was elected by the 'proctors and councillors'[4]
chosen by the five faculties, canon and civil law ranking as
separate faculties and theology being included in spite of the
prohibition of graduation therein. The general congregation included students of all grades, but the ordinary government was in the hands of a college composed of nobles ('living
as such') above twenty years of age, all licentiates, all *bacca-
larii formati* in theology, the regents,[5] the proctors and councillors of faculties, and the *procurator generalis*. The rector
had a full jurisdiction in causes of scholars,[6] but in criminal
cases involving 'pena sanguinis' he was to try lay scholars in
conjunction with the ducal bailiff; such offenders when clerks
were, of course, sent to the bishop.

A body of three external 'distributors', originally appointed

[1] Beaune, pp. 7, 21; Fournier,
iii, Nos. 1614, 1615, 1617, 1622.

[2] *Ibid.*, No. 1623.

[3] Cf. above, p. 177. The statutes
(1424) are printed by *ibid.*, No.
1616.

[4] How many of each does not
appear: § 12 might suggest that
each nation had one 'proctor or
councillor', and § 58 confirms that

interpretation. Yet in § 53 we have
'procuratores Facultatum, consiliarii earundem'.

[5] Fournier prints 'regentes, pensionati', as if two classes. It should
be of course 'regentes pensionati',
i.e. salaried regents.

[6] From the rector an appeal lay
to the college, and from the college
to the university.

CHAP. VIII, by the duke merely to superintend the administration of the
§ 10.   public funds devoted to the support of the *studium*, eventually
acquired an increasingly extensive control over its affairs.[1]
The appointment of the regents was transferred from the
college to the distributors. Their position, in fact, was
exactly that of the 'governors' or 'curators' of the Italian
Colleges. universities. The Cluniac College of S. Jerome was founded
by Antoine de Roche, Grand Prior of Cluny, in 1494, and a
Cistercian College in 1498.[2]

Rival uni-   In 1445 there broke out at Besançon one of those quarrels
versity at
Besançon. which were of such frequent occurrence in the Middle Ages
between the great feudal prelates and their semi-autonomous
see-towns. In the course of the quarrel the citizens burned
the archbishop's château of Brégille. An interdict followed,
and the city was obliged to send a deputation to Rome to get
it taken off. In 1450 the Pope condemned the citizens to re-
build the palace and pay an indemnity; but, at the same time,
by way of relief to the civic *amour propre*, the envoys succeeded
in obtaining from the reigning pontiff, Nicholas V, a Bull for
the erection at Besançon of a *studium generale* in arts only.[3]
This unusual limitation was no doubt introduced out of consideration for the rights of the neighbouring University of
Dôle, which was for the most part a university of theology
and law. The archbishop was named chancellor; the abbot
of S. Paul, the chanter of the cathedral, and the dean of
S. Mary Magdalene, conservators. War, pestilence, civil
commotion, and the unwillingness of the House of Burgundy
to allow of even a restricted rivalry to Dôle long prevented
any real execution being given to the Bull. It was not till
Besançon took the side of France in the last conflict between
Louis XI and his great Burgundian feudatory that Besançon
was rewarded and the Burgundian Dôle punished by the transfer of the university in all its faculties from the former to the
Suppres- latter town. The pillage and burning of Dôle by the French,
sion of
Dôle,
1481.   [1] Beaune, pp. lxi *sq.*, lxxiv;   [2] *Ibid.*, p. xcviii; the statutes of
Labbey de Billy, i. 45. As usual in   the former in Fournier, iii, No.
French universities the chairs were   1643.
filled 'au concours', i.e. by public   [3] Beaune, pp. clxxx, 24;
competition. Beaune, p. lxxix.   Fournier, iii, No. 1626.

in spite of a gallant resistance, in which the students of the university distinguished themselves, took place in 1479: the king's letters patent in favour of Besançon were issued in 1481.[1] A curious accident, however, prevented the people of Besançon from enjoying their triumph. The king's physician Coitier, a native of Poligny, used his influence to persuade his dying patient to transfer the university of the conquered and ruined Dôle to Poligny by letters patent of 1483.[2] The univer- Transfer-sity not having been actually established either at Besançon or ence to Poligny, at Poligny, Dôle was, however, able in the following year to 1483. procure the restoration of its privileges from Charles VIII, and Besançon did not obtain a full foundation-charter till 1565.[3]

Meanwhile, a municipal college was erected at Besançon in 1511,[4] which may possibly, on the strength of the old Bull of Nicholas V, have claimed the privileges of a *studium generale* in the faculty of arts. Even after the issue of the Bull, the restored university—though for a time a flourishing Protestant law-school—enjoyed but an intermittent existence; and it was not till 1691, after the final conquest of Franche-Comté by Louis XIV, that its triumph over its ancient rival was completed by the final transfer of the University of Dôle to Besançon.[5]

§ 11. POITIERS (1431)

De l'Université de la Ville de Poictiers . . . Extract d'un ancien Manuscript latin, gardé en la bibliothecque de M. Iean Filleau, Poitiers, 1643. A copy of this rare book, or rather pamphlet, which contains the foundation-charters and the *procès-verbal* of the proceedings at the inauguration of the university, is in the University Library of S. Andrew's (now printed by Fournier, iii, No. 1721). There is a very short notice in Dreux DU RADIER, *Bibliothèque du Poitou*, Paris, 1754; i. 387 *sq.* The article by DE LA LABORDIÈRE in the *Bulletin de la Soc. des Antiquaires de l'Ouest* (1844, p. 68 *sq.*) and his notices in *Vieux Souvenirs de Poitiers d'avant 1789* (Poitiers, 1846), relate chiefly to a more modern period. The same may be said of the 'Essai historique sur l'ancienne Université de Poitiers', by PILOTELLE, *Bulletin*, xxvii (1863), 251 *sq.*

DURING the English occupation of Paris the great French Origin. university, of course, passed under English influence, and it

---

[1] Beaune, pp. xci, 28; Fournier, iii, No. 1632.

[2] Beaune, p. 31; Fournier, iii, Nos. 1634, 1955. At the same time Coitier was named conservator of

privileges. *Ibid.*, No. 1657.

[3] Beaune, p. 33; Fournier, iii, No. 1638.

[4] Beaune, p. clxxxix.

[5] *Ibid.*, pp. clxxxix–cxcii, 62.

became an object with the exiled king to weaken that influence, and to draw students away from what had become his enemy's capital. It was not, however, till 1431 that Charles VII obtained from Eugenius IV a Bull for the erection of a university in his temporary capital at Poitiers;[1] a charter of privilege was issued in the following year (1432), when the university was solemnly opened.[2] The papal Bull conferred upon the university all the privileges of Toulouse, and declared that it was to be on the model of that *studium*.[3]

Constitution.
The actual constitutional arrangements of the university would, however, appear to have very imperfectly carried out this injunction, except in so far as they exhibit (like those of Toulouse) a compromise between the Parisian and the Bolognese pattern. There was a single rector; and the university, or rather the two legal faculties only, were divided into four nations: (1) France, (2) Aquitaine, (3) Touraine, (4) Berry. Each nation elected a proctor.[4] All graduates—masters, licentiates, and bachelors—were admitted to the general congregation except bachelors of arts. But there is a special provision that the faculty of law was to be governed after the manner of Orleans, which would imply the possession of some rights by mere students in that faculty. The abbot of S. Maixent was to be made apostolic conservator, and the seneschal conservator of the royal privileges. The new university—doubtless through some private influences of which we know nothing—was totally disconnected with the cathedral, the chancellor being the treasurer of the collegiate church of S. Hilary.

Subsequent history.
In the year 1448 the municipality began the construction of the 'Great Schools' of the university.[5] At about this time the city is found, in obedience to royal orders, making certain grants in payment of salaries to the regents,[6] and the city magistrates frequently invoke the royal authority for the cor-

---

[1] Printed in Bulaeus, v. 842; Fournier, iii, No. 1719.

[2] Bulaeus, v. 844; Fournier, iii, No. 1720.

[3] 'Ad instar ipsius studii Tholosani.'

[4] Fournier, iii, No. 1721. Cf. No. 1748.

[5] *Ibid.*, No. 1730 *sq.*; also a library in 1459 (No. 1744).

[6] *Ibid.*, Nos. 1724, 1735, 1736, &c.

rection of the numerous 'abuses' which at this time prevailed CHAP. VIII,
in the university, especially graduation without sufficient § 11.
residence or qualification, and the absence or negligence of
the regents.[1] It is not till the close of the century (1488) that
we meet with any actual statutes of the university,[2] and then
the constitution appears somewhat different from that contemplated at its first foundation. It is now clear (whatever
may have been the case earlier) that only noble students have
a deliberative voice with the doctors, licentiates, and bachelors
in the jurist nations. The choice of a rector rotated, in a
manner not very clearly defined, between the four nations and
the other faculties (represented by their doctors).[3] In the
faculty of law there were four regents, who co-opted each
other after a public disputation in which the candidates were
required to dispute with all comers.[4]

In 1478 a College of Puygareau, for a prior and eight scholars College of
in theology and arts, was founded by Françoise Gillier, Lady Puygareau.
of Puygareau and widow of an advocate-fiscal in the Parlement of Paris.[5]

§ 12. CAEN (1432, 1437)

There are slight notices in Ch. DE BOURGUEVILLE (Sieur de Bras), *Les
Recherches et Antiquitez de la province de Neustrie . . . mais plus spécialle-
ment de la Ville et Université de Caen*, Caen, 1588 (reprinted 1883);
HUET, *Les Origines de la Ville de Caen*, Rouen, 1702 (2nd ed., 1706); and
DE LA RUE, *Essais historiques sur la Ville de Caen*, Caen, 1820, and *Nou-
veaux Essais hist. sur la Ville de Caen*, Caen, 1842. A full account of the law
faculty is given by CAUVET, *Le Collége des Droits de l'ancienne Université
de Caen*, Caen, 1858, and *L'ancienne Université de Caen*, Caen, 1874
(*Mémoires de l'Acad. des Arts et Belles-lettres de Caen*). The work of
Le Comte Amédée DE BOURMONT, 'La Fondation de l'Université of Caen'
(in *Bulletin de la Soc. des Antiquaires de Normandie*, xii, Caen, 1884), is
a very careful history with full collection of documents (also *La Bibliothèque de l'Université de Caen au XVe siècle*, 1881). Other documents were
published by CHARMA in *Mém. de la Soc. des Ant. de N.*, 3rd ser., ii (1876).
There is also a 'Liste des Recteurs de l'ancienne Université de Caen'
by CHATEL (*Bull. de la Soc. des Ant. de Norm.*, xi, 1881-2. [H. PRENTOUT,

---

[1] *Ibid.*, Nos. 1742, 1758, 1759.
[2] *Ibid.*, No. 1765.
[3] The university is 'directa et
gubernata per duas Facultates et
quatuor nationes, videlicet per
Facultates artium et Theologie, cui

Facultati adiungitur Facultas medicine'. Presumably each nation and
each faculty had one turn in six.
[4] *Ibid.*, Nos. 1723, 1767.
[5] *Ibid.*, No. 1763.

'Esquisse d'une histoire de l'Université de Caen', in the quincentenary volume, *L'Université de Caen, son passé, son présent*, Caen, 1932, especially pp. 19–65.]

Law-university, 1432.

LIKE Poitiers, the University of Caen owes its existence to the French wars of the English king, Henry VI. A university of canon and civil law was erected here in 1432 by the regent, the duke of Bedford, under letters patent of Henry VI.[1] The consent of Martin V [to the establishment of a university in arts and civil law 'in some city in the province of Rouen'] had already been obtained in 1424, but no Bull granted. As Paris was in the hands of the English, and the new university was to be purely legal, it is evident that it was intended as a rival rather to such places as Orleans and Angers than to Paris. Nevertheless the scheme met with a violent opposition from that university. Its masters vainly petitioned the Parlement of Paris, the Council of Basel, and afterwards Eugenius IV, against this addition to the number of its competitors.[2] After the expulsion of the English from Paris in 1436, the scope of the university was extended to the other faculties,[3] and in

Bull of Eugenius IV for all faculties, 1437.

1437 a Bull of erection was granted by Eugenius IV.[4] The diocesan, the bishop of Bayeux, was appointed chancellor, and shortly afterwards the bishops of Lisieux and Coutances conservators.[5] The solemn inauguration of the university took place in 1439, the first rector being an Englishman, Michael of Tregury, B.D., of Exeter College, Oxford, Archdeacon of Barnstaple, and afterwards Archbishop of Dublin.[6]

Confirmation by Charles VII, 1450 and 1452.

The measure was as usual popular in the neighbourhood: the Bull had been granted on the petition of the estates of Normandy, and the university was therefore not interfered

---

[1] De Bourmont, p. 477; Fournier, iii, No. 1644.

[2] De Bourmont, p. 328 *sq.*; Fournier, iii, Nos. 1645, 1646, 1650. [Prentout, pp. 28, 32–5; the opposition was mainly directed against the establishment of a faculty of civil law.]

[3] Theology and arts in 1437, medicine in 1438: de Bourmont, pp. 480, 482; Fournier, iii, Nos. 1647, 1650.

[4] De Bourmont, p. 564; Fournier, iii, No. 1644.

[5] De Bourmont, p. 568; Fournier, iii, Nos. 1648, 1651.

[6] De Bourmont, pp. 337 *sq.*, 373; Fournier, iii, No. 1653. Tregury is said to have written a tract 'de origine illius studii', cf. Boase, *Reg. of Exeter College*, ed. 2, i. 22, which, however, is not known to survive.

with, in spite of the renewed efforts of Paris,[1] on the re- CHAP. VIII,
annexation of the duchy to the French crown. Upon the § 12.
petition of the estates it received a temporary continuation
in 1450 and in 1452 a new charter from Charles VII[2] [and a
Bull of solemn confirmation from Pope Nicholas V].[3]

The university, in the form which it assumed after the loss Constitu-
of Paris, was deliberately intended to divert the Norman sub- tion.
jects of the English king from attending the university of
the capital. It was completely modelled on that university,
with a few slight constitutional modifications necessitated by
the smaller numbers and different circumstances of Caen.
Students and bachelors have no more power than at Paris;
but the licentiates of the four superior faculties (the civil and
canon laws being reckoned as distinct) are admitted to vote
in congregation,[4] and the voting is by faculties. The rector
is elected by intrants from the five faculties;[5] he may himself
be a master of any faculty, but, if a master of arts, must be
also a bachelor in one of the superior faculties. The change
necessitated a dean of arts.[6] There are no nations or proctors.
None but purely academical jurisdiction is conferred upon
the rector; and the statutes, which are enacted by authority of
the English king, betray an anxious desire to confine the privileges of the university to *bona-fide* students, and to restrict
even in their case the jurisdiction of the royal conservator—
the bailiff of Caen—to purely 'personal causes and injuries'.[7]

---

[1] Bulaeus, v. 426, 536, 554;
Fournier, iii, No. 1666.

[2] De Bourmont, pp. 557, 560;
Fournier, iii, Nos. 1674, 1678. The
faculty of law was suppressed by
the first edict but revived by the
second.

[3] [Prentout, p. 53.]

[4] The university statutes of 1439
are printed in de Bourmont, p.
484 *sq.*; Fournier, iii, No. 1652.
It is observable that in this university the privileges of graduates were
not limited to a small co-opting
college of regents. In 1480, however, the interference in academical
affairs of non-academical graduates

became so serious that the faculty
of arts found it necessary to deny a
vote to non-teaching masters residing in the neighbourhood, on the
ground that the privileges of the
university were limited to those
residing 'studii causa' (Fournier,
iii, No. 1689).

[5] An arrangement already adopted at Dôle, though there doctors
were ineligible. See above, p. 191.

[6] The jurist college and the theological faculty had priors as well as
deans.

[7] The jurisdiction was slightly
extended in 1445: de Bourmont, p.
540 *sq.*; Fournier, iii, No. 1664.

CHAP. VIII, §12.

In the strictness of these statutes of 1439 in reference to 'night-walking'[1] and other conduct of the students, it may, perhaps, not be fanciful to trace the effects upon university discipline of an army of occupation, whose purposes the university itself was intended to serve.[2]

The college of law.

A small constitutional peculiarity of the university remains to be noticed. Civil and canon law formed, as we have seen, distinct faculties; but the two faculties were from 1443 housed in an ancient court-house known as *La Cohue*. The two faculties thus united formed a college under a prior, the two deans remaining at the head of their respective faculties in their separate deliberations and their relations to the university as a whole.[3] Schools for the remaining faculties were given by Mary, Duchess of Orleans, in 1476.[4] In 1452 one of the

Colleges.

smallest colleges on record was endowed (for artists) by one Le Cloutier, a neighbouring *seigneur*, consisting only of a principal and two bursars.[5] By the beginning of the sixteenth century there were several small endowed colleges (mostly, if not all, for artists) in the town, besides the unendowed pedagogy or 'College of Arts' under the control of the faculty.[6] Of these the most important was the Collège du Boys, founded —it is thought as an expiatory offering—by the infamous Pierre Cauchon, bishop of Lisieux and burner-in-chief of Joan of Arc, who died in 1442, though the college was not actually established before 1491.[7] The congregations and

[1] Scholars captured by the watch after 8 or (in summer) 9 p.m. are to be imprisoned for the night and surrendered on the requisition of 'suos iudices', who are not to fine them, but 'imponetur eisdem salutaris pena'.

[2] In 1444 the privileges of all other universities were declared by Henry VI to be forfeited for disobedience. De Bourmont, p. 534; Fournier, iii, No. 1662.

[3] De Bourmont, pp. 354 *sq.*, 432 *sq.*, 522; Fournier, iii, Nos. 1659, 1710. The membership of the college was eventually limited to seven regents.

[4] *Ibid.*, No. 1688.

[5] *Ibid.*, No. 1676. One of the

two might be a religious named by the abbey of Barbery.

[6] 'Et alia collegia in eadem Facultate artium nunc fundata, preter collegium Montis, collegium de Boult, collegium Cingal, et cetera.' *Ibid.*, No. 1718 (§ 38). Cf. de Bourmont, pp. 456, 458–76.

[7] Fournier, iii, Nos. 1701, 1705–8, 1713. [Prentout summarizes his story (p. 63): The bishop's will was annulled and Jean de Gouvis, one of his executors, bought the 'maison du Bois' in 1467; *bursarii* were established then, but the college was not definitely founded until 1491. It was incorporated with the university in 1493.]

courts of the university were held in the Franciscan convent, which was eventually, in 1486, made over by the order to the university in a very peculiar and unprecedented manner, the order being henceforth placed 'under the protection and guardianship' of the university.[1]

In strict accordance with the whole aim of the foundation, and the better to attach its members to the English connexion, the university was endowed out of the revenues of Parisian colleges and of various ecclesiastics, sequestrated for non-submission to the English rule. It is remarkable that the chairs endowed included rhetoric and poetry as well as theology, canon law, and medicine. When, in accordance with the treaty of 1448, these revenues had to be restored to their rightful owners, a sum of 450 *livres tournois* was divided among six masters, the payment being charged upon a wine and beer tax.[2] Loyalty was also encouraged by the reservation in 1445, during the next seven years, of half the English king's benefices in France for graduates of Caen.[3] After the expulsion of the English the university appears, although apparently without any other endowment than its buildings and its artist colleges, to have enjoyed considerable prosperity as a local *studium*.[4]

§ 13. BORDEAUX (1441)

The *Statuta Universitatis Burdigaliae* were printed in 1694. Of this volume only one copy is known to exist. They have been reprinted (the original manuscript being lost) with a preface and other documents by BARCKHAUSEN, in *Statuts et Règlements de l'ancienne Université de Bordeaux*, Libourne and Bordeaux, 1886 (which contains the documents now printed by Fournier). GAULLIEUR, *Histoire du Collège de Guyenne*, Paris, 1874.

LIKE Caen, the University of Bordeaux arose during the English domination in France. It was founded in 1441 by

[1] Fournier, iii, Nos. 1699, 1704. Such a step can only have been taken under pressure of grievous financial embarrassment.

[2] De Bourmont, p. 551 *sq.*; Fournier, iii, No. 1672.

[3] De Bourmont, p. 551 *sq.*; Fournier, iii, No. 1663.

[4] The numbers at the beginning of the sixteenth century may be estimated from the manuscript *Matrologium*, f. 369 (in the archives of the Department), where there is a list of sixteen doctors and seventy-six other resident graduates of the superior faculties and twenty-two regents in arts.

a Bull of Eugenius IV upon the petition of the archbishop, of the seneschal and Aquitanian councillors of the English King Henry VI, and of the mayor and jurats of the city,[1] but (strange to say) did not receive a direct royal confirmation.[2] Its foundation was mainly the work of the municipality, though it was a project of which the English authorities had every reason to approve. Situated at the mouth of the river by which the students of Bordeaux might have ascended to

On the model of Toulouse. Toulouse, the new university was naturally modelled on that studium.[3] It was governed mainly by the masters, the student-rights being only recognized in the enactment that two of the rector's four councillors should be bachelors.[4] The then archbishop of Bordeaux was named chancellor for his lifetime. After his death the chancellorship was to pass to the first archdeacon in the church of Bordeaux, the archdeacon of Médoc. The bishop of Bazas, the abbot of La Sauve, and the archdeacon of Cernès were to be apostolical conservators: the conservation of the royal privileges was entrusted to the seneschal of Guienne.[5] The university nominally embraced all faculties, but no regular teachers were appointed in medicine,[6] and the faculty of arts represented little more than the incorporation of the existing college of arts or town-school, afterwards known as the College of Guienne.[7] By the original statutes there were to be one regent master in theology (in addition to the theological teachers of the Mendicant convents), two in canon law, two in civil law, one in arts, and

---

[1] Statuts, p. 3 sq.; Fournier, iii, Nos. 1768, 1769. [The Bull was dated 7 June 1441; the petition 30 April 1439; cf. Denifle, La Désolation des églises, i. 129 sqq.]

[2] Till the reign of Louis XI: Statuts, p. 19; Fournier, iii, No. 1772.

[3] The Bull declared that it was to be 'ad instar Studii Tolosani'.

[4] Statuts, p. 9; Fournier, iii, No. 1771. By the statutes of 1482 there were to be two proctors, one a bachelor of law, the other of arts, and two councillors. Statuts, p. 30; Fournier, iii, No. 1774. The councillors might be licentiates or bachelors.

[5] The mayor and sub-mayor of Bordeaux were in 1487 joined with him in the conservation. Statuts, p. 47; Fournier, iii, No. 1777.

[6] A regent in medicine occurs in 1491. Fournier, iii, No. 1780; Statuts, pp. xxiv, 440.

[7] The 'Magnae Scholae Civitatis'; Statuts, p. xix. No books are prescribed for the faculty of arts except 'Doctrinale et Graecismum'. Later we find a regular arts faculty; ibid., pp. 25, 35.

one in grammar.[1] None of the chairs were endowed, though the right of teaching was limited to their occupants; the professors were left to be supported by a fee of half a golden noble from each scholar.[2] Under these circumstances it is not surprising to find statutes very particular in their injunctions to examiners to treat the candidates 'with all tenderness and charity, preferring pity and lenity to the rigour of the law', so as 'to increase the university rather than diminish it'; while the prelates, nobles, and sons of doctors and masters are unblushingly excused 'the private examination'.[3] The reader will by this time be sufficiently familiar with the fate of small unendowed universities to anticipate that the career of the University of Bordeaux was far from a brilliant one. During the sixteenth and seventeenth centuries we find that extreme difficulty was experienced in getting university professors (who were here, it must be remembered, the only teachers) to deliver any lectures at all, and at times we find the university reduced to little more than an establishment for the sale of 'bogus' absentee degrees.[4]

§ 14. VALENCE (1452, 1459)

NADAL, *Hist. de l'Université de Valence*, Valence, 1861; a full history with a few documents. Fournier speaks of a very rare edition of the statutes, *Institutio, privilegia et statuta Universitatis Valentinae*, Turnone, 1601.

THE University of Valence owes its existence substantially to Origin. the efforts of its consuls, and formally to the dauphin Louis (afterwards Louis XI), who frequently resided in the place and bore (like his predecessors) the title of count of Valence. His charter of foundation was issued in the year 1452.[5] It is worded so as to be rather an announcement of the dauphin's

---

[1] *Statuts*, p. 12; Fournier, iii, No. 1771. After the French reconquest the university received a confirmation of its privileges from Louis XI (1474), and the number of regents was slightly increased: *Statuts*, pp. 19, 31; Fournier, iii, No. 1773 *sq.* The chairs were filled by co-optation.

[2] Together with 'pro scamno seu banquo suo . . . duodecim albos sive arditos monetae usualis Burdigaliae', and twenty for the bedel. *Statuts*, p. 13; Fournier, iii, No. 1771.

[3] *Statuts*, p. 16; Fournier, *loc. cit.*

[4] *Statuts*, pp. xxxviii *sq.*, 55, &c.

[5] Nadal, pp. 13, 361; Fournier, iii, Nos. 1784–9.

intention to found a university than an actual foundation,[1] though he goes on actually to found it in so far as lay in him —the rights of the Pope being thus respected. The university, however, came into being forthwith, though no papal Bull was issued till the year 1459, and the rector of the university was the envoy dispatched to Rome to procure its *ex post facto* erection. The language of the Bull granted by Pius II is remarkable. It both recognizes the university as already existing and also, 'for greater caution', founds it anew.[2] It was clearly intended to take the place of Grenoble as the university of the Dauphiné, the existence of any other university within its limits being ignored, or rather denied, by the dauphin's charter.[3] The bishop was appointed chancellor; the archbishop of Lyons, the bishop of Grenoble, and a neighbouring abbot conservators apostolic; and the seneschal of Valence conservator of the dauphin's privileges. The rector is spoken of (after the chancellor) as the 'rector or *primicerius*'—a title which we have previously met with in the neighbouring universities, Avignon and Aix.

Constitution and history. The university enjoyed the privileges of Orleans, Toulouse, and Montpellier. The earliest statutes are not extant, but a code belonging to the last years of the fifteenth or beginning of the sixteenth century makes it plain that it was a university of students under a student rector and council of twelve students.[4] Though it nominally embraced all the faculties,

---

[1] 'Universitatem studentium in facultatibus sacre Theologie, Iurium canonici, civilis, medicine et artium, in eadem nostra civitate perpetuo residendam, creavimus et instituimus, creamusque et instituimus, *quantum in nobis est*, ut eadem universitas, cancellarius, primicerius seu rector dictorum scholarium eiusdem, et quicunque alii illic aggregati secura studio intendant libertate.'

[2] 'Pro potiori cautela et presentium firmitate . . . studium huiusmodi de novo facimus, creamus et instituimus, . . . concedentes ut in eadem civitate sit studium ge-

nerale.' Fournier, iii, No. 1796; Nadal, p. 368. The Bull is also remarkable as recognizing the *ius ubique docendi* 'in singulis aliis studiis generalibus et *quibuscunque aliis locis* in quibus voluerint'. It is observable that it was thought necessary—not till 1459—to ask the bishop 'quod permittat legere et exercere studium' (Fournier, iii, No. 1802).

[3] 'Cum rari sint principes in quorum territoriis universitas non sit fundata, in nostris vero nulla.'

[4] Fournier, iii, No. 1842. It is observable that the *collegium doctorum* seems to have been open to

the university was mainly a law-school. The expenses of its chap.viii, § 14. foundation and the *honoraria* of the professors were paid by the consuls and council of the city,[1] to whose liberal patronage was due the considerable fame which the university attained in the sixteenth century, when Cujas, the illustrious reformer of Roman law-studies, was only one, though the greatest, of a succession of eminent professors of civil law.[2]

§ 15. NANTES (1460)

Teulé, 'L'ancienne Université Nantaise', in *Revue de Bretagne et la Vendée*, 3rd series, i, Nantes, 1867, 337 *sq.* Léon Maître, 'L'Université de Nantes', *ibid.*, 4th ser., ix, x; 5th ser., i, iii (1876–8). A few very slight notices occur in Travers, *Hist. de Nantes*, ii, 1837, 5 *sq.* The *Leges et Statuta inclyte Universitatis Nannetensis* were published at Nantes in 1651 (32 pages), and there are several editions of the foundation, privileges, &c.

In 1414 a Bull was issued by John XXIII sanctioning a Origin. scheme of John, Duke of Brittany, for the erection of a university at Nantes by the levy of a third upon all ecclesiastical revenues within the duchy.[3] But nothing came of this enactment, and no actual Bull of foundation appears to have been granted till the time of Martin V, whose Bull was confirmed by another Bull of Nicholas V in 1449.[4] All three Bulls, however, remained without effect, and it was not until 1461 that a university in all faculties was actually opened under a new Bull of Pius II granted in the preceding year.[5] Another Bull enabled the then duke, Francis II, to endow the university with a sum of 4,000 *saluts d'or* owing by him to the dean and chapter of S. Brieuc as an atonement for simony.[6] An annual grant of 200 livres was also made from the revenues of the duchy.[7]

The Bull of foundation entrusted the power of making Constitution.

all doctors who cared to lecture: was this the cause of the university's vigorous condition early in the sixteenth century?

[1] Fournier, *passim.*
[2] Nadal, p. 47 *sq.*
[3] Fournier, iii, No. 1588. According to Travers (ii. 5) the failures were due to the refusal of the earlier Popes to allow a faculty of theology,

but this is improbable.
[4] Fournier, iii, Nos. 1589, 1590.
[5] *Ibid.*, Nos. 1591, 1594.
[6] Maître, *Revue*, 1876, p. 418; Fournier, iii, No. 1593 (where the amount is wrongly stated in the heading as 5,000 *saluts*).
[7] Maître, *loc. cit.*, p. 421; Fournier, iii, No. 1599.

statutes to the bishop as chancellor, the rector and resident doctors, 'together with a competent number of licentiates and students' and two councillors of the duchy. But, after the establishment of the university and the promulgation of the first statutes, we hear no more of such a board. The constitution and statutes of 1462[1] are inspired by, but not copied from, those of its two nearest neighbours, Caen and Angers. They exhibit a kind of compromise between the mainly Parisian system of the former and the very modified student-democracy of Angers. Simple students have no share in the government of the university, unless they are 'dignitaries or canons of important churches';[2] but licentiates and bachelors of the superior faculties (together with the 'dignitaries and canons') have seats in congregation as well as the doctors or masters of all faculties. As at Caen, the rector is elected by five intrants representing the five faculties, and is selected from each faculty in turn. Unlike Caen, the five faculties of Nantes elect five proctors as well. In the faculty of arts, indeed, the proctorship is held by the same person as the deanship; but in the other faculties the dean is distinct from, and superior to, the proctor, who was usually a licentiate or bachelor. The rector must be a licentiate or bachelor of a superior faculty, or a master of arts. As at Orleans, the ordinary administration of university affairs is in the hands of a 'college' composed of the rector, the doctors, the regent masters of arts, and the proctors. The composition of the college seems to be suggested by the similar arrangement at Angers, though the proctors at Nantes are representatives of faculties, not of nations. Voting in both college and university is by faculties. At Paris college teaching had by this time become so essential a part of the university system in the faculty of arts that two pedagogies (with not less than three regents in each) were established at Nantes by the statutes from the first, and its students subjected to the schoolboy discipline now established in the Parisian colleges and pedagogies.[3]

---

[1] Fournier, iii, No. 1595.

[2] 'Nisi fuerit in dignitate constitutus, aut ecclesie cathedralis seu collegiate insignis canonicus.'

[3] By the papal Bull of 1460 the 4,000 *saluts d'or* owed by the duke

Under the liberal patronage of its founder the university CHAP. VIII,
enjoyed a short prosperity, but declined after his death, and §15.
almost totally collapsed during the last unsuccessful struggle History.
for Breton independence. In 1494 it was revived, chiefly as
a school of law, by the joint action of Charles VIII of France
and the city.[1] The faculty of law was transferred to Rennes
in 1735.

§ 16. BOURGES (1464)

There are very scanty notices in CHENU, *Recueil des Antiquitez et Privilèges de la Ville de Bourges*, Paris, 1621, and DE LA THAUMASSIÈRE, *Histoire
du Berry*, Bourges, 1689. Most of the documents printed by FOURNIER
in his *Statuts* appear also in *Mémoires de la Soc. historique du Cher*,
4th ser., ix, Bourges, 1893, with a short introduction by the same editor.
See also articles by MARTONNÉ in *Revue de Berry*, 1865, and by DUCHAS-
SEINT, *ibid.*, 1866. Fournier refers to GRANDMAISON, *De la splendeur de
l'Université de Bourges et de son rétablissement*, Bourges, 1829, and to
various works by CATHERINOT (seventeenth century).

THE University of Bourges was founded for all faculties by Origin.
Bull of Paul II, granted on the petition of Louis XI of France
(a native of Bourges) and his brother Charles, Duke of Berry,
in 1464.[2] A long but eventually unsuccessful effort was made
by the universities of Paris, Orleans, and Angers to procure
the recall of the Bourges privileges.[3] The university was

to the chapter of S. Brieuc was to
be spent in the foundation of a college. As to whether it was actually
spent upon the pedagogies there
appears to be no information. Mention is made of a Collège de Launay
and a Collège de Mellerai (Travers.
Hist. de Nantes, ii. 258). Maître
makes the former an addition to the
already existing 'College of S. John'
connected with the cathedral school
(*Revue*, 1876, p. 422). Cf. Teulé,
Revue, 1867, p. 343.

[1] Maître, *loc. cit.*, p. 424; 1878,
p. 180; Fournier, iii, Nos. 1602–8.
We hear, prior to the revival, of the
'penuriam doctorum atque perito-
rum legentium . . . et quod propterea nulli aut saltem pauci et rari
scolares ad civitatem et urbem Nan-
netensem accedebant seu ibidem
remanebant' (Fournier, iii, No.
1608). Charles VIII provided for

four professors with 100 *livres* each.
No. 1607 *sq.*

[2] Fournier, iii, Nos. 1850, 1851.
It confers also a general dispensation from residence, the *privilegium
fori*, leave for all secular clergy to
study the civil law, and (a very
exceptional feature) a prohibition
to practise medicine in the city
without leave of the faculty.

[3] Bulaeus, v. 678, 689–91, 715.
The proceedings before the Parlement of Paris are printed in Fournier, iii, Nos. 1858, 1860, 1861.
After reciting the original transference of the university from
Athens to Paris via Rome, and the
Carolingian privileges, the plea of
the University of Paris goes on
to notice the evils arising from a
multiplication of universities. It
declares that originally there were
only four universities, 'la premiere

designed for all faculties,[1] and was actually opened in 1467.[2] In 1470 the king by a twice-repeated order compelled the Parlement of Paris to register his letters of erection.[3]

Constitution and history.   The chancellor of the metropolitan church became chancellor of the university, and the bailiff of Bourges was the royal conservator. Some provision was made for the support of the university partly by the civic authorities and partly by a tax on ecclesiastical property;[4] but it is not clear how far these arrangements were really carried out. The statutes assign to the doctors of law a *collecta* of twenty-seven and a half *solidi turonenses* from each student.[5] Little information is forthcoming as to the character of the university constitution, but, as the rector was often a student,[6] and the university was mainly a university of law, we may presume that it was more or less a student-university of the modified French type. There were originally four nations, afterwards five, viz. France, Berry, Touraine, Aquitaine, and Germany, and the nations were, it appears (as at Poitiers), divisions of the jurist faculty only.[7] Charles VIII in 1498 had to issue an edict against gross neglect of duty on the part of certain regents of law who were also canons of the cathedral, officials of the archbishop, and considerable landed proprietors;[8] but in the sixteenth century the university rose to great importance as a school of law, when great jurists like Alciat, Refussus, and Cujas were among its teachers.

à Paris, la seconde en Italie, la tierce en Angleterre, et la quarte en Espagne'. It also alleges that Bourges gave degrees to those 'refusez in graduatione propter insufficientiam'.

[1] I have not elsewhere noticed the following curious custom: 'At Bourges in France,' says Luther, 'at the public creation of doctors in theology, which takes place in the metropolitan church there, each doctor has a net given him, as a sign, seemingly, that their business is to catch men.' Michelet's *Life of Luther* (Eng. trans. in the Universal Library), p. 64. There is no trace of this in any medieval statute.

[Professor Potter has found this story in *D. Martini Lutheri Colloquia, meditationes, consolationes,* edit. H. E. Bindseil (1863), ii. 15: 'Ita et Burgis Doctores theologiae promotos ornant, *geben ihnen fisch reusen, das sie die leutte damit fahen sollen'.*]

[2] Fournier, iii, No. 1853.

[3] *Ibid.,* Nos. 1859, 1860.

[4] *Ibid.,* No. 1854.

[5] *Ibid.,* No. 1862.

[6] *Ibid.,* No. 1866.

[7] *Mém. de la Soc. Hist. du Cher,* p. 9, referring to Raynal, *Hist. du Berry,* iii. 364.

[8] Fournier, iii, No. 1865.

BESANÇON (1485)

A Bull for a *studium generale* in arts only was issued by Nicholas V CHAP. VIII, in 1450, but apparently remained unexecuted. For the further § 16. history of the successive attempts to found a university in this place, the reader may be referred to the section on Dôle (p. 192). There *may* have been some kind of school or college in arts, technically entitled to university privileges, from the year 1483; but it is extremely doubtful whether there was a university here in anything but the name till a university in all faculties was formally established in 1565.

§ 17. SUMMARY

AFTER the somewhat bewildering mass of constitutional details Summary. with which we have been engaged, it may be well to sum up in a few sentences the leading characteristics of the French universities other than Paris:

(1) In their origin the older of them—such as Orleans and Origin. Angers—were spontaneous developments of ancient cathedral schools, or at least of episcopally governed schools (such as Montpellier), which eventually obtained papal Bulls. The later were erected by papal Bull as elsewhere. In the older *studia* the organization is in part of independent origin— especially the system of nations, which does not seem to be copied from either Paris or Bologna.

(2) At the beginning of our period the internal government Modified student-rights. of the universities is originally in the hands of the masters or doctors, though there is sometimes a more or less nominal recognition of the students as members of the university corporation. In the old universities of Orleans, Angers, and perhaps Montpellier, there was probably from an early period an organization of the students into nations side by side with the university proper. And through these nations the students, in the course of the fourteenth century, gradually acquired a much larger share in university government, including especially the election of the rector. The ultimate result of this change is a constitution in which the doctors and students together are recognized as the ultimate governing body of the university, but in which its actual government and administration were practically left in the hands of a college composed of a rector, the whole or a portion of the doctors,

and the representatives of the student nations, whether styled proctors or councillors, most or all of whom are in practice licentiates or bachelors. At Toulouse a somewhat scantier admission of students to the council or college dates from the original constitution of the university. The typically French university system thus represents a fusion between the magisterial or Parisian and the Bolognese or student constitution. Caen and Poitiers must be regarded in some measure as exceptions to this generalization, being framed on the model of Paris, but even they are not unaffected by the prevailing type. At Avignon the efforts of the students in the fourteenth century to acquire an elective and legislative rectorship were baffled, and the power remained in the hands of the masters. The medical university of Montpellier also retained to the last the ancient system of government by the college of doctors; but in both cases there is a student organization outside the university proper, which eventually enables the students' representatives to conduct corporate negotiations with the doctors, though not to obtain admission to their college.

Authority of bishop.

(3) In almost every case the bishop has a much more important and powerful position in the university than he enjoyed either at Bologna or at Paris. The spontaneously developed *studia* were originally entirely under the control of the bishop and an episcopal chancellor or *scholasticus*. In many cases statutes are issued by his authority. Later, his prerogatives were gradually diminished by the powers acquired by the doctors or the universities under royal or papal privilege. But to the last the bishop retained considerable authority in nearly all the French universities. The municipalities, on the other hand, though in the south of France often interesting themselves in the foundation or development of the universities, possessed much less control over them than in Italy. Towards the close of our period, however, the system of *salaria* brought with it increased subordination to the secular power, whether king, prince, or town council.

Limited college of doctors.

(4) The rights of regency were—in some cases from the beginning, in almost all sooner or later—limited to a small

body of teachers whether supported by *salaria* or only by fees.
A permanent professoriate was thus formed very like that
established in the German universities by the totally different
system of endowed *collegiaturae*. The French and German
professoriate differs from the Italian in being for the most
part co-opted, instead of being periodically elected either
by the students or the city government. Moreover, in France
the privilege of the co-opting college was usually limited to
the monopoly of 'ordinary' lectures and the resulting fees.
Salaries only become common towards the close of our
period.[1]

(5) Law-studies were the most prominent in all these uni- Promi-
versities, except at Montpellier, whose fame was originally nence of
based on medicine. This was especially the case with the law.
older schools of Angers and Orleans, which long remained
without any other faculty.

(6) Endowed colleges for poor students played a much Impor-
more important part in these universities than in Italy. Many tance of
of the smaller *studia* were kept alive during the less prosperous colleges.
periods of their history mainly by the colleges. Their constitution in southern France usually approximates to the
Italian type: at all events the headship is usually held for
short periods, though at Toulouse the head was usually a
chaplain. College teaching never became important except
in colleges for monks or friars, and perhaps at Caen, where
there was an important arts faculty modelled on Paris.

(7) One consequence of the prominence of law in the Position
French provincial universities was the unimportance of the of arts.
faculty of arts. Towards the close of our period we see,
however, a tendency on the part of towns to erect 'colleges'
which were really schools for boys, in connexion with a
newly erected university, or to bring old grammar-schools
into connexion with the newly created faculty of arts. This
is not the place to attempt to trace the effects of such arrangements upon the French educational tradition down to the

[1] Even before the end of the fifteenth century we find the law-professors claiming the privileges of nobility, a claim which was eventually recognized in all French universities; Pilotelle, in *Mém. de la Soc. des Ant. de l'Ouest*, xxvii (1863), 367 *sq.*

CHAP. VIII, present day, but it would probably be found that the system
§ 17. by which the bachelor's degree *precedes* the beginning of the
strictly university course, while 'rhetoric and philosophy' are
taught in the highest form of the lycée, is to some extent an
inheritance from the scholastic organization of the Middle
Ages.

CHAPTER IX

THE UNIVERSITIES OF GERMANY, BOHEMIA, AND THE LOW COUNTRIES[1]

[An exhaustive bibliography of work done before 1904 will be found in W. ERMAN and E. HORN, *Bibliographie der deutschen Universitäten*, 3 vols., Leipzig, 1904; cf. DAHLMANN-WAITZ, *Quellenkunde der deutschen Geschichte*, 9th ed., Leipzig, 1931, especially pp. 206–17, and L. J. PAETOW, *A Guide to the Study of Medieval History*, revised edition, London, 1931, pp. 481, 482. Karl VON RAUMER, *Die deutschen Universitäten*, 6th ed., Stuttgart, 1898 (Part IV of his *Geschichte der Pädagogik*), deals slightly with the medieval period. The first systematic study is in G. KAUFMANN, *Die Geschichte der deutschen Universitäten*, 2 vols., Stuttgart, 1888–96. Studies of particular universities by various scholars will be found in *Das akademische Deutschland*, herausg. M. DOEBERL, O. SCHEEL, W. SCHLINK, &c., vol. i, Berlin, 1930. See also F. PAULSEN, *Geschichte des gelehrten Unterrichts auf den deutschen Schulen und Universitäten*, ed. 3, by R. LEHMANN, 2 vols., Leipzig, 1919–21; Th. ZIEGLER, *Geschichte der Pädagogik mit besonderer Rücksicht auf das höhere Unterrichtswesen* (Part I of A. BAUMEISTER's *Handbuch d. Erziehungs- und Unterrichtslehre*), 5th ed., by A. NEBE, Munich, 1923; and S. D'IRSAY, *Histoire des Universités*, i. 174–91.

The following articles deserve special mention: F. PAULSEN, 'Die Gründung der deutschen Universitäten im Mittelalter' (*Hist. Zeitschrift*, xlv, 1881, 251–311), and 'Organization und Lebensordnungen der deutschen Universitäten im Mittelalter' (*ibid.*, pp. 385–440); B. GEBHARDT, 'Die deutschen Universitäten im Mittelalter' (*Preussiche Jahrbücher*, lxxxviii, 1897, 374–406); F. VON BEZOLD, 'Die ältesten deutschen Universitäten in ihrem Verhältnis zum Staat' (*Hist. Zeitschrift*, lxxx, 1898, 436–67, reprinted in his collected papers, *Aus Mittelalter und Renaissance*, Munich, 1918, pp. 220–45, 417–23); A. VON WRETSCHKO, 'Universitäts-Privilegien der Kaiser aus der Zeit von 1412–56' (*Festschrift zur O. Gierkes 70. Geburtstag*, Weimar, 1911, pp. 793 *sqq.*); M. MEYHÖFER, 'Die kaiserlichen Stiftungsprivilegien für Universitäten' (*Archiv für Urkundenforschung*, iv, 1912, 291–418).]

§ 1. PRAGUE (1347–8)

VOLCKMAN, *Gloria Universitatis Carolo-Ferdinandae Pragensis* (Prague: no date) [1672] is rather a 'eulogium' than a history; of which VOIGT, *Acta Litteraria Bohemiae et Moraviae* (Prague, 1776, pp. 119–35), gives a summary with a few extracts from documents. There is also a slight sketch of the history of the university by the same writer, entitled *Versuch einer Gesch. d. Univ. zu Prag* (Prague, 1776). *Monumenta Historica Universitatis Pragensis* (Prague, i, 1830, ii, 1834, iii, no date), edd. DITTRICH and SPIRK, is a valuable and tolerably complete collection of documents. V. V. TOMEK, *Geschichte d. Prager Univ.* (Prague, 1849) is

---

[1] [We have received much assistance in the revision of this chapter from Professor G. R. Potter.]

CHAP. IX, a good book somewhat spoiled by the absence of references to authorities.
§ 1. HERBST, *Das juridische Doctorencollegium in Prag* (Prague, 1861), deals almost entirely with post-medieval history. C. HÖFLER, *Magister Johannes Hus und der Abzug der deutschen Professoren und Studenten aus Prag, 1409* (Prague, 1864), is a useful study of the subject. Many notices and documents relating to the university may be found in HÖFLER, 'Geschichtsschreiber der husitischen Bewegung in Böhmen', in *Fontes Rer. Austriacarum: Scriptores (Kais. Akad. d. Wissenschaften in Wien,* 1856–65), which includes the *Chronicon Universitatis Pragensis,* [also edited by J. GOLL in *Fontes rerum Bohemicarum,* v. 565 *sq.* (Prague, 1893)], on which there is a dissertation by M. RUSTLER, *Das sogenannte Chron. Univ. Prag.* (Leipzig, 1886). Of later works on the Hussite movement by far the most important is J. LOSERTH, *Huss und Wiclif. Zur Genesis der husitischen Lehre,* Prague and Leipzig, 1884; edit. 2, Munich, 1925; trans. M. J. EVANS, *Wiclif and Hus,* London, 1884.

[F. DOELLE, 'Ein Fragment der verlorengegangenen Prager Universitätsmatrikel aus dem 14. Jahrhundert' (*Miscellanea Francesco Ehrle,* Rome, 1924, iii. 88–102); G. E. GUHRAUER, 'Die Anfänge der Prager Universität' (*Deutsche Vierteljahrschrift,* iii (1848); *L'Université de Charles IV dans le passé et dans le présent,* Prague, 1923 (a pamphlet published by the Senatus Academicus); W. WOSTRY on the German University of Prague in *Das akademische Deutschland,* i. 349; A. BLASCHKA, 'Das Prager Universitäts-privileg Karl IV', in *Jahrbuch des Vereins für Geschichte der Deutschen in Böhmen,* iii (1932); K. SPIEGEL, 'The origin of the University of Prague', in *Catholic Historical Review,* ix. 179–82 (Washington, 1929); S. D'IRSAY, i. 174–6, 186–91; A. BACHMANN, 'Der älteste Streit zwischen Deutschen und Tschechen an der Prager Universität' (*Historische Vierteljahrschrift,* vii (1904), 39–52; F. MATTHAESIUS, *Der Auszug der deutschen Studenten aus Prag,* 1409, Prague, 1914. This dissertation appeared in the *Mitteilungen des Vereins für die Geschichte der Deutschen in Böhmen,* lii. 451–99; liii. 58–110, a series of publications which illustrates the range of the controversy between German and Czech. Cf. F. PALACKÝ, *Die Geschichte des Husitenthums und Prof. C. Höfler,* Prague, 1868; F. PAULSEN in the *Historische Zeitschrift,* xlv (1881), 266 *sqq.,* and F. STIEVE, *Abhandlungen, Vorträgen und Reden,* Leipzig, 1900, pp. 28 *sqq.*

The books and articles mentioned above are, indeed, but a fragment of the extensive literature relating to the University of Prague; for the history of the university is bound up with the history of national feeling, ecclesiastical criticism, heresy, and especially the career of John Hus. The most convenient bibliographies, for those who do not read Czech, are to be found in J. LOSERTH, *Geschichte des späteren Mittelalters,* Munich and Berlin, 1903, pp. 455–7; the articles of J. ŠUSTA in the *Revue historique,* cl (1925), 67–89, and clxxi (1933), 162–205; *La Fin du Moyen Âge,* i (Paris, 1931), 331–2 in *Peuples et civilisations,* ed. L. HALPHEN and P. SAGNAC, vii; HEFELE-LECLERCQ, *Histoire des conciles,* VII. i (1926), 110 *sqq.;* cf. for bibliographies in Czech, *Cambridge Medieval History,* vii. 848. Among the more important collections of texts, in addition to the *Fontes rerum Austriacarum* mentioned above, are: *Fontes rerum Bohemicarum,* edit. J. EMLER, iii–v, Prague, 1882–93; *Concilia Pragensia,* ed. HÖFLER, Prague, 1862 (in Abhandl. der K. Böhmischen Gesellschaft der Wissenschaften, ser. v, vol. xii); J. LOSERTH, 'Beiträge zur Geschichte d. huss. Bewegung' (in *Archiv für österreichische Geschichte,* 55, 57, 60,

75, 82). General histories: F. PALACKÝ, *Geschichte von Böhmen*, Prague,
1836–67 (5 vols. to 1526), especially vol. iii, edit. 3, Prague, 1896;
A. BACHMANN, *Geschichte Böhmens*, 2 vols. to 1526, Gotha, 1899–1905;
A. FRIND, *Die Kirchengeschichte Böhmens*, 4 vols., Prague, 1864–78;
F. H. V. LÜTZOW, *The Life and Times of Master John Hus*, London, ed.
1921; Joseph T. MÜLLER, *Geschichte der böhmischer Brüder*, 1400–1572,
2 vols., Herrenhut, 1922–31.

The bibliographies noted above contain references to the chief collections and monographs in Czech and German relating to the religious life
of Bohemia in this period, to the movements prior to Hus, and to Hus
himself and his companions. On the whole the standpoint of Palacký
(d. 1876), who found the roots of the Hussite movement in the previous
history of Bohemia, has been maintained, but various writers have looked
for other influences especially to the Waldensians, or to the University
of Paris, or to Wyclif. See especially (for Parisian influence) V. KYBAL,
'Étude sur les origines du mouvement hussite en Bohème: Matthias de
Ianov' (*Revue historique*, ciii, 1910, 1–31); V. NOVOTNÝ, 'Les origines
du mouvement hussite en Bohême', in *Revue de l'histoire des religions*,
lxxxix (1924), 77–90; O. ODLOŽILÍK, 'Wycliffe's influence upon Central
and Eastern Europe', in *The Slavonic Review*, vii (1928–9), 634–8; and
(for the Waldensians) S. H. THOMSON, 'Pre-Hussite heresy in Bohemia'
(*English Hist. Review*, xlviii, 1933, 23–42). The two last articles contain
valuable bibliographical information.]

NOTHING can more strikingly illustrate the cosmopoli- No university in
Germany
in the
earlier
Middle
Ages.
tanism of the medieval university system than the fact
that up to the middle of the fourteenth century Germany
possessed no university at all. Germany was certainly not
untouched by the great intellectual movement of the twelfth
century; but its two great centres were Paris and northern
Italy. To England, indeed, the impulse transferred itself in
the infancy of the university system. But when the earliest
universities arose, Germany was too far behind the rest of
Europe in culture and civilization for the spontaneous development of a university; and when the period of artificial
foundations arrived, its political dissensions were not favourable to such an experiment. Feudal magnates were perhaps
less likely to become patrons of learning than either independent kings or independent cities. However this may be, the
fact remains that for two centuries the university-movement
affected Germany mainly by drawing away students to foreign
schools. German students abounded in all the more important *studia* both of France and Italy. At Paris, after the rise
of the English universities, they must have formed an increasingly large proportion of the English nation; while the

CHAP. IX,
§ 1.

special privileges which they enjoyed at Bologna, Padua, and other Italian universities no doubt contributed to reconcile the wealthier class of students to the non-existence of a national *studium*.

Designs of Charles IV.

The foundation of a university was a scheme exactly suited to the character and position of Charles IV, King of the Romans and King of Bohemia. It was his policy at once to assert the imperial prerogative in so far as that could be done by the issue of charters and privileges, and to make his imperial position an instrument for strengthening and developing his Bohemian kingdom and capital. He was himself a scholar, had lived long in France, and was much influenced by French ideas.[1] Paris naturally, therefore, became the model for Charles's university; and, partly no doubt in consequence of that precedent, for all subsequent German universities. A nucleus for the new foundation was already in existence. There had been a *studium particulare* of considerable importance in Prague at least from early in the thirteenth century.[2] In 1271-4 we hear of masters teaching under the *scholasticus* of the cathedral, and the instruction included not merely grammar and logic but the Aristotelian natural philosophy. The students were drawn from a considerable area—from Austria, Styria, and Bavaria, as well as from all parts of Bohemia.[3] Had the *studium* attained to this point of development a little earlier, and had it succeeded in maintaining its prestige continuously, there would probably have been a spontaneous development into a *studium generale*. But the outbreak of hostilities between the Emperor Rudolf of Hapsburg and the Bohemian king Ottokar II in 1274 drove away the students from the Hapsburg dominions, and lowered the importance of the *studium*.[4] From more distant

Existing studium particulare.

[1] Pelzel, *SS. Rer. Boh.* ii (Prague, 1784), 350. [W. Klein, *Kaiser Karls IV Jugendaufenthalt in Frankreich und dessen Einfluss auf seine Entwicklung* (Dissertation), Berlin, 1926; cf. H. Friedjung, *Kaiser Karl IV und sein Antheil am geistigen Leben seiner Zeit*, Vienna, 1876.]

[2] In 1248, after the capture of

Prague by the Margrave Ottokar, we read that 'Studium Pragae perit', *Ann. Pragens.* in *Mon. Germ. Scriptores*, ix. 172.

[3] *Ep. Engelberti Abbatis ad mag. Ulricum schol. Wienn.* in Pez, *Thes. Anecd. Nov.* i, cc. 429, 430.

[4] Pez, *loc. cit.*

regions students could not at the close of the thirteenth century be attracted without chartered privileges and authenticated degrees. The idea of obtaining the now indispensable parchments had already presented itself to the enlightened Bohemian monarch, Wenceslaus II,[1] but the plan had failed through the opposition of the nobles, who feared an increase in the power and influence of the clerical order[2]—a significant indication alike of what the universities had done for the clergy and therefore for the people elsewhere and of the causes which had kept Germany without a university for so long a period. It seems probable too that the scheme was connected, or supposed to be connected, with another project of Wenceslaus— the substitution of 'written laws', which would practically mean the civil and canon law, for the customary law of the kingdom.[3] In 1346, however, Charles IV forwarded to the Pope a petition for a Bull of foundation. The Bull was issued by Clement VI in January 1347,[4] and on 7 April was followed by an imperial charter, which not unnaturally shows the influence of Frederick's epoch-making charter for Naples—like Prague the capital of a national sovereign who also wore the imperial crown.[5]

Previous attempt of Wenceslaus II: opposition of the nobles.

Foundation.

All the conditions essential to the success of a university were present, and the new institution prospered from the first. The large number of German students who had previously found their way to foreign universities only shows how many possible students must have been previously deterred by the

Importance of event.

[1] *Chron. Aulae Regiae* ap. *Fontes Rer. Austr.*, *Scriptores*, viii, ed. Loserth (1885), 130.

[2] *Chron. Aulae Regiae*, pp. 130, 131.

[3] *Ibid.*, pp. 129, 130. The chronicler says that the nobles opposed this project 'ne . . . fructus, quem de abusivis eorum adinventionibus hactenus consueverant tollere, ipsis forsitan deperiret'.

[4] *Mon. Univ. Prag.* ii. 219. [See also *Monumenta Vaticana res gestas Bohemiae illustrantia*, i (ed. L. Klicman), Prague, 1903, No. 845. Prague was raised to be the seat of

an archbishopric in 1344, and the necessity for a school of theology had been pressed.]

[5] *Ibid.*, p. 223. This charter is granted by Charles as king of the Romans and of Bohemia, and confers all the privileges of Bologna and Paris. [The charter was sealed with the golden bull, used on the same day for other important acts; Wostry in *Das akademische Deutschland*, i. 350.] A purely imperial charter of 1349 conferred all the privileges ever bestowed by the emperors on any university. *Reg. Imp.* viii (ed. Huber), No. 834.

distance and consequent expense. The bulk of the Germans at foreign universities were probably young nobles and well-born or well-beneficed ecclesiastics: hence perhaps in part their exceptional privileges at Bologna and elsewhere. The erection of a university in Germany was therefore an event in the social as well as the intellectual emancipation of the German people: the 'career open to merit' was henceforth brought within reach of the sons of the tradesman and the artisan. Martin Luther could hardly have enjoyed a university education if he had had to go to Paris for it; and without a university education for Luther, and such as Luther, the German Reformation could not have been. From other points of view the growth of the German universities exercised a less entirely favourable influence upon the national development. They are largely responsible for the ascendancy of Roman law in Germany—an ascendancy which, however satisfactory from the point of view of the scientific jurist, has not always made for personal liberty or political progress.[1]

Rapid success of university. The foundation of the university came at a moment when the Bohemian nation was making immense strides in civilization and culture. The fourteenth century is the golden age of Bohemian literature; and the country is said to have been exceptionally well provided with grammar-schools.[2] We have

[1] 'The universal employment of torture founded on an appeal to the Roman law and the Italian jurists; the Roman theory of the absolute freedom of the monarch in legislation; the principle of the jurists that every landlord on his own estate is to be held as supreme as the Roman Emperor himself; the privileges of the Roman Fiscus; the horrible doctrine of high treason, and the Draconian laws against it; and lastly, the legal axiom that the Sovereign is not amenable to the laws.' Döllinger, *Universities Past and Present*, translated by Appleton, Oxford, 1867, pp. 5, 6.

It may be doubted, however, how far the Roman law did more than supply a vehicle for the expression of ideas whose growth was due to other causes. The same ideas were growing up in England (where the influence of the Roman law was almost at its *minimum*), but the resistance offered to the civil law by our common lawyers was doubtless one of the forces which prevented their complete ascendancy. [See also Vinogradoff, *Roman Law in Medieval Europe*, ed. 2, Oxford, 1929, pp. 118–45, esp. p. 127.]

[2] See Wratislaw's interesting *Native Literature of Bohemia in the Fourteenth Century* (London, 1878), p. 3 *sq.* Even within the single city of Prague there appears to have been a number of grammar-schools attached to parish churches, the master or *rector scholarum* being

fairly satisfactory means of tracing the progress of the univer- sity in numbers and popularity. All faculties (except civil law) were represented from the first. A rectorial election was held in 1353, which probably indicates the actual opening of the university; and at that time there were five masters of theology, two of decrees, one of medicine, and several of arts.[1] A roll of supplicants for benefices sent to the Roman court in 1355 contains the names of one doctor and one bachelor of decrees, five masters of arts, and nineteen bachelors of arts (many of whom are described as 'actually teaching'), with a large number of students in various faculties;[2] and later notices testify to gradually increasing numbers in the faculties of arts and law from all parts of Germany[3]—especially after the year 1370. By the beginning of the following century contempo- rary chroniclers declared that the number of foreign students Numbers. in Prague amounted to two thousand or more.[4] The total numbers of the university at this time cannot have fallen far short of four thousand.

It has been said above that on the whole the constitution of Constitu- the university was framed on the Parisian rather than on the tion. Bologna model. This statement, however, requires to be

appointed by the parish priest. But after the foundation of the univer- sity, that body claimed a certain jurisdiction over the schools which led to collisions with the *plebani*. (*Mon. Univ. Prag.* i, pt. 2, 242; iii. 65; Tomek, p. 41.)

[1] *Chron. Aulae Regiae*, p. 600.

[2] Denifle, i. 593, 594. [One chronicler refers to the multitudes of scholars from other countries, including England, France, Lom- bardy, Hungary: *Fontes rerum Bohemicarum*, iv. 460. In 1399 Uberto Decembrio noted the strength of the theological faculty: 'studium hic satis magnum viget in artibus, potissimum in theologica facultate: in legibus vero et medi- cina non est ita'; quoted by S. d'Irsay, p. 176 note, from *Archeo- grafo Triestino*, vii, no. 3, 1880, p. 9.]

[3] See extracts from the Vatican registers, Denifle, i. 594 *sq.*, and *Mon. Univ. Prag.*, i. 133 *et passim*.

[4] See below, p. 228. Tomek (p. 38) estimates the average number of students between 1372 and 1409 at 11,000. This is far too high. The most trustworthy data are the facts (1) that between 1397 and 1408, 844 persons graduated as masters, and 3,823 as bachelors (*ibid.*, p. 30); (2) that 722 students were enrolled in one semester of 1374 (*Mon. Univ. Prag.* i, pt. 2, 240). [See F. Eulen- burg, *Die Frequenz der deutschen Universitäten von ihren Gründung bis zur Gegenwart*, Leipzig, 1904 (Abhandl. d. konigl. Sachs. Gesell- schaft d. Wissenschaften, phil.-hist. Klasse, xxiv. 2).] For further dis- cussion of the question see below, vol. iii, ch. xiii.

CHAP. IX, understood with certain modifications. The foundation Bull
§ 1.   assigned the right of promotion to the archbishop of Prague,
and in the early days of the university's existence the archbishop, in his capacity of chancellor, exercised something of
that paternal control over it which was exercised in the infancy of Oxford and Cambridge, and more permanently and
successfully in French universities like Montpellier and
Angers, by their respective diocesans.[1] By its original constitution the University of Prague embraced all the four faculties, as at Paris, under the government of a single rector.[2] But
the law-students became ambitious of the student-liberties

Indepen- enjoyed by their class at Bologna and Padua. Hence in 1372
dent uni- they were allowed to form a separate university under a rector
versity of
jurists, of their own.[3] We do not possess any early statutes of the
1372. jurist university, but we may presume that its constitution
was more or less influenced by Italian traditions.

Nations. Even the university of the other three faculties was not a
faithful reproduction of Paris. The statute relating to the
rectorship is copied from the corresponding statute at
Bologna,[4] and does not require the person elected to be a
master. It appears, however, that he usually, if not invariably,
was so; and we have no evidence that students had a vote in
his election or in other university congregations.[5] Each university was divided into four nations, (1) Bohemia, (2) Poland,
(3) Bavaria, (4) Saxony.[6] In the non-jurist university all its

[1] See, for instance, *Mon. Univ.
Prag.* ii. 229. [While Charles had
memories of Paris, the archbishop,
Ernest of Pardubice, had studied
law in Bologna.]

[2] So the *Chron. Univ. Prag.* (ap.
Höfler, *Geschichtsschreiber*, i. 13).
But the chancellor's order of 1360
(*Mon. Univ. Prag.* ii. 230), that
henceforth 'in dicto studio sit unus
rector et una universitas' (with a
vicar taken from the faculty to
which the rector for the time being
did not belong), would seem to
imply that there had already been
some controversy about the matter.

[3] *Mon. Univ. Prag.* ii. 28; Höfler,
Geschichtsschreiber, i. 13. [The

rector of the jurists was not a
master.]

[4] *Mon. Univ. Prag.* iii. 1.

[5] [In 1385 it was stipulated that
the electors must be graduates; cf.
the remarks of Matthaesius, *op. cit.*,
p. 12.]

[6] Bavaria included the whole of
south Germany; Poland included
also Prussia and east Germany;
Saxony the adjoining German
states, England, Finland, and the
Scandinavian countries (*Mon.
Univ. Prag.* iii. 10; Tomek, p. 9).
It does not seem clear whether at
first the students voted on the
election of *consiliarii*, but certainly
by 1415 the masters appear to be

members belonged to the nations, and not, as at Paris, the
faculty of arts only. This constitutional change brought with
it another. The special connexion of the rector with the
faculty of arts did not exist in Prague, and it was necessary
for the artists to have a dean like the superior faculties.[1] The
heads of the nations were usually called by the Bolognese
name of *consiliarii*, though occasionally styled 'councillors' or
'proctors'. The councillors, who were (at least, in all probability, until 1392) students or bachelors, sat with the masters
in the congregation or council of the university.[2]

In the council of the university the voting was by heads, in
congregation by nations. All faculties were apparently included in the nations until the secession of the jurists.[3] The
university was, however, even more completely split up for
practical purposes into distinct faculties than the mother
University of Paris. These faculties were at first composed
of the whole body of masters; but at some date prior to 1393
the ordinary business of the faculty of arts was entrusted to
a council consisting of the dean and the masters of four years'
standing, the 'full congregation' of the faculty being summoned only for the admission of new masters and bachelors
and on occasions of exceptional importance.[4] These constitutional changes we shall find reproduced with more or less
fidelity in the other German universities.

The rector had from the first jurisdiction in civil causes
and 'injuries' over members of the university, subject to an
appeal to the chancellor.[5]   In 1392 the university was

the only electors (*Mon. Univ. Prag.*
iii. 46). Besides the *consiliarii* we
hear of certain *directores*, whose
position I cannot precisely explain.
[1] [He appears from 1368 in the
faculty of arts and later in the other
two faculties. The deans were
elected by the masters; Wostry,
p. 352.]
[2] *Mon. Univ. Prag.* iii. 17. [Cf.
Matthaesius, p. 21, for the statute
of 1392.]
[3] *Ibid.*
[4] *Ibid.* i, pt. i, p. 93.

[5] *Ibid.* ii. 252; iii. 5. [In 1384
the rector and masters protested
strongly against interference (Höfler, *Geschichtsschreiber*, ii. 128–
30). Tomek, pp. 8, 14, followed
by Kaufmann, ii. 126, regards the
intervention of the archbishop of
Prague as due to his archiepiscopal
concern for the university and not
to his rights as chancellor. Cf. the
whole section on the position of the
chancellor in German universities
in Kaufmann, ii. 125–57.]

exempted from the jurisdiction of the ordinary civil tribunals,[1] and in 1397 the court of the rector and *consiliarii* obtained an apparently unlimited jurisdiction—civil, criminal, and spiritual—over causes in which one party was a scholar, and the university was totally exempted from all metropolitan and episcopal jurisdiction by a Bull of Boniface IX, the pontiff to whom Oxford owes a similar exemption.[2]

Endowments.

We have seen that, though originally the professors alike in the student and in the magisterial universities were supported by the fees of their scholars, the system of salaried professors early became characteristic of the *studia* of the Bologna type. But while the masters of Paris and Oxford long continued without direct salary (an indirect endowment was supplied by the colleges), new universities rarely succeeded without some kind of endowment. At Prague this was at first supplied from the royal exchequer; but after 1352, with the consent of the archbishop, the expense was defrayed by contributions from the revenues of the monasteries and chapters throughout the kingdom.[3] Each of the faculties was early provided with a building for its lectures.[4] A college (from the first supplied with a considerable library) was erected in 1366 for twelve masters by the founder of the university—

Collegium Carolinum, 1366.

and this *Collegium Carolinum* was soon afterwards connected in an entirely novel manner with the royal Collegiate Chapel of All Saints, the members of the academical college being appointed to prebends in the chapel as they fell vacant.[5] It is observable that in one respect the *Collegium Carolinum* seems to have approximated to the Oxford model rather than to the Parisian, the vacancies being filled by co-optation. The hall of the college was the ordinary place of assembly for the university congregations and other public functions. Residence in a college or a hall kept by a master or bachelor was here required at a much earlier period than at Paris or Oxford[6]

---

[1] *Mon. Univ. Prag.* ii. 325.

[2] *Ibid.* ii. 370. This presumably did not supersede the jurisdiction of the apostolic conservators (*ibid.*, p. 346).

[3] Pelzel, ii. 350; Denifle, i.

598. Fees were still paid by the students.

[4] Tomek, pp. 26, 27.

[5] *Mon. Univ. Prag.* ii. 231 *sq.*; Pelzel, ii. 351, 405; Tomek, p. 21 *sq.*

[6] *Mon. Univ. Prag.* iii. 8, 9.

—another indication of the real supremacy of the masters in spite of the democratic character of the nations. A *domus pauperum* was established by a private founder in 1379. The College of King Wenceslaus was founded by that monarch before the year 1381; and in 1397 a college was projected for students from Lithuania and the surrounding countries by his kinswoman Hedwig, Queen of Poland.[1] Most of the masters of Prague appear to have resided and taught in the colleges; the college lectures were open to non-foundationers and were recognized by the faculty; and, as the collegiate masters lectured in arts while pursuing their own studies in theology, the colleges supplied the place of an additional endowment to the university.[2] The example set by Charles IV was followed in the other German universities. The German colleges differed from those of Paris, Oxford, or any earlier university in being intended from the first as colleges for teachers, and only secondarily (if at all) for students. They often formed part of the original plan of the universities in which they were set up, and were at all events much more closely connected with the university and enjoyed much less corporate independence than was the case at Oxford or Paris.

For seventy years after its foundation the internal affairs of the University of Prague have an important bearing upon general European history. The university plays a conspicuous part in a great national and a great religious movement. The maturity of each of the foremost European nations is marked by a profound intellectual movement, of which one of the results necessarily was a collision with the medieval ecclesiastical system. In France it came in the twelfth and thirteenth centuries, and was stamped out by the Albigensian crusades and the inquisition. In England it came in the fourteenth century, and was crushed out for the moment, and

---

[1] Tomek, pp. 25, 27; *Mon. Univ. Prag.* ii. 359, 374. [Cf. Morawski, *Hist. de l'université de Cracovie*, i. 68. This college is said not to have become effective till the foundation of Vladislaus II in 1411; see V. Novotný in *L'Université de Charles IV*, p. 31.]

[2] The bachelors of arts took a much more important position in the teaching of the faculty here than at Paris (Tomek, p. 29; Denifle, i. 593 *sq.*). [Cf. A. Franz, *Der Magister Nikolaus Magni de Jawor*, Freiburg-i.-B., 1898.]

with it all the intellectual life of the great English university, by the persecution of Lollardism. In Bohemia too the fourteenth century was marked by a great outburst of national vitality. The Bohemian religious revival inaugurated by Milicz and Matthias of Janow was originally independent of the very similar Wyclifite movement in England, though it was only under the influence of Wyclif that the movement advanced beyond the limits of medieval orthodoxy. At first, indeed, the academic culture of Prague had little connexion with the popular religious movement which was going on all the while in the university city; but ere long a national party grew up in the university itself, which was ultimately brought into connexion with the religious life outside in the person of John Hus, at once a schoolman and a popular preacher, a reforming theologian and nationalist leader.

Quarrels between Czechs and Germans. The first rumblings of a storm which was to convulse all Europe might have been heard in the intestine feuds of the Bohemian university. The older universities were essentially cosmopolitan institutions: at Paris and Bologna students of all nationalities met and, in spite of occasional quarrels, managed on the whole to tolerate each other's existence. The division into formal 'nations', securing to the foreigners an equal or a preponderating share in the government, no doubt largely contributed to this result. But at Prague the nation-organization threw the government of the university practically into the hands of a single nationality—the nearest neighbours and the bitterest foes of the Bohemian people. Two of the nations, the Bavarian and the Saxon, were wholly German; while in a third—the Polish—the Teutonic element seems to have predominated over the Slavonic. But the most substantial part of the Czech grievance was that the colleges, built by the Bohemian kings Charles IV and Wenceslaus, were being filled with German students. At last, in 1384, the smouldering feud broke out in a petition from the Bohemians to the king and the archbishop. The archbishop ordered that in future only Bohemians should be admitted to places on the college foundation, except in the absence of duly qualified candidates. The Germanic nations appealed to the Pope, and

meanwhile the German rector ordered a suspension of lectures. The Bohemians disobeyed. The result was a series of
disturbances of the usual medieval type, in the course of which
the rector himself was grievously maltreated. At last a slight
concession was made to the Germans, but the dispute smoul-
dered on till it was merged in the wider issues raised by the
Hussite movement.[1]

When the quarrel broke out afresh, it was upon more
serious ground. We have already had occasion to notice the
importance of universities as centres for the growth of reform-
movements, particularly of universities which possessed a
faculty of theology. From the old religious orders no reform-
movement could reasonably be expected: the Mendicants,
who alone showed much pastoral activity, were the sworn
champions of the Holy See and the friends of every popular
superstition. When they revolted against authority, their
revolt was not usually in the direction of greater enlighten-
ment. It was only where there was a secular faculty of theology that any considerable number of instructed parish priests
were to be found as distinguished from the clerical lawyers
and administrators who appropriated to themselves most of
the valuable preferments of the medieval Church. In Italy
and in Spain, where theology was abandoned to the Mendicants, no voice was raised against the Papacy and the myriad
abuses which it sheltered. In England, on the other hand,
Oxford had become the cradle of the Wyclifite movement. In
France the theologians of Paris were even now agitating for
the compulsory retirement of the rival pontiffs and the suppression of the curialist abuses. Prague became the scene of
a reform-movement far deeper, more earnest, more closely

---

[1] 'Quinque collegiatos Bohemos
in collegio Karoli et sextum in-
differentem admiserunt. Et con-
formiter in collegio Regis Wenceslai
secundum numerum collegiatorum
fuit concorditer pronunciatum.'
[The remaining six places would go
to the other three nations.] Höfler,
Geschichtsschreiber, i. 14. The documents are printed *ibid.* ii, 128-
32. [Trouble broke out again in
1390 over the election of a master,
Konrad Beneschow; the issue was
raised whether natives of his district 'deberent esse de natione
Bohemorum' (*Mon. Univ. Prag.* ii.
294).] As to the nature of the compromise see Paulsen's note, *Hist.
Zeitschrift*, xlv. 266 *sqq.* [and the
criticism of Bachmann, *Hist. Vierteljahrschrift*, vii, 1904, 39–52].

connected with the popular religious life. The leading theologians of Prague held parochial cures in the town, and
preached in Czech to townsmen and students. Partly perhaps
for this reason the reform-movement in the university con-
Nominal- fined itself to the Bohemian nation. But in the factions of a
ism v.
realism. medieval university it was almost inevitable that philosophical
differences should play their part side by side with religious
and racial animosities. We have already seen how the daring
nominalism of the fourteenth century spread from Oxford to
the English and German schools at Paris, how it was pro-
scribed as a philosophic heresy, and how, in spite of proscrip-
tion, it grew and spread and contributed, with the ecclesiastical
controversies generated by the Schism, to reawaken the intellectual life of the university. When Prague took the place of
Paris as the chief seminary of German ecclesiastics, nominalism naturally took possession of its schools. The attempts
made at Paris to stifle nominalism by authority may well have
contributed to swell the numbers who elected to exchange the
most famous university in the world for the new imperial
institution in the Bohemian capital. Among the Teutonic
nations at Prague nominalism carried all before it;[1] and this
was almost sufficient reason for the Czechs to turn realist.
Intercourse between Prague and Oxford is supposed to have
been promoted by the marriage of Charles IV's daughter
Influence Anne with Richard II of England.[2] At all events, the philo-
of Wy-
clif. sophical writings of the great representative of the new post-
Ockhamite realism early found favour in the schools of the

[1] A statute of *circa* 1370 forbids
the 'scandal', 'quod magistri quaestiones Buridani et aliorum magistrorum accurtabant per ianuas inti-
mando'. *Mon. Univ. Prag.* i, pt. i,
p. 82.

[2] The high authority which Oxford enjoyed at Prague is illustrated
by a statute of the latter university
passed in 1367, enacting that scholars who dictated books to their
fellow - students (*pronunciatores*)
were only to dictate works 'ab
aliquo vel aliquibus famoso vel
famosis de universitate Pragensi,

Parisiensi vel Oxoniensi magistris
vel magistro compilata', while
bachelors were also required to
confine their comments to the
'dicta' of such masters. (*Mon.
Univ. Prag.* i, pt. l, p. 13.) Cf.
Loserth (Eng. trans.), p. 69 *sq.*
[Prague was mainly realist before
Hus; just as it was in close touch
with Oxford thought before Wyclif:
Ehrle, *Der Sentenzenkommentar
Peters von Candia*, p. 146; Franz,
op. cit., p. 31; cf. R. F. Young,
in *Eng. Hist. Rev.* xxxviii (1923),
72].

Czech masters. This realism of the reforming Bohemian divines effectually tended to prevent the reform-movement spreading to the German nations: it stamped the Bohemian reform-movement with that impress of nationality which it never lost. From about the year 1401 or 1402 the theological works of Wyclif gradually began to circulate in Prague,[1] and John Hus soon became prominent as the exponent, defender, and imitator of his writings. The reputation of Wyclif as a philosopher secured a welcome for his heretical theology among the Bohemian masters. Henceforth the faction fights that raged in the streets of the university town in the earlier years of the fifteenth century became a battle not merely of Czech against Teuton and of realist against nominalist, but of reformer against conservative, of heretic against orthodox.[2]

The first open collision between the two parties occurred in 1408. Five years before, the university congregation, upon the demand of the chapter *sede vacante*, had formally condemned forty-five articles extracted from Wyclif's books.[3] But the writings of the heresiarch continued to be read and

Condemnation of Wyclif and resistance in university.

---

[1] [The *Dialogus* was known and widely read in Bohemia from 1402. Nine of the surviving ten manuscripts were copied in Bohemia (see A. W. Pollard's introduction to his edition, London, 1886, p. v). According to Aeneas Sylvius, Nicholas Faulfisch first brought Wyclif's books to Bohemia, and though this is not the case, Faulfisch probably brought *some*, including the *De Dominio divino*, about 1407 (see R. L. Poole's preface to his edition of the *De Dominio divino*, London, 1890, p. x). The close connexion between Wyclifite and Hussite writings indeed makes it difficult to distinguish *quaestiones*, &c., ascribed to Wyclif from those of Bohemian origin; see S. H. Thomson, 'Some Latin Works erroneously ascribed to Wyclif' (*Speculum*, iii, 1928, 382-91). On the relationship in general see Loserth's book, *Hus und Wyclif*, and his various papers, which are noticed in his *Geschichte*

des Späteren Mittelalters, p. 392; cf. R. L. Poole in *Eng. Hist. Rev.*, vii, 1892, 306.]

[2] How closely the two last antagonisms were connected may be inferred from the lines:

'Facta nunc adultera profert realistas

Chymeras et vetera monstra Wyclevistas

Jam mater ignobilis, meretrix inmunda

Fel emittit heresis velut petram unda.'

Bericht d. deutschen Gesellschaft in Leipzig, 1841, p. 22.

[3] [Höfler, *Concilia*, pp. 43 *sqq.* The propositions contained the 24 censured at London in May 1382 (H. B. Workman, *John Wyclif*, Oxford, 1926, ii. 266-7, 416-17) and 21 others compiled by John Hübner, a master of Prague. The date was 28 May 1403: cf. Hefele-Leclercq, VII. i. 123-4 and notes.]

taught in the schools; and John Hus, who was elected rector of the university in 1402, had ardently championed their orthodoxy.[1] Another congregation was held upon the subject on 18 May 1408, when the forty-five articles were again condemned, but two days later, a meeting of the Bohemian nation, attended, it is said, by 64 doctors and masters, 150 bachelors, and about 1,000 students, while forbidding the articles to be taught, added the qualification, 'in their false and heretical sense.' Lectures and disputations on the *Dialogus*, *Trialogus*, and *De Eucharistia* were forbidden, and only masters were at liberty to read Wyclif's writings.[2] The modified character of the condemnation shows plainly the strength of Wyclifite sympathies in the university. In the same year Wyclif's books, which, of course, found no favour with the Bohemian hierarchy or with the mass of the parochial clergy, were condemned at a synod; and all masters, bachelors, and students who possessed them were required to surrender them to the ecclesiastical authorities. As at Oxford in the time of Wyclif, the reforming divines took refuge behind their academical privileges. There were, however, only five students (Hus was not among the number) who had the courage to refuse to surrender their copies, and to appeal to the Holy See against the synodical decree as an infringement of the privileges of the university, and also on the ground that the definition of eucharistic doctrine prescribed by the synod was itself heretical.[2]

The Schism. But now the embroglio was complicated, and the inevitable catastrophe hastened, by the introduction of a political element into the struggle. The very year in which the heretical tendency of the Bohemian reformers first definitely proclaimed itself was the year in which a momentous breach was made in the system of medieval Christendom by the cardinals of the Holy Roman Church itself. At a council summoned by a

---

[1] [The sympathy of Hus was expressed more gradually and cautiously than Rashdall suggests.]

[2] [Höfler, *Concilia*, pp. 51–64 *passim*; the same, *Magister Hus und der Abzug*, &c., pp. 189–200.]

These champions of orthodoxy had blundered into the assertion that nothing remained in the host after consecration but the body of Christ, thereby ignoring the doctrine of concomitance.

section of the cardinals of the two obediences, both pontiffs were deposed and a new pontiff was elected under the title of Alexander V. Wenceslaus, King of Bohemia, was still struggling for the imperial crown against Rupert, Count Palatine of the Rhine, who was favoured by the Roman Pope, Gregory XII. Hence the king was anxious to withdraw his realm from the allegiance of Gregory, and to proclaim its neutrality in the triangular contest for the papacy. This design was vehemently opposed by the archbishop and his clergy. In the university the measure was naturally welcomed as a step to the reform of ecclesiastical abuses by the Bohemians, and was consequently opposed by the German element. As, however, the Germans virtually commanded three votes in the university congregations against the Bohemian one, the king could get no assistance from the academical body. Under these circumstances a deputation from the Bohemian nation, headed by Hus, waited upon the king with the petition that the voting-power of the nations should be altered so as to secure a preponderance for the king's own subjects. On 18 January 1409 a royal decree was issued which ordered that in future the Bohemian nation should enjoy three votes, while the other three nations were to have only one between them. The Germans promptly had recourse to the old weapon which had once proved so mighty an engine against royal or civic tyranny in Paris and Bologna: they bound themselves together by an oath[1] to secede from Prague in a body if the decree were not withdrawn. A petition was sent to the absent king, and meanwhile his commands were contemptuously disregarded by the hitherto dominant majority. But the old weapons had lost some of their power; the decree was not withdrawn; national passions were becoming too strong for the continuance of the cosmopolitan universities of the thirteenth century. At last on the 9th of May, the masters were summoned to the hall of the Caroline College to hear the royal decision. The German

Royal decree against Germans, 1409.

---

[1] The oath, given in *Geschichtsschreiber*, ii. 166, is a formal instrument before a notary, subjecting the violator to excommunication and a penalty of 60 marks.

CHAP. IX, rector was peremptorily ordered to surrender the insignia
§ 1. of office to a Bohemian nominated by the King. In one day
Exodus of
Germans. Prague was forsaken by the vast horde of German students
who had been attracted by the policy of the Bohemian
emperor-king to the city which he had designed to make
the German as well as the Bohemian capital. To the number,
it was said later, of 5,000, to the number, actually, of about
1,000, the Teutonic masters and scholars departed; a few,
perhaps, to reinforce younger universities like Heidelberg and
Cologne, a larger contingent to found at Leipzig the most
illustrious of the ancient universities of Germany proper.[1]

Impor-   The German exodus from Prague constitutes something
tance of
this event more than an epoch in the history of universities and of the
on Hus- university system of Europe. A knowledge of the academic
site move-
ment. conflicts which terminated in May 1409 is essential to a just
appreciation of the general history of the period, and particularly of the causes which led up to the tragi-comedy of
Constance and the darker tragedy which sealed the fate of the
Bohemian nation. The final split between the German and
the Czech elements at Prague was immediately occasioned,
we have seen, by the ardour of the Bohemians for ecclesiastical
reform. Although sympathizing more or less overtly with

---

[1] Tomek, pp. 60–9; Docs. in
Höfler, *Geschichtsschreiber*, ii. 156
sq. The 15th cent. chronicler Pro-
copius (*Geschichtsschreiber*, i. 70)
says that over 2,000 left in one day
and went to Leipzig. Aeneas Sylvius (*Hist. Bohem.*, cap. 35) adds
that 3,000 followed shortly afterwards. The total number Höfler estimates at 20,000 (*Hus und der Abzug*,
p. 247)! But the 602 admitted
at Leipzig (see below, p. 259 n.),
even allowing for a small proportion
having found their way to Erfurt
and Heidelberg (at neither is there
any large increase of matriculations), do not support such an
extravagant estimate. It is said that
some of the students went to
Cologne, but here there were only
eighteen matriculations between 28

June and 9 Oct. 1409, and but thirty
in the following quarter (Keussen,
Matrikel d. Univ. Köln, i. 112 *sq.*).
[The numbers of students show a
great increase at Erfurt in 1409, i.e.
370 as against 278 in 1408 and 229
in 1410. The numbers at Cologne
were 73, 119, 98 in the three years;
at Vienna 223, 231, 303; at Cracow
35, 57, 88. There was no increase
at Heidelberg. At Leipzig the
numbers were 368 (1409), 247
(1410). It is improbable that more
than 660 students entered Prague
annually, even during the years
1380–9, or that the exodus in 1409
was more than 1,000. We owe the
substance of this note to Professor
Potter. See also Matthaesius,
op. cit.]

Wyclif, Hus declined to follow him in his most startling heresy as to the sacrament of the altar: the aims of his party were not very different (though its zeal was more unquestionable) from those of the small group of comparatively liberal divines which had at this time acquired so much influence in the mother university of Paris. The revolt against the contending pontiffs, which the Bohemians had joined and which the Germans refused to join, was in the main the work of the University of Paris. Yet at this time we find the reformers of Paris joining with the anti-reformers of Germany to condemn and to burn the reformers of Prague. What is the explanation of this strange transformation? Partly, no doubt, the fact that the Bohemian movement represents a genuine outburst of popular religious fervour, while the Parisian movement was at bottom a merely ecclesiastical demonstration. The Bohemian movement seriously threatened the inordinate wealth, the luxury and immorality, the idleness and secularity of the clergy as a body; while the Parisian movement was little more than an outcry of the educated clerical class against abuses by which they did not profit. To some extent it is true also that the doctrinal heresies of Wyclif (including, in some cases, his denial of transubstantiation) had found sympathizers at Prague, while the reformers of Paris were men of the most rigid orthodoxy. But the total absence of sympathy from first to last between the Hussite party at Prague and the Gerson party at Paris cannot be completely understood without taking into consideration the philosophical antagonisms in the schools and the streets of the Bohemian university. By the time of the Council of Constance nominalism was in the ascendant at Paris as well as in Germany. Hus was condemned almost as much for being a realist in philosophy as for being a heretic in theology. By a strange irony of fate Hus, though he professed to accept the doctrine of transubstantiation, was condemned because the nominalists of the fifteenth century had persuaded themselves that a realist could not firmly hold in its integrity a doctrine which owed its existence as an article of faith to the extravagant realism of an earlier age. And the outcry against Hus was, of course, largely the work of his old

CHAP. IX, antagonists in the Bavarian, Saxon, and Polish nations: the
§ 1.   exiles from Prague had carried with them into their new universities the tradition of hostility to Hus and the Bohemian
reformers. At the Council of Constance the very men who
had been beaten in the encounter with Hus and his party at
Prague clamoured for his blood. The national insult of 1409
was wiped out at Constance. And the quarrel did not end at
Constance. The Bohemian nation itself fell a victim to the
racial animosities which had been so loudly emphasized and
so sorely aggravated—though unquestionably they had not
been engendered—in the scholastic debates, the academic
parties, and the student street-fights of the Bohemian capital.

Rupture
between
Czech and
Teuton
inevitable.

Sooner or later the disruption of the bi-racial university
was inevitable: Teuton and Czech could not live and study
together in the same schools. Even at the present day, be-
neath the strong hand of a military monarchy, the separation
seems inevitable, and the Bohemian capital now embraces
two distinct universities, a Czech university which still holds
aloft the standard of nationality, and a German university
ministering to the wants of students whose patriotism does
not rebel against the wider culture to which the German
tongue is now the indispensable key. [1895.]

Progress of
Hussite
movement.

In the earlier stages of the reform movement at Prague the
Bohemian element in the university appears as a united body.
But, when Hus gradually drifted into open disobedience to
ecclesiastical authority, the inevitable moment arrived when
the more conservative or more lukewarm of his disciples
were offended at him and walked no more with him. From
about the year 1412, when Hus publicly disputed against the
papal indulgences granted in aid of the crusade against
Ladislaus of Naples, the theological faculty—that is to say,
the doctors—was definitely hostile.[1] The ardour of at least
two of these elderly reformers had in any case been effectually
cooled by a sharp touch of persecution. Hus's old master,

---

[1] [Hus was excommunicated by
the archbishop of Prague on 15
March 1411. His thesis against the
crusading Bull of Pope John XXIII
was sustained on 7 June 1412. For
the subsequent dispute with the
faculty of theology see Palacký,
Documenta M. Joannis Hus pp. 448
sqq. There is a good summary in
Hefele-Leclercq, VII. i. 146–8 note.]

Stanislaus of Znaïm (who had at one time gone to greater
lengths in the direction of Wyclifism than his pupil) and his
most intimate friend, Stephen Palecz, had been imprisoned
at Bologna in December 1408, while they were with a royal
embassy to the cardinals at Pisa.[1] But the university as a body
—including, it must be remembered, all the younger theologians, who were masters of arts and bachelors or students
in theology—were in Hus's favour. And their support was
steadily continued throughout his trial and after his condemnation.

To trace the various steps by which their sympathy was
shown would be possible only in a special history of the
university, and would almost involve writing the history of
Bohemia during this momentous crisis in her national existence. Suffice it to say that the university as a body refused
to submit to the Council of Constance as strenuously as they
had refused to submit to the decisions of archiepiscopal
synods or papal delegates. In 1417 the privileges of the university were suspended by a decree of the Council; while the
university unflinchingly maintained the principle of com-
munion in both kinds.[2] The revolt of Prague, not only against
ultramontanism but against what for want of a better term we
may call medievalism, was thus far more complete, as it was
far more unanimous, than the revolt of Oxford in the days of
Wyclif.

It has been said that moral movements come from below,
intellectual movements from above. The remarkable feature
of the Oxford movement in the fourteenth century and the
Prague movement of a generation later—a feature which
completely distinguished them from the Gersonite movement
at Paris—was that in them an intellectual current from above
united itself with a moral current from below. Wyclif and
Hus were both of them great preachers and popular leaders
as well as professors, the creators of a vernacular literature

---

[1] [They had been seized by
Baldassare Cossa, later Pope John
XXIII, who was papal legate at
Bologna. They were presumably
regarded as supporters of Gregory

XII. See Hefele-Leclercq, VI. ii.
1381.]
[2] Höfler, *Geschichtsschreiber*, ii.
237, 243. Tomek, pp. 105–6.

as well as scholastic theologians. Both at Prague and at Oxford the movement was eventually suppressed because the two elements—the movement from above and the movement from below—could not hold together. At Oxford Wyclif's teaching aroused or became identified with socialistic tendencies which alienated the court and the upper classes of lay society generally. At Prague, after the revolt of Bohemia against the decrees of Constance, the university divines led a party of moderate reform, which failed permanently to control the popular movement which had been set on foot by its great master. The fanaticism of the Taborites ruined the cause, and prepared the way for the humiliation of the Bohemian people, for the triumph of the catholic, the anti-national, the ultramontane reaction in the country whose heroic spirit had anticipated the final revolt of one half of Europe from medieval Christianity.[1]

Influence of universities on Reformation.

When the standard of revolt was raised once more, it was raised by the very nation which had most strenuously set itself against the Hussite movement. The Teutonic nation was the last of the nations of Europe to attain to moral and intellectual maturity: it was the last to assert its manhood by a rebellion against Roman usurpation, but it was the first to carry its revolt to a successful issue. The Reformation which succeeded, like the earlier reform-movements of the Middle Ages which had failed, was born in a university. There only were the culture and the learning, the leisure and the possibilities of co-operation, which were necessary for the growth of intellectual and religious revolt, found in union with that measure of liberty which was essential for an even temporary resistance to authority. The mass of the higher clergy was incapacitated for the work of reform, not so much because they were ecclesiastics as because they were primarily politicians and lawyers: the lower clergy were incapacitated by their ignorance and their obscurity: the monks by their wealth and their essential conservatism. An individual friar might, indeed, be a reformer, but the religious orders were opposed on principle to individual liberty, and were decidedly ultra-

[1] Höfler, *Geschichtsschreiber*, ii. 475 *sq.*

montane in their traditions, except when they were carried CHAP. IX, § 1.
away by visionary and unpractical enthusiasms like those of
the spiritual Franciscans and the Fraticelli. It is hardly too
much to say that the existence of universities—universities of
the northern type with secular faculties of theology—made
the Reformation a possibility.

One other feature of the Hussite movement serves to illus- Inter-course between medieval univer-sities.
trate an essential characteristic of the medieval university
system—the close, intellectual solidarity which it established
between the different parts of Europe. At the beginning of
the fifteenth century it is true that the majority of average
students in England, France, and Germany no longer went
abroad to study. But the most enterprising students still, as
a rule, studied, at one period or other of their career, in more
than one university and very often in the universities of more
than one country. A distinguished teacher, anywhere but at
Paris, was sure to promulgate his views, either personally or
through some ardent pupil, in other universities than his own.
The Hussite movement, as a religious revival, was indeed of
purely indigenous origin; but very early in its history it was
profoundly modified by the intimate connexion which was
kept up between Prague and Oxford. The use of Latin as the
language of academical life threw open the lecture-rooms of
a university to every part of Europe. The universal validity
of the academic licence made the teacher of one university
a potential teacher in all others. Books spread from one
country to another, in a sense, more easily before the invention
of printing than after it: a single copy of an Oxford master's
lectures, carried to Prague in a traveller's baggage, could be
instantly republished in the *scriptoria* of the university writers,
and had not to wait for a translator. In this way it came about
that in the Middle Ages, ideas, systems, and movements
spread more easily from Paris to Oxford or from Oxford to
Prague than they spread at the present day from Berlin to
Oxford or from Oxford to Berlin.

While it is the 'movements' which the universities originate Condition of uni-versity movements during Hussite troubles.
that constitute a large part of the interest of our subject,
movements are by no means uniformly favourable to the quiet

educational work which is the primary, though by no means the only, purpose for which universities exist. The national movement of 1408 deprived Prague of its cosmopolitan character; the Utraquist movement of 1416 enormously diminished the influx of students. After the triumph of the Utraquists the theological, legal, and medical faculties seem to have almost ceased to exist. The men who came to the university only to advance their fortunes in the Church now advanced them best by staying away. After the siege of Prague by Sigismund promotions even in arts were suspended for no less than ten years, though for the last seven years of that troubled period lectures were not wholly dropped.[1] During the course of the Hussite war most of the property of the university and its colleges found its way into the hands of the Emperor and other lay owners. But the foundation of New colleges. numerous colleges during the latter half of the century[2] to some extent repaired these losses, and testify that the educational activity of the Utraquist university was not entirely suspended by the political and theological discords of the time.

§ 2. VIENNA (1365)

[Wolfgang LAZIUS, *Vienna Austriae* (Basel, 1546); G. EDER, *Catalogus Rectorum et illustrium virorum Archigymnasii Viennensis*, Vienna, 1559.] *Conspectus historiae universitatis Viennensis* (Vienna, 1722) is a book of annals with copious extracts from the registers and other documents. COLLAND, *Kurzer Inbegriff von den Ursprunge der Wissenschaften, Schulen, Akademien, und Universitäten in ganz Europa, besonders aber der Akad. und hohen Schule zu Wien* (Vienna, 1796) contains a short summary of the uni-

---

[1] Tomek, p. 108 *sq.* [There was a strong German element in Prague between 1433 and 1448, in which year the Germans again left the university. But by 1461 the university had excluded all Catholic teaching and was reduced to one small faculty : Wostry, p. 357.]

[2] The *Collegium Recek* or *Sanctissimae Virginis*, founded by a wealthy citizen, John Recek de Ledecz (1438), and the *Collegium Laudae* or *Apostolorum* (1439), were what was called at Paris *Collèges de plein exercice* (vol. i, p. 528). There were

besides some smaller houses which merely lodged their scholars. One of these (*Collegium Nazareth*) was closely connected with Bethlehem Chapel, the scene of Hus's preaching, and the starting-point of the Hussite movement. *Mon. Univ. Prag.* iii. 54. Volckman (p. 21) mentions a College of SS. Matthew and Matthias, and a *Collegium Angelicum*. Exhibitions were also founded by Adelbertus Ranconis in 1388 to enable Prague students to study at Paris or Oxford. See Loserth, pp. 40, 41.

versity's history. Geusau, *Gesch. d. Stiftungen . . . in Wien* (Vienna, 1803), chap. ix,
and Hormayr, *Wien, seine Gesch. u. seine Denkwürdigkeiten* (Vienna, 1823)　§ 2.
have only short notices of the university. Kink, *Gesch. der Kaiserl. Univ.
zu Wien* (2 vols., Vienna, 1854), is a satisfactory work with a large collection of documents. Aschbach, *Geschichte der Wiener Universität* (3 vols.,
Vienna, 1865, 1877, 1882), gives a full account of the first century of the
university's existence, chiefly from the point of view of the history of
learning, with biographies of the professors. Large extracts from the
matriculation-book and other documents are also printed by Steyerer,
Commentarii pro hist. Alberti II (Leipzig, 1725, *c.* 409 *sq.*). The documents up to 1384 are also printed by Schlikenrieder, *Chron. diplomat.
Univ. Vindob.* (Vienna, 1753); and the Statutes in Kollar, *Analecta
monumentorum Vindobonensia* (Vienna, 1761).

[K. Schrauf, *Acta facultatis medicae Universitatis Vindobonensis*, i
(1399–1435), Vienna, 1894; ii, Vienna, 1904 (with L. Senfelder); the same,
Die Matrikel der ungarischen Nation an der Wiener Universität (Vienna,
1902); also *Die Wiener Universität im Mittelalter* (Vienna, 1904), printed
separately from *Geschichte der Stadt Wien*, published by the Wiener
Altertumsverein, vol. ii, part 2; O. Redlich, *Die geschichtliche Stellung
und Bedeutung der Universität Wien*, a rectorial address (Vienna, 1911);
the same, in *Das akad. Deutschland*, i. 401; G. Sommerfeldt, 'Aus
der Zeit der Begründung der Universität Wien' (*Mitthl. d. Instituts
für österr. Geschichtsforschung*, xxix, xxx, Innsbrück, 1908); *Die Universität Wien, ihre Geschichte*, &c., herausg. vom Akad. Senat (Düsseldorf,
1929); G. M. Haefele, *Franz von Retz: ein Beitrag zur Gelehrtengeschichte
des Dominikanerordens und der Wiener Universität am Ausgange des
Mittelalters* (Innsbrück, 1918); L. Glückert, 'Hieronymus von Mondsee
(Magister Johannes de Werdea): ein Beitrag zur Geschichte des Ein-
flusses der Wiener Universität im xv. Jahrhundert' (*Studien und Mitthl.
zur Geschichte des Benediktinerordens*, xvii, 1930, 99–201). For humanism
see G. Bauch, *Die Reception des Humanismus in Wien* (Breslau, 1903);
K. Grossmann, 'Die Frühzeit des Humanismus in Wien' (*Jahrbuch
für Landeskunde von Niederösterreich*, n.s. xxii, 1929, 150–325). In his
Mittelalterliche Bibliothekskataloge Österreichs, i, Vienna, 1915, 463–504,
T. Gottlieb has tried to reconstruct, with the aid of the *acta* of the
faculties and other documents, the medieval libraries of the university,
faculties and *bursae*.]

We have seen how closely connected with the political aims
of the Emperor Charles IV was the foundation of the University of Prague. The inspiring motive of the second German
university was not less political. It owed its origin to the most
formidable rival of the Bohemian monarchy in the Germanic
commonwealth, the house of Habsburg, whose jealousy had
been recently stimulated by the precedence over all other
princes assigned to the electors in the Golden Bull issued by
the founder of Prague in 1356.

The only previously existing nucleus for a university in the
Austrian capital was the school of S. Stephen. From the end

Motives of foundation.

Existing school of S. Stephen.

of the twelfth century we have frequent notices of an important school held in or close to S. Stephen's church. By the
charter granted to the town by Frederick II in 1237 the school
of S. Stephen's is to be placed under the authority of an
officer—afterwards called *scholasticus* or rector[1]—to be appointed by the Emperor with authority to appoint other
masters.[2] Albert I[3] gave the nomination to the town council.
The school enjoyed some reputation at the end of the thirteenth and the beginning of the fourteenth centuries; the
praises of the then *scholasticus*, Ulrich, are sung by a poet who
describes clerks from all parts of the world as flocking to hang
on the master's lips.[4] Some allowance must, however, be
made for the rhetoric of a pupil addressing complimentary
verses to his schoolmaster; but an allusion to 'faculties' shows
that the school was something more than a mere grammar-
school.

First
foundation
of univer-
sity by
Rudolf IV
1365.
The foundation of a university is due to Duke Rudolf IV.
His charter was issued on 12 March 1365. It does not follow
the model of any earlier charter of the kind, but contains a very
ample grant of privilege and fixes the constitution of the university in much detail.[5] It orders that a 'general and privileged
studium' shall henceforth be established in Vienna, 'according
to the ordinances and customs observed first at Athens, then
at Rome, and after that at Paris'. It is needless to say that the

---

[1] So Denifle (i. 604) calls him.
In the charter of Albert III (Kink,
ii. 63) he is called 'rector scolarium Sancti Stephani'.

[2] 'Volentes etiam commodo studio prouideri . . . potestatem damus
plenariam magistro, qui Wienne
per nos vel successores nostros ad
scolarum regimen assumetur, ut
alios doctores in facultatibus sub-
stituat de consilio prudentium
uirorum ciuitatis eiusdem, qui
habeantur sufficientes et idonei
circa suorum studium auditorum.'
*Archiv für Kunde österr. Geschichts-
quellen*, x, (1853), 126.

[3] Document in *Sitzungsberichte
d. Kais. Acad. d. Wissensch.*, phil.-

hist. Kl. xiii (1854), 337: 'So geben
wir vollen gewalt dem Schulmaister
datz Sant Stephan der Pfarrechir-
chen, der von dem rate der Stat de
wirt gesetzet ze schulmaister, ander
Schul under sich ze stiften in dem
stat, und doch der si erleich und
gewohnleich sein. . . . Swer dauider
dehain Schul ze seiner Chirchen
oder in seinem hause hiet wider des
Maisters willen und der purger, daz
sulen di Purgo wenden mit allen
sachen.' The true date appears to be
1296, though the editor gives 1196.

[4] Ap. Leyser, *Hist. poetarum et
poematum medii aevi*, p. 2034, l. 647
sq.

[5] Printed by Kink, ii. 1-24.

influence of the last-mentioned university is more distinctly discernible in the Rudolfian constitution than that of its supposed predecessors. The constitution prescribed by Rudolf
is the Parisian constitution with a few modifications. The
ancient town church of All Saints (more usually known as
S. Stephen's)[1] was to be made collegiate, and its provost to
become chancellor of the university: the university chest was
to be placed in its sacristy.

The anomalous arrangement by which at Paris the four Proposed
organiza-
tion.
nations of artists elected the rector of the whole university is
perpetuated at Vienna, the nations being styled (1) Austria,
(2) Saxony, (3) Bohemia, (4) Hungary.[2] The main difference
between the system established at Vienna by Rudolf and that
which had grown up at Paris was in connexion with the
administration of justice. The Viennese students enjoyed
much more extensive exemptions than the Parisian. Charges
against a master or a scholar, which would be capital in the
case of an unprivileged layman, were to be tried, not (as at
Paris) by the bishop, but by the chancellor.[3] Other criminal
charges and civil plaints were to go before the rector, who had
also jurisdiction in ordinary civil actions and minor criminal
charges where the plaintiff was a scholar. More serious
offences against a scholar were to go before the ordinary
secular courts,[4] but a special scale of punishment—a curiously
minute *lex talionis*—is prescribed for the punishment of such

[1] Schlikenrieder, p. 142. [It
seems that Rudolf IV changed the
dedication from S. Stephen to All
Saints, 16 March 1365; Kink, ii. 4.]
[2] The division was made by the
first statute of the University
passed in June 1366. Kink, ii. 32.
[3] One exception to the extensive
protection accorded to students is
too significant of the actual condition of student and clerical morality
to be omitted: 'Sane vt magis disciplina Scholastica clericalis religionis,
Katholice institucionis ac humane
discrecionis cerimonie a membris
dicte Vniuersitatis purius et rigidius
obseruentur, declarantes presenti-

bus quo supra nomine volumus,
quod si quis in Magistrum uel
Studentem dicte Vniuersitatis, sue
honestatis et salutis immemorem,
cum sua uxore agentem turpiter
deprehensum manus violentas inie-
cerit uel sibi offensam irrogauerit,
pro eo per nos, Rectorem uel ipsam
Vniuersitatem, non est aliqualiter
puniendus, Nolentes aliquam per-
sonam dicte Vniuersitatis quo ad
hunc casum indultis sibi priuilegiis
et iuribus perfrui et gaudere' (*loc.
cit.*, p. 18).
[4] 'Exceptis duntaxat causis mor-
tis et criminibus honorem seu
famam rei concernentibus.'

crimes.[1] A number of special and unprecedented privileges are conferred for the protection of scholars and the benefit of the university. Property confiscated for outrages on scholars was to be divided between the university and the injured party. The assailant of a scholar lost the benefit of sanctuary. Special protection in travelling was promised with the usual exemptions from tolls and municipal taxes. If a scholar was robbed, the duke would compensate the loss. In Vienna itself a special quarter of the town was granted for the accommodation of students with a right to demand such houses as they pleased for their residence, the rent to be fixed by the usual method of arbitration. The system of a specially assigned students' quarter (which had grown up spontaneously in the older universities) was, it will be remembered, artificially reproduced in some of the Spanish universities; and it was no doubt a measure highly conducive to the security of the students and the peace of the town. But at Vienna this Latin quarter was by the terms of Rudolf's charter positively to be fortified against assailants by a special wall.

Bull of Urban V, 1365. Before the issue of Rudolf's charter, the consent of the Pope, Urban V, had been obtained,[2] and shortly after it (1365) a papal Bull of foundation of the usual type was granted.[3] In one point there is a discrepancy between the terms of the ducal and the papal charters. Rudolf provided for a theological faculty: Urban V expressly excluded theology from the faculties in which the ecumenical licence might be granted at Vienna. The popes had begun to relax their earlier policy of confining theological graduation to Paris, but not in all cases. Prague had been granted a theological faculty from the first; and it was through the intrigues of that university and its imperial patron that a similar concession was not granted to Vienna. Charles IV had gone in person to Avignon to

[1] e.g. 'Si quis Magistrorum uel Studencium ab ullo sauciatus uel ex violenta manuum uel pedum incussione taliter lesus fuerit, quod ex eo membrorum suorum officia non amittit, quod eidem Lesori pro eo deprehenso debet manus pugione transfigi, nisi id redimat quadra-

ginta marcis argenti' (*loc. cit.*, p. 14).

[2] Denifle, i. 605; Doc. in Kink, I. ii. 1, from which also it appears that the municipality had granted privileges to the projected university.

[3] Kink, ii. 26. [18 June 1365.]

prevent the erection of any university at all at Vienna, but CHAP. IX, § 2. had to content himself with this very modified triumph.[1]

We are by this time familiar with the difficulties which, Failure. except under peculiarly favourable circumstances, attended the establishment of a new university. Ample endowments were absolutely essential to secure professors whose reputation would attract students. Rudolf's foundation (unlike the more successful venture of Charles IV at Prague) consisted chiefly in the grant of paper-privileges. Of more substantial assistance we hear nothing, except the impropriation of a single benefice, which was to take effect on the resignation of the then incumbent, Albert of Saxony.[2] Above all, the university lost its founder in the very year of its birth. From that time till 1383 Austria was distracted by the dissensions of the rival dukes, Albert III and Leopold III, between whom Rudolf had divided his dominions. During the civil war neither brother was likely to concern himself much about academical affairs. As a matter of fact we do not know the name of a single master who taught at Vienna in the earliest years of the university, except the first rector,[3] Albert of Saxony, a former rector of Paris (1355),[4] to whom, in consultation with the ducal chancellor, the bishop of Passau, the arrangements for the foundation of the university had been entrusted. From 1366 to 1377 no documents are forthcoming except a deed of 1370 for the foundation of a small college.[5] That document is sufficient to show that the university was at the very lowest ebb, and that the possibility of its actual extinction was contemplated. From 1377 to 1383 a fragmentary matriculation-book supplies somewhat clearer evidence of a continued though very feeble vitality.[6]

---

[1] Aschbach, i. 17.

[2] Doc. in Kink, i. 34. Four proctors are mentioned in the statutes (*ibid.*, p. 40), but it is not clear whether they were masters or students.

[3] Steyerer, *Commentarii pro hist. Alb. II.* (Leipzig, 1725), pp. 429, 453.

[4] Aschbach, i. 12. [For this important scholar, who became bishop of Halberstadt in 1366, see Ueberweg-Geyer, pp. 600–2, 784 and the authorities there noted. Cf. above, vol. i, p. 563, note.]

[5] A college of bachelors, founded by Master Albert, pastor at Gars, in 1370. Hormayr, v, p. clxxiv.

[6] Steyerer, p. 455.

CHAP. IX,
§ 2.
Revival by
Albert III,
1383.

In 1383 Albert III came into possession of the whole Austrian dukedom, and from that year the university dates its regeneration. The moment was an auspicious one for the revival of a German university. Paris was still distracted by the disputes which the Schism of 1378 had brought with it. The German masters were more or less decidedly in favour either of neutrality or of the recognition of Urban VI, and found it difficult to maintain their independence in opposition to the pressure put upon them to declare for the French Pope, Clement VII. Moreover, by remaining dissentient members of a university which as a body adhered to Clement VII, they would lose all hope of preferment by means of the *rotulus beneficiandorum*. Hence about the year 1383 the duke found it easy to attract to Vienna the distinguished doctor of theology, Henry of Langenstein, one of the strongest opponents of Clement at Paris.[1] Henry became the 'soul' of the new university.[2] Other masters followed him. In the year 1384 a new ducal charter of privilege was issued, a papal Bull was procured from Urban VI authorizing promotions in the theological faculty, not under the chancellor but under the provost of All Saints,[3] and the real life of the university began.

Albertine
reorganiza-
tion.

The Rudolfian constitution was the work of the master of arts, Albert of Saxony; the Albertine was mainly inspired by the theologian Henry of Langenstein.[4] The former preserved in the main, the latter entirely destroyed, the anomalous ascendancy enjoyed by the faculty of arts at Paris. As at Prague, the rector and proctors might now be elected from any faculty,[5] so that the superior faculties are included in the nations. This measure made it necessary for the faculty of arts to have a dean of its own. In the method adopted for the endowment of the university, too, the influence of Prague is

[1] There is no positive evidence of an actual institution by the duke. See Denifle, i. 618, 619.

[2] O. Hartwig, *Leben und Schriften Heinrichs von Langenstein* (Marburg, 1858), p. 37 *sq*. [See also Ueberweg-Geyer, pp. 604, 610–11, 785; and cf. above, vol. i, p. 560 *n*.]

[3] 'Prout in Bononiensi uel Parisi-ensi aut Cantabrigie uel Oxoniensi Studijs generalibus insimilibus est fieri consuetum.' Doc. in Kink, ii. 46.

[4] Doc. in *ibid*., pp. 49–71.

[5] The statutes prescribe an elaborate system of rotation among the faculties, so that each faculty has one proctor. *Ibid*., p. 79.

unmistakable. A *Collegium Ducale* is founded to house twelve CHAP. IX, § 2. *Collegium Ducale*.
masters of arts and two or three of theology; and the college
is to be connected with the collegiate chapter of All Saints,
in exactly the same way as the Carolinum of Prague was connected with the church of All Saints at Prague. The members
of the *Collegium Ducale* were to succeed to the vacant canonries. The town grammar-school of S. Stephen's was also
incorporated with the university, which was henceforth to
have the appointment of its rector and the three other
masters.[1] At the same time the connexion with the municipality was kept up by the appointment of a 'conservator of
privileges' from among the royal nominees in the town
council.

In the year after the foundation (1384) the duke granted Statutes.
a formal licence to the university to make statutes for itself.
A code of general statutes for the whole university was drawn
up in the following year, and in 1389 statutes for the respective faculties.[2]

Since in the infancy of the university the number of masters Altered position of faculty of arts.
might be insufficient to form a congregation, it is enacted that
'till masters and doctors be sufficiently multiplied', bachelors
shall have seats in that assembly;[3] and provision is made
against an individual master exercising the vote of a whole
faculty.[4] It should be noticed that the division into nations
adopted by the Rudolfine constitution is slightly modified in
the Albertine. The nations are now styled: (1) the Austrian
(including Italy); (2) the Rhenish (including western Germany and all western Europe); (3) the Hungarian (embracing
also all Slavonic nationalities); (4) the Saxon (including

---

[1] The rector's salary was to be 'triginta due libre preter accidencia Chori Sancti Stephani': of other masters (each) 'sedecim libre denariorum Wiennensium'. These were to be masters of arts: the masters of the other schools in the town ('Rectorem Scolarium ad Sanctum Michahelem, et in Hospitali, necnon et quibuscunque alijs') were, if they pleased, to enjoy the privileges of the university. No new school was to be set up without leave of the rector (*ibid.*, p. 63).

[2] *Ibid.*, pp. 72, 73 *sq.*, 95 *sq.*

[3] *Ibid.*, p. 83. It seems that this transitional state of things passed away, as least as regards the faculty of arts, before 1389 (*ibid.*, p. 184). In the faculty of law, licentiates apparently had votes, but not bachelors (*ibid.*, p. 138).

[4] *Ibid.*, p. 86.

northern and eastern Germany, the Scandinavian kingdoms, and the British Isles).[1]

Albertine Constitution.

Vienna, after the Albertine reorganization, was still in the main a university of masters. But its constitution admits the students to a larger share in the government of the university than was the case at Paris or Oxford. They have no share in legislation; but they have apparently[2] a vote in the election of proctors, and are eligible to the office. The importance of the proctors is, indeed, to a considerable extent modified by the transfer of many of their functions to the deans; but they still elect the rector, who, though no longer the president of the faculty of arts, remains the head of the whole university; and the rector and proctors, together with the deans, form the 'consistory' or executive council. In many other respects we notice an infusion of Bologna ideas in the university institutions.[3] There is far more magisterial discipline at Vienna than at Bologna or Montpellier, but perhaps rather less than at Paris and Oxford. Marriage, though married students are described in the registers in a by no means complimentary manner, is not absolutely a bar to graduation.[4]

Curriculum.

The educational system of the university is likewise Parisian. But whereas the official arts curriculum of Paris consisted, as we have seen, almost entirely of Aristotelian treatises, Vienna is less conservative, and introduces, in addition to the books of the Paris course, several modern books, which were no doubt in extensive use at Paris, but were not 'taken up' for the schools, such as the *Summulae* of Petrus Hispanus, and a

---

[1] *Ibid.*, p. 51.

[2] The statutes are not clear on this point; but they do not limit the power of voting to masters. As a matter of fact, scholars were rarely elected. See the lists in Aschbach, i, 593.

[3] [The unpublished *acta* of the theological faculty (1, f. 34ʳ) show that on 20 Oct. 1426 the faculty decided to adopt (*pro se servare*) the revised Bologna statutes, a copy of which Thierry Rudolf de Hammelburg had brought to Vienna; see Ehrle, *I più antichi statuti della*

facoltà teologica dell'università di Bologna, p. ix.]

[4] Under 1397 there appears the entry 'Baccalarius Johannes de Bertholtzdorf, primus qui duxit uxorem'. Again, 'uxorem duxit versus in dementiam'. Kink, 1, i. 133. In the statutes of Ingolstadt, a university modelled on Vienna, absence from lecture is (in 1526) condoned 'si quis sanguinis minutione aut propter honestas nuptias . . . impediretur'. Prantl, *Gesch. d. Un. Ingolst.* ii. 178.

much larger amount of mathematics than appears (though the CHAP. IX,
point is not quite clear) to have been exacted at Paris.[1] 'Some §2.
book of Music' is also required. In some of these innovations
it is possible that we may trace the influence of Oxford transmitted to Vienna by the Englishmen[2] and other members of
the English nation at Paris who were the first masters of the
University of Vienna. Possibly the influence of Oxford may
be traced also in the conferment of regular degrees in grammar, of which we hear nothing at Paris.[3]

[1] For B.A.: 'Debet audiuisse ...
Summulas Petri Hyspani, Supposiciones, Ampliaciones et Appellaciones, Obligaciones, Insolubilia,
consequencias, Veterem artem,
Priorum, Posteriorum, Elencorum,
Physicorum, De Anima, Spheram,
Algarismum, Primum librum Euclidis, aut alios libros equiualentes';
together with 'Primam et secundam
partem Doctrinalis, Secundam partem Grecismi, Vnum librum in
Rhetorica'. These last might be
heard 'vbicunque', i.e. not necessarily 'in scolis publicis alicuius
Vniuersitatis'. Kink, ii. 189. The
licence examination further included 'De Celo et mundo. De
Generacione et Corrupcione. Meteora. Parua Naturalia communiter
legi consueta. Theoricas Planetarum. Quinque libros Euclidis.
Perspectiuam communem. Aliquem Tractatum de Proporcionibus, et aliquem de Latidudinibus
formarum. Aliquem librum de
Musica et aliquem in Arithmetica.
Sex libros Ethicorum, Metaphysicam et Topicorum.' Ibid., p. 199.
The table of lecture-fees given
in the same code (p. 213) contains
several books not mentioned in the
above list, e.g. 'Politicorum decem
grossi . . . Yconomicorum duo
grossi. Boethius de consolacione
philosophie quinque grossi . . .
Proporciones longe Bragwardini
tres grossi . . . Summa Naturalium
Alberti quatuor grossi.' The fees
vary from twelve *grossi* (for the

Ethics) to two. A scale is also given
for 'particularia siue Cameralia
exercicia . . . in questionibus consuetis seu precognitis' (p. 215): e.g.
'Magister disputans in priuato
exercicio questiones Byridani . . .
habeat de ipsis octo libris physicorum Viginti quatuor grossos a
quolibet exercitancium' (p. 216).
The fees are throughout much
higher. The prominence of these
'private lectures' (A.D. 1389) affords
interesting evidence of the progress
of college teaching at Vienna. Cf.
the statute of 1413 (*loc. cit.*, p. 254)
which enforces attendance at the
'exercitium Bursale' (i.e. disputations in the *bursae* or halls) every
evening. In 1509 students were
further required to attend the
private grammar-lessons (*resumptiones*) of a master (p. 317).

[2] Aschbach, i. 31.

[3] The statute of 1423 makes the
earliest allusion to such degrees that
I have been able to find in any continental university north of the Alps
(Kink, ii. 274; 'baccalariatus in
grammatica'). Maximilian I, in
1501, founded a 'collegium poetarum', including a 'lector ordinarius
in poetica', with authority to examine and to confer the 'laurea' upon
aspiring poets approved by him
(pp. 305–7). The word 'poeta' was
of course used very much in the
sense of a 'classical scholar' as opposed to the logician or scholastic
philosopher.

CHAP. IX.
§ 2.
Later
privileges.

Of later accessions of privilege two only need be mentioned—the appointment of the bishops of Ratisbon and Olmütz and the abbot of the Scots' monastery in Vienna as papal conservators in 1411,[1] and the conferment of spiritual jurisdiction upon the rector by Martin V in 1420, a jurisdiction which, however, does not seem to have excluded that of the diocesan bishop of Passau.[2] At some time before the end of the fifteenth century a general superintendence of the university, including the payment of the *stipendia*, was entrusted to certain 'superintendents' commissioned by the archduke.

The decline of Prague in consequence of the Hussite troubles put Vienna at the head of the German universities.[3] Vienna long resisted the tendency observable in older German universities towards the concentration of power in the hands of an inner circle of senior masters. It was not till 1458 that it was proposed to deprive the masters of arts of their votes, though not of seats, in the council of the faculty and in the congregation of the university. The three superior faculties voted for the measure, but the young masters of arts had a majority in their faculty, and refused to vote their own disfranchisement. A threat of appealing to the Holy See induced the other faculties to consent to reduce the period of exclusion from six years to four.[4] Later we hear of a university council composed of the 'seniors of all faculties'.[5]

[The history of the University of Vienna between 1365 and 1500 illustrates many aspects both of internal organization and of the movements in academic thought. Kink and Aschbach, following the work begun by Rosas in 1842 on the *acta* of the faculty of medicine (whose publication was begun by Schrauf in 1894), explored the proceedings of the faculties; and Kaufmann, in the second volume of his *Geschichte der deutschen Universitäten* (1896),

[1] Kink, ii. 238.
[2] *Ibid.*, p. 269. (Cf. *Conspectus*, ii. 32.) The exact extent of his jurisdiction is not clear, and he certainly had great difficulty in enforcing it. Vienna had no bishop till 1480.
[3] *Conspectus*, i. 62 *sq.*

[4] *Ibid.* i. 183–6. The excluded masters were allowed to speak by permission of the four senior masters. They were further excluded from votes for a fifth year 'in graciosis', i.e. in granting dispensations.
[5] *Ibid.* ii. 31 (1480).

made free use of these and other Viennese material, e.g. to illustrate
the tendency in German universities towards the organization of a
'lecture list' (pp. 323–42, especially pp. 328–9, 333, 336 n., 339 n.,
cf. S. d'Irsay, p. 180). Kaufmann also deals with the comparatively
unimportant position of the chancellor in Vienna (pp. 134–8). In
spite of the supervision, indeed co-operation, of the duke and the
city (e.g. *ibid.*, p. 34) and of the difficulties in which the turbulence
of the students frequently involved the masters (as in 1455, *ibid.*,
pp. 242–3), great respect was paid to the corporate opinion of the
university in Vienna itself. This opinion was especially influential
in the outside world during the period of the Schism and Councils.
For the 'conciliar' views of the university, and the activity of its
spokesmen, e.g. Peter of Pulka at Constance, cf. L. Dax, *Die Universitäten und die Konzilien von Pisa und Konstanz* (Freiburg-i.-B.,
1910), and, generally, Kaufmann, ii. 429 *sq.* (See also above, vol. i,
pp. 568–80.)

The University of Vienna has a high place in the history of
mathematical and astronomical study. This is due mainly to the
work of John of Gmund (d. 1442) and George of Peurbach (d. 1461),
the teacher of the famous Johannes Müller of Königsberg (Regio-
montanus). Cf. Kaufmann, ii. 480–2. On other aspects of the
intellectual life at Vienna see the bibliographical note, above, p. 235.
As a leading humanist centre, endowed with chairs of poetry and
rhetoric, the university was at its height during the reign of Maximilian I, when its numbers exceeded 1,000.

The University of Vienna looked to Paris as her *alma mater*; her
own daughters were Freiburg-i.-B. and Ingolstadt; see below,
pp. 273, 276.]

§ 3. ERFURT (1379, 1392)

MOTSCHMANN, *Erfordia literata*, Erfurt, 1729. J. C. H. WEISSENBORN,
'Acten der Erfurter Univ.' in *Geschichtsquellen der Provinz Sachsen*, viii
(Halle, three parts, 1881, 1884, 1899). In the last-mentioned work is printed
the statute-book of 1347, a project or short draft for the original statutes
made before the actual beginning of the university, and the matricula.
The same writer's *Hierana*, i (*Beiträge zur Gesch. des erfurtischen Gelehr-
tenschulwesens*, Erfurt, 1862) deals chiefly with the post-Reformation
grammar-schools. He has also published *Amplonius Ratingk de Berka
u. seine Stiftung*, Erfurt, 1878, and *Die Urkunden für d. Geschichte des
Amplonius Ratingk*, Erfurt, 1879. Denifle's section on Erfurt (i. 403) is
largely based on unpublished documents. KAMPSCHULTE, *Die Univ. Erfurt
in ihrem Verhältnisse zu dem Humanismus und der Reformation* (i, Trier,
1858) of course refers chiefly to a later period. [W. SCHUM, *Beschreibendes
Verzeichnis der Amplonianischen Handschriftensammlung zu Erfurt*, Berlin,
1887; G. OERGEL, *Das Collegium Majus zu Erfurt*, Erfurt, 1894; G. BAUCH,
Die Universität Erfurt im Zeitalter des Frühhumanismus, Breslau, 1904;
H. GRAUERT, 'Auf dem Weg zur Universität Erfurt', in *Historisches
Jahrbuch*, xxxi (1910); F. BENARY, *Zur Geschichte der Stadt und der Uni-
versität Erfurt am Ausgang des Mittelalters*, Gotha, 1919; P. KALKOFF,

CHAP. IX, *Humanismus und Reformation in Erfurt*, Halle, 1926; L. MEIER, 'De
§ 3.   schola Franciscana Erfordiensi saeculi XV', in *Antonianum*, v (1930), 57–
94, 157–202, 333–62, 443–74.]

Ancient THE *origines* of the University of Erfurt are perhaps more
schools
of arts. interesting than those of any other German university. The
schools of Erfurt (a town comprised in the territory of the
archbishop of Mainz), though not the first to acquired university rank, may claim a greater antiquity than any other
schools of the same calibre in Germany. Towards the end of
the twelfth century the conventual schools of the place were
of considerable importance, though by this time secular students were excluded from them in accordance with the custom
which had become or was becoming universal throughout
Europe.[1] In the middle of the following century we read of
1,000 boys studying in the town.[2] Many of the churches had
magistri scholarum, and at the end of the thirteenth century
(and probably throughout that century) the four 'principal
schools' of Erfurt, i.e. the schools of the four collegiate
churches of the place, had been schools of arts in the fullest
sense, and not mere grammar-schools, and were united together by some kind of organization under a *rector superior*;
they were governed by statutes made by the chapters and
approved by the archbishop of Mainz.[3] To such an extent
had these schools assumed a university character, that the
place appears to have been popularly spoken of as a *studium*
Disputed *generale*, at least by its own ambitious officials. At all events
claim to be
studium in a roll of supplications for benefices sent to Urban V by
generale. German masters in 1362–3, the then rector, Henry Totting,
procured the insertion of his name as 'Rector superior studii

[1] Doc. in Denifle, i. 403. [See
also Grauert's article in the *Hist.
Jahrbuch* for 1910.]

[2] Denifle, i. 404, refers to *Chron.
Ecclesie* (ed. Wegele, Jena, 1855,
p. 354 *sq.*). The same number is
given at the end of the century by
the versifier Nicolas de Bibera, ap.
Geschichtsquellen der Prov. Sachsen,
Halle, 1870, i. 90. From the earlier
part of the same poem, it would
seem that classical studies were

pursued at Erfurt almost as exten-
sively as at Orleans; but see
Denifle's remarks (*loc. cit.*).

[3] 'Anno 1293 facta fuerunt statuta pro scholaribus et Rectoribus
Scholarum Erffordiae per omnia
ibi Capitula; et per judices S.
sedis Moguntinae confirmata: quae
merito starent et servarentur in
omni schola.' *Chron. Engelhusii*,
ap. Leibnitz, *SS. Rerum Brunsvic.*
ii (Hanover, 1710), 1123.

generalis et solennioris Alamannie artium Erfordensis'.[1] The CHAP. IX,
fate of the petition is an instructive illustration of the notions § 3.
by this time attached to the conception of a *studium generale*.
In the thirteenth century the *studium* of Erfurt would probably have been recognized as 'general', in the technical sense
of the word, except perhaps for the non-existence of one of the
superior faculties.[2] But now the rival applicants for benefices
lodged a complaint against the petition of Henry Totting as
'surreptitious', on the ground that he had described himself
as the rector of the University[3] of Erfurt, when in fact no
university existed in that town. A few years later the Emperor
wrote to the Pope in support of the applicant's petition, and
in his letter describes the school as a *studium generale* 'according to the custom of that and of other surrounding countries';[4]
but he does not defend the technical accuracy of the description. The recognition of its position had not been sufficient to
constitute a *studium generale ex consuetudine*. In particular it
had never received (like the acknowledged *studia generalia ex
consuetudine*) any grant of privilege; and by this time privilege

---

[1] Denifle, i. 406.

[2] Denifle (i. 409) suggests that
it is possible that in the thirteenth
century, when the use of the term
originated, law or theology was
taught here, and that it was then
a *studium generale ex consuetudine*. Kaufmann dogmatically pro-
nounces that Erfurt was a *studium generale* (*Deutsche Zeitschrift
f. Geschichtswissenschaft*, i. 146–50),
ignoring the opposition to its claims
and the qualification 'secundum
usitatam loquendi consuetudinem
illius patrie'. The fact is, Erfurt
was in the fourteenth century a
studium generale in the thirteenth-
century sense, not in the technical
sense of the fourteenth century,
which implied the *ius ubique docendi*.

[3] 'Rector universitatis studii Erforden.' (Denifle, i. 407.) As a
matter of fact he had used the
term 'studium generale', not 'universitas studii'; the circumstance is
interesting as showing how completely the latter term had come
to have the same meaning as the
former.

[4] Denifle (i. 407) prints an interesting extract from this unpublished document: 'Quia in dicto
loco Erforden. secundum usitatam
loquendi consuetudinem illius patrie et aliarum circumiacentium
dicebatur, prout adhuc dicitur, esse
studium generale propter magnam
studencium multitudinem, qui ad
prefatum locum plus quam ad
aliquem alium locum tocius Alamannie confluere consueverunt, et
eciam ex eo, quia ibidem sunt et
fuerunt quatuor scole principales,
in quibus philosophia tam naturalis
quam moralis cum aliis libris arcium
copiose legebatur, quarum scolarum superiorum prefatus Henricus
rector existebat, licet ibidem non
fuerit, nec adhuc sit un iversias
privilegiata.'

had come to be regarded as of the essence of a *studium generale*. Moreover, its teachers appear to have come from Paris and other universities, so that it is doubtful whether at this time graduation was practised at Erfurt.

Bull of Clement VII, 1379.   The foundation of Prague and Vienna naturally inspired in the students and citizens of so ancient and distinguished a *studium* a desire for university privileges. A Bull of foundation was granted by Clement VII in September 1379.[1] But no important change seems to have immediately taken place in consequence of the new charter. The first rector was not

Not executed till 1392.   elected till 1392, after the foundation of two more German universities at Heidelberg and Cologne.[2] Meanwhile, the city had been transferred to the obedience of the Roman pontiff.

Bull of Urban VI, 1389.   A new Bull was accordingly, in 1389, procured from Urban VI, which naturally took no cognizance whatever of the previous charter from the Avignon Antipope.[3] As a matter of fact, however, the university appears to have dated its own existence from the earlier Bull; for the provisions of the former as to the grant of the licence were still enforced, and the change introduced by the latter entirely ignored. Urban VI had assigned the right of promotion to the dean of the collegiate church of S. Mary's in Mainz; while as a matter of fact the archbishop of Mainz retained the rights of chancellor in accordance with the provisions of the Clementine bull.

Constitution; no nations.   The University of Erfurt is the first university of the Parisian type in whose constitution the four nations disappear altogether.[4] The place of the proctors is to some extent taken by the two *consiliarii* from each faculty.[5] The rector may be chosen from any faculty; and, in consequence, the faculty of arts naturally has a dean as well as the other three. As at

---

[1] Motschmann, i. 18; Weissenborn, *Acten*, i. 2: 'Ut in eodem oppido de cetero sit studium generale . . . in grammatica, logica, et philosophia nec non in iuribus canonico et civili et etiam in medicina et qualibet alia licita facultate.' The order in which the faculties are mentioned is, Denifle tells us, unique, and points to the pre-existing schools of philosophy.

[2] *Acten*, i. 36.
[3] *Ibid.* i. 3. Denifle places the university after Heidelberg and Cologne, though it is elsewhere his practice to date a university from the issue of the first Bull of foundation, even if it remained long unexecuted.
[4] *Acten*, ii, 2. Cf. below, p. 256.
[5] *Ibid.* i. 17.

Prague and at Vienna, the university or rather the higher CHAP. IX,
faculties were endowed by the annexation of prebends in the   § 3.
churches of S. Severus and S. Mary's in Erfurt[1] to professorial
chairs—a method which became universal in German universities. The judicial power over scholars was divided—prob- Jurisdic-
ably very much on the Parisian lines—between the ordinary, tion.
the rector, and the apostolic conservators; but the rector
could cite a townsman, as he could not at Paris, for an offence
against a scholar, and the scholar's right to be tried by his own
master is to some extent recognized.[2] It is not always possible
to define the exact limits of the rectorial jurisdiction in German universities; but speaking generally, we may say that the
judicial powers of the rector made some nearer approach to
those of the Oxford chancellor than was the case with the
Parisian rector. He did not always, however, possess direct
spiritual jurisdiction.

The earliest college, the *Collegium maius*, for masters of arts Colleges.
perhaps dates from the earliest days of the *studium*;[3] the
Collegium Amplonianum or *Porta Caeli*, for jurists, was
founded by the ex-rector Amplonius Ratingk in 1433.[4]

In the first year of its real existence as a *studium generale* Growth.
523 persons matriculated at Erfurt.[5] The matriculations show
that the academic population must have been usually considerably above that number in the succeeding years. In 1409
the influence of the German exodus from Prague is just traceable;[6] but after that the numbers fall off, no doubt owing to
the competition of Leipzig. The period of the greatest prosperity and importance of Erfurt was not reached till the

---

[1] *Acten*, i. 25.

[2] *Ibid.* i. 12, 21, 28.

[3] *Ibid.* ii. 8. [Oergel has shown
that the town built the *Collegium*.
It comprised a lecture hall and
buildings for eight masters, who
supervised the *bursarii*. See also,
for the foundation at Erfurt, Kaufmann, ii, 34–7.]

[4] *Acten*, i. 43. On Ratingk cf. the
preface to Schum, *Beschreibendes
Verzeichnis der Amplonianischen
Handschriftensammlung*, Berlin,

1887. [The great Amplonian collection of manuscripts is one of the
most illuminating records of medieval academic interests. It is especially rich in Biblical works and in
the writings of Parisian and Oxford
scholars. Erfurt was a 'nominalist'
university.]

[5] *Ibid.* i. 42.

[6] There were 370 matriculations
as compared with 278 in the preceding year.

CHAP. IX,
§ 3.

middle of the fifteenth century, when it was the scene of the teaching and studies of one of the most distinguished precursors of the Reformation—John of Wesel.[1] It was thus perhaps something more than an accident that Erfurt was the university of Martin Luther. It is melancholy to notice that the university of the great reformer's younger days should have been destroyed by the government of a Protestant country in 1816.

§ 4. HEIDELBERG (1385)

PAREUS, *Historia de Academia Heidelbergensi*, and other old writers who touch on the history of the university, are mentioned by WUND, *Beiträge zur Geschichte d. Heidelberger Universität*, Mannheim, 1786. J. F. HAUTZ, *Geschichte der Universität Heidelberg* (2 vols., Mannheim, 1862-4), which supersedes his *Zur Geschichte der Univ. Heid.* (Heidelberg, 1852), is the most important modern work, containing the statutes and some other documents. More recently, a fuller and very careful study of the earliest period is supplied by A. THORBECKE, *Die älteste Zeit der Universität Heidelberg, 1386-1449* (Heidelberg, 1886), and a full collection of documents has been edited by E. WINKELMANN, *Urkundenbuch der Universität Heidelberg* (Heidelberg, 1886). G. TOEPKE has printed the matriculation-book from the foundation to 1662 (*Die Matrikel d. Univ. Heidelberg*, Heidelberg, 1884-1916)—a most important contribution to University history. The following may also be mentioned: HAUTZ, *Geschichte der Neckarschule in Heidelberg*, Heidelberg, 1849; STOCKER, *Die theologische Fakultät an der Universität Heidelberg, 1386-1886*, Heilbronn, 1886; KUNO FISCHER, *Die Schicksale d. Univ. Heid.*, Heidelberg, 1888; HAUTZ, *Lycei Heidelbergensis origines et progressus* (Heidelberg, 1846), which touches on the colleges or *contubernia* of the university, but relates chiefly to later periods.

[F. W. E. ROTH, *Aus der Gelehrtengeschichte der Universität Heidelberg, 1456-1572* (Neues Archiv für Geschichte der Stadt Heidelberg, vi); E. STÜBLER, *Geschichte der medizinischen Fakultät der Universität Heidelberg, 1386-1925*, Heidelberg, 1926; G. RITTER, *Geschichte der Universität Heidelberg*, Heidelberg, 1922; the same, 'Aus dem geistigen Leben der Heidelberger Universität am Ausgang des Mittelalters', in the *Zeitschrift für die Geschichte des Oberrheins*, n.s. xxxvii. 1-32 (Heidelberg, 1922), and his article in *Das akademische Deutschland*, i. 205.]

Growth of universities in Germany.

WHEN once the university movement was started in Germany, it advanced with rapid steps. As in medieval Spain and modern America the foundation of a university in one State excited the jealousy or ambition of others, and universities

---

[1] Kampschulte, i. 17. [The reader should note that Rashdall's meagre account of Erfurt does injustice to the importance of the part taken by the university in the academic and spiritual life of the fifteenth century.]

multiplied till every considerable principality had one of its CHAP. IX, § 4.
own. Thus the growth of a national or provincial spirit in
Europe, while it destroyed the brilliant intellectual life of the
old cosmopolitan universities, enormously fostered the spread
of ordinary education. The tendency to multiply universities
in Germany gained further strength from the Schism, since
the Roman Popes were always ready to grant the necessary
Bulls as a means of weakening Paris, the great champion of
the Avignon pontiffs.[1] In the case of these minor universities
we must be content with a very brief statement of the main
facts regarding their foundation and constitutional structure.

The University of Heidelberg was founded by the Pals- Founda-
grave Rupert I. The Bull of foundation was issued by Urban tion of
Heidel-
VI in 1385.[2] In the following year a number of charters of berg.
privilege[3] were granted by the founder. Marsilius of Inghen,
an ex-rector of Paris (one of the strong Urbanists who had
left the university), was elected first rector of Heidelberg, and
is often styled in its documents 'founder' of the university.[4]
Lectures were begun by him and two other masters in October
1386. Both the papal and the electoral charters declare that
the university is to be on the model of Paris, and the constitution is a closer imitation of Paris than Vienna or even Prague.
The bishop of Worms is *judex ordinarius* of scholars (at least
if clerks), with a special official and a prison in Heidelberg,[5]
though with some restriction upon his jurisdiction; the provost of the cathedral church of Worms is chancellor; as at
Paris, there is a faculty of theology, but none of civil law.

---

[1] [On the political situation in
the Palatinate at the time of the
foundation of the University of
Heidelberg, see G. Ritter in *Das
akademische Deutschland*, i. 206.]

[2] Hautz, ii. 313; *Urkundenbuch*,
No. 2. That the founder's intention
to found a university dates from
1346, and that an imperial as well
as a papal authorization was obtained, are traditional theories for
which there is no real basis. See
Denifle, i. 381, 383. Cf. also Thorbecke, p. 5 *sq.*

[3] Hautz, ii. 315 *sq.*; *Urkundenbuch*, No. 4 *sq.* [The formal act
of foundation is dated 1 October
1386.]

[4] [See Ueberweg-Geyer, pp.
602–3, 609–10, 785, and the
authorities there cited.]

[5] 'Ut Episcopus Wormaciensis
iudex ordinarius clericorum studii
nostri carceres et officiatum pro
criminosorum clericorum deten-
tione in opido nostro Heidelberg
habeat.' *Urkundenbuch*, No. 8;
Hautz, ii. 319.

CHAP. IX,   A division into nations is mentioned in the foundation-
§ 4.   charter, but it is not clear how far the national organization
Constitu-   really came into existence.[1] The rector was always to be
tion.
taken from the faculty of arts, which apparently voted as
one body in the general congregations.[2] The rectorship was
not thrown open to the other faculties, as it was from the first
in most German universities, till 1393.[3] The change necessitated the appointment of a dean of arts. Few universities of
the Middle Ages, not founded by migration from an existing
Numbers. university, could boast so large a membership in the very year
after its foundation. By October 1387, 589 persons had been
matriculated, including six masters of theology, five doctors
and a licentiate of canon law, three doctors of medicine, and
thirty-four masters of arts.[4] A year later the university was
nearly emptied[5] by pestilence, quarrels with the town, and
the establishment of a rival university at Cologne. But
Heidelberg recovered its ground in the following year, and
permanently took its place as one of the most important in
Germany.

Colleges   As in other German universities, the endowment without
and other   which a young university could not long flourish was partly
endow-
ments.   supplied by the foundation of colleges. The first was the
Cistercian *Collegium Jacobiticum*, erected by Rupert I in
1389.[6] The first secular college, a *Collegium Artistarum*, was
founded by the first chancellor of the university, Conrad von
Geylhausen, in 1390, for twelve teaching masters 'on the
model of the Sorbonne', and was further endowed by the

[1] Paulsen (*Hist. Zeits.* xlv. 389)
assumes that it had no effective
existence. [Kaufmann's view is
that, as at Ingolstadt, nations were
contemplated, but were never
formed (ii. 65).] In the older universities of Germany the nations
retained a formal existence to the
present century.

[2] *Urkundenbuch*, No. 17; Hautz,
ii. 345.

[3] *Urkundenbuch*, No. 31. At the
same time it was provided that in
case of 'dissension' between the
faculties, the matter was to be

determined by a smaller council
consisting of one doctor of each
superior faculty and three delegates
of the faculty of arts. Later (1437)
we find a sort of inner Council of
'seniores magistri' in the faculty
of arts. *Urkundenbuch*, No. 97.

[4] *Matrikel*, i. 1–24. [Ritter gives
the total as 579, including 20
masters from Prague and nine from
Paris, *op. cit.* i. 207.]

[5] Doc. in Hautz, ii. 359, and
Matrikel, i. 34.

[6] Hautz, i. 184; *Urkundenbuch*,
No. 27.

university's 'second founder', Count Rupert II, in 1391,
with 3,000 gulden. It was established in the confiscated
houses of Jews.[1] The *Contubernium Dionysianum*[2] was
founded by Gerlach von Homburg, master of the schools of
S. Stephen's at Mainz, as a house for poor scholars, in 1396.
A further endowment was supplied, under Rupert II and
Rupert III (according to the example already set at Prague
and Vienna) in 1398, by the appropriation of twelve prebends
at Speyer, Worms, and elsewhere for university masters.[3] In
1400 the collegiate churches of S. Peter and of the Holy Ghost
in Heidelberg and other benefices were also impropriated for
the use of the university.[4] A valuable library was bequeathed
to the university by Count Lewis III, who died in 1436.[5]

The university, treading in the footsteps of its first great The two
teacher, Marsilius, was originally entirely nominalistic.[6] In 'viae'.
1412 we find a prohibition not merely of the 'perverse and
condemned doctrines' of Wyclif, but of all realistic teaching.[7]
After the Council of Constance, however, we find symptoms
of the realistic reaction which was everywhere in progress.
In 1452 there is a rectorial injunction against members of the
'via modernorum' using contumelious words against the 'via
antiquorum' and its books, or vice versa, and a prohibition
against trying to prevent scholars attending the lectures or
disputations of any particular master.[8] A few years later
(1455) it becomes evident that the faculty of arts is regularly

[1] Hautz, i. 188; *Urkundenbuch*, Nos. 28–30. The Jewish school was turned into S. Mary's Chapel, used as a university chapel and for meetings of congregation.

[2] Hautz, ii. 362 *sq.* The method of nomination to this college was remarkable. Vacancies were to be filled by the *rectores bursarum* (principals of Halls) and the *rector scolarium sive bachantrie*, who seems to have been an unauthorized rector elected by the students. (See the statutes in Hautz, ii. 371.) No doubt such offices existed in other master-universities where we do not hear of them.

[3] *Urkundenbuch*, No. 46.

[4] *Ibid.*, No. 50 *sq.*

[5] *Ibid.*, No. 98.

[6] [See especially G. Ritter, *Studien zur Spätscholastik*, i, *Marsilius von Inghen und die okkamistische Schule in Deutschland*, Heidelberg, 1921.]

[7] 'Quod nullus magistrorum aut baccalarius dogmatiset aut dogmatisare presumat perversa condempnataque dogmata Wyckleff eciam universalia realia, verum pocius contraria.' *Urkundenbuch*, No. 70. It should be observed, however, that this emanates from the theological faculty only.

[8] *Ibid.*, No. 110.

divided into two 'viae'—so much so that it is necessary to make a statute ensuring to the scholar freedom to pass from one to the other, though with the restriction that he must have heard all the books required for the 'via' in which he wishes to be promoted.[1] There was a separate set of lecturers and of examiners for each 'via'.[2] The division in the magisterial body naturally led to the erection of separate 'bursae' or halls for nominalists and realists.[3] A *bursa* for jurists was founded by count Philip in 1498.[4]

§ 5. COLOGNE (1388)

[HARTZHEIM], *Prodromus Historiae Universitatis Coloniensis*, Köln, 1759. ENNEN, *Geschichte d. Stadt Köln*, iii (Köln, 1869), p. 833 *sq.* BIANCO, *Die alte Universität Köln*, Köln, 1855; which supersedes an earlier *Versuch einer Geschichte der ehemaligen Universität u. d. Gymnasien d. Stadt Köln* (Köln, 1833); Bianco prints the statutes and some documents. H. KEUSSEN, *Die Matrikel der Universität Köln, 1389 bis 1559* (vol. i, to 1466; vol. ii, 1476 to 1559: Bonn, 1892; index, 1928). A few additional documents appear in ENNEN, *Quellen zur Gesch. d. Stadt Köln*, v, vi, Köln, 1875, 1879.

[H. KEUSSEN, *Regesten und Auszüge zur Geschichte der Universität Köln, 1388–1559* (Mitth. aus d. Stadtarchiv. von Köln, xv, 1918); A. WREDE, *Geschichte der alten Kölner Universität*, Köln, 1922; Chr. ECKERT, in *Das akad. Deutschland*, i. 265; and especially H. KEUSSEN, *Die alte Universität Köln, ... Festschrift zum Einzug in die neue Universität Köln*, Köln, 1934, which brings the subject up to date and includes valuable tables and discussions. See also the following articles by the same scholar, 'Die Rotuli der Kölner Universität', in the *Mitteilungen aus dem Stadtarchiv von Köln*, xx (1891), 1 *sqq.*; *Die alte Kölnische Universitäts-Bibliothek* (Jahrb. Köln. Gesch. Ver. xi, 1929); and 'Die Stellung der Universität Köln im grossen Schisma und zu den Reformkonzilien des 15. Jahrhunderts' (in *Annalen des historischen Vereins für den Niederrhein*, cxv (1929), 225–54). For the Dominican schools: G. LÖHR, *Beiträge zur Geschichte des Kölner Dominikanerklosters im Mittelalter*, 2 vols., Leipzig, 1920, 1922; for scholastic exercises the same writer's *Die theologische Disputationen und Promotionen an d. Universität Köln im ausgehenden 15. Jahrhundert*, Leipzig, 1926.]

Ancient schools. COLOGNE appears from very early times to have boasted schools of some repute. In countries which possessed no universities of their own the old church-schools naturally retained an importance which was elsewhere lost after the full development of the universities in the thirteenth century.

[1] *Urkundenbuch*, No. 114.
[2] *Ibid.*, Nos. 135, 138.
[3] *Ibid.*, No. 176. [Cf. Kaufmann, ii. 358–9.] [4] *Ibid.*, No. 145.

The most important of these in Cologne was of course the cathedral school under its *magister scholarum*. As the most prominent and central of the educational and ecclesiastical centres of Germany, Cologne was selected by the Dominicans as the chief *studium* of their order in that country—a *studium* made illustrious by the teaching of Albert the Great and Thomas Aquinas. Here too, in the convent of the rival order, taught and died their great opponent Duns Scotus.[1] But it is a mistake to regard the university as a mere outgrowth or incorporation of these early schools, whether secular or regular. No graduations took place here before the foundation of a university. Like so many of the Italian universities, but unlike the three earlier universities of Germany,—Prague, Vienna, and Heidelberg, which were created by princes,—the great commercial city of Cologne owed its university to the public spirit of its own municipality, which on 21 May 1388 procured a Bull from Urban VI erecting a university on the model of Paris and conferring the right of promotion upon the provost of the cathedral.[2] The papal Bull was proclaimed on 22 December 1388 and the *studium* opened at the beginning of the following year with twenty-one masters, i.e. one D.D., two *baccalarei formati* of theology, a master and a licentiate of medicine, and a bachelor of laws, the rest being masters of arts.[3] Most of the teachers were graduates of Paris, Prague, Vienna, or Heidelberg. A large proportion of the students no doubt came from the same universities. An endowment was gradually provided for the university by the annexation of prebends[4] to academic chairs, and, in respect

CHAP. IX, § 5.

University founded by municipality, 1388.

---

[1] Ennen, *Gesch.* iii. 836. [A. G. Little, in *English Historical Review*, xlvii, 1932, 582.]

[2] Printed in Bianco, i. *Anl.*, p. 1. The university afterwards obtained privileges, conferring protection on journeys and exemption from tolls, &c., from the duke of Guelders (1396) and the Emperor Frederick III (1442): *Ibid. Anl.*, p. 3 *sq.* [For the extensive control exercised by the city over the university and its affairs, see Kaufmann (ii. 121, 142–

3), who cites H. Keussen, 'Die Stadt Köln als Patronin ihrer Hochschule von deren Gründung bis zum Ausgange des Mittelalters', in the *Westdeutsche Zeitschrift*, 1890–1, ix. 344–404, x. 65–104. Cf. F. von Bezold, *Aus Mittelalter und Renaissance*, pp. 233–4.]

[3] Doc. in Bianco, i. 87. Denifle, i. 396. The licentiate and the two bachelors were also M.A.s.

[4] Docs. in Bianco, i. *Anl.*, p. 126 *sq.* (Ennen, *Quellen*, No. 185.)

of the chairs of law and medicine, by the town council.[1] The pecuniary affairs of the *studium* and the appointment of the salaried professors rested jointly with the rector and the municipal *provisores*.[2] The constitution of the university was the Parisian constitution modified by the admission of masters in all faculties to the rectorship,[3] by the admission of non-regents to electoral power,[4] by the introduction of a dean of arts[5] and by the total suppression of the nation-organization.[6] We have seen that in the earlier Germanic reproductions of Paris, the importance of the nations and the proctorships were increasingly diminished. At Cologne they disappear altogether.[7]

The jurisdiction over members of the university belonged in minor cases to the rector, in more serious ones to the rector and deans, and in the last resort to the university itself.[8] For the exercise of spiritual jurisdiction, however, the university had to appeal to the apostolic conservators.[9]

The *Bursa Coronarum* or *Collegium Hervordianum* was founded for a rector and twelve poor students in 1430, and few other foundations of colleges or endowed *bursae* followed.[10]

[Keussen, *Die alte Universität Köln*, pp. 21–38, shows that in the provision of prebends by the pope the city councillors exercised much influence on behalf of their friends and relatives, not always to the advantage of the university. Cf. above, vol. i, p. 556, note.]

[1] Ennen, *Gesch.* iii. 869. [The city also paid salaries to theologians. The masters in arts were expected to live on their pupils' fees. See the interesting chapter in Keussen, *Die alte Universität Köln*, pp. 103 *sqq.*]

[2] Bianco, i. *Anl.*, p. 125.

[3] *Ibid.* i. 147.

[4] *Ibid. Anl.*, p. 59. Bachelors in the higher faculties were to be admitted till they possessed a sufficient number of doctors. (*Ibid.*, p. 17.)

[5] *Ibid.*, *Anl.*, p. 60.

[6] *Ibid.* i. 83.

[7] Their *de facto* existence at Heidelberg is somewhat doubtful. See above, pp. 248, 252. [Kaufmann (ii. 59–68) shows that the nation-organization existed only at Prague, Vienna, and Leipzig among medieval German universities.]

[8] Ennen, *Gesch.* iii. 864. The extent of this jurisdiction, however, does not clearly appear from the published documents; but it seems to have been more than merely disciplinary.

[9] Bianco, i. *Anl.*, p. 119. [The conservators were the abbot of S. Martin, Cologne, and the deans of S. Paul, Liége, and S. Salvator, Maestricht; Ennen, *Quellen*, v. 605–7.]

[10] Ennen (*Gesch.* iii. 859 *sq.*) mentions a *Collegium Ruremundanum* and other 'domus' or 'bursae'; but it is not clear how many of them were really colleges. [Cf. Bianco, p. 253.]

In the first three rectorships of the university's actual existence (9 Jan. 1389–7 Jan. 1390) there were 738 matriculations, the numbers being swelled by the misfortunes which had overtaken Heidelberg a year after its prosperous inauguration. At this time there were twenty-one masters.[1] The recovery of Heidelberg would seem to have injured its rival, since from 1391 the matriculations begin to fall off. After the beginning of the fifteenth century the numbers on the whole slowly increase, amid considerable fluctuations, till in 1461–5 the total is 1,348.[2]

§ 6. WÜRZBURG (1402)

BÖNICKE, *Grundriss einer Geschichte von der Universität zu Wirzburg* (Würzburg, 1782) is superseded by the fuller work by WEGELE, *Geschichte der Universität Wirzburg* (Würzburg, 1882), who prints the few medieval documents. [J. F. ABERT, *Aus der Geschichte der ersten Würzburger Universität unter Bischof Johann v. Egloffstein*, Würzburg, 1923.]

THE idea of founding a university in the ecclesiastical principality of Würzburg originated with the bishop Gerhard of Schwarzburg, who, however, died in 1400 without having accomplished his design.[3] The scheme was carried out by his successor, John of Egloffstein, who, in 1402, obtained a Bull for all faculties from Boniface IX, conferring the privileges of Bologna and the *ius ubique docendi*.[3] The bishop became chancellor, and in 1406 the bishop of Augsburg, the dean of Mainz, and the dean of the collegiate church of S. John at Haug outside the walls of Würzburg were named conservators apostolic.[4] At that date it appears that the university had some formal, though possibly only a formal, existence.[5] The founder's charter of privileges was not issued till 1410.[6] Spiritual and temporal jurisdiction over students was conferred on the rector with a right of appeal to the university: only if both rector and university failed to do justice could they be cited before the ordinary tribunals. The endowment

[1] Keussen, i. 1–45.
[2] *Ibid.*, p. lxxix. There are, however, indications that the matriculations were at times not properly entered.
[3] Wegele, i. 10 *sq.*; ii. 4.

[4] *Ibid.* ii. 6.
[5] The papal Bull speaks of a petition from the university. It is true that this may be a mere 'common form'.
[6] Wegele, ii. 8.

CHAP. IX,
§ 6.

was supplied by the assignment to the university of a *collecta* due from the clergy of the diocese to the bishop. The death of the founder in 1411 was followed, in November 1413, by the murder of the rector,[1] and the outrage was followed by a total dispersion of the masters and scholars. The bishops, becoming involved in the Hussite wars, had no leisure to bestow upon the revival of the university, which seems to have been practically suspended till its gradual restoration in the following century (1561–82), when it became a main-stay of the Counter-Reformation.[2]

§ 7. LEIPZIG (1409)

A magnificent collection of materials exists in B. Stübel, *Urkundenbuch der Univ. Leipzig* (*Codex Diplomaticus Saxoniae Regiae*, pt. ii, vol. xi), Leipzig, 1879, and F. Zarncke, *Die Statutenbücher der Univ. Leipzig*, Leipzig, 1861, and *Acta rectorum Univ. Stud. Lipsiensis*, Leipzig, 1859. There are short sketches of the university's history by Kreussler (*Gesch. d. Univ. Leipzig*, Dessau, 1810), Gretschel (*Die Univ. Leipzig*, Dresden, 1830), and Gersdorf ('Die Univ. Leipzig in ersten Jahre' in *Berichte der deutschen Gesellschaft*, Leipzig, 1847). The following may also be mentioned: *Collegium Beatae Mariae Virginis in Univ. Lips.*, Leipzig, 1859; Zarncke, *Causa Nicolai Winter, Ein Bagatellprocess bei d. Univ. Leipzig*, Leipzig, 1891; Th. Brieger, *Die theologischen Promotionen auf der Universität Leipzig, 1428–1539*, Leipzig, 1890.

[P. W. Ulrich, *Die Anfänge der Universität Leipzig*, i, Leipzig, 1895; G. Erler, *Die Matrikel der Universität Leipzig*, i (*1409–1559*), Leipzig, 1896; R. Kötzschke, in *Das akad. Deutschland*, i. 289; *Beiträge zur Geschichte der Universität Leipzig im fünfzehnten Jahrhundert, zur Feier des 500-jährigen Jubiläums der Universität*, 4 vols., Leipzig, 1909 (this includes R. Helssig, *Baccalaureat in artibus et Magisterium im ersten Jahrhundert der Universität*, and E. Friedberg, *Die Leipziger Juristen-fakultät*); G. Buchwald and Th. Herrle, *Redeakte bei Erwerbung der akademischen Grade an der Universität Leipzig im 15. Jahrhundert*, Leipzig, 1921. Older books, not included above, comprise: F. Zarncke, *Die deutschen Universitäten im Mittelalter*, Leipzig, 1857 (containing the *Libellus formularis universitatis studii Lipczensis* of John Faber of Werden, 1495, *op. cit.* i. 155–209); E. Friedberg, *Das Collegium Juridicum*, Leipzig, 1882. Add also, W. Bruchmüller, *Beiträge zur Geschichte d. Univ. Leipzig und Wittenberg*, Leipzig, 1898; G. Bauch, *Geschichte des Leipziger Frühhumanismus*, Leipzig, 1899. Leipzig, in the beginning of the sixteenth century, as again in later times (e.g. 1872–8), was the most frequented of the German universities.]

Founded by Prague migration, 1409.

The story of the great Prague migration of 1409 has already been told. Some of the students no doubt transferred them-

[1] Wegele, ii. 19 *sq.*

[2] [The story is well summarized

by S. d'Irsay, i. 344–9, with a full bibliography.]

selves to the already existing universities of Germany. A body CHAP. IX,
§ 7.
of over forty masters and some 400 bachelors and students
accepted the invitation of Frederick and William, Landgraves
of Thuringia, to establish a university in Leipzig.[1] The
rapidity with which the scheme was carried into execution is
remarkable. The foundation-bull of Alexander V is dated
Pisa, September 9, 1409.[2] A dean of the philosophical faculty
was elected, and lectures no doubt began, in October, though
the formal opening of the *studium* and the election of a
rector were deferred till the beginning of December.[3] The
first meetings of the university are said to have been held in
the ancient building still used for examination in the faculty
of philosophy [1895]. The bishop of Merseburg became
chancellor and chief conservator apostolic;[4] but the degrees
were usually conferred (as, indeed, was very generally the
case in many universities) by a vice-chancellor. Spiritual
jurisdiction over all students, including clerks, was delegated
to the rector by the bishop.[5]

To supply the place of the *Carolinum* of Prague, the Colleges
and en-
dowments.
masters of arts were from the first lodged by the landgraves in
two houses known as the *Collegium maius* and the *Collegium
minus*, which served both as places of residence for themselves
and their pupils and as lecture-rooms.[6] Soon afterwards the

---

[1] *Urkundenbuch*, p. 3; Gersdorf, p. 25 *sq.*, where the names are given. The list of students is the list of those who matriculated in December. By the end of the first year 602 students had been matriculated.

[2] *Urkundenbuch*, p. 1.

[3] Gersdorf, pp. 25, 35.

[4] *Urkundenbuch*, p. 5.

[5] *Ibid.*, p. 18. It was often renewed (*Acta Rectorum*, p. 15). But in the *Causa Nicolai Winter* we find the rector obliged to apply to the bishop for the enforcement of his sentence by ecclesiastical censure.

[6] *Urkundenbuch*, p. 4; *Statuten-bücher*, p. 96. [Zarncke edited the earliest statutes of the *Collegium minus* from a transcript. The

original text was found and edited by K. Boysen in the *Beiträge zur Geschichte der Universität Leipzig*, 1909.] In S. Mary's College (founded 1416) the 'bursa' of the boarders or pensioners seems to be distinguished from the 'collegium' of the masters (*Statuten-bücher*, p. 277). After the Reformation, Leipzig seems to have been troubled by the 'married don' difficulty. It is interesting to see how it was met. A statute of 1565 recites that, though celibacy is required by the existing statutes, 'domo sua aliquem necessitate promissionis iuratae abstrahere, noctu praesertim, inhumanum sit . . . propterea quod plerique iam coniuges sint, et accidere possit, ut brevi fiant uni-

CHAP. IX, faculties of theology and canon law were endowed with
§ 7.   prebends in various churches.[1]

Constitu-   In some points the constitution of Leipzig naturally differs
tion.
from that of the other north-German universities which we
have been hitherto considering, and follows the example of
its mother-university of Prague. It was divided into four
nations—(1) the Polish, (2) the Misnian, (3) the Saxon, (4)
the Bavarian;[2] and the nations possessed rather more individuality than they enjoyed in other German universities,
since they had separate statutes, congregations, and *consiliarii*
(but no proctors) of their own.[3] The rector is not necessarily
a master;[4] and the faculty of arts has a dean as well as the
superior faculties.[5] Only masters, however, sit in the congregations of the university or of the separate nations, which
include masters of all faculties.[6] In the German universities
we have noticed many indications of the growing tendency
to transform the ever-changing regents of the old Parisian
system into a permanent professoriate. The tendency was
promoted by the colleges and other endowments for masters
which tended to establish a class distinction between the
university teacher and the mere graduate. Another instance
of this tendency meets us at Leipzig, where in the faculty of
arts the chief power seems lodged with a council composed
of the senior members of the faculty, whose numbers were
gradually reduced.[7]

§ 8. ROSTOCK (1419)

I am chiefly dependent on O. KRABBE, *Die Universität Rostock im 15.
und 16. Jahrhundert*, Rostock, 1854. The statutes (*c.* 1435) are printed
in J. VON WESTPHALEN, *Monumenta inedita rerum Germanicarum*, iv,

versi'. A kind of academic caretaker
('Curator') is appointed to live in
college, to maintain discipline and
superintend the 'seriotinarum dis-
putationum exercitationes' (*ibid.*, p.
216). [The problem of marriage
had disturbed German universities
before the Reformation; cf. Kaufmann, ii. 86–7. At Leipzig the
rector was expected to care for the
widows and children of deceased

married professors: Bruchmüller,
Beiträge, p. 17.]

[1] *Urkundenbuch*, pp. 9, 19.
[2] *Ibid.*, p. 4.
[3] *Statutenbücher*, p. 158 *sq.* The
voting in the faculty of arts was not
by nations (*ibid.*, pp. 374, 382).
[4] *Ibid.*, p. 48.
[5] *Ibid.*, p. 306.
[6] *Ibid.*, p. 167.
[7] *Ibid.*, pp. 345, 368, 377, 385.

Leipzig, 1745. *Die Matrikel der Universität Rostock* has been edited by CHAP. IX,
A. HOFMEISTER (Rostock, 1889, &c.). [G. KOHFELDT in *Das akad.* § 8.
Deutschland, i. 363–6; S. D'IRSAY, i. 198–9. For the earlier literature see
Erman and Horn.]

IN the fifteenth century Rostock was one of the most flourish- Founda-
ing of the semi-independent Hanse towns. Its university was tion.
founded by the co-operation of John III and Albert V, then
dukes of Mecklenburg, with the city municipality. The dukes
granted the requisite charters: the city supplied an endowment of 800 florins annually.[1] Hitherto many of the students
from the Baltic countries had been accustomed to study at
Prague; and Rostock must no doubt be reckoned among the
universities which indirectly owe their origin to the great
secession of the Germans from Prague in 1409. In 1419 a
papal Bull was issued sanctioning the erection of a university
in all faculties except theology if the requisite arrangements
for its endowment should be made.[2] The bishop of Schwerin
was made chancellor.[3] The first masters came from Erfurt
and Leipzig, and 160 students were matriculated within the
first half-year of the university's existence.[4] In imitation of
Leipzig the masters of arts were from the first established in
two colleges, the *Collegium maius* and the *Collegium minus*.[5]
Martin V viewed all university faculties of theology with dis-
favour: for doctors of divinity meant councils, and Martin V
was not likely to forget that councils could make and unmake
popes. Accordingly the efforts made, not only by Rostock but
by other Hanse towns, to acquire a faculty of theology proved
fruitless till the accession of Eugenius IV, who granted a Bull
for the purpose in 1431.[6]

[1] Krabbe, i. 31, 32; Krantz, *Wandalia*, Köln, 1518, L. x, c. 30.

[2] The rector does not appear to have enjoyed any very extensive judicial powers till 1468, when he received jurisdiction from the bishop. Krabbe, i. 152.

[3] *Ibid.*, p. 37.

[4] *Ibid.*, pp. 47, 48.

[5] Kosegarten, *Die Univ. Greifs-wald*, i. 55.

[6] Krabbe, i. 54–6, 61. For the migration of the university to Greifswald in 1437–43 see below, p. 270. From 1487 to 1488 the university was similarly transferred, by papal authority, to Lübeck. (Krabbe, i. 202–7.) The dispute arose out of a fusion of certain parish churches into the collegiate church of S. James by the bishop and grand duke for the benefit of the university in 1485—an arrange-ment which was resented by the citizens. Popular feeling ran so high against the chapter that the new

CHAP. IX,
§ 8.
No
nations.

The national subdivisions of Paris and Bologna were clearly out of place in a merely provincial university; and by this time the German universities were becoming essentially provincial. Leipzig was founded by students from three distinct nations of Prague; here the national distinctions were naturally perpetuated. But Leipzig was almost the last German university in which this part of the old Parisian system was reproduced. There is no trace of nations at Rostock, or any of the subsequently founded universities of Germany except Louvain.[1]

The 'promotor.'

The only constitutional innovation which calls for special notice at Rostock is the introduction of a new official, or the glorification of an old one, under the style of the 'promotor et superintendens' of the university. The name 'promotor Universitatis' is occasionally applied at Paris to the university advocate or syndic;[2] but there he never seems to have acquired the prominence and importance of his analogue at Rostock and elsewhere in Germany, where he becomes a sort of public prosecutor or executive officer of the university entrusted with the enforcement of the statutes, even when an offence was committed by the rector himself.[3] He becomes in fact a sort of permanent and acting representative of the merely honorary, often very youthful, and ever-changing rector of

provost was beaten to death with clubs and thrown into the river. (Krabbe, i. 197 *sq.*; Krantz, L. xiv, c. 6.) [Cf. Erman and Horn, ii. 16099.] Later on, we still find the citizens complaining of the connexion between the collegiate church and the university as fatal to the interests of the latter. It is interesting to notice some of the reasons alleged against it: 'Quia omnes civitates stagnales proclamant Universitatem perire propter collegium ... Per dominos universitatis canonicos fiunt lectiones negligentius ... Distrahuntur concordie per diversos diverse sortis dominos et generantur periculosa suspicia. Diversa sunt canonicorum et dominorum de Universitate officia. Illi

cantabunt, hi docebunt et studebunt' (Krabbe, p. 219). Similar arrangements in more modern times have been attended with results not wholly dissimilar.

[1] See above, p. 256, n. 7.
[2] See above, vol. i, p. 420.
[3] Krabbe, i. 88; Westphalen, iv, c. 1020. So at Louvain: cf. Lipsius, *Lovanium*, p. 96. In the *Jura et Privilegia Acad. Lovan.* (p. 12) he is described as the *oculus rectoris*. At Louvain we hear that he 'vicos Urbis perambulat, aliquando solus, nonnunquam cum urbano Praetore. Suos habet Satellites', &c.' (Vernulaeus, *Acad. Lovan.*, p. 38)—one of the few traces of such proctorial perambulations which I have met with in continental universities.

those days. In other respects the constitution was closely
modelled on Leipzig.

The university matriculation-book shows 160 matriculations between November 1419 and April 1420: between that
time and October, 226; in the following half year, 101. After
this the matriculations for the semester are usually between
50 and 100. After a migration to Greifswald, which came to
an end in 1443, the total number of members of the university
appears to have been 278. The average numbers remain much
the same till the close of our period, with the exception of a
slight increase from about 1470–7 and a great depletion between the years 1487 and 1490, during part of which time
the university was transferred to Lübeck.[1]

§ 9. LOUVAIN (1425)

There is a meagre account of the university by LIPSIUS, *Lovanium*
(Antwerp, 1605, p. 90 *sq.*), and a still more meagre one in GRAMAYE,
Antiquitates Brabantiae (Louvain, 1708, p. 20 *sq.*). There are two histories
of the old type: Valerius ANDREAS, *Fasti academici studii generalis
Lovaniensis* (Louvain, 1635; ed. 2, 1650), and VERNULAEUS, *Academia
Lovaniensis* (Louvain, 1667), of which the latter is the more valuable.
The *Privilegia Academiae Lovaniensis* (Louvain, 1728) and *Jura et
Privilegia Academiae Lovaniensi* (Strasbourg, 1787) are of little use.
The *Statuts primitifs de la faculté des arts de Louvain* have been edited
by DE REUSENS in *Bulletins de la commission royale d'histoire*, sér. 3,
ix, and the *Anciens Statuts de la faculté de médecine*, by DE RAM (*ibid.* v),
who has also published 'Considérations sur l'histoire de l'Université', in
Bulletins de l'Acad. royale de Belgique, xxi, 1859, and edited a series
(continued by NAMÈCHE) of *Analectes pour servir à l'histoire de l'Un. de
Louvain* (Louvain, 1850–80), which, however, contain hardly anything
relating to our period. The statutes of the university are printed by
the same editor in his ed. of MOLANUS, *Historia Lovaniensium* (Com.
royale d'histoire: Brussels, 1861), and separately as *Codex veterum statutorum Academiae Lovaniensis*, Brussels, 1861. The statutes of the colleges
are printed in the *Analectes pour servir à l'histoire ecclésiastique de la
Belgique*; sér. 2, xvii, &c., and *Documents relatifs à l'hist. de l'Univ.
de Louvain*, ed. DE REUSENS (Louvain, 1881, &c.). See also A. J. NAMÈCHE,
Jean IV et la fondation de l'Université de Louvain, Louvain, 1888.
[*Bibliographie de l'Université de Louvain* (1834–1900) and supplements
(Louvain); H. DE VOCHT, *Inventaire des archives de l'Université de Louvain*,

---

[1] *Matrikel*, pp. xxii *sq.*, 1 *sq.* See
above, p. 261, n. 6. [For the later
revival cf. Kaufmann, ii. 552, and
S. d'Irsay, i. 328. The humanist
Gisbertus Longolius was called in

to advise about the reconstitution
of the faculty of arts. For his
Restauratio, printed Rostock, 1544,
see Erman and Horn, ii. 15329.]

CHAP. IX, *1426–1797, aux Archives Générales du Royaume à Bruxelles,* Louvain,
§ 9.   1927; F. DE REIFFENBERG, 'Mémoire sur les deux premiers siècles
de l'Université de Louvain', in *Nouv. mém. de l'Académie royale de
Belgique,* 1829, 1832; P. DELANNOY, *L'Université de Louvain,* Paris, 1915;
L. VAN DER ESSEN, *Une institution d'enseignement supérieur sous l'ancien
régime: L'Université de Louvain* (1425–1797), Brussels and Paris, 1921;
the same and others, *L'Université de Louvain à travers cinq siècles: études
historiques,* Brussels, 1927 (cf. the *Liber memorialis,* Bruges, 1932);
S. D'IRSAY, i. 254–9; A. VAN HOVE, 'Statuts de l'Université de Louvain
antérieur à l'an 1459' (*Bull. de la commission royale d'histoire de Belgique,*
lxxvi (1907), 597–662); E. REUSENS, 'Documents relatifs à l'histoire de
l'Université de Louvain' (*Analectes pour servir à l'histoire ecclésiastique
de la Belgique,* and separately, Louvain, 1901); A. VAN HOVE, *Actes ou
procès-verbaux des séances tenues par le conseil de l'Université de Louvain,*
2 vols., covering years to 1455, Brussels, 1903, 1919 (Publ. de l'Académie royale de Belgique); E. REUSENS, *Le Matricule de l'Université de
Louvain,* i (1426–53), Brussels, 1903 (Publ. de l'Académie royale de
Belgique); H. DE JONGH, *L'Ancienne Faculté de théologie de Louvain au
premier siècle de son existence,* Louvain, 1911; A. FIERENS, 'Les Ambitions
de la faculté des arts de Louvain au début du xvie siècle' (*Mélanges
Moeller,* 1914, ii. 56–68); A. VAN HOVE, 'La Bibliothèque de la faculté
des arts de l'Université de Louvain au milieu du xve siècle' (*ibid.* i. 603–
25); the same, 'L'Enseignement à la faculté de droit canonique de Louvain
au début de son existence' (*Mélanges Camille de Borman,* 1919, pp. 191–
202); H. DE VOCHT, 'Excerpts from the Register of Louvain University
from 1485–1527' (*English Historical Review,* xxxvii (1922), 89–105);
J. H. BAXTER, 'Scottish Students at Louvain University, 1425–84'
(*Scottish Historical Review,* xxv (1928), 327–34); B. LEFEVRE, 'Les Sciences
mathématiques et physiques à l'ancienne Université de Louvain au
xve siècle' (*Revue des questions scientifiques,* xv (1929), 29–58.]

Decline of   IN the fifteenth century Louvain had lost most of its old
Louvain.   commercial prestige. The violence of its civic factions—
culminating in the horrible massacre of seventy patricians
in 1378—had led to a large migration of weavers to England,
a blow to its commercial prosperity from which it never fully
recovered. According to Lipsius, its university was erected,
as was so often the case in Italy, in part at least as an expedient
for reviving a declining town.[1] In 1425[2] a Bull was obtained
from Martin V for a university of all faculties with the exception (as in the case of Rostock) of theology: as with Rostock
too the deficiency was supplied by the next pope, Eugenius IV

Founda-   (1432).[3] The university was actually opened in 1426.[4] Its
tion of   founder was the territorial sovereign, John IV, Duke of
university. Brabant, and the leading part in the promotion of the scheme

---

[1] Lipsius, p. 91.   [3] *Ibid.* i. 499.
[2] Molanus, i. 455.   [4] *Statuts,* p. 19.

was taken by his councillor Engelbert, Count of Nassau. The CHAP. IX, chancellor was the provost of the collegiate church of S. § 9. Peter. It was one of the conditions upon which the Bull of erection was granted that the duke should confer upon the Jurisdic- rector full criminal and civil jurisdiction over scholars; and tion of rector. this condition was immediately complied with. The rector's jurisdiction extended to all cases except those which fell to the apostolic conservators,[1] who were the archbishop of Trier, the abbot of Tongerloo, and the dean of S. Peter's at Louvain.

The constitution of the university seems to be partly copied Constitu- direct from Paris, partly from the modification of the Parisian tion. constitution presented by the earlier German universities.[2] All the doctors or masters appear at first to have had seats in the governing body of the university. The faculty of arts alone was divided into nations, each of which had a proctor, (1) Brabant, (2) the Walloon country (*Gallia*), (3) Flanders, (4) Holland;[3] but the rector was taken from the four faculties in turn, the faculty of civil law counting as a distinct faculty; and the voting was by faculties.[4] The nations were, however, of little importance. At first the teaching was left (it would appear) as at Paris to any regents who chose to lecture; but after 1466 teaching in the faculty of arts was confined to four *paedagogia*, except in ethics and rhetoric, for which there were university professors.[5] These professorships and those of the superior faculties, by a Bull of Eugenius IV (23 May 1443),

[1] Molanus, i. 459 *sq.*, 495; ii. 896 *sq.*; Vernulaeus, p. 28 *sq.*

[2] Gollnitz (*Ulysses Belgico-Gallicus*, p. 96) describes the university as 'e Coloniensi nata'. [See Ehrle, *Der Sentenzenkommentar Petrus von Candia*, p. 158.]

[3] *Statuts*, p. 47; Andreas, ed. 1650, p. 240; Vernulaeus, p. 57. The dean of the faculty is sometimes called in the statutes 'Procurator Facultatis Artium'. There are allusions to a 'Consilium Facultatis Artium', but its composition is not clear.

[4] I infer this from the sixteenth-century statutes. [Cf. Van der Essen, pp. 64–6.] At a later time the government was monopolized by a senate consisting of the rector, deans, salaried professors, and heads of colleges. Vernulaeus, p. 10 *sq.* [The *acta* of the council or senate survive, with some gaps, from May 1432. Those prior to 1455 have been edited by A. van Hove. Two volumes, containing the *acta* for the years 1474–1522, perished in the fire of 25 August 1914.]

[5] Vernulaeus, p. 64; Molanus, ii. 942.

were provided for by the annexation of stalls in the collegiate church of S. Peter and of various parochial churches, the nomination to them being bestowed upon the burgomasters and consuls of the city.[1] The high prestige which the university had attained by the end of the century goes far to justify a municipal or at least a governmental system of university patronage.

Colleges and Paedagogies. The College of the Holy Ghost was founded by a Flemish knight, Louis de Rycke, in 1445 for seven students of theology, and rapidly grew through later benefactions.[2] For law-students the College of S. Ivo was founded by Robert van de Poel (de Lacu), a doctor of both laws, in 1483; the College of S. Donatian by Doctor Antonius Haneron in 1484. For the last decade of the fifteenth century Louvain was the abode of the famous Jean Standonck, who in 1499 left behind him a 'domus pauperum', organized on the rigid and ascetic principles which he had applied to his College of Montaigu at Paris. The College of Malines for Artists was founded by Arnold Trot, bedel of the faculty of theology, in 1500. The four paedagogia, (1) lilii, (2) falconis, (3) castri, (4) porci, which (unlike the colleges proper) were under the direct management of the faculty of arts, also began to receive various small endowments towards the end of the century. But the most famous college at Louvain was the Collegium Trilingue,[3] founded, circa 1517, by Jerome Busleiden for the study of Greek, Latin, and Hebrew, which confirmed the position which Louvain had already won as one

[1] Molanus, i. 109, &c. [These privileges led to repeated disputes with the bishops of Liége; see de Jongh, pp. 255–7, and P. S. Allen's note in Opus epistolarum D. Erasmi, v. 527.]

[2] De Ram, Analectes, i. 56 sq. For the colleges generally see Molanus, i. 622 sq. [and especially the calendar of documents in H. de Vocht, Inventaire des archives, from which the dates given by Rashdall have been corrected. The Collège de Houterlé, which Rashdall described as a confraternity of the 'innocent boys of S. Peter', and as founded in 1496, was founded in December 1510 for three students in theology by Henri de Houterlé and seven choristers of Saint-Pierre; ibid., Nos. 2446, 2459].

[3] There is an elaborate history of this college by Félix Nève, in the Mémoires couronnés of the Académie royale de Belgique, xxviii (1856). [See also some delightful pages in P. S. Allen, Erasmus: Lectures and Wayfaring Sketches (Oxford, 1934), pp. 156–63.]

of the earliest and for a time by far the most famous home of the new learning in Europe.

Louvain retained the character of a federation of many colleges until the Reformation; and even in the revived Roman Catholic University of Louvain a nearer approach to the college life of Oxford and Cambridge may be found than is to be met with elsewhere on the continent of Europe; while Louvain preserves or has revived the full graduation ceremonial which has disappeared everywhere else north of the Pyrenees.[1] In another respect Louvain reminds us of an English university. Here was established, as early as the year 1441, a much nearer approach to our English system of competitive honours than is perhaps to be found at the present day upon the continent of Europe. The candidates for the mastership were after examination placed in three classes, in each of which the names were arranged in order of merit. The first class were styled *rigorosi* (honour-men), the second *transibiles* (pass-men), the third *gratiosi* (charity-passes), while a fourth class, not publicly announced, contained the names of those who could not be passed on any terms.[2] These competitive examinations contributed largely to raise Louvain to the high position as a place of learning and education which

[1] A full account of these ceremonies is given in *Documents relatifs à l'érection et à l'organisation de l'Université catholique de Louvain* (Brussels, 1844), p. 134 *sq.* [1895.]

[2] 'Ita est, si aliqui reperiantur rigorosi, sint de primo ordine, transibiles de secundo, si gratiosi, capaces tamen gracie, sint de tertio; si autem (quod absit) aliqui inveniantur simpliciter gratiosi seu refutabiles, erunt de quarto ordine' (*Statuts*, p. 55). It is noticeable that rivalry between the colleges called for a statutable provision 'quod . . . non respiciunt ad conditiones domorum seu pedagogiorum' (*ibid.*; cf. p. 59). At a later time it would appear that the division into classes was done by the professors *before* the examination, and the competition was only for places in the class.

An interesting account of the examinations is given (from Vernulaeus, p. 60 *sq.*) in Sir W. Hamilton's *Discussions* (London, 1852), pp. 407-8, and App. III (B). Hamilton was at one time inclined to trace the origin of the Cambridge tripos to the Louvain Examination, but the suggestion was afterwards withdrawn (*ibid.*, p. 418). The examinations certainly seem to have kept up the studious character of the place, if not its intellectual eminence, at a time when Oxford had sunk into absolute lethargy; in 1787 the author of the *Jura et Privilegia* (p. 20) declares 'Nullus hic locus otio, soli studio duodecim fere horas quotidie impendunt, reliquas aut pietati aut modicae relaxationi animi' (!).

CHAP. IX,
§ 9.

it attained before the universities elsewhere were roused from their fifteenth-century torpor by the revival of learning. Pope Adrian VI and (at a later date) Jansen were among the many celebrated men who attained the position of *primus* in the Louvain examinations.[1] The intolerant realism which pre-vailed in the university prepared it for its role as the chief stronghold of anti-reformation learning later in the sixteenth century.[2]

Realism and con-servatism.

§ 10. TRIER (1454, 1473)

BROWERUS et MASSENIUS, *Antiquitatum et Annalium Trevirensium libri xxv*, Liége, 1670, ii. 288 *sq.*; MARX, *Geschichte des Erzstifts Trier*, Trier, 1859, ii. 454 *sq.* [KEIL, *Akten und Urkunden zur Geschichte der Trierer Universität*, 2 parts, 1917, 1926 (Trierisches Archiv).]

No ancient studium generale.

KAUFMANN[3] claims the position of *studium generale* for Trier in the twelfth or thirteenth century, on the ground that a student song contains the apostrophe 'Urbs salve regia, Trevir, urbs urbium'. 'Urbs regia' is, he contends, used in allusion to the theory that the teaching of law was confined to 'civitates regiae' by the constitution *omnem*.[4] It is impos-sible to say that the schools of this metropolitan city may not have been what would have been considered a *studium generale* in the loose thirteenth-century sense; but there is no real evidence to show that they were so. And there are certainly no traces of an existing *studium generale*, or of any-thing like it, in the place in 1454, when the archbishop, James of Sirck, procured a Bull of creation from Nicholas V,[5]

Bull of 1454.

---

[1] A list is given in Vernulaeus, p. 146. Molanus (i. 467) quotes the testimony of Erasmus in 1521: 'Academia Louaniensis frequentia nulli cedit hodie praeterquam Parisianae. Numerus est plus minus tria milia, et affluunt quotidie plures.' [*Opus epist.*, ed. P. S. Allen, iv. 548.] The college which had produced the *primus* enjoyed three days' holiday, during which the bell was continually rung day and night. Gramaye, p. 24; Ver-nulaeus, p. 61. Cf. below, App. iv.

[2] 'Anno 1486 Marsilius de Crae-nendonck reconciliatus est Facul-tati, qui in actu formali asseruerat Aristotelem nominalem fuisse, agnoscens se ex levitate fecisse' (Molanus, i. 581). In 1427 some nominalists were suspended for three years, and in 1446 it was con-sidered a sufficient defence of an incriminated thesis to say that it was found in Scotus, 'quem repro-bare Facultati non licebat' (*ibid.*, p. 582).

[3] *Gesch. d. deutsch. Univ.* i. 159.

[4] Cf. above, vol. i, p. 11 n.

[5] Browerus et Massenius, ii. 288.

who also authorized the impropriation of six canonries and CHAP. IX, § 10.
three parochial churches in the city for the sustentation of
masters.[1] The date, however—the year after the capture of
Constantinople—was an ill-omened one for such an undertaking. The war with the Turk called away the founder to
other tasks, and the actual birth of the university was post- No actual
poned to the year 1473.[2] university
till 1473.

It would appear, however, that the credit of this revival is
due not to the then archbishop but to the city, which had to
bribe that prelate with a sum of 2,000 *aurei* to hand over to
them the old Bull of Nicholas V and to assist them in obtaining a fresh one.[3] The archbishop was chancellor, and the
foundation-Bull conferred upon the university the privileges
of Cologne, which seems to have been the model for its
constitution.

§ 11. GREIFSWALD (1456)

KOSEGARTEN, *Geschichte der Universität Greifswald, mit urkundlichen
Beilagen*, 2 vols., Greifswald, 1856–7. See also authorities for Rostock,
above p. 260. [PALTHENIUS, *Historia ecclesiae collegiatae Gryphiswaldensis*,
Greifswald, 1704; J. ZIEGLER, *Geschichte der Stadt Greifswald*, Greifs-
wald, 1897; E. FRIEDLÄNDER, *Aeltere Universitätsmatrikeln*, ii, *Universität
Greifswald*, 2 vols., Leipzig, 1893–4 (Publ. aus den K. Preussischen
Staatsarchiven); *Aus der Geschichte der Universität Greifswald* (Fest-
schrift), Stettin, 1906; F. CURSCHMANN, 'Die Stiftungsurkunde der
Universität Greifswald' (*Pommersches Jahrbuch*, vii, Greifswald, 1906);
R. ENGELBRECHT, *Der Grundbesitz der Universität Greifswald, seine
Entwicklung und Bedeutung* (thesis), Greifswald, 1926; F. KRÜGER in
Das akad. Deutschland, i. 173; A. HOFMEISTER, *Die geschichtliche Stellung
d. Univ. Greifswald*, Greifswald, 1932.]

IN the year 1428 a democratic revolution took place in the Interdict
town of Rostock, in consequence of the failure of the town at Ro-
council in their expedition against Eric of Pomerania, King of migration
Denmark. The existing burgomasters—the representatives of univer-
of the hitherto ruling oligarchy—were expelled, and betook Greifs-
themselves to the council of Basel to get the assistance of wald,
ecclesiastical thunders for the promotion of their recall. As 1437.
a consequence of this appeal, the city was laid under interdict,

[1] *Ibid.*
[2] *Ibid.*, p. 299. As to the date, cf.
Marx, ii. 459.

[3] Wyttenbach and Müller, *Gesta
Trevirorum*, ii (Trier, 1838), 343;
Browerus et Massenius, ii. 299.

and the university in particular was ordered to have no dealings with the excommunicated city magistrates. The university was evidently disposed to sympathize with the citizens, but the place was at length rendered uninhabitable for it; and a decree of the Council of Basel was procured authorizing its transference to any other place within the dioceses of Kammin and Ratzeburg. The place selected was the neighbouring Hanse town of Greifswald in Pomerania, to which the university removed from 1437 till 1443. The Basel decree only authorized the transference of the *studium* so long as the

Removal of interdict, 1439. interdict on Rostock lasted. This was removed in November, 1439, when a kind of coalition government was arranged between the aristocracy and the craftsmen. The university at Greifswald was, therefore, *ipso facto* brought to a conclusion. But the town council of Rostock were not at first disposed to renew the endowment of the truant university; and for more than three years the *studium* practically ceased to

Return of university to Rostock, 1443. exist in either city. In 1443, however, it was permanently transferred back to Rostock; but the six years during which it had enjoyed the dignity of a university town left academical aspirations in the minds of the burghers of Greifswald; and it is not surprising to find a movement arising for the erection of a permanent university not many years after the departure of the Rostock professors.[1]

Bulls from Calixtus III, 1455-6. In 1455 a Bull[2] was procured from Calixtus III addressed to the bishop of Brandenburg, authorizing the erection of a university if it were found that the allegations of the petitioners as to the suitability of the place and other circumstances were true. The project, however, was opposed by the duke of Mecklenburg and the University of Rostock, and the actual Bull of erection was not granted till 1456.[3] The issue of a preliminary commission of inquiry, it may be remarked, seems to be a very usual method of procedure at the

Commission of inquiry. Roman Court in the erection of a university at about this period. In this case there appears to have been a very

[1] Krantz, *Wandalia*, L. xi, c 11 *sq.*, L. xii, c. 28. Kosegarten, i. 27–33, 293–4; Krabbe, i. 110–29.
[2] Kosegarten, ii. 3.

[3] *Ibid.* ii. 14. An imperial charter of privilege was obtained from Frederick III in the same year. *Ibid.*, pp. 49, 50.

elaborate inquiry,[1] and the definitive Bull was not procured without the expenditure of 300 ducats on the part of the envoy of the city, no less than 200 of which went in gratifications to the cardinals or the inferior hangers-on of the ecclesiastical Court.[2] Even when the Bull was issued, its operation was conditional on the actual endowment of the university to the extent of 1,000 ducats annually in rents by Wratislaus, Duke of Pomerania-Stettin, whose supremacy Greifswald now acknowledged, and other local benefactors. This sum was supplied as usual by the impropriation of churches: in particular, the town church of S. Nicholas in Greifswald was made collegiate, and the patronage of the canonries bestowed on the university. The city likewise contributed to the endowment, and also—a more unusual circumstance—the bishop of Kammin and the neighbouring abbeys.[3] The bishop of Kammin became chancellor and (jointly with the bishop of Brandenburg) conservator apostolic. The chancellor, however, early appointed as perpetual vice-chancellor Henry Rubenow, one of the burgomasters of Greifswald, who had taken the largest share in promoting the erection of the university, towards which he contributed on a munificent scale out of his private purse.[4] He has always been considered the true

Impropriations.

Henry Rubenow.

[1] These precautions would appear not to have been altogether uncalled for. The first Bull of Calixtus III declares that the duke's representatives had made the astounding assertion 'quod infra Centum miliaria prope ipsum Opidum (ab una parte) aliquod generale studium, quod ad presens vigeat, non existit', thus ignoring Rostock. The words 'ab una parte' seem to be a later correction. Kosegarten, ii. 3, 4. [See also Kaufmann, ii. 26–31, and Engelbrecht.]

[2] See the amusing letter in Kosegarten, ii. 18, 19: 'Vix valeo facta universitatis cum ccc ducatis expedire, propter impedimenta nobis facta. Quasi cc ducatos habeo dare in propinis. Nisi hoc fecissem, nihil obtinuissemus', &c. The envoy stayed at Rome to procure further privileges; and on 28 April 1457 (*ibid.*, p. 59) writes to Rubenow giving further particulars of the gratifications which he had given to the cardinals. He explains that the first envoy of the enemies of the university had died of chagrin at its success—'Credo quod ex melanconia (*sic*) obiit'—and he hopes that their present agent will likewise die at Rome: 'ebriosus est; credo quod nunquam revertetur, quia aer Romanus non patitur homines talis modi'. He asks for more money 'sine quibus nichil'. [Cf. Hofmeister, p. 29.]

[3] Kosegarten, ii. 4, 8, 10, 12, 38, 164 *sq.*

[4] *Ibid.* ii. 24 (this document also authorizes the rector to have a prison), and p. 159.

CHAP. IX, founder of Greifswald.[1] Rubenow was also elected first
§ 11.   rector of the university, and 173 students were matriculated
during his rectorship, i.e. during the first half-year of the
university's existence.[2]

First pro-   The universities of Greifswald and Rostock are remarkable
fessorship
founded for the large number of private citizens who contributed to
by private their foundation or endowments. They may be said to supply
persons.
Colleges. the first recorded instances of the foundation of professorships
(*collegiaturae*) by private persons.[3] The masters of arts, as at
Leipzig and Rostock, were divided between a *Collegium maius*
and a *Collegium minus*. The houses were given by the duke;[4]
the colleges were richly endowed; and the masters further
derived a considerable income from letting out rooms to non-
foundation students. At Greifswald the *Collegium maius* was
adapted for six rectors or regents and 200 students; the
Collegium minus for four regents and 140 students. In the
ducal deed of gift the average net income derivable from room-
rent is estimated at a florin per student.

§ 12. FREIBURG-IM-BREISGAU (1455–6)

The chief history (with extracts from documents) is H. SCHREIBER,
Gesch. der Stadt und Albert Ludwigs Universität Freiburg im Breisgau,
ii, Freiburg, 1857. A few documents are given in J. A. RIEGGER, *Analecta
academiae Friburgensis* (Ulm, 1774), and SCHREIBER, *Urkundenbuch der
Stadt Freiburg im Breisgau*, ii (Freiburg-i.-B., 1829). *Die Urkunden über
die der Universität Freiburg-i.-B. zuhörigen Stiftungen* (Freiburg-i.-B.,
1875), refers but little to our period. It contains the statutes of the
'Sapientia', a college founded in 1501, on which there is also a 'Pro-
gramme' by F. X. WERK (*Das Collegium Sapientiae in Freiburg*, Freiburg,

---

[1] Rubenow's total expenditure
upon the foundation of the university was 3,012 marks, besides the
patronage of eight benefices and
400 'florenos renenses' spent in procuring the Bulls. He bequeathed
further property to the university
by will, including a library which
'pro mille florenis,' he says, 'nulli
darem'. Kosegarten, ii. 259.

[2] *Ibid*. i. 65; ii. 259 *sq*. [Some of
these were students only in name.]

[3] Krabbe, i. 57; Kosegarten, ii.
101 *et passim*.

[4] The duke gives a house 'cum

cameris siue commodis pro sex
Rectoribus et ducentis Studentibus,
pro collegio maiori et pedagogio
artistarum bene preparatis, a quibus
Regentes in illo ultra ducentos
florenos pro conductura solum-
modo absque liberis expensis et
collecta leccionum percipere valeant
ad omne minus', &c. Kosegarten,
ii. 20. Later on, in both universities, the 'Collegium minus' was
made into a stricter school or
paedagogy for the younger stu-
dents·('pedagogium cum clausura
et directione'). *Ibid*. ii. 213.

1839). KRAUS, *Die Universitäts-Kapelle im Freiburger Münster* (Freiburg- CHAP. IX
i.-B., 1890). [F. X. WERK, *Stiftungsurkunden*, Freiburg-i.-B., 1875; § 12.
H. MAYER, *Die Matrikel der Universität Freiburg-i.-B.*, 1460–1656, 2 vols.,
Freiburg-i.-B., 1907, 1910. The statutes of the theological faculty have
been edited by J. KÖNIG in the *Freiburger Diözesanarchiv*, xxi, xxii, xxiv.
E. PFISTER, *Die Finanziellen Verhältnisse d. Univ. Freiburg*, Freiburg-i-B.,
1889. Articles in the *Zeitschrift der Gesellschaft für Geschichtskunde zu
Freiburg-i.-B.*, include J. REST, 'Beiträge zur Geschichte der Universität
Freiburg' (xxvii, 1912), P. P. ALBERT, 'Gründung und Gründer der
Universität Freiburg' (xxxvii, 1923). F. SCHAUB, 'Die älteste Stipendien-
stiftung an der Universität Freiburg und ihr Stifter Konrad Arnolt von
Schorndorf' (xxxviii, 1925). H. MAYER, *Die alten Freiburger Studenten-
bursen*, Freiburg-i.-B., 1926. See especially F. SCHRAUB, 'Geschichte des
Archives der Universität Freiburg-i.-B.', in the *Finke-Festschrift*, 1925;
H. FINKE'S lecture, *Universität und Stadt Freiburg in ihren wechselseitigen
Beziehungen*, Freiburg-i.-B., 1920; and the same scholar's article in *Das
akad. Deutschland*, i. 127 *sq.*]

A BULL was granted in April 1455[1] authorizing the erection Founda-tion.
of a university at Freiburg-im-Breisgau, on the petition of
Machtildis, archduchess of Austria; and in August 1456 a
ducal charter followed erecting the university and conferring
upon it the privileges of Paris, Heidelberg, and Vienna. It
was endowed by the impropriation of rectories and prebends
in the ducal patronage. The bishop of Basel was chancellor,
and the jurisdiction over students was divided between the
bishop and the rector.[2] [The deans oi the cathedrals of
Strasbourg and Constance and the abbot of the Benedictine
monastery of S. Trudpert in Breisgau were appointed 'con-
servatores et iudices academiae'.][3]

The accessible data do not admit of any further account Constitu-tion: the
of the constitution. It was, no doubt, more or less based on two *viae*.
that of Vienna; but before the end of the century[4] a curious

[1] This Bull does not appear to have been a direct Bull of erection, but conferred upon the bishop of Constance the power to erect the university, which he exercised in the following year.

[2] Schreiber, *Gesch.* ii. 7–14. Albert's charter is printed in Riegger, *Analecta*, pp. 277–89; also (p. 297) a Bull of Innocent VIII in 1484 conferring on the rector jurisdiction over clerks as well as laymen, and giving power of absolution for assaults on clerks to the senior

doctor of theology. [The university also obtained an imperial confirmation: Frederick III's charter, December 1456, is printed in Riegger, *Opuscula ad historiam et jurisprudentiam praecipue ecclesiasticam pertinentia*, Freiburg-i.-B., 1773, p. 436.]

[3] [Riegger, *Analecta*, p. 302.]

[4] Schreiber, *Gesch.* ii. 11. [The rector, *consiliarii* and deans of faculties appear. The first teachers came from Vienna and Heidelberg.]

2994.2　　　　　N n

modification was introduced. It was in the English universities, and through the antagonism between the nominalists
of the English nation and the rest of the university at Paris,
that the quarrel between the nominalists and realists first
assumed the form of a great faction-fight, dividing masters
and scholars into two hostile camps alike in the battles of the
streets and in the debates of the congregation-house. In the
German universities of the fifteenth century this feud reached
a climax of bitterness and absurdity. We have seen how it
had already contributed to the disruption of the University
of Prague in 1409. At that time the Germans were nominalists
almost to a man; and in the purely German universities—at
Vienna and in the universities which received the dissidents
from Prague—nominalism for a time carried all before it. But
as the memories of Prague and of Constance began to die out,
realism, no longer incompatible with patriotism, seems to
have revived. The Freiburg faculty of philosophy was, however, like the parent University of Vienna, predominantly
nominalist till the year 1484, when we find the archbishop
Siegmund ordering the university to provide a *via realium*.
A little later a realistic section of the faculty was actually
formed under the direction of Master Northofer, who had
been fetched from Tübingen for the purpose. From this time
distinct lectures were given on each book by a nominalist and
by a realist master; and it was provided that the two per-
suasions should be equally represented upon the council of
the faculty.[1] It is a singular fact that that liberty of conscience,
about which so much ado has been made in the sphere of what
is technically known as theology or 'religious instruction',
should never, in modern times, have been extended to the
sphere of philosophy, in which men's differences are no less
fundamental, no less fraught with consequences alike for
religious belief and for practical ethics.[2]

---

[1] Schreiber, ii. 43, 59–63. The
via antiquorum at Freiburg was
also styled *via scotistarum*. [Cf.
Kaufmann, ii. 360, 361.]

[2] It is interesting to notice that
in the 'Magnum Convictorium', or
college of this university, college
life seems to have lasted till about
1774. Werk, p. 34.

§ 13. BASEL (1459)

LUTZ, *Geschichte d. Universität Basel,* Aarau, 1826. W. VISCHER, *Geschichte* CHAP. IX, *der Universität Basel von der Gründung 1460 bis zur Reformation, 1529,* § 13. Basel, 1860. The latter supersedes the former, and publishes more documents. Cf. also OCHS, *Geschichte der Stadt und Landschaft Basel,* iv, Basel, 1819. [*Festschrift zur Feier des 450 j. Bestehens der Universität Basel,* Basel, 1910; C. C. BERNOUILLI, *Die Statuten der juristischen Fakultät der Universität Basel,* Basel, 1906; the same, *Die Statuten der theologischen Fakultät der Universität Basel,* Basel, 1910; M. ROTH, *Aus den Anfängen der Basler medicinischen Facultät,* Basel, 1896; A. BURKHARDT, *Geschichte der medizinischen Fakultät in Basel, 1460–1900,* Basel, 1917; R. WACKER-NAGEL, *Geschichte der Stadt Basel,* ii (Basel, 1916), 551 *sqq.,* and iii (Basel, 1924: *Humanismus und Reformation in Basel*).

The *Matricula studiosorum universitatis Basiliensis* (Basel MS. A.N. ii. 3) shows that the average number which matriculated each year was 126 between 1460 and 1479, and 61 between 1480 and 1499; 226 matriculated in 1460, 35 in 1499, but 1499 was an exceptional year, for only 6 matriculated in the first half-year (1 May) and the note is added 'tempore erat bellum Sueuicum'. We owe the details on which these calculations are based to Mrs. H. M. Allen.]

AENEAS SYLVIUS, who resided at Basel during the sessions of the council, testifies to the educational zeal of its burgomaster and council, who supported masters of grammar, logic, and music [1] When Aeneas mounted the papal throne as Pius II, the council took the opportunity of petitioning their old friend for university privileges. A Bull was granted in 1459 for the erection of a university in all faculties.[2] The bishop was chancellor; and the *studium* was actually opened in the following year.[3] The university was under the control of a body of deputies (*deputati*) named by the magistrates. A college was provided and funds supplied by the town council; and a further endowment was obtained by the annexation of prebends varying in value from 40 to 200 florins.[4] The statutes were based on those of Erfurt.[5]

Aeneas Sylvius' account of Basel schools. As Pius II, grants bull for university, 1459.

§ 14. INGOLSTADT (1459, 1472)

ROTMARUS, *Almae Ingolstadiensis academiae tomus primus,* Ingolstadt, 1581; J. R. MEDERER, *Annales Ingolstadiensis academiae* (4 vols.: vol. iv is a *Codex diplomaticus*), Ingolstadt, 1782. PRANTL, *Gesch. der Ludwig-*

[1] *Scriptores Rerum Basil. minores* (ed. Brucker, i, Basel, 1752), p. 374.
[2] Vischer, pp. 268–70.
[3] *Ibid.,* pp. 282, 290. *Basler*

Chroniken, iv (Leipzig, 1890), p. 332.
[4] Vischer, pp. 21–2, 85, 272, 307–8. [Cf. Kaufmann, ii. 42.]
[5] Vischer, pp. 311–14.

Maximilians-Universität in Ingolstadt, Landshut, München (2 vols.,
Munich, 1872) is one of the most serious and learned of university
histories, with a full collection of 'Urkunden'. [F. X. FRENINGER, *Das
Matrikelbuch der Universität Ingolstadt-Landshut-München*, Munich, 1872
(gives a list of rectors, professors, doctors, but is not a full edition);
M. STADLBAUR, *Über die Stiftung und älteste Verfassung der Universität
Ingolstadt*, Munich, 1849; Ch.-H. VERDIÈRE, *Contre-réforme religieuse
et réforme littéraire: histoire de l'Université d'Ingolstadt*, Paris, 1887;
G. BAUCH, *Die Anfänge des Humanismus in Ingolstadt*, Leipzig, 1901;
SCHAFF, *Geschichte der Physik an der Universität Ingolstadt*, Erlangen,
1912.]

Founda-
tion. BAVARIA was the next German principality to grow ambitious
of having a university of its own. A Bull was obtained by
Lewis the Rich, Duke of Bavaria and Count Palatine of the
Rhine, from Pius II in 1459; but the actual erection of the
university was delayed in consequence of the war in which
the duke was engaged against the Emperor Frederick III and
Albert of Brandenburg. The university was not opened till
1472,[1] when 489 students were matriculated within the year.[2]
In the following year there were 321 matriculations, in the
next 220. From this to the end of the century the average
number of annual matriculations is about 200.[3] The university received from its founder the privileges of Vienna, which
had no doubt hitherto served as the university-town of most
Bavarians.[4]

Constitu-
tion. The bishop of Eichstädt became chancellor. In the main
the constitution and statutes of the university were modelled
on those of Vienna. The original draft of the university

[1] *Annales*, i, pp. xx. 1; Prantl, i.
15. The Bull and ducal charters
are given by Mederer, iv. 16, 39,
42. *Inter alia* the duke confers
the privileges of the University of
Athens [as was not uncommon at
this time]. Though the Bull is in
the usual form, a special Bull was
procured to authorize promotions
in the superior faculties in 1477.
Annales, iv. 113.

[2] Prantl, i. 64. [Verdière gives
the number 794.]

[3] *Annales*, i. 1–59. The numbers
fluctuate between 130 and 373. We
may perhaps conclude that the
actual numbers of the university

were at least 500 or 600 (Prantl,
loc. cit.).

[4] *Ibid.*, pp. xxi, xxxiii. A plan
for making the church of S. Mary's
collegiate, and giving the stalls to
professors nominated by the duke,
for which the papal consent was
obtained, broke down, but the
revenues were applied to the benefit of the university: Prantl, i. 15;
Annales, iv. 19, 25. In the same
way other churches were saddled
with pensions to masters without
the latter serving the cures. *Ibid.*
i. 31 *sq.* A prebend at Eichstädt
seems to have been actually held by
the *lector theologiae*. *Ibid.* iv. 25.

charter professed to reproduce the Vienna division of the CHAP. IX,
whole university into four nations;[1] but in the actual statutes § 14.
of 1472 we find no nations, and as a consequence the student-
rights disappear. But the voting by faculties is retained. The
rector is to be chosen in turn from each faculty,[2] and the whole
of the masters have seats in the general council of the university and of their respective faculties.[3] Soon afterwards, however, in accordance with the prevailing tendency throughout
Germany, we find the masters of below four years' standing
excluded from the councils of the faculty of arts unless
specially invited.[4] But the most striking innovation in the The two
Ingolstadt constitution arose out of the now stereotyped and viae.
traditional feud between the nominalists and the realists. The
faculty of arts divided itself into two distinct sections, each
with a dean, council, *matricula*, chest, and *bursae* of its own.
They met only at disputations. This expedient, however,
appears rather to have fomented than appeased the heat of
the metaphysical combatants, and in 1478 the two *viae* were
compelled to reunite by the strong hand of the duke.[5]

The *Collegium Georgianum*, founded by the son and suc- *Collegium*
cessor of the founder of the university in 1494, is remarkable *Georgia-*
as being one of the few colleges in German universities organ- *num.*
ized on the Parisian model. Most of the colleges in German
universities were primarily colleges for masters who were
engaged in university teaching: the *Collegium Georgianum*
was a college for eleven poor students under a regent.[6]

The university was moved in 1800 to Landshut, and in Transfer-
1826 to Munich.[7] The papal Bull for Ingolstadt contains the ence to
Landshut
wholly exceptional provision that candidates for degrees and
Munich.
should take an oath of obedience to the Holy See—almost the

[1] Prantl, i. 25.

[2] *Annales*, iv. 60.

[3] *Ibid*. ii. 59, 70.

[4] Prantl, ii. 88. In the statutes
of 1519–20 we find the exception
'nisi collega, regens, aut alicuius
contubernii praefectus esset'. *Ibid.*
ii. 154–5.

[5] *Annales*, i. 16; ii. 70, 71, 73;
Prantl, ii. 50, 52, 77. The voting
was by faculties, the two *viae* only

counting as one. Prantl, ii. 72.

[6] *Annales*, i. 44, 47. Prantl, i.
96–100; ii. 117 *sq.*

[7] *Ibid*. i. 697, 720. [For Ingolstadt as a source of the Counter-
Reformation in the sixteenth century, see Ch.-H. Verdière, *Contre-
réforme religieuse et réforme littéraire: histoire de l'Université
d'Ingolstadt*, 2 vols., Paris, 1887;
cf. S. d'Irsay, i. 351, 352.]

CHAP. IX, first instance of anything in the nature of a test in university
§ 14. history.[1] Candidates for degrees at Paris or elsewhere had,
indeed, been required before this to assent to various con-
clusions of the university itself, but no such provision had
been imposed from without upon a university at its foundation. In recent times the Bavarian university has elected to
its rectorial chair the leader of the most notable modern revolt from within the bosom of the Roman Church itself
against the authority of the Roman See. [1895.]

§ 15. MAINZ (1476)

A few documents in WÜRDTWEIN, *Subsidia diplomatica*, Heidelberg,
iii, 1774, and a *Catalogus chronologicus rectorum magnificorum*. [This
last is part of H. KNOD, *Historia universitatis Moguntinae*, Mainz,
1751. Add F. FALK, 'Die Mainzer Hochschule 1477 und ihr Lehrstuhl
für Bibelkunde' (*Mitteilungen der Gesellschaft für d. Erzieh.- und Schul-
geschichte*, ix (1899), 123 *sqq.*); A. L. VEIT, 'Aus der Geschichte der
Universität zu Mainz, 1477–1731,' in *Historisches Jahrbuch*, xl (1920),
106–36.]

Founda- THE university of Mainz was founded by a Bull of Sixtus IV,
tion. granted on the petition of Diether, archbishop of that see in
1476, and was endowed with one canonry and prebend in each
of fourteen churches of the neighbourhood, which were placed
in the patronage of the rector and 'provisors' of the university.
The provost of S. Mary-at-steps in Mainz became chancellor;
and the university was endowed with the privileges of Paris,
Bologna, and Cologne.[2] The archbishop's first charter to the
university was issued in 1477,[3] and the first privileges in 1479.
The first rector was elected in 1478.[4] A document of 1483
shows that the 'Provisors' were the rector (who was a D.D.)
and the deans of the four faculties.[5]

§ 16. TÜBINGEN (1476–7)

A. F. BÖK, *Geschichte der herzoglich Würtenbergischen Eberhard Carls
Universität zu Tübingen* (Tübingen, 1774), largely occupied with biographies; KLÜPFEL, *Geschichte und Beschreibung der Univ. Tübingen*,

[1] [For the position of the duke,
and the oaths taken to him by the
rector, *consiliarii*, and *bedelli*, see
the statutes of 1472 in Mederer (iv.
45, 68); and cf. Kaufmann, ii. 117.]
[2] Würdtwein, iii. 182, 197 *sq.*
[3] *Ibid.*, pp. 187, 223.

[4] *Catalogus*, p. 1.
[5] *Ibid.*, p. 3. A work entitled
'Modernorum summule logicales'
and published by the 'Magistri
collegii moguntini regentes' in 1490
indicates the existence of a *Collegium*.

Tübingen, 1849, and *Die Univ. Tübingen*, Leipzig, 1877; *Urkunden*
zur Gesch. der Univ. Tübingen aus den Jahren 1476–1550 (ed. R. Roth),
Tübingen, 1877; STEIFF, *Der erste Buchdruck in Tübingen*, Tübingen,
1881. [C. WEIZSAECKER, *Antiquissima tria statuta facultatis theologicae
Tubingensis*, Tübingen, 1867; F. X. LINSENMANN, 'Gabriel Biel und die
Anfänge der Universität Tübingen' (*Theologische Quartalschrift*, xlvii,
Tübingen, 1865, 195–226); H. HERMELINK, *Die Matrikeln der Univer-
sität Tübingen*, i (1477–1600), Stuttgart, 1906 (index, 1931); *Beiträge zur
Geschichte der Universität*, edited for 450th anniversary, Tübingen,
1927. There is now a full study of the early history of the university by
J. HALLER, *Die Anfänge der Universität Tübingen, 1477–1537*, 2 vols.,
Stuttgart, 1927–9; cf. A. RAPP in *Das akad. Deutschland*, i. 385. Add
H. HERMELINK, *Die theologische Fakultät in Tübingen vor der Reforma-
tion, 1477–1534*, Stuttgart, 1906 (an important study); the same, 'Die
Anfänge des Humanismus in Tübingen' (*Württembergische Viertel-
jahrschrift für Landesgeschichte*, new series, xv (1906), 319 *sqq.*), and
F. ERNST, *Die wirtschaftliche Ausstattung der Universität Tübingen in ihren
ersten Jahrzehnten (1477–1534)*, Stuttgart, 1929.]

WÜRTTEMBERG obtained a university of its own by the founda- Foundation of Tübingen in 1477. Its founder was Eberhard, Count tion.
of Württemberg, with the 'co-operation' of his mother, Machtildis, Archduchess of Austria,[1] and his uncle Count Ulric.
Its endowment was supplied by impropriations, and especially
by the annexation to magisterial chairs of the ten canonries
and prebends in the church of S. George at Tübingen, whose
provost became chancellor of the university.[2] The Bull
authorizing the erection of the university was issued by Sixtus
IV in 1476, but was not executed till 1477, when the university was actually founded and the first statutes drawn up by
the abbot of Blaubeuren acting as papal delegate.[3]

In 1484 the university obtained a confirmatory charter Imperial
                                                         Bull for
                                                         laws.

[1] *Urkunden*, pp. 28–9. [Mach-
tildis, who was also concerned in
the foundation at Freiburg (above,
p. 273), has been called 'the Lady
Margaret of German university
history'.]

[2] *Ibid*, pp. 1, 11 *sq.* The
count afterwards added the first-
fruits or *decimae novalium* (which
he had appropriated to himself),
with papal licence. *Ibid.*, p. 68.

[3] *Ibid.*, p. 11 *sq.*, 39. It is
observable that the original purpose
of the papal Bull has now passed
out of sight: there is no express

grant of the *facultas ubique docendi*,
merely a general conferment of all
privileges enjoyed by other universities. The Provost of S. George's
is appointed *studii cancellarius*,
with the powers which the Archdeacon of Bologna exercises 'in
universitate Studii Bononiensis'. It
will be noticed that 'universitas
studii' and 'studium' are now
practically synonymous. In the
words used by the chancellor in
conferring the licence, the 'hic et
ubique terrarum' has disappeared.
Ibid., p. 260.

CHAP. IX, from the count's kinsman, the Emperor Frederick III. The
§ 16. language of this charter is remarkable since it seems to assume
that the imperial permission was specially requisite to authorize teaching and graduation in the Roman or 'Imperial' laws
—the first indication of such a theory with which we have
met.[1] By this time the true idea of the purpose for which the
papal or imperial Bull was originally sought was becoming
confused. The Tübingen charter is no doubt a somewhat
unhistorical assertion of prerogative on the part of the Emperor. At an earlier period the imperial charter would not
have been limited to the faculty of law; although an imperial
charter was sometimes obtained as well as a papal one, each
authority had fully recognized the prerogative of the other in
respect of all faculties alike. The Emperor as little denied the
Pope's power to found a law university as the Pope denied
the Emperor's to erect a *studium generale* in theology.[2]

Numbers: Forty masters and 256 students were enrolled by the first
early dis-
tinction. rector.[3] Among its earliest masters appears the name of one
who has sometimes been called the last of the schoolmen,
Gabriel Biel, a name of very great importance in the develop-
ment of that nominalist theology against which the revolt of
German protestantism was in an especial manner directed.[4]
There were, however, two *viae* at Tübingen as well as at
Freiburg and Ingolstadt; but Tübingen was one of the earliest
universities to welcome first the new learning and then the
Reformation. It numbers Reuchlin among its teachers, and
Melanchthon and Eck among its students.

§ 17. GENERAL CONCLUSIONS

Summary. IT may be well at the conclusion of this brief sketch to sum
up the chief characteristics of these German universities

[1] *Urkunden*, p. 76.

[2] [The authorization to teach
imperiales leges appears also in
Frederick III's charters for Freiburg in 1456 (cf. above, p. 273) and
for the abortive University of Lüneburg, 1471; see Kaufmann, ii. 12–
14, 563–5. Kaufmann, in accordance with his well-known views,
regards the imperial action as a
form of protest against papal
pretensions.]

[3] *Urkunden*, pp. 462, 471.

[4] [See Hermelink, *Die theologische Fakultät*, and the literature
mentioned in Ueberweg-Geyer, pp.
604, 612, 786.]

in the form which they have assumed by the end of our period.[1] Paris was on the whole the model from which they all started. In all essential respects in which we have not noticed a change, it may be assumed that the customs and institutions of Paris were reproduced in her German offshoots. The changes which we have noticed in successive foundations exhibit a gradual modification of the Parisian constitution; all these changes tended in the same direction, and culminated in the evolution of a form of university constitution in which it is not always easy to recognize the resemblance to the Parisian prototype. It remains for us to recapitulate the main points of difference between the German university of the fifteenth century and its Parisian original.

(1) An important reservation must be made when it is said *Survival of* that the German universities were founded on the model of *student-rights.* Paris. The two earliest universities—Prague and Vienna— exhibit a mixed type of university constitution. At Prague after 1372 the jurists had a separate student-university of their own; while in the four nations of Vienna students had a place as well as masters, and all participated in the election of a rector. Gradually, however, the constitution of the last university was so far modified as to place in the hands of the masters all real academic power. This was effected by transferring most of the authority from the nations to the council of the university in which the masters predominated and to the councils of the respective faculties which were wholly composed of masters. In later universities the student-rights disappear with one exception; in many of them the rector may still be a student though not elected by the students. The exception was of little practical importance. It perpetuated itself because it conduced to the honour and advantage of a university to have a young prince or count for its rector. It is probable that it was only in such cases that a student was ever elected. Sometimes a young aristocrat was elected even if under age: in that case he was assisted and practically controlled by a vice-rector.

---

[1] [Kaufmann, in his second volume, analyses the general features and developments with much wealth of detail.]

CHAP. IX,   (2) The connexion of the rector with the faculty of arts
§ 17.   which had its root in the peculiar historical development of
Rector and
faculty of the Parisian constitution had by the date of the earliest Ger-
arts.   man university become an unintelligible anomaly. It early
disappeared both at Prague and at Vienna, and in the later
universities (with the exception of Heidelberg) the rector
might from the first be chosen from any faculty. The faculty
of arts always had a dean of its own.

Nations.   (3) The special connexion of the nations with the faculty
of arts had likewise become meaningless. When nations
existed in the German universities they existed as a division
of the whole university. They were from the first less important than at Paris; and in the later medieval foundations they
disappear altogether.

Collegiati   (4) A fundamental difference between Paris and her Ger-
and
councils. man daughters lay in the fact that in the latter the teachers
were from the first endowed. The endowment was usually
effected, at least in the faculty of arts, by the erection of one
or more colleges. The universities were thus provided with a
permanent professoriate, and this professoriate succeeded in
time in ousting the unendowed regent masters from all real
academic power. Sometimes all regents voted for the election
of rector and dean; but in every case the real power was
gradually transferred to the councils, which practically constituted both the university and the faculties.[1] The composition of these councils varied. Nearly always they included
only *collegiati* with such honorary members as they might
think fit to co-opt:[2] sometimes all *collegiati* sat in the council,

---

[1] At Greifswald, in 1456, all the
regent masters voted in the election
of dean (Kosegarten, ii. 297). But
all academic power seems to be in
the hands of a council of twelve
senior masters, of at least four
years' standing (*ibid.*, p. 300), who
are also the *collegiati* (*ibid.*, i. 77; ii.
215), though extraordinary mem-
bers might be added to the former
(*ibid.*, ii. 220). The *collegiati* are a
co-opting body, but the election to
a *collegiatura* or to the prebends,

with which the endowment was
completed, requires the confirmation of the university (*ibid.*, ii. 221
&c.). Here (as in other cases) many
functions are reserved to a still
smaller *concilium secretum* of the
university or faculty (*ibid.*, p. 229).

[2] At Rostock only the professors
of the more valuable chairs in the
superior faculties and two masters
of arts with extraordinary members
co-opted by them (Westphalen,
Diplomatarium, iv, c. 1010).

sometimes only a limited number—those of a certain standing or the holders of the better-endowed chairs. In the university council the faculty of arts was often represented by only a limited number of its members, while all the professors of the superior faculties had seats in it.[1] Throughout the period which we have been studying there is a tendency to transfer academic power from popular congregations, such as still rule our English universities, to an oligarchy of permanent and endowed professors. The change is virtually complete by the end of the fifteenth century.

(5) The colleges stood from the first in a different relation to the university from that which they occupied at Paris. At Paris the colleges had sprung up later than, and independently of, the university, and their original purpose was merely to provide for poor students. In the German universities the larger colleges were designed primarily to supply the university with teachers. Many of them formed part of the original founder's design: at all events they were in most cases under the direct government of the university, or rather of its faculties. The old haphazard regent system was necessarily inefficient. At Paris and Oxford it was gradually supplanted by the growth of college teaching, at least in the faculty of arts. In Germany the same change may be traced, but here the college teachers were from the first university teachers as well, and gradually passed into the position of a university professoriate pure and simple. At first there was, indeed, a distinction between university lectures and college disputations or 'exercises', the latter being given in the colleges by the endowed regents or in the private *bursae* by their rectors or conventors. For a time college teaching and university teaching existed side by side (though given to a large extent by the same persons), but even the college or domestic teaching

Colleges.

---

[1] In some universities, however, as late as the sixteenth century, the unendowed regent masters are still required to reside for two years and do a certain amount of lecturing, probably *extraordinarie*, unless dispensed by the faculty. So at Leipzig (1471–90), Zarncke, *Statutenbücher*, p. 403; and at Greifswald, Kosegarten, ii. 303; but here they are only required to lecture 'per duos menses . . . et octies disputare extraordinarie'. [This was to complete their *biennium*.]

was regulated and required by the university,[1] so that, long before the colleges began to disappear, all teaching was practically in the hands of the university. The college or colleges of a faculty were in fact practically identical with the faculties themselves, and in most cases had hardly any existence independently of the university.[2]

Evolution of professoriate.
(6) Another step towards the evolution of the modern professoriate was taken when the subjects to be lectured on were systematically distributed among the masters of the faculty. We are entirely in the dark as to the manner in which the distribution of books among lecturers was effected at Paris. But perhaps in a university like Paris, where 120 regents in arts are said to have been teaching simultaneously, the distribution may have been left to the natural operation of the law of supply and demand. In smaller universities (especially when newly founded) where the same number of subjects had to be divided among a very small staff of teachers, this was impossible. Hence we find on the foundation of Leipzig that it was resolved that the books should be distributed among the regents by lot.[3] In other universities it would appear that the distribution was effected by mutual arrangement or the decision of the faculty. To convert these endowed regents into

[1] At Leipzig 'serotinae disputationes' are required for a degree in 1471–90 (Zarncke, *Statutenbücher*, p. 420). Private *paedagogia* often existed side by side with the colleges, and the 'exercises' in them were recognized by the faculty as equivalent to those conducted by *collegiati* in the colleges. (See, e.g., Kosegarten, *Greifswald*, ii. 301 *sq*.) But some students still lodged with citizens (*ibid.*, p. 252—a document from which it appears that most of the arts students were Danes).

[2] This appears with peculiar clearness at Greifswald, where the faculty of arts is found ordering the most minute repairs of the *Collegium maius* and *Collegium minus* and of the 'bursae', which seem to have been houses included in or annexed

to the *collegia* proper. Kosegarten, ii. 243, 249 *sq*. The former passage throws light on the state of sanitary arrangements in a medieval college in 1484. Money was voted 'pro quodam loco secreto erigendo ad commodum magistrorum, ne eos contingeret dispariter vulgari suppositorum concursu permisceri, tum eciam quia cloace . . . fuerunt supereffluenter replete sordibus, et sic cum difficultate expurgabiles'. The requirements of undergraduates do not seem to have been considered; hence perhaps the partiality of the latter for the private 'regentia' so bitterly lamented by the *collegiati*.

[3] Zarncke, *Statutenbücher*, p. 309.

professors of distinct subjects it was only necessary that the chap. ix, §17. teacher should continue to teach the same subject permanently instead of having a fresh book assigned to him at the beginning of each academical year. To trace the steps by which this change was effected would carry us beyond the chronological limits to which this work is confined.

When the power of voting at faculty-meetings, and especially the control of the examinations, was reserved to a council, and the emoluments of the ordinary lectures to a college, a single step only was necessary for the complete evolution of the regent master into a professor—i.e. to make the two restrictions coincide. This change appears to have been completed in the course of the sixteenth century, when membership of the faculty became dependent upon a place in the college: faculty and college became identical.[1] To trace further the development of the ancient college-system of modern Germany into the professorial system of to-day, would again be beyond our province. Suffice it to say that the professor ordinarius[2] of modern times is the successor of the medieval collegiatus or doctor-prebendary; while the extraordinary professors and the 'Privat-dozenten' may be considered to represent the old extra-collegiate regents, authorized to teach and to take what fees they can get for doing so, but with no endowment or share in the government of the university.

Additional Note to Chapter IX.

[The distinction often drawn between the Middle Ages and the sixteenth century—a distinction which made Rashdall regard the foundations of Frankfurt-on-Oder and Wittenberg as outside his subject—is never a happy one, and it is especially unhappy when it is applied to the history of the German universities. If a line is to be drawn anywhere, it might more appropriately distinguish the later fifteenth-century foundations between 1456 and 1477, Greifs-

---

[1] Cf. Paulsen, *Hist. Zeitschr.*, xlv. 396. The full development of the system involved also (1) the making of *collegiaturae* permanent, which in the faculty of arts had usually not been the case; (2) the extinction of the ordinary regent's role in the university as well as the faculty; (3) the restriction of particular chairs to particular subjects.

[2] [For the title *ordinarius* in the faculties of law see Kaufmann, ii. 209, 210.]

CHAP. IX. wald, Freiburg-im-Breisgau, Basel, Ingolstadt, and Tübingen, from those which preceded them; for it is impossible to separate the theological and humanistic movements of the later fifteenth century from the powerful and perplexing forces which disturbed mankind during the age of Maximilian I and Charles V. Yet even this earlier division would be arbitrary, since the stirring of mind and spirit was as profound in some of the older universities—Vienna, Heidelberg, Erfurt, Leipzig—as it was in the newer foundations.

From the first, academic opinion, and in some degree even the foundation of universities, in Germany were influenced by the disputes in Paris. The conflict between the Ockhamists and their opponents, the agitations caused by the Schism and the Conciliar movement, all of which began, or tended to centre, in Paris, reacted violently upon the German universities. The influence of princes and cities combined with local feeling in the universities themselves to prevent anything like a united body of university opinion during the period of the councils, but the movement undoubtedly increased intercourse between the universities, and sometimes led to the formation of mutual understandings. Similarly the disputes between the realists and nominalists, which very often divided universities against themselves and, especially at Ingolstadt, led to a duplication of academic organizations (see above, p. 277), was a means of bringing together the followers of the *via antiqua* or the *via moderna*. Louvain followed Cologne in the *via antiqua*; Heidelberg followed Vienna in the *via moderna*. And, just as it is impossible entirely to separate the Ockhamite controversies from opinion about the Schism or the Conciliar movement, so, as Ritter has pointed out, it is impossible to treat the rapid development of humanism apart from the philosophical conflict about the 'two ways'. The connexion in both cases was not necessarily logical; it was as often as not the result of personal influence, of local rivalries, or of vested interests; but it was none the less a real connexion. The inner history of the German universities from the foundation of Prague in 1348 to the foundation of Wittenberg in 1502 is not, as a reflection of mental processes, a coherent development, but it is in fact unbroken, and it leads, by way of pietism, philosophical and theological discussion, and humanism, to the Reformation.

A detailed study of these aspects of German academic life would demand a volume. Any attempt to summarize the results of recent scholarship would require a long chapter, such as would be out of place in a new edition of this work. Rashdall regarded his book primarily as a treatise on the development of university organization in Bologna, Paris, and Oxford. He confined his treatment of other universities to a description of their origin and constitution. Yet it may be helpful to his readers if we close with some references to the more important books and papers which have been devoted to the subject mentioned in this note.

The German universities and the Conciliar movement: Hermann CHAP. IX.
BRESSLER, *Die Stellung der deutschen Universitäten zum Baseler
Konzil, zum Schisma und zur deutschen Neutralität* (Dissertation),
Leipzig, 1885; KAUFMANN, *Geschichte der deutschen Universitäten*, ii
(Stuttgart, 1896), 419–68; Lorenz DAX, *Die Universitäten und die
Konzilien von Pisa und Konstanz* (Dissertation), Freiburg-i.-B.,
1910. The collections of documents and the studies of FINKE
and others make a revision both necessary and possible. V. RED-
LICH, 'Eine Universität auf dem Konzil in Basel' (*Histor. Jahrbuch*,
xlix, 1929, 92–101); and cf. Hermann KEUSSEN on Cologne in the
Annalen des historischen Vereins für den Niederrhein, cxv (Düsseldorf, 1929), 225–54. Keussen brings out clearly the importance of
the problem of the *rotuli* or lists of graduates seeking benefices, in
shaping opinion. He points out that the practice, so prevalent in
German universities, of incorporating collegiate churches for the
benefit of the masters, was increased by the need for benefices
(p. 233).

The Nominalist school and the controversy about the 'two ways':
UEBERWEG-GEYER, pp. 583–7, 609–13, 782, 785–6, for a good summary and bibliography; F. EHRLE, *Der Sentenzenkommentar Peters
von Kandia, des Pisaner Papstes Alexanders V: ein Beitrag zur
Scheidung der Schulen in der Scholastik des XIV. Jahrhunderts und
zur Geschichte des Wegestreites* (Franziskanische Studien, ix, 1925).
G. RITTER, *Studien zur Spätscholastik*, 2 parts (Sitzungsberichte d.
Heidelberger Akademie, Phil.-hist. Klasse, 1921, 1922). The first
part deals with Marsilius of Inghen, the second with the *viae* in
the German universities in the fifteenth century. For the works of
Benary and Hermelink see above, under Erfurt and Tübingen. An
illustration of the way in which the supremacy of one *via* over
another could be established as the result of a particular dispute is
described by Paul FRÉDÉRICQ, *L'hérésie à l'Université de Louvain vers
1470* (Académie royale de Belgique: Bulletin de la classe des lettres,
1905, no. 1).

The German universities and humanism: KAUFMANN, ii. 490–562;
S. D' IRSAY, *Histoire des Universités*, i (Paris, 1933), 270–303, a good
short account; the recent historians of particular universities, e.g.
J. Haller on Tübingen, Wackernagel on Basel, Friedensburg on
Wittenberg, also the studies of G. Bauch on humanism at Vienna,
Erfurt, Heidelberg (see above). But, needless to say, it is not
possible to dissociate the literature of this movement from that on
humanism and religious tendencies in Germany generally. Cf.
G. RITTER's paper on romantic and revolutionary movements in
German theology in the *Deutsche Vierteljahrschrift für Literatur-
wissenschaft und Geistesgeschichte*, v (1927), and the school of learning
led by Konrad Burdach. See G. ELLINGER in *Gebhardts Handbuch
der deutschen Geschichte*, edited R. HOLTZMANN, i (Stuttgart, Berlin,
Leipzig, 1930), 547–55.

Wittenberg and Frankfurt-on-Oder: the University of Wittenberg was founded by the Emperor Maximilian I and the Elector of Saxony, July 1502. Nicholas Marschalk, the jurist and historian, came from Rostock to teach and was followed by other scholars. The university, under the influence of Luther and Melanchthon, was the first to adopt the principles of the Reformation. For documents see J. C. A. GROHMANN, *Annalen der Universität zu Wittenberg*, Meissen, 1801; R. FÖRSTEMANN, *Album Academiae Vitebergensis*, i, Leipzig, 1841, reprint, 1906 (the *matricula* from 1502 to 1540); Th. MUTHER, *Die Wittenberger Universitäts- und Fakultätsstatuten vom Jahre 1508*, Halle, 1867; later edition in W. FRIEDENSBURG, *Urkundenbuch der Universität Wittenberg*, 2 vols., Magdeburg, 1926–7; F. ISRAËL, *Das Wittenberger Universitätsarchiv, seine Geschichte und seine Bestände*, Halle, 1913. For the history of the university, W. FRIEDENSBURG, *Geschichte der Universität Wittenberg*, Halle, 1917.

The university at Frankfurt-on-Oder was founded by the Elector of Brandenburg. An imperial Bull was granted in 1500, but the university did not come into existence until 1506. The statutes were based on those of Leipzig. The university at once became a centre of both orthodoxy and humanism. For documents see: J. C. BECKMANN, *Notitia universitatis Francofurtanae*, Frankfurt-a.-O., 1707; P. REH, *Die allgemeinen Statuten der Universität Frankfurt-a.-O., 1510–1610*, Breslau, 1898; E. FRIEDLÄNDER, *Aeltere Universitätsmatrikeln*, i. *Universität Frankfurt-a.-O.*, 3 vols., Leipzig, 1887 *sqq.* For early studies, G. BAUCH, *Die Anfänge der Universität Frankfurt-a.-O.*, Berlin, 1900; cf. S. D'IRSAY, i. 300–1.

Paper Universities: These were Kulm (1366), Lüneburg (1471), and Breslau (1505). See below, Appendix i, pp. 329, 330.]

CHAPTER X

THE UNIVERSITIES OF POLAND, HUNGARY, DENMARK, AND SWEDEN

[HUNGARIAN UNIVERSITIES. In addition to the works, general or particular, mentioned below, see H. SCHÖNEBAUM, 'Die ungarischen Universitäten im Mittelalter' (*Archiv für Kulturgeschichte*, xvi, 1925–6, 41–59; cf. S. D'IRSAY, i. 183, 184). The latter refers somewhat misleadingly to a letter from King Louis of Hungary to the Pope, printed in the *Chartul. Univ. Paris.*, ii, No. 1114 (Sept. 1345). The King begs the Pope to promote a Dominican from Hungary, who had studied at Paris and in the *studia generalia* of his order in Hungary and Toulouse.]

§ 1. CRACOW (1364, 1397)

[There is a good collection of documents, *Codex Diplomaticus Universitatis studii generalis Cracoviensis*, 5 vols., 1364–1605 (Cracow, 1870–1900); H. VON ZEISSBERG edited some extracts from the Matriculation-book in *Das älteste Matrikelbuch der Universität Krakau* (Innsbrück, 1872); for the whole see *Album studiosorum Universitatis Cracoviensis*, 3 vols., 1400–1606 (Cracow, 1887–1904), ed. B. ULANOWSKI and A. CHMIEL. The *Acta rectoralia almae Universitatis studii Cracoviensis*, vol. i, 1469–1537, ed. W. WISLOCKI (Cracow, 1879), vol. ii, 1537–80, ed. S. ESTREICHER (Cracow 1909), consist of the records of the rector's court. Other important publications are *Statuta Universytetu Krakowskiego*, ed. J. SZUJSKI (Cracow, 1882); *Conclusiones Universitatis Cracoviensis ab anno 1441 ad annum 1589*, ed. H. BARYCZ (Cracow, 1933); *Regestrum Bursae Hungarorum Cracoviensis* (1493–1559), new edition by K. SCHRAUF (Vienna, 1893); *Statuta necnon liber promotionum philosophorum ordinis in universitate studiosorum Jagellonica ab anno 1402 ad annum 1849*, ed. J. MUCZKOWSKI (Cracow, 1849); *Liber diligentiarum facultatis artisticae Universitatis Cracoviensis*, part i, 1487–1563 (Cracow, 1886). For the statutes of other faculties see L. FINKEL, *Bibliografja historji polskiej* (Cracow, 1906), pp. 55–6, 920–3. Indeed, few universities can show so rich a collection of published records, illustrating university life in the later Middle Ages, as the University of Cracow. The most important modern histories are K. MORAWSKI, *Historya Universytetu Jagiellonskiego* (Cracow, 1900), trans. into French by P. RONGIER, *Histoire de l'Université de Cracovie, moyen âge et renaissance* (Paris, 1900–5), and H. BARYCZ, *Historja Universytetu Jagiellonskiego w epoce humanizmu* (Cracow, 1935). See also S. D'IRSAY, i. 184–6.]

THE University of Cracow was originally founded by a charter of Casimir the Great, King of Poland, in 1364.[1] A Bull of Urban V followed in the same year.[2] The royal

First foundation by Casimir the Great, 1364.

---

[1] Printed in *Cod. Dipl.*, pt. i, p. 1. [This was apparently a confirmation of an earlier foundation by Casimir in 1362, about which the Pope had been consulted.]

[2] *Ibid.*, p. 6.

CHAP. X, charter confers in general terms the privileges of Bologna and
§ 1. Padua, and describes in some detail the constitution of the
A student contemplated university. This constitution is entirely of the
university. Bologna type, and the fullest student-rights are conferred.
Both rector and professors are to be elected by the students,
and a master is ineligible to the rectorship.[1] The rector is
Jurisdic- accorded a full and exclusive civil jurisdiction over students,
tion. and in criminal cases his judicial competency extends to cases
of 'hair-pulling, slapping, and striking'.[2] In serious criminal
matters a clerk is to be handed over to the bishop, a layman
to the royal tribunals. Even in such cases he was not to be
arrested without the rector's consent. Salaries were assigned
to masters of law, 'physic', and arts, and charged upon the
revenue arising from the salt-tax of a certain district.[3] The
university was nominally founded for all 'lawful faculties'; but
law was evidently intended to be the prominent subject, and
the Pope expressly excepted theology from the privileges conferred by his Bull. In another important point Urban V refused his assent to the provisions of the royal charter. The
king, in imitation no doubt of Frederick II's Neapolitan constitution, ordered that the royal chancellor should superintend
the 'private examination', but the Pope's Bull secured his
usual rights to the bishop of the diocese.[4]

Second   Whether the existence of Casimir's university was ever
founda-
tion by more than nominal is far from certain: still more doubtful is
Ladislaus, it whether it outlived the death of its founder in 1370, and
1397-1400.
the political confusion which ensued.[5] The resuscitation of
the extinct university is due to King Ladislaus Jagello, who
in 1397 procured from the Roman Pope, Boniface IX, a Bull

[1] *Ibid.*, pp. 2, 3.

[2] 'Veluti pro verberali iniuria, vel
si scolaris . . . aliquem capillando
vel offendendo palma vel pugno ad
effusionem sanguinis laeserit.' *Cod.
Dipl.*, pt. i, p. 3.

[3] *Ibid.*, p. 3.

[4] See Urban's letter to the king.
Ibid., p. 9.

[5] The charters of 1400, though
ostensibly issued on account of the
new faculty of theology, involve

complete reorganization of the *studium*. Moreover, a letter of the
university to the Council of Constance, in 1416, speaks of itself as
being 'in sua novitate' (*ibid.*, p.
113). [Although the university
languished, there appears to be no
doubt that it continued to exist
between 1370 and 1397. For example, graduation of bachelors is
known to have occurred during
this period.]

for a theological faculty,[1] and in 1400 issued a fresh charter
for the whole university.[2] The university was actually opened
or reopened in that year.[3] In the form given to it by the new
charter, it appears very doubtful whether the university was
really a university of students. It would appear that the
students still elected the rector, but the clause requiring the
rector to be a student disappears. And from the list of rectors[4]
it is evident that the office was generally, if not invariably, held
by a master; and the masters seem—at least in all matters
relating to the property of the university—to be in possession
of the powers of their Parisian brethren. A College of Jurists
and a College of Arts—known also as the College of King
Ladislaus—were provided for the masters.[5] A *collegium minus*
for the artists was afterwards added, as at Leipzig and its
daughters, Rostock and Greifswald.[6] These colleges were
colleges of regent masters on the German model. No non-
foundationers appear to have been admitted to them as students, but several slightly endowed halls or *bursae*[7] were
founded in the course of the fifteenth century. The salaries
of the professors in all faculties were now supplied mainly by
the impropriation of ecclesiastical dignities,[8] canonries, and
other benefices. In this, as in other respects, the University
of Ladislaus—so far as the extant documents enable us to
judge—now follows the precedents of Prague, Leipzig, and

[1] *Cod. Dipl.*, pt. i, p. 24. Kaufmann (*Zeitschr. für Geschichtswissenschaft*, i. 26), points out that the
mere fact that the Bull purports to
found a new university does not
absolutely disprove the existence of
the old one: still, where the Bull is
from the same authority, it makes
it improbable.

[2] *Cod. Dipl.*, pt. i, p. 25.

[3] Zeissberg, p. 6.

[4] *Cod. Dipl.*, pt. i, p. 203 *sq.*

[5] *Ibid.*, pp. 43, 48, 73, 100, 139,
&c. *Collegiati* of the College of
Arts often proceeded in theology.
[The faculty of medicine was reorganized by Johannes de Saccis
of Pavia in 1433.]

[6] *Cod. Dipl.*, pt. ii, p. 98; pt. iii,
p. 45.

[7] A *bursa pauperum* was founded
in 1410 (*ibid.*, pt. i, pp. 82, 83), and
in 1454 a *bursa Jerusalem* for 100
'studentes nobiles et plebei' (p. 156).
These *Bursae*, founded by private
liberality, but with slender if any
endowments, seem to stand mid-
way between the private-adventure
bursa or *hospitium* and the 'College' of Paris or Oxford. So, in
1473, a house is given 'pro Canoni-
starum Bursa' (*Cod. Dipl.*, pt. iii,
p. 38.) Among the *bursae* mentioned in the *Acta rectoralia* is a
bursa divitum.

[8] *Cod. Dipl.*, pt. i, pp. 35, 38, 66,
70 *et passim*.

CHAP. X,
§ 1.

other German universities, rather than the Bolognese traditions which had influenced the abortive scheme of Casimir the Great. The charter of Ladislaus confers the same rights on the royal chancellor as that of his predecessor; but it is doubtful whether the bishop was not in actual possession of the university chancellorship.[1] The rector possessed an ample jurisdiction in the causes of scholars, whether civil, criminal, or spiritual.

Numbers.

From the re-foundation under Ladislaus the university enjoyed considerable prosperity, drawing students not only from Poland, but from Hungary, Silesia, and Germany[2] (especially from Bavaria, Franconia, Swabia, and even from the north of Switzerland). Two hundred and five students were matriculated in the first year, including no doubt some honorary incorporations of ecclesiastics who had graduated elsewhere. Between 1401 and 1410 the annual number fluctuates between 35 and 130. In 1411 the continued troubles at Prague may be the cause of the matriculations going up to 150, and from this time the number is seldom below 100, and often exceeds 200. In 1483 the matriculations go up with a bound from the 130 of the preceding year to 388, and (with some falls) the prosperity of the university was fully maintained till the end of our period. In 1500 there were 406 matriculations, representing probably an academic population of between 1,500 and 2,000.[3] [Altogether 18,338 students

---

[1] See *Cod. Dipl.*, pt. i, p. 79. The bishop directs the distribution of the ecclesiastical revenues annexed to the *studium*. The *Cod. Dipl.* contains an immense collection of documents relating to the property of the university, but no statutes.

[2] [G. Bauch, *Deutsche Scholaren in Krakau in der Zeit der Renaissance, 1460 bis 1520*, Breslau, 1901.]

[3] Zeissberg, p. 19 *sq.* [Papal influence was strong in both the earlier and later foundation at Cracow. Queen Hedwig, the wife of Ladislaus, 'catholicae fidei in Lithuania plantatrix', regarded the work of the university as part of the

civilizing activity which she encouraged in her husband's great duchy. She left her fortune to the university. Yet a remarkable chapter in the early history of the university was its consistent and, on the whole, moderate support of the conciliar movement. It is possible that Matthew of Cracow, a professor in the university and an adviser of King Ladislaus, was the author of the famous *De squaloribus Romanae curiae*. During the period of the Council of Basel the university supported Felix V, and was ultimately left in isolated resistance to Nicholas V, until unity was re-

matriculated in the course of the fifteenth century, and of these CHAP. X,
7,611 were foreigners.] § 1.

[The most numerous group among the foreign students at Cracow was the Hungarian (16 per cent.), a fact which explains the slow development of Hungarian universities in our period.[1] Cracow was also the principal university for the Silesians, who formed 14 per cent. of the foreigners. The principal attraction for the Germans was the flourishing state of mathematical and astronomical studies which had two chairs at Cracow, whereas no other university north of the Alps had such chairs before 1500. Some of the *magistri* of these studies enjoyed wide authority, as, e.g., Martinus Krol de Zorawica, Martinus Bylica de Olkusz, Albertus de Brudzewo (probably the teacher of Copernicus, who studied at Cracow in the years 1491–4). Some of the well-known German humanists also studied at Cracow, among others: Laurentius Corvinus, John Virdung, Conrad Celtis, Henry Bebel, Thomas Murner. Among the Swiss students there were two historians: Valerius Anshelm de Rottweil and Jean Aventin (Turmair).

In theology and canon law the widest recognition was won by the following masters of Cracow: Paul Wlodkowicz, i.e. Vladimiri, who presented to the Council of Constance in 1415 a celebrated treatise *De potestate papae et imperatoris respectu infidelium*, in which he protested against propagating Christian faith by force of arms, Stanislaus de Scarbimiria, and Nicolaus de Blonie, the author of a much reprinted *Sacramentale*.

The University of Cracow contributed considerably to the work of the christianization of Lithuania, and in the course of the fifteenth century no fewer than six of its *magistri* occupied the episcopal see of Wilno.

---

stored in 1449. The doctors, faced by the danger of expulsion, for the king and prelates sided with the papal legate, appealed in July 1448 to the Universities of Paris, Vienna, Leipzig, Erfurt, and Cologne. The debates and correspondence which ensued give a lively picture of academic opinion on the question.

See *Cod. Dipl.*, pt. ii, pp. 73–96 *passim*, and cf. H. Keussen in the *Annalen des historischen Vereins für den Niederrhein*, cxv (1929), 252, 253.]

[1] [We owe the following paragraphs to the kindness of Professor Stanislaw Kot, of the University of Cracow.]

CHAP. X,
§ 1.

From the time of the Council of Basel onwards there were considerable penetrations of humanism, which developed under the influence of the Italian *émigré* Philippo Buonaccorsi, called Callimachus, who matriculated in 1472.

The university was closely associated with the political life of the country. One of its graduates, John Dlugosz, compiled a large Polish history, and some of its professors, e.g. John Dabrowka, commented on old Polish chronicles. Finally, the whole of Poland and Silesia depended upon Cracow for the bachelors who taught in the schools and developed the educational life of the country.]

§ 2. PÉCS OR FÜNFKIRCHEN (1367)

WALLASZKY, *Tentamen Historiae Litterarum . . . in Hungaria*, Leipzig, 1769, p. 51 *sq*. Ábel JENÖ, *Egyetemeink a Középkorban*, Budapest, 1881, which contains many extracts from documents. [R. BÉKEFI, *A pécsi egyetem története*, Budapest, 1890.]

Cathedral schools at Veszprim, &c.

A DECREE of Ladislaus III, setting apart an estate for the 'reformation' of the schools at Veszprim,[1] declares that a *studium* of the liberal arts had flourished there 'as at Paris since the acceptance by Hungary of the catholic faith'.[2] Such a comparison might seem to suggest that the *studium* was regarded to some extent in the light of a *studium generale respectu regni*; but there is no express evidence that such was the case, and as a matter of fact the first recognized Hungarian University did not develop by spontaneous evolution out of the schools of Veszprim or any other ancient *studium*, but was founded entirely *de novo* in the episcopal city of Fünfkirchen, where it appears to have no special continuity with any older school.

Foundation of Fünfkirchen, 1360–7.

The foundation of the university was begun by King Lewis I of Hungary in 1360,[3] but the Bull of erection was not granted by Urban V till 1367.[4] The *studium* was to be 'as well in canon and civil law as in any other lawful faculty', except

---

[1] 'Ut ibidem studium quod hactenus floruerat, reformetur.' Doc. in *Cod. Diplom. Hungariae*, ed. Fejér, v. ii. 347.

[2] 'Liberalium artium studia . . .

prout Parisius in Francia' (*loc. cit.*).

[3] Wallaszky, p. 51.

[4] Ábel Jenö, p. 50: sometimes wrongly dated 1382 (see Denifle, i. 415, note).

theology. It was clearly for the faculties mentioned that the university was chiefly intended, and—since Hungarian law was not based on Roman—primarily for the study of the canon law. To teach it the Bolognese doctor, Gabranus Bettinus, was provided by the bishop with a salary of 300 silver marks or 600 golden florins, which was made (with the consent of the Chapter) a permanent charge upon the episcopal revenues; and the provostships of the cathedral and two neighbouring churches were also annexed to three chairs of law.[1] A few allusions in papal Bulls suffice to show that the *studium* really came into being; but the latest of them is dated 1376,[2] and how long after that the university survived it is impossible to say. The allusions to schools at Fünfkirchen in the fifteenth century[3] are certainly not of a kind which prove the existence of a university.[4]

CHAP. X,
§ 2.

§ 3. BUDA (1389, 1395)

WALLASZKY, *Tentamen Historiae Litterarum . . . in Hungaria*, Leipzig, 1769, p. 51 *sq.* Ábel JENÖ, *Egyetemeink a Középkorban*, Budapest, 1881, which contains many extracts from documents.

THE University of 'Old Buda' was founded in 1389 by Sigismund, King of Hungary, with a Bull granted by Boniface IX appointing the provost of S. Peter's chancellor; but in 1395 a Bull was issued by the same Pope[5] appointing the bishop of Veszprim to the provostship and chancellorship, in spite of the want of a doctor's degree.[6] In the following year the extant register of the faculty of arts begins, and shows that the university was now in working order, at least as far as

Foundation, 1389.

---

[1] Ábel Jenö, pp. 51, 52, 54. [He is called Galvanus Bethinus (p. 52), or Galvano Bethininck (p. 12).]

[2] Denifle, i. 417. Cf. below, p. 296.

[3] Ábel Jenö, p. 55.

[4] The statement of Zeilerus that there were at one time 2,000 (afterwards multiplied to 4,000) students at Fünfkirchen before the 'Turkish Captivity' appears to rest only on the statements of seventeenth-century writers. Wallaszky, p. 51. [Ábel Jenö says (p. 55): 'floruisse

eam (*sc.* universitatem) immo minorem quoque scholam ibi extitisse ad finem usque seculi'.]

[5] The authority for the statement is Inchofer, *Annales ecclesiastici regni Hungariae*, Rome, 1644, i. 328. Denifle (i. 419) tells us that the Bull cannot be found at Rome, but it is mentioned in Garampi's Catalogue, and the fact that a *studium generale* was founded by Sigismund is attested by a Bull of John XXIII. Cf. Ábel Jenö, p. 57.

[6] *Ibid.*, p. 59.

that faculty is concerned.[1] In 1410 a Bull is addressed by John XXIII to the papal referendary in Hungary, which, after alluding to Sigismund's intention of founding a university in that country, directs him to report on the most suitable site for such a university.[2] [The new foundation-bull or rather Bull for the extension of the older foundation into a full *studium generale* 'in qualibet licita facultate', was issued on 1 August in the same year.][3] From this time the life of the university becomes more vigorous. It sends three doctors in theology and two of decrees to the Council of Constance;[4] and for some years after this there is evidence of the existence of a considerable *studium*, especially in theology. But it is probable that it did not outlive its founder, who died in 1437, and certain that both Fünfkirchen and Buda must have been

Extinc-
tion. practically extinguished before 1465, when a Bull of Paul II declares that there now exists no *studium generale* in the kingdom of Hungary. This Bull was called forth by a petition of King Matthias, and authorizes the archbishop of Gran and the bishop of Fünfkirchen to erect a university in any city of the realm approved by the King.[5] It seems that the immediate effect of this Bull was a new university at Pressburg; but some years afterwards we find a new college erected at Buda by King Matthias. It appears, however, difficult to say whether this was regarded as a revival of an earlier university or as a wholly new institution. The fact that its first rector was a friar seems to indicate that its organization was not altogether upon the usual university lines.[6]

---

[1] Ábel Jenö, p. 60.

[2] *Ibid.*, pp. 18, 57, 58.

[3] The only trace of this Bull known to exist before 1892 was the entry in Garampi's Catalogue: 'Erectio studii generalis in oppido veteris Budae Vesprimien. dioec. *AB. Johannis 23, II, 1, p. 74.*' Denifle, i. 421. [The publication of the text by Bishop Fraknói in the *Történelmi Tár* of Budapest, 1892, pp. 398–401, revealed both the true date and the nature of the new privileges; see Lewis L. Kropf in *The Academy*, 9 Nov. 1895.]

[4] Ábel Jenö, p. 61.

[5] *Ibid.*, pp. 64, 65; Schier, *Memoria Acad. Istropolitanae*, p. 7.

[6] In the dedication to King Matthias of his *Clypeus Thomistarum* (Venice, 1481), the rector, Petrus Niger, thus describes the college: 'Instituisti namque hac ciuitate Buda, florentissima regni tui sede, apud Praedicatorum ordinis fratres uniuersale gymnasium, ubi cuncti generis disciplinae, philosophiae, theologiae, sanctaeque scripturae, ubertim possint quod quisque cupit haurire' (Echard, *SS. Ord. Praed.*

§ 4. PRESSBURG (1465–7)

SCHIER, *Memoria Academiae Istropolitanae*, Vienna, 1774. Ábel JENÖ, CHAP. X, *Egyetemeink a Középkorban*, Budapest, 1881. § 4.

ALLUSION has already been made to Paul II's Bull of 1465, Founda-conferring on the archbishop of Gran and the bishop of early Fünfkirchen powers to erect a university in any town of history. Hungary selected by the King.[1] In pursuance of these powers a university was erected in 1467 at Poszony or Pressburg, situated on the great water-way of the Danube near the Austrian frontier. The house of a wealthy citizen, who had opportunely died intestate, was set apart for the schools, and also for a college of masters and scholars founded by the king.[2] The *studium* actually opened in the same year under masters of theology, canon law, and arts, hired from Vienna, France, and Italy.[3] The documentary allusions to the university are sufficiently numerous to show that it enjoyed a robuster life than its predecessors, and lasted till the war between King Ladislaus and the Emperor Maximilian made peaceful studies impossible in Hungary. Both the King and the archbishop, who concurred in its foundation, were much given to judicial astrology, and such fame as the university acquired was due to the astrological eminence of its masters.[4]

The original Bull of Paul II gave the apostolic delegates Constitu-named therein power to frame statutes 'on the model of the tion. University of Bologna', and that clause contains the only clue which appears to be forthcoming as to the constitution of this and other Hungarian universities.[5] The archbishop of Gran

i. 862). Cf. Wallaszky, pp. 5–7 *sq.* Some of the accounts here quoted border on the fabulous.

[1] See above, § 3.

[2] Ábel Jenö, pp. 66, 68, 78; Schier, p. 12. The date is given by a horoscope preserved in the Civic Library at Vienna, inscribed 'Figura Coeli hora Institucionis Universitatis histropolitane Anno domini 1467°'. The town of Poszony was not previously known as *Istropolis*, and on this account Schier supposes that the university was originally founded at Gran, and afterwards transferred to Poszony, higher up the Danube, where it would be less exposed to Turkish inroads, and enjoy easier communication with the civilized West.

[3] Ábel Jenö, p. 69; Schier, p. 22. It is not clear, however, whether those from France and Italy ever actually arrived.

[4] Ábel Jenö, pp. 70 *sq.*, 78; Wallaszky, *Tentamen*, pp. 20 *sq.*, 26.

[5] 'Ad instar studii Bononiensis,' Ábel Jenö, p. 65.

CHAP. X,
§ 4.

was chancellor, and an archiepiscopal ordinance conferred
on the vice-chancellor, the provost of the church of Pressburg, a comprehensive jurisdiction in all cases—spiritual,
civil, and criminal—in which a scholar was engaged, reserving, however, an appeal to the archbishop.[1]

§ 5. UPSALA (1477)

C. ANNERSTEDT, *Upsala Universitets Historia*, i, Upsala, 1877. This may
be a convenient place to mention L. DAAE, *Matrikler over Nordiske
Studerende ved fremmede Universiteter*, the first part of which (Christiania,
1885) gives the list of Scandinavian students for Prague and Rostock.
[CORNELIUS, *Några bidrag till Upsala Theologiska Fakultets Historia*,
Upsala, 1874. Axel NELSON, *Om Uppsala Universitet under Medeltiden*,
Upsala, 1927. This useful essay (46 pages) contains new bibliographical
material on the wanderings of Scandinavian students in the Middle Ages,
e.g. Ellen JORGENSEN, in *Historisk Tidsskrift*, eighth series, v (1915),
331–82, vi (1916), 197–214; also a drawing (p. 27) from J. B. BUSSER,
Utkast till beskrifning om Upsala, ii (1769), 24, of the earliest *lectorium* of
the University, a building of 1422–31, rebuilt in 1778.]

Founda-
tion and
early
history.

A BULL for a university at Upsala was issued by Sixtus IV
in 1477, on the petition of the archbishop of Upsala and
the bishops and clergy of Sweden.[2] The Bull declares that the
university was to be on the model of Bologna, and confers the
privileges of that university.[3] No early statutes of Upsala
are extant, but there can be little doubt, in spite of this de-
claration, that some German university, such as Cologne or
Rostock, with which Swedish ecclesiastics were familiar, was
the real model for the new university. The archbishop, Jakob
Ulfsson, was its true founder. It was closely connected with
the cathedral: it is even said to be founded 'in the Metropolitan Church of Upsala'.[4] No royal charter was issued,
though the archbishop's ordinance recites that Steno the
Governor and the Council of the Realm had conceded to his
foundation the royal privileges of Paris.[5] Such endowments

---

[1] Ábel Jenö, p. 76.

[2] [At a provincial council held at
Süderköping thirty-six years earlier
(1441) the archbishop, Nils Rag-
valdsson, and the bishops undertook to found a *studium privilegiatum*; see H. Reuterdahl, *Statuta
synodalia veteris ecclesiae Sueogo-
thicae*, Lund, 1841, p. 125; and

Hefele-Leclercq, *Histoire des conciles*, VII. ii (Paris, 1916), 1161.]

[3] Annerstedt, i, Docs. pp. 1–4.

[4] *Ibid.*, Docs. p. 6: 'apud metropolitanam ecclesiam Upsalensem.'

[5] *Ibid.*, i, Docs. p. 7. [A. Nelson
(pp. 18–21) brings new evidence to
show that Upsala was a 'Studium
generale ad instar Bononiensis'.]

as the university possessed came from the annexation of
prebends in the cathedral church. There is evidence that
lectures in theology and arts really began in the foundation
year and continued till the close of the century.[1] At that time
we find a professor of theology endowed with a cathedral
prebend, a professor of law and a 'college' of four regent
masters of arts.[2]

§ 6. COPENHAGEN (1478)

BARTHOLINUS, *De Ortu et Progressu et Incrementis Regiae Academiae Hafniensis*, Copenhagen, 1620 (no pagination). H. MATZEN, *Kjøbenhavns Universitets Retshistorie, 1479–1879*, Copenhagen, 1879. WERLAUFF, *Kiøbenhavns Universitet fra dets Stiftelse indtil Reformationen*, Copenhagen, 1850. H. F. RØRDAM, *Kjøbenhavns Universitets Historia*, 2 vols., Copenhagen, 1868, 1869. The same, *Fra Universitets Fortid*, Copenhagen, 1879. [W. NORVIN, *Københavns Universitet i Middelalderen*, Copenhagen, 1829.]

THE University of Copenhagen—since 1443 the capital of
the Danish kingdom—was founded under a Bull granted by
Sixtus IV in 1475 on the petition of King Christian I.[3] The
Bull runs in a form not unusual at this period: it authorizes
the primate, the archbishop of Lund, to erect a *studium
generale* in any place selected by the king, to frame statutes
for it, and to make the bishop of the diocese chancellor. The
chancellor is to have all the powers of the archdeacon of
Bologna, but in the conferment of degrees he is to observe
the constitutions of Vienna.[4] In 1478 the university was
actually planted at Copenhagen by royal letters-patent.[5] By
these letters the bishop, dean, and provost of Roskild, together
with the dean of Copenhagen, were appointed royal conservators with an apparently unlimited jurisdiction over students.
In 1479 a code of statutes was promulgated by the archbishop of Lund.[6] They are little more than a transcript of the
statutes of Cologne, which were themselves based on those

---

[1] The evidence is chiefly derived from MS. notes or dictates by students.

[2] See the archiepiscopal ordi-nance of 1504, which assigns 130 marks from the cathedral revenues (Docs. p. 414). But it would seem that some endowment out of cathe-dral funds must already have been provided, since the college of arts is assumed to be in existence.

[3] Matzen, i, Docs. p. 1. Accord-ing to Bartholinus, a Bull had been granted in 1420 by Martin V, but remained unexecuted.

[4] See above, vol. i, p. 231.

[5] Matzen, i, Docs. p. 3.

[6] *Ibid.* i, Docs. p. 4.

CHAP. X,
§ 6.

Collapse
and re-
foundation,
1539.
of Vienna. Cologne had, no doubt, hitherto been one of the chief places of education for Danish students; and thence came the first professors of Copenhagen.[1] The university was brought to an end in 1530 by the civil and religious commotions of Denmark, and was re-founded as a Protestant university in 1539 by Christian III, three years after the definitive triumph of Protestantism in that country.[2] The university had originally been endowed with a few impropriations, but it remained poor and obscure until its re-foundation by Christian III.

[1] Werlauff, p. 6; Rørdam, p. 19.   [2] Bartholinus; Matzen, i. 78.

CHAPTER XI

THE UNIVERSITIES OF SCOTLAND

[Rashdall's book marked a great advance in the history of the Scottish universities, but the discovery of fresh material and the appearance of new studies make it particularly difficult to bring his chapter up to date. Professor R. K. Hannay has prepared the sections which follow on S. Andrews and Glasgow, with careful regard to Rashdall's observations on certain features of academic development. The section on S. Andrews was written in co-operation with Professor J. H. Baxter, and that on Glasgow after consultation with Sir Robert Rait. The only general work which has appeared in recent times is by J.-B. COISSAC, *Les Universités de l'Écosse depuis la formation de l'université de S. Andrews jusqu'au triomphe de la réforme, 1410–1560*, Paris, 1915; cf. *Scottish Historical Review*, xiii (1916), 92. There is some discussion of the early history of the Scottish universities in an essay by A. MORGAN, *Scottish University Studies*, London, 1933. Neither work adds anything to previous knowledge.]

§ 1. S. ANDREWS (1413)

The most important documentary sources are (1) the *Evidence* before the University Commissioners for Scotland (vol. iii, 1837), (2) the MS. *Acta Facultatis Artium* (from 1413), (3) the MS. *Acta Rectorum* (from 1470), (4) the reformed statutes of the faculties of arts and theology. The *Acta Facultatis Artium*, unlike the corresponding Glasgow minutes, are not yet in print; but J. MAITLAND ANDERSON edited in *Early Records* (Sc. Hist. Soc., 1926) the graduation lists, with the matriculations from the *Acta Rectorum*. The *Statutes of the faculties of arts and theology at the Reformation*, not presented in the *Evidence*, have been restored from some very imperfect copies by R. K. HANNAY (*Univ. Pub. No. vii*) with an historical introduction. No general history of the university has appeared to supersede the sketch by MAITLAND ANDERSON (Cupar, 1878: with Supplement, 1883); but for the early period his articles in the *Scottish Historical Review*, vols. iii (1906) and viii (1911), 333–60, and his preface to *Early Records* are indispensable, and for the later developments the introductory matter in his *Matriculation Roll, 1747–1897*. Useful information was gathered by T. MCCRIE in his *Life of Andrew Melville*, ed. 2, Edinburgh, 1824. Papers on the history of the university were written for its Quincentenary (*Votiva Tabella*, 1911); cf. also HANNAY, 'Early University institutions at St. Andrews and Glasgow: a comparative study' in the *Scottish Historical Review*, xi (1914), 266–83. J. HERKLESS and R. K. HANNAY, *The College of St. Leonard*, gives particulars of that foundation. Recently a number of documents and notes relating to the earlier years (1411–50) have been contributed by J. H. BAXTER in his *Copiale Prioratus S. Andree* (Oxford, 1929). His *St. Andrews University before the Reformation* (S. Andrews, 1927) deals with the circumstances attending the foundation and with the effect of the Conciliar movement on the life of the university; and his *Collections towards a bibliography of St. Andrews* (S. Andrews, 1926) devotes a large section to university history.

CHAP. XI, §1.
The Scottish student abroad.

THE foundation of the first Scottish university was due to a situation which developed towards the close of the great Schism. Academic intercourse with England in the thirteenth century was interrupted by the war of independence; and a Scots college at Paris, begun under Robert I by the bishop of Moray, is the first evidence of the diversion of Scottish students from England to the Continent. Between the release of David II in 1357 and the Schism in 1378 many of them still attended the English universities; but within a year or two after the beginning of the Schism the difference in papal obedience precluded this intercourse. Henry Wardlaw, for instance, who was to found the University of S. Andrews, and who had a safe-conduct from Richard II in 1380, graduated in arts at Paris, studied civil law at Orleans, and appeared later at Avignon.[1] The prior and the archdeacon of S. Andrews, while Wardlaw was bishop, had been students in France;[2] and the eight teachers named at the inception of the new school had all been educated at French universities.[3]

Foundation.

For some twenty-five years after the beginning of the Schism no urgent need for a Scottish university was felt; but the persistent adherence of Scotland to Benedict XIII during the two periods of French withdrawal from him before the deposition attempted by the Council of Pisa in 1409, coupled with the turbulence and depression in Paris after the assassination of the duke of Orleans in 1407, made the resort of Scots to Paris university both unprofitable and dangerous. Somewhere between 1407 and 1410 the situation compelled Scotland to consider the establishment of a national university. Possibly the appearance of Lollardy also exerted some influence upon the project.[4] In 1411, accordingly—and it may have been even in 1410—*incepit studium generale universitatis sancti Andree.*[5]

[1] J. M. Anderson in *Sc. Hist. Rev.* viii (1911), 231.

[2] *Ibid.*, pp. 232–3.

[3] *Ibid.*, p. 235.

[4] There is considerable emphasis upon defence of the faith in the foundation Bulls; and cf. *Copiale Prioratus S. Andree*, pp. 230–6.

[5] Bower (*Scotichronicon*, xv, c. 22) describes the battle of Harlaw (1411), alludes to operations in 1412, and reverts to the beginning

It was probably from the lesser French universities, such as Orleans and Angers, in which the Bologna system of student-election was modified by the reservation of greater rights to the bishop on the one hand and to the masters on the other, that the founders of the Scottish universities derived the ideal which their earliest constitutions and charters seem to imply. Circumstances were not, however, favourable to rapid growth. When Scotland decided in 1418 to obey Martin V, ambitious students tended to resume emigration to famous continental schools, nearer the central power of the Papacy, whose patronage might be the reward of distinction. A man might 'determine' in Scotland, and complete his arts course abroad. Even when the master's degree was taken at home, those who had the funds aimed at graduation in the higher faculties at foreign places of repute. About 1420, at S. Andrews, measures had to be adopted to insist upon graduation and post-graduate residence.[1] It is certain, nevertheless, that the faculties of theology and canon law existed there from the outset, while medicine must have been represented during the fifteenth century.[2]

The theologians were at first closely associated with the Higher faculties. priory, in which the canons regular constituted the chapter of the cathedral. James Biset, whose rule was drawing to a close when the university began, had fostered learning; and James Haldenston, one of his canons, was elected prior at the end of the Schism with special regard to his academic attainments.[3]

---

of the university 'in the preceding year', specified (possibly by interpolation) as 1410: Major accepted 1411 in his *Greater Britain*.

[1] *Univ. Pub.* vii. 8, 15.

[2] *Ibid.*, p. 67: *Sc. Hist. Rev.* viii. 344. David Crannoch, afterwards physician to James II, became dean of the faculty of arts in 1446 (*Copiale Prioratus S. Andree*, p. 487). There was a doctor of medicine at Glasgow in 1469: later, William Manderston, a Glasgow student, who became doctor at Paris and rector of that university, subsequently taught medicine at Glas-

gow before passing to S. Andrews (Coutts, *Univ. of Glasgow*, p. 477; *Early Records*, pp. 225–7); but William Schevez, Archbishop of S. Andrews (1478–97), had resorted to Louvain for medical study. (Herkless and Hannay, *Archbishops of St. Andrews*, i, Edinburgh, 1907, p. 82.)

[3] *Scotichronicon*, vi, c. 56: Hannay, in *Scottish Hist. Rev.* xiii (1916), 324. Bower says of Haldenston (*Scotichronicon*, vi, c. 57) 'in facultate sacre pagine precellenter rexit et in theologia decanus graduandos cathedrizavit'.

CHAP. XI, The prior was dean *ex officio* until 1428–9, when, in the
§ 1. presence of James I, the monopoly was brought to an end,
and statutes were adopted which have been shown to bear the
mark of Paris.[1] For lack of record the history of the faculty
cannot be traced. Recruited from teaching masters in the
faculty of arts, the canons of the priory, the friars, and others,
it was probably never insignificant. In 1541 at least a dozen
members answered the summons of John Major as dean.[2]

Of the lawyers even less is known. Bower mentions four
canonists who taught at the beginning. The marketable value
of legal knowledge in the fifteenth century, if it induced rising
churchmen to study abroad, also encouraged pursuit of the
law at home.[3] In 1457 a *schola decretorum* adjoined the school
of the faculty of arts in South Street;[4] and there must have
been some demand for civil law. Archbishop Forman (*c.*
1516) sought to revive 'the old and laudable custom' of
attendance by regulars for the study of theology and canon
law.[5] Later, in Cardinal Betoun's time, we hear of the
doctores venerandi collegii iuris civilis, and of 'the new schools
of the laws'.[6] Legal studies, however, did not flourish to any
considerable extent, though it is probable that many graduates
in arts took advantage of the available instruction with a view
to practising as notaries. Apart from inducements to foreign
graduation and the appearance of universities at Glasgow and
Aberdeen, the evolution of the civil court of Session tended
to attract legal interests to Edinburgh. The first proposal for
an academic institution there, in 1558, contemplated especially
education in the laws.[7]

---

[1] *Univ. Pub.* vii. 80, 112. A
very important description of the
ceremony in connexion with the
doctorate survives in the amended
statutes (*ibid.*, pp. 76–80).

[2] *College of St. Leonard*, p. 220.
Richard Hilliard, the English
refugee, was a member (*Rentale S.
Andree* (Sc. Hist. Soc.)); and there
was graduation in Cardinal Betoun's
time (*Archbishops*, iv. 234). On
Major's connexion with S. Andrews see *Early Records*, p. xxxix.

[3] A secretary of James II was a
licentiate of S. Andrews in canon
law (J. Dowden, *The Bishops of
Scotland*, Glasgow, 1912, p. 74).
For lawyers of standing at the
university see *Copiale Prioratus
S.Andree*, pp. 398–9, 406, 442, 465.

[4] Acta Fac. Art. (Univ. MS.).

[5] Robertson, *Statuta*, i. 284.

[6] *Archbishops of St. Andrews*, iv.
235.

[7] *Univ. of Edinburgh, 1883–1933*,
p. 1.

That the main influence of the university was exerted CHAP. XI,
§ I.
through the faculty of arts upon the rank and file of Scottish
clerics is indicated by the graduation lists.[1] Towards the Faculty
of arts.
close of the fifteenth century lay students must have begun to
matriculate, with a view to graduation and obtaining subsequently, perhaps, a smattering of law.[2] The development of
the college system brought most of the resident doctors and
bachelors of the higher faculties inevitably into connexion
with the faculty of arts, through interest in organization and
discipline, or as actual teachers. By the middle of the sixteenth
century it was possible to describe the minute-book of the
faculty as *liber conclusionum universitatis sancti Andree*, and
the rector of the university concerned himself *ex officio* with
business which formerly was appropriate to the faculty alone.[3]

The traditions of the faculty of arts, like those of the
theologians, were derived ultimately from Paris. It was
ordained *quod more Parisiensi libri consueti legantur ordinarie*:
certain regulations against touting for scholars were adopted
word for word: when the statutes were revised in 1439, a book
was produced *de statutis et privilegiis studii Parisiensis*.[4] The
Parisian nominalism reigned.[5] Laurence of Lindores, the
dominant figure till 1437, read lectures on the *De Anima* and
the *Physics* of Aristotle, which remained, until the time of
Copernicus, a standard text-book in universities where the
doctrina Buridani was prevalent.[6] After his death there was
a reaction, under influence from Cologne, whither Scottish
students had been resorting since 1420; and in 1438 Bishop
Wardlaw persuaded the faculty to allow the *via Alberti*.[7]

On 28 February 1411–12, some time after teaching had Papal
actually begun,[8] Wardlaw granted a charter stating the privileges.

---

[1] *Early Records*: the oldest graduation lists in Britain.

[2] *Acts of Parl.* ii. 238, c. 3.

[3] *Univ. Pub.* vii. 23–4, 56.

[4] *Ibid.*, pp. 3 *sqq.*

[5] 'Quod doctrina Alberti adhuc
non legatur in isto studio sed
Buridani' (1417). For the books
to be heard see *Copiale Prioratus
S. Andree*, p. 456.

[6] *Ibid.*, p. 382: J. H. Baxter in
Scottish Hist. Rev. xxv (1927–8), 92.

[7] Acta Fac. Art.: a large majority
had voted against the *doctrina
Alberti* and the *summule Petri
Hispani*. At Glasgow in 1482
Hispanus was the text-book.

[8] 'Universitas vestra a nobis . . .
de facto instituta et fundata et a
vobis . . . iam laudabiliter inchoata.'

CHAP. XI, relation of the new body to the bishopric, the priory, and
§ 1. the two diocesan archdeaconries, and defining the jurisdiction
of the rector.[1] With the support of James I, then a captive in
England, a petition was presented to Benedict XIII suggesting that the bishop should be chancellor, with powers to
regulate graduation and frame statutes. Benedict, however,
adopted (28 August 1413) the terms he had used for Turin
(1404), based upon the foundation Bull of Cologne (1388);
and he did not, as Alexander V had done in the case of Leipzig (1409), expressly designate the bishop as chancellor.[2]

No fewer than six separate Bulls were issued: (1) erecting
the *studium generale*; (2) confirming Wardlaw's diocesan
indult for residence, and extending it to all beneficed persons
in Scotland, (3) executorial of this indult, (4) ratifying Wardlaw's charter, (5) conservatorial of the university privileges,
(6) providing for study and graduation by Scots who had
begun at universities not under Benedict's obedience. According to a very unusual condition, the rector was required
to be a graduate in some faculty and in holy orders.

Some months after the reception[3] of the Bulls the university of Paris sought to enlist Scottish interest in the Council
of Constance, and appealed to the new foundation.[4] It was
not, however, till the year after the election of Martin V that
Scotland resolved to abandon Benedict. Early in the autumn
of 1418, the faculty of arts by a large majority decided for the
change of obedience; and the rector of the university played
a prominent part in swaying the Estates.[5]

James I
and the
university.
After James I returned home he opened an anti-papalist
campaign, with a willing minister in John Cameron, who became bishop of Glasgow.[6] Relations with Wardlaw, owing

---

[1] The jurisdiction was modified
in favour of the citizens of S.
Andrews by Bishop Kennedy in
1444, after inquiry as to practice at
Cologne (*Scottish Hist. Rev.* xi.
272).

[2] The Bulls are printed in *Evidence*, iii. 171: a facsimile of the
Bull confirming Wardlaw's charter
is in *Nat. MSS. of Scot.*, pt. ii. For
the petition to Benedict see *Scottish*

Hist. Rev. iii. 213; and for a summary of the Bulls, *ibid.* viii. 337.

[3] 3 February 1413–14 : *Scotichronicon*, xv, c. 22.

[4] *Copiale Prioratus S. Andree*,
p. xl.

[5] *Scottish Hist. Rev.* viii. 347–60;
cf. xiii. 327.

[6] *Ibid.* xv. 290; *Acts of Council
in Public Affairs*, p. xlv.

to a difference over the controversy, were not cordial; and in CHAP. XI, § 1.
1426 the king actually petitioned Martin V that the university
be transferred to Perth, a place represented as being under the
immediate authority of the crown, and more suitable than
S. Andrews both geographically and economically. The
proposal, which might have led to a national university, pre-
cluding the later episcopal enterprises at Glasgow and Aberdeen, could hardly in the circumstances be entertained by
the Pope. James appears to have been dissatisfied with the
condition of affairs. He intervened repeatedly in university
politics, and did not confirm the bishop's original charter
until 1432.[1] The facts are obscure; but the antagonism between supporters of the Pope and of the Council caused a
dispeace not completely cured until the latter's defeat.

The real power in the university lay with the magisterial
body. From the outset there were four nations. The divisional
arrangement, due in part to academic tradition, was not a
meaningless survival, for in the fifteenth century a common
law was still in process of development. The two nations of
the south, Lothian and Britain, corresponded roughly to the
archdeaconry of Lothian and to the dioceses of Glasgow and
Galloway, where racial factors had affected ecclesiastical
boundaries.[2] Each nation had its procurator, whose duties
required constant attendance, personally or by proxy, and
included as a rule the function of rector's assessor. The
comitia or congregation of the University was a meeting of
the nations. Protests recorded by the faculty of arts, as well
as a considerable number of university statutes,[3] testify to
legislative action; but it is chiefly in connexion with the choice
of a rector that the nations are mentioned. Each nation, under
the presidency of its procurator, appointed an intrant to give
the vote. If the votes were equal, the decision lay with the
retiring rector. Our information indicates a desire to preserve
the independence of university authority in face of the predominant faculty of arts; and the electors seem to have
avoided heads of colleges or members of the teaching staff.

---

[1] *Univ. Pub.* vii. 18, 24, 112.
[2] For the nations see *Early Records*, pp. ix–xi.   [3] *Evidence*, iii. 232.

CHAP. XI, At first all supposts had a voice in deliberation; but a statute
§ 1.   of 1475 deprived those below the bachelor grade of the
rectorial franchise.[1]

The   In 1414 it was enacted 'that no schools be conducted in the
Pedagogy. faculty of arts but by way of community, hall, or paedagogy
under the daily direction and control of masters', and that no
extra commensales, known elsewhere as 'martinets', should be
admitted, except poor students and the sons of burgesses.
The scholars of a pedagogy seem to have been taught exclusively by resident masters.[2] Rivalries ensued: discipline
suffered; and there was little scope for the post-graduate
lectura upon which the growth of the university would depend. The faculty of arts had an interest in what was loosely
styled the 'college' of S. John the Evangelist in South Street.
There, in 1430, Wardlaw proposed to concentrate masters
and scholars in 'one pedagogy'. The project of concentration
failed; but the faculty acquired a residential place—the
Pedagogy, which was ultimately merged in the college of
S. Mary—and a 'school' for public lectures and acts. This
school was *in vico*, by adoption of the Parisian technicality;
and some sort of lecture-system developed, whereby each
teaching master, whether 'regent' or merely 'reading', selected
his 'book' before the faculty.[3]

S. Salva-   It was Bishop Kennedy (1440–65) who conceived the plan
tor's Col- of a properly endowed college, and initiated developments
lege, 1450. which gave S. Andrews a marked advantage over the university which Bishop Turnbull was establishing in Glasgow.
S. Salvator's, begun in 1450, was a collegiate church with
an academic intention, providing for three theologians, four
masters of arts, and six poor foundation scholars. A pro-
longed controversy with the faculty of arts and its pedagogy
was ended (1470) in the provincial council of the Scottish

[1] *Early Records*, pp. xi–xxii. For
the subsequent history of the franchise and the ultimate effect of the
provision requiring the rector to be
in holy orders, see *Matric. Roll,
1747–1897*, pp. xvii–xxii.
    [2] This appears to be the meaning
of the rule 'quod non audirent sub

aliquo magistro vel aliquibus magistris nisi tenentibus domicilium'.
For details of teaching and graduation see *Univ. Pub.* vii.
    [3] A book is still handed to a
professor at the ceremony of in-
stallation.

Church, when Kennedy's college renounced a Bull permitting CHAP. XI, independent degree examinations.[1] But the quarrel dis- § I. couraged public lecturing *in vico*. By the close of the century these public lectures had almost disappeared: the class of non-regent 'readers', and the hearing of 'extraordinary' books, diminished; and a result was the unfortunate arrangement whereby a regent master conducted his class through the whole course to graduation. Instead of a shifting body of graduates teaching in virtue of their oath of residence, or by the inherent right given them by their degrees, the masters tended to pass into a permanent co-optative professoriate.

Early in the sixteenth century a new collegiate enterprise was undertaken. In 1512 Prior Hepburn turned the hospital of S. Leonard, an appendage of his monastery tracing its origin to the Celtic Church, into a college of poor clerks, with special regard to the training of Augustinian novices. More liberal provision was made than by Kennedy for the maintenance of foundationers; and, as the Pedagogy was almost defunct for lack of endowment, the new foundation could justifiably be styled *principale Sanctiandree collegium*. Though the control by the priory led at first to difficulties with the faculty of arts,[2] the college was soon admitted to full status as a constituent of the university, and its monastic character tended to fix the collegiate system.[3]

S. Leonard's College, 1512.

The heretical leanings for which S. Leonard's became notorious led Archbishop James Betoun to plan what became the New College of S. Mary in place of the decayed Pedagogy, with which the disaster at Flodden had prevented Archbishop Alexander Stewart, the pupil of Erasmus, from dealing. Cardinal Betoun carried on his uncle's design; but the advice of his relative Archibald Hay, of Montaigu College at Paris, who recommended the teaching of Greek, Hebrew,

S. Mary's College, 1537.

[1] *Univ. Pub.* vii. 22 *sqq.*; *Archbishops of St. Andrews*, i. 36. The Bull (1468) provided for teaching and examination within the college, reserving the rights of the bishop as chancellor.

[2] *College of St. Leonard*, p. 101.
[3] The statutes (*ibid.*, p. 167) show that members of the college resorted to the schools at the Pedagogy only for public acts and examinations.

CHAP. XI, Syriac, and Arabic, was not accepted.[1] In 1553 Archbishop
§ 1.   Hamilton modified the foundation in view of the contemporary movement for the reform of the Church from within.
He laid emphasis upon theology,[2] and intended that the new
college should be dominant in the university.

After the   The development of the colleges, and the constant efforts
Reforma- of the faculty of arts to control the persons and matters in
tion.   which it was directly interested, go far to explain the post-
Reformation plan of annexing a faculty to each college. The
radical scheme of the *First Book of Discipline* and the *Opinion*
of George Buchanan[3] are alike based upon this idea; but they
were carried out in one particular only, when in 1579 S.
Mary's was permanently appropriated to the study of theology. S. Salvator's and S. Leonard's continued to serve
students in arts, till in 1747, after an abortive attempt to
combine all three foundations, economic pressure brought
about a united college of S. Salvator and S. Leonard.[4]

Residence Losses in revenue sustained since the Reformation, and the
ceases.   insufficiency of the endowments to keep the buildings in
repair, caused the decline of residence in college. By 1820 the
ménage of the common table, which probably continued the
old medieval scholar's mode of life more completely than any
other institution surviving in Europe, was given up in
S. Mary's College, just when the complete reconstruction of
S. Salvator's—where the united college had been established
—could no longer be delayed. The rights of the foundationers
were commuted for a money payment, while the colleges
existed mainly as endowments for professors and non-resident
'bursars'.[5]

The cur-   That the Reformation left the curriculum in arts still
riculum.

[1] Hay became principal of S.
Mary's for a brief period from 1546:
his *Panegyricus* addressed to the
Cardinal (Paris, 1540) is an important educational document.

[2] Posts in civil law and medicine, arranged by the Betouns, were
excluded (McCrie's *Melville*, notes
to ch. xi): an *orator* and a *grammati-
cus* were not striking concessions to

humanism.

[3] P. Hume Brown, *Vernacular
Writings of George Buchanan* (Scottish Text Soc.), Edinburgh, 1892.

[4] *Matric. Roll, 1747–1897*, p.
xxvi. University College, Dundee,
was brought into the university in
1897 (*ibid.*, p. lix).

[5] *Ibid.*, pp. xxxviii, lv.

medieval in character is shown by the account which James chap. xi,
Melville gives in his *Diary*, and by the faculty statutes as § 1.
purged and revised in 1570.[1] George Buchanan effected
little; and Andrew Melville's prospects were clouded by
ecclesiastical controversies in which he was opposed to
James VI, a king who might in other circumstances have
béen his educational ally.[2]

§ 2. GLASGOW (1450–1)

Unlike S. Andrews, Glasgow has long possessed in the *Munimenta
Universitatis Glasguensis*, edit. Cosmo INNES (Maitland Club, 1854), a
complete collection of documents down to 1727. The *Evidence* (vol. ii)
before the Commissioners for the Universities of Scotland (1837) is also
important, though necessarily less useful, owing to the publication of the
Munimenta, than the companion volume relating to S. Andrews. A
synopsis of the history, still valuable, was prepared by Thomas REID, the
well-known professor of moral philosophy, for SINCLAIR's *Statistical
Account of Scotland* (vol. xxi, 1799). Cosmo INNES, editor of the *Munimenta*, has a chapter on Glasgow in his *Sketches of Early Scottish History*,
Edinburgh, 1861. J. COUTTS, *A History of the University of Glasgow*,
Glasgow, 1909, contains much miscellaneous information; but it is valuable for the later rather than for the earlier developments. H. BLACKBURN
wrote (1858) a *Short Sketch of the Constitutional History of the University
of Glasgow*, London, 1858. R. RENWICK and J. LINDSAY, *History of
Glasgow*, i, Glasgow, 1921, has some topographical matter relating to the
university. See also R. K. HANNAY in the *Scottish Historical Review*, xi.
266–83.

THE University of Glasgow was founded under a Bull of The
Nicholas V, in response to a petition of James II presented founda-
at the instance of William Turnbull, who had recently ob-tion.
tained the bishopric. Turnbull seems to have been a graduate
in arts of S. Andrews.[3] Eleven years later (1431) his name
appears on the matriculation roll of Louvain;[4] and, as cus-
todian of the King's privy seal from 1440 till his episcopal
consecration in 1448, he is described as doctor in decrees.[5]

[1] *Univ. Pub.* vii. 86.
[2] For a general account of the
position see John Burnet in *Votiva
Tabella*, pp. 129–38.
[3] He may be identified with the
William Turnbull licensed in 1420
(*Early Records*): when he matriculated at Louvain in 1431 he was
accompanied by Nicholas Otterburn, who also graduated at S.

Andrews in 1420 (*Scottish Hist.
Rev.* xxv. 330).
[4] During the Conciliar controversy papalist Scots gravitated
towards Louvain, while anti-
papalists favoured Cologne (*Copiale
Prioratus S. Andree*, p. 494).
[5] *Reg. Mag. Sig.* ii: Otterburn
had the same degree.

In 1450 the king, an honorary canon of Glasgow, granted to his 'well-beloved councillor' rights of regality in the city and barony, and submitted to the Pope his request for the erection of a *studium generale*.[1]

The university began in 1451, favoured by a jubilee indulgence which the bishop had procured for his church.[2] The Bull of Nicholas V (7 January 1450–1) does not appear to have been based upon any documentary instructions or writs prepared at Glasgow. It erected a *studium generale* in the various faculties: bestowed on individual members all the privileges and exemptions enjoyed at Bologna; declared Turnbull and his successors to be *rectores cancellarii nuncupati*, with the powers exercised by the Bologna *rectores scholarium*; provided for graduations after the customary fashion, and for the universal validity of the degrees.[3]

Nicholas V had been a student and, later, Bishop of Bologna. He happened to be deeply interested in the fortunes of that city and university when the royal petition was submitted;[4] and he granted to prospective members of the University of Glasgow a body of privileges which he assumed to be well understood.[5] There was some misapprehension, however, from the very outset; for a Glasgow clerk described the new foundation as *instar studii et universitatis Bononiensis*, and propagated the belief, still surviving, that the university was after the Bologna 'model'.[6]

The Bull left Turnbull with a free hand to adjust his arrangements according to local conditions. The new institution was intimately connected with the cathedral: the chapter-

[1] *Registrum Episcopatus Glasguensis* (1843), ii. 325; *Munimenta*, i. 3.

[2] 'That samyn yer [1451] the privilege of the universite of Glasqw come to Glasqw throw the instance of King James the Secund and throw instigacioun of master William Turnbull . . . and was proclamit at the croce of Glasqw on the Trinite Sonday the xx day of June; and on the morne thar was cryit ane gret indulgence' (*Auchinleck Chronicle*, p. 45).

[3] *Munimenta*, i. 4–5.

[4] Pastor, *History of the Popes* (Eng. trans.), ii. 14, 17, 70.

[5] In the case of Aberdeen, Elphinstone petitioned for and obtained a university in which there should be teaching and study 'sicut in Parisiensi et Bononiensi et quibusvis aliis generalibus studiis ad hoc privilegiatis' (*Fasti Aberd.*, pp. 4–5).

[6] *Munimenta*, ii. 178.

house was the customary place of congregation;[1] and the powers of the bishop in his regality were sufficient to set the school in motion. It was not until 1453 that the king exempted members from general taxations and services,[2] or that the bishop and chapter defined the rectorial jurisdiction in relation to the city, adopting Wardlaw's regulations for S. Andrews, with modifications after the letter and spirit of the revision made in 1444 by Kennedy.[3]

The university has no record of the appointment of conservators. It is known, however, that Turnbull's successor approached Calixtus III in 1456; explaining that the privileges enjoyed at Bologna were very hard to ascertain, he asked the Pope to exempt all supposts in actual residence from the jurisdiction of ordinaries (including the conservators of S. Andrews University) and to subject them henceforth to the bishop of Dunblane, the abbot of Paisley, and the dean of Glasgow. Calixtus granted the request, and ordered a commission; but there is no further notice of the provision.[4]

The emphasis laid upon Bologna in the Bull of Nicholas V may have had no more than an accidental connexion with the hope that a school of law would develop. The hope without doubt was entertained. Turnbull's antecedents and interests pointed in that direction; and the royal charter dwelt upon the civil benefits to be expected.[5] The only higher faculty to leave traces of its activities in statute was that of canon law.[6]

---

[1] The first assembly was in the chapter-house of the Blackfriars (*Munimenta*, ii. 55); but from 1452 down to the Reformation, meetings of the university were usually at the cathedral. After 1480 some meetings are specified as held *in inferiori capitulo*, others as *in superiori capitulo*. The minutes cease to draw this distinction in 1537.

[2] *Munimenta*, i. 6.

[3] *Evidence*, iii. 176: *Munimenta*, i. 7. Kennedy's revision was made in the light of Cologne practice.

[4] *Reg. Supp.* (Vatican MS.), July 23, 1456: a reference due to

Dr. Annie Cameron. Some conservatorial arrangement must have been required.

[5] *Munimenta*, i. 6: 'per quos . . . populus . . . virga equitatis et iusticie corripiatur, orthodoxa fides solide defensetur, querele iurgiose determinentur et reddatur unicuique quod debetur'. The first rector, David Cadzow, was a lawyer, and Official of Glasgow.

[6] *Ibid.* ii. 17–20. In 1463 there was a small endowment for canon law (*ibid.* i. 17) and in 1482 the faculty contributed for the repair of the canon law schools

CHAP. XI,
§ 2.

The records of the fifteenth century show that a certain number of graduates from other places and some clerics of standing joined the university; but it is not possible to say how they were distributed between law and theology, or whether there was regular instruction in medicine.[1] After the first fifty years or so, it would appear that the higher faculties had to depend mainly upon the cathedral staff, a few local Dominicans, the teaching masters, and the supply, always limited, of graduates from the faculty of arts.[2] There would be, as at S. Andrews, a certain amount of post-graduate study in the elements of law, indispensable for the notarial practice to which so many clerics looked. The verdict of John Major, whose advent in 1518 stimulated enrolments, was that the university, poorly endowed, was not rich in scholars.[3]

Constitution.

The constitution was very much on the lines of S. Andrews. There were the faculties, with their deans, of whom only the dean of the faculty of arts figures upon record; four nations, with their proctors elected by the whole body of masters and students; the rector, chosen by the four intrants of the nations;[4] his assessors; a promoter or syndic, appointed by the intrants, and charged to see that delinquents were called to account; and the bishop-chancellor, who granted the licence.[5]

Faculty of arts.

The geographical arrangement of the nations[6]—Clydesdale, Teviotdale, Albany, and Rothesay—indicates that, while S. Andrews had contemplated the whole of southern Scotland and the northern Lowlands, without much expectation from the Highlands,[7] Glasgow looked mainly to the region which became in 1492 the archiepiscopal province, and to the west generally, not without regard to Ireland. There was

---

(*ibid.* ii. 93, 95). In 1460 there is a reference to reading in civil law (*ibid.*, p. 67).

[1] A doctor of medicine was incorporated in 1469 (*ibid.* ii. 74).

[2] Arts graduations at Glasgow were on an average about one-third of those at S. Andrews.

[3] John Major, *History of Greater Britain*, trans. by A. Constable (Scot. Hist. Soc., 1892), p. 28.

[4] Cf. *Early Records* (S. Andrews), p. xiii.

[5] Cf. *Munimenta*, i. 5; ii. 6–11, with *Evidence*, iii. 171–2, 233–4.

[6] *Munimenta*, ii. 6.

[7] *Evidence*, iii. 233: *Early Records* (S. Andrews), pp. ix–xi.

some attempt to attract men from S. Andrews;[1] but, on the whole, supplementary effort is suggested rather than competitive rivalry.[2]

Upon the faculty of arts the usage of S. Andrews exerted an influence; and some features of the faculty were avowedly borrowed from Cologne. After 1420, when the number of Scots at Paris diminished, owing to the disturbed state of France, a steady connexion with Cologne was established. A Scottish graduate in arts at Cologne was received by the faculty at S. Andrews in 1448. Invited to Glasgow in 1451, he was mainly responsible for the arts statutes there, which are compounded of regulations derived from the statutes of Cologne and S. Andrews.[3]

The Glasgow arts statutes differ from those of S. Andrews in the absence of any allusion to 'touting' for scholars. The competitive difficulty never arose. The first regents seem to have hired a house in the Ratounraw—traditionally known as 'the Auld Pedagogy'—to provide for residence.[4] The public schools of the university, on the other hand, were accommodated at the Blackfriars in the High Street.[5] In 1460 Lord Hamilton granted to the principal regent in arts, for the benefit of the faculty, a tenement adjoining the Blackfriars; and he was to be instituted *ad regimen collegii*.[6] Thereupon the faculty began to expend surplus funds upon building, and in 1478 was still contributing *circa collegium artium*,[7] which

The Pedagogy.

---

[1] *S. A. Univ. Pub.* vii. 21, 36.

[2] Turnbull and Kennedy were on intimate terms in the earlier stages of their careers (cf. Annie Cameron, *Apostolic Camera and Scottish Benefices*, p. 112), and there is no indication that Kennedy was hostile to Turnbull's university.

[3] The borrowings from Cologne related specially to usage in graduation. The debt to S. Andrews was not known until its arts statutes, as revised at the Reformation, were restored in 1910, in the light of the Glasgow text (*S. A. Univ. Pub.* vii). For a comparative account see *Scottish Hist. Rev.* xi. 266.

[4] This was their own enterprise: in 1457 they had help from the faculty 'pro firma pedagogii . . . quod eorum laboribus crevit bursa facultatis ymmo et futuris temporibus uberius augmentari posset' (*Munimenta*, ii. 191).

[5] *Ibid.* ii. 182. In 1453 the faculty of arts subscribed 'pro reparatione scole in loco predicto'; and the schools there were *in vico*, after the Parisian technicality. In 1460 public lectures in law were given in the chapter-house of the Blackfriars (*ibid.*, p. 67).

[6] *Ibid.* i. 9–13.

[7] *Ibid.* ii. 195, 204, 210, 220.

CHAP. XI, was enlarged by the gift of a manse immediately to the north.[1]
§ 2. Thus the operations of the faculty of arts were now con-
centrated, and at the site of the public schools of the university, in what was by 1467 already known as the *collegium
facultatis*.[2] No additional halls were required to house the
arts students: the higher faculties had a very slender hold
upon life. During the thirty or forty years before the Reformation only the faculty of arts had a serious existence.

The university always had upon its roll a sufficient number
of senior men, not officially connected with the faculty of
arts, to participate effectively in the election of the rector.[3]
The extreme youth of pupils in the Pedagogy and their
limited number must have made any influence upon affairs
by them negligible. In 1532 the faculty of arts, the rector
presiding, enacted that any student who was caught out of
his bed-chamber after the bell for silence had rung, or who
should 'rashly and temerariously' meet the rector, dean, or
one of the regents in the streets without seeking to avoid his
awful glance, or even play any game, 'otherwise lawful', in
their presence, should be subjected to humiliating corporal
chastisement.[4]

Lack of   The lack of endowment, remarked by Major, remained a
endow-   fatal handicap to expansion. Early in the sixteenth century
ments.   Archbishop Blackadder proposed to annex benefices to 'his
College of the University of Glasgow'; and in 1537 Archbishop Dunbar had similar plans to create a proper collegiate
institution for the maintenance of masters and scholars.[5]

[1] *Munimenta*, i. 18; ii. 220.
[2] *Ibid*. ii. 204.
[3] Canons of the cathedral and the
holders of neighbouring benefices
were incorporated; but it may be
doubted whether study was the
prevailing motive.
[4] *Ibid*., p. 41. The statute seems
to insist on a boy who met a
regent in the streets showing his
respect for authority by running
away or 'shirking', as Eton boys
were required to do when they met
a master in Windsor. The notion
that this was because Windsor was

out of bounds may, therefore, be a
case of false analogy. The custom
of 'shirking' is very ancient, being
prescribed to the *clericuli*, when
they met a canon, by the statutes
of the Church of Lyons in the
twelfth century. If they could not
run away, they were to pretend
that they were not there by holding
their hands in front of their faces
(Migne, *Patrol. lat.* cxcix. 1104).
[Most of the above paragraph and
this note are taken from Rashdall
(ed. i, vol. ii. 307).]
[5] *Munimenta*, i. 42, 493.

Neither design took effect. The constitutional usage of the CHAP. XI,
§ 2.
university was observed; but by the eve of the Reformation
'Pedagogy' and 'university' had become for practical purposes convertible terms.[1]

The original location of the university centre and the initial After the
Reforma-
tion.
hospitality offered by the adjoining Blackfriars proved to have
important consequences. Visiting the city in 1563, after the
Reformation, Queen Mary saw 'the decay of ane Universite'
rather than 'ane establisst foundatioun'; and she granted,
among other property, the place of the Blackfriars and certain
of their rents which the religious revolution had rendered
available.[2] This was the prelude to a revival. In 1566-7 the
royal burghs obtained gift of all friars' houses and revenues,
along with the endowments for masses.[3] In 1572 the provost
and magistrates, at the instance of Master Andrew Hay, who
was rector of the university and commissioner of the
General Assembly for the superintendence of Clydesdale,
conveyed their gift to the Pedagogy for the maintenance of
a principal, who was to be an exponent of theology—the
higher faculty of dominant interest at the time—two regents
in arts, and twelve poor students.[4]

The additional endowment was not adequate, though the *Nova
erectio.*
services of Andrew Melville were obtained. Under Melville's
influence, and with hearty support from George Buchanan,[5]
the regent Morton was induced to grant additional resources,[6]
providing for a theological prefect, three regents in arts, and
now only four poor foundationers.[7] This *nova erectio* imposed
for the first time upon the Pedagogy a collegiate organization
within the university; and its ordinances were remarkable for

<hr>

[1] 'Pedagogium seu Universitas'
(*ibid*. i. 62–6).

[2] *Ibid*., p. 67.

[3] *University of Edinburgh* (*1883–
1933*), p. 6; *Munimenta*, i. 71. The
mass endowments, subject to life-
rent interest, were not immediately
available.

[4] *Ibid*., pp. 84–5.

[5] Buchanan was a witness to
the royal charter (*ibid*., p. 112)

and had showed 'singular favour'
(*ibid*., p. 123).

[6] 'Ad colligendas reliquias
Academie Glasguensis quam pre
inopia languescentem et iam pene
confectam reperimus' (*ibid*., p.
105).

[7] The provision for poor students seems to have been abused
(*ibid*., p. 154).

the attempt, not in the end successful, to induce specialism
among the regents.[1]

Upon this new foundation, within the medieval scheme,
the modern University of Glasgow was built. The beginnings
of revival, to which the city made its contribution, had a
similarity, in respect of this municipal interest, to the contemporary movement which brought about in 1583 the College of Edinburgh.[2] Both places benefited from the posses-
sions of the old Church: both were supported by burgess
enthusiasm for the advancement of the new; but, while the
growth in Edinburgh was from the initial status of a town's
college, the College of Glasgow preserved for fuller realization
the dignity, the traditions, and the constitution of a university
conferred by its founders.

§ 3. ABERDEEN (1494)

Report of Commissioners for visiting the Universities of Scotland, 1831, and
Evidence, iv, 1837, with *App. of Documents. Fasti Aberdonenses*, ed.
C. INNES, Aberdeen (Spalding Club), 1854. C. INNES, *Sketches of Early
Scotch History*, Edinburgh, 1861, p. 254 *sq*. Cf. KENNEDY, *Annals of
Aberdeen*, London, 1818, ii. 357 *sq*.

Founda-
tion, 1494. ABERDEEN, like the two other medieval Scottish universities,
was founded by a bishop. William Elphinstone, Bishop of
Aberdeen, was personally a more remarkable man than the
two earlier university-founders. He is said to have studied
arts and canon law at Glasgow, canon law at Paris, and civil
law at Orleans.[3] Sir Alexander Grant[4] suggests that he may
have been the original inspirer of the Scots Act of 1496
which required all barons and freeholders to have their eldest

[1] 'Nolumus prout in reliquis
regni Academiis consuetudo est
[regentes] novas professiones quo-
tannis immutare quo fit ut dum
multa profiteantur in paucis periti
inveniantur' (*ibid.*, p. 109). The
modern professorial system was a
development of the eighteenth
century.

[2] *University of Edinburgh, 1883–
1933*, pp. 6–11.

[3] *Fasti*, p. xi *sq*. [The William
'Elcomsten' of S. Andrews, whose

name appears on the *matricula* of
Louvain in 1431, was probably the
bishop's father. His lecture notes,
on civil, canon, and feudal law, are
preserved in King's College, Aberdeen; see J. H. Baxter in *Scot.
Hist. Rev.* xxv (1928), 329 and
note, 330.]

[4] *Story of the University of Edinburgh* (1884), i. 27. The Act is
printed in *Miscellany of the Maitland Club*, 1840, p. 5.

sons instructed in 'Arts and Jure'. At all events it is clear chap. xi,
that, even more certainly than the founders of S. Andrews §3.
and Glasgow, Elphinstone aimed at making his university a
school of law. It was especially intended to be a means of
promoting the civilization of the highland clergy, of whose
extreme ignorance an appalling picture is drawn in the petition
of King James IV recited in the Bull of foundation. This Bull
was granted by Alexander VI in 1494,[1] but not published
till February, 149⅚.[2] The royal charter of the same year in-
corporates certain benefices, and confers a scanty endowment
for the support of a doctor of medicine.[3] The decayed
Hospital of S. German's was also made over to the university;[4] and from the first it was part of the founder's plan to
endow the university by the erection of a college, which was
actually established in 1505 with the title of the College of
the Holy Virgin in Nativity—now King's College—which The
provided teachers in all the faculties.[5] The college was College.
endowed with impropriations; and the resemblance to the
German colleges is increased by the annexation to the college
of a church, of which the masters became prebendaries and
the 'bursars' choristers or clerks.[6] The university does not
appear to have entered upon actual existence till the year
1500, when the teaching of Hector Boece, whom Elphinstone
had brought from the College of Montaigu at Paris and
eventually made principal of his new college, soon placed
Aberdeen at the head of the Scotch universities—a position
which it retained for at least forty years. A comparison of the
early history of those universities which started with sufficient
endowments with the fate of those attempts at university-
founding which were not thus supported supplies ample
illustration of the absolute necessity—at ordinary times and
under ordinary circumstances—of endowment or some other

---

[1] *Fasti*, p. 6.
[2] *Ibid.*, p. 7.
[3] *Ibid.*, p. 11.
[4] *Ibid.*, pp. 9, 17, 18 *sq.*
[5] See Hector Boece's Life of
Elphinston, ap. *Aberdonensium Episcoporum Vitae*, 1552, f. xxvii *sq.*;
cf. *Fasti*, pp. xvii, 53 *sq.*

[6] *Ibid.*, p. 53 *sq.* A remarkable
provision of this charter is that
'nulle in quacumque facultate per
annum integrum fiant vacantie'
(p. 58). The wishes of the 'pious
founder' do not seem to have had
much influence on the length of
Scottish vacations.

CHAP. XI, extraneous support for the maintenance of higher education.
§ 3.   To this day Aberdeen is kept alive and flourishing, in spite
of the competition of the great city universities of Edinburgh
and Glasgow, by the number and wealth of its bursaries.

Constitu-   The constitution of Aberdeen was on the same lines as that
tion. of the two earlier Scottish universities, but the influence of
Orleans is plainly discernible in the constitution of its governing body. At Orleans it will be remembered that power was
shared between the professors and certain representatives of
the students. So at Aberdeen the power of making statutes
is entrusted to the chancellor, rector, and resident doctors,
'calling unto them' a competent number of licentiates and
scholars, and—a quite original feature—at least two privy
councillors of Scotland.[1] This state of things does not appear,
however, to have lasted long: real power here, as elsewhere,
passed to the principal and professors or regents who, together
with the rector, formed the Senatus Academicus.[2]

§ 4. CONCLUSION

[It should be remembered that this section was published in 1895. We
have thought it wiser to leave it, with one modification, as it appeared in
the first edition.]

Subse-   A WORD must be said as to the educational organization of the
quent
develop- Scottish universities and the process by which it has become so
ment of widely differentiated from that of the English universities.
the Scottish
universi- The future of the Scottish university was largely determined
ties. for it by the fact that its teachers from the first, or almost from
the first, were college teachers and university teachers at the
same time. Here, according to the North-German precedent,
college and university were more or less completely fused into
one. At Paris and Oxford the college teaching, which gradually supplanted the university teaching, was never modelled
on the lines of the old university system at all. In particular,
the Oxford tutorial system, by ultimately making every tutor
responsible for the whole education of his pupils, tended to
narrow the range as well as to lower the efficiency of the

[1] *Ibid.*, p. 5.   appear to have at one time existed.
[2] The nations and proctorships   *Documents*, pp. 167, 169.

college teaching, while the university teaching practically CHAP. XI,
§ 4. disappeared, and the university degree system, having no organic relation to the real studies of the colleges, degenerated into a farce. The consequence was that lecturing—in anything like the sense which the word bears in ordinary usage—almost died out. Education was reduced to lessons in logic and catechetical instruction on classical books. In the Scottish universities the instruction of the colleges always bore a direct relation to the subjects of the degree examination.

In Scotland the old medieval *trivium* and *quadrivium* and Survival the old medieval 'three philosophies' (natural, moral, and of the metaphysical), enlarged by the gradual infusion of the Renais- curri- sance Greek, have continued, almost down to the present [1895]. moment, to supply the outline of the university curriculum through all changes in the subject-matter actually taught in each department. At first the subjects were divided at the beginning of the academical year, in the way usual at the German universities, among the regent masters, i.e. practically the paid regents of the colleges.[1] Very early in the history of the Scottish universities a system—of which there is no distinct trace in the history of any other university—established itself, by which one regent took the entire instruction of a class, consisting of the men of a single year, through the whole of their four years' curriculum. The subjects of each year thus 'rotated' among the regents.[2] Only very gradually, as the standard of efficiency demanded of the teacher rose and the area covered by each subject expanded, was the system of 'rotation' abandoned in favour of the 'fixation' of each regent to a particular subject.[3] The system of 'rotation' has only quite recently disappeared from the leading 'High-schools'

[1] The Glasgow Statute-book retains the oath to lecture for two years unless dispensed, but this was practically no doubt insisted upon only in the case of the college regents. See *Documents*, p. 287.

[2] The origin of this system is very obscure. The Glasgow statute provides that the regents shall choose their books in order of seniority, according to the German

system. *Ibid.*, p. 285. But the system grew up in the Middle Ages; the reformers indeed wisely attempted to abolish it. See Grant, *Story of the University of Edinburgh*, i. 146 sq., and the *Documents*, *passim*.

[3] The first step, about the beginning of the eighteenth century, was to assign Greek to a separate professor.

CHAP. XI, of Scotland. This revolution in the universities was not com-
§ 4. pleted till after the middle of the eighteenth century.[1] Still
more recently and still more gradually has the title of professor, formerly appropriated only to the single teachers of
each of the superior faculties, supplanted the old medieval
regent or master.[2]

The   The consequences of this retention of the old medieval
Scottish
philo- curriculum in the Scottish universities, and the subsequent
sophy. evolution of distinct chairs of philosophy out of it, have been
of the utmost importance, not only in the history of Scottish
education, but in the history of British and even of European
thought. Scotland gained from it an education at once stimulating and practical, however grave its deficiencies on the
score of sound preparation and classical discipline; while to
the seemingly accidental circumstance that the Scottish universities provided philosophers, not merely with chairs but
with classes to teach, Europe probably owes in no small
measure the development of an important and influential
school of philosophy. Between the time of Hutcheson and
that of J. S. Mill a majority of the philosophers who wrote in

---

[1] This was a great Reform-era in
the Scottish universities, especially
at Aberdeen. The spirit of the
movement may be illustrated by
the following resolutions of Mari-
schal College:

'That the students may have the
benefit of those parts of Education
which are not commonly reckoned
Academical, such as dancing, writing, book-keeping, French, &c.,
without losing time in attending
Masters at a distance from the
College, the Sub-Principal and
Regents shall appoint proper rooms
in the College, and proper hours
when these things may be taught,
and shall bespeak Masters of the
best characters and qualifications
for instructing those who choose to
attend them.' (*Documents*, p. 176.)

'The Professors of Philosophy,
with the concurrence of the other
Masters, have unanimously agreed

to employ much less time than has
been usually done in the Universities, in the Logic and Metaphysick
of the Schoolmen, which seem con-
trived to make men subtle dispu-
tants—a profession justly of less
value in the present age than it has
been in some preceding ones; and
to employ themselves chiefly in
teaching those parts of Philosophy
which may qualify men for the
more useful and important offices
of society.' (*Ibid.*, p. 177.)

Every line of these resolutions
breathes the spirit of Locke's
Treatise on Education, and of that
Scottish 'common-sense' philosophy whose best representative
(Reid) was one of the regents who
voted for these changes.

[2] The Answers to the Commission of 1830 speak of the change as
made 'of late years'.

the English language were professors, or at least *alumni*, of CHAP. XI,
Scottish universities.

The reader of the preceding chapters will have remarked Disappear-
how closely parallel this transformation of the old regent- ance of the
system into the modern professorial system has been to a system.
similar development in the German universities. In both
cases the germ of the evolution was contained in the original
constitution of the university. The gradual disappearance of
the old college life which has taken place in both the Scottish
and the German universities is perhaps to be similarly accounted for. The characteristic feature of both systems in
their medieval form was the close fusion of the college with
the university system. At Paris and Oxford the college life
lasted on because it was inseparably bound up with the only
educational system which the university possessed. In Germany and Scotland the colleges were created primarily to
supply the universities with teachers; the common life could
disappear without destroying the *raison d'être* of the college-
foundations. Another influencing circumstance has been no
doubt the different attitudes of the universities towards the
marriage of the teaching body. At the revolutionary Reformation of Scotland and Germany it was assumed as a matter of
course that the compulsory celibacy of regent masters disappeared with the celibacy of the clergy; and it is not long
before we find difficulties arising about the maintenance of
discipline in the colleges.[1] In England, where the breach
with the past was less violent, and where the college fellowship was still looked upon mainly in the light of an endow-

[1] But it was a long time before
the Scottish mind reconciled itself to
the anomaly of women in college.
Thus at Morton's visitation of
S. Andrews in 1574, it was ordered
'that the wyffis, bairnis, and ser-
vandis of the Principallis and utheris
Maisteris in the Universitie be put
apart in the cietie out of the Col-
legis, sua yat wemen, to a slanderus
and evill exempill, haif not residence amangis the zoung men
studentis, nor zit that the same

wemen have ony administratioun
and handilling of the common
guidis of the College, to ye greit
prejudice yairof, and of sic as frelie
wald gif thame selffis to the study
of Lettres' (*Documents*, p. 189). At
a later date the difficulty seems to
have been met by requiring the
regent on duty for the week, or
hebdomadarius, also to sleep in
college. As to marriage in German
universities see above, pp. 242, 259,
n. 6.

ment for students to which educational functions were only accidentally annexed, the abolition of celibacy appears never to have suggested itself even to Puritan reformers. And the preservation of the common life for graduate-fellows has tended to its preservation for undergraduate students.

Boy-students and student-elections.
It is not only in its curriculum—in the wide range and the regular succession of subjects prescribed to its students—that the Scottish university preserves to this day the impress of the Middle Ages. Here alone perhaps in Europe were the bulk of the students in the arts faculty, till very recently, boys of about the same age as the artists of medieval Paris or Oxford. The average age is still below that of most universities. Here alone does the ancient chancellorship—no longer held by a bishop—survive side by side with the rectorship. Above all, here alone do the students—students still at Glasgow and Aberdeen divided into nations under the government of proctors—elect the head of a university. These Scottish rectorial elections, now used as the means of paying a triennial homage to some distinguished public man, reproduce perhaps more both of the outward mechanism and of the ancient spirit of medieval student-life than any feature of the more venerable, but also in some respects far more altered, constitutions of Oxford and Cambridge [1895].

APPENDIXES

I. PAPER UNIVERSITIES

THE following is a list of universities for which Bulls were granted, but which never came into actual existence. Down to 1400 the list (with one exception) has the authority of Denifle (*Die Univ. des Mittelalters*, i. 630–52): after that it is probably very incomplete.

GRAY (1290). A Bull was granted in 1290 by Nicholas IV on the petition of Otto IV, Count of Burgundy. See above, p. 190.

PAMIERS (1295). A Bull granted by Boniface VIII in 1295 erects in this city 'studium generale in quo magistri doceant et scolares libere studeant et audiant in quavis licita facultate' (*Registres de Boniface VIII*, ed. Thomas, Paris, 1884, No. 658 (c. 227); Fournier, *Stat. et Priv. des Un. françaises*, ii, Paris, 1891).

DUBLIN (1312). In 1311, the year after his accession to the see, John Lech, Archbishop of Dublin, petitioned Clement V for a *studium generale* in his metropolitical city. The petition refers to the non-existence of any university in Ireland or in the most nearly neighbouring countries of 'Scotland, Man, and Norway' (the geography of the Irish prelate seems tinged by Home-rule aspirations), the absence of learned men in Ireland, and the perils of the Irish Channel. The Bull was issued on 13 July 1312 and is printed in W. Monck Mason, *The History and Antiquities of the Collegiate and Cathedral Church of S. Patrick near Dublin*, Dublin, 1819, App. VII, i (where it is wrongly dated 1310), and in *Regesta Clem. V*, Rome, 1887 (No. 8634). It is remarkable in that it makes the establishment of the university at Dublin dependent upon the approval of the archbishop and his suffragans, confers no *ius ubique docendi*, and, while authorizing the *licentia docendi*, does not determine the authority by which it is to be conferred. The death of the archbishop and a long vacancy in the see prevented the immediate execution of the design. On 10 February 1320 the new archbishop, Alexander de Byckenore, with the assent of his two Chapters of the Holy Trinity (now Christ Church) and S. Patrick's, issued a body of statutes (Mason, App. VII, ii; also in Ware, *De Hibernia et Antiquitatibus eius*, London, 1658, p. 77), by which the chancellor is to be elected by the regents (subject to confirmation by the archbishop), but, if there is a doctor of theology or canon law in either of the Dublin chapters, he (or one of such doctors, if there are more than one) is to be elected. The university is to be governed by the chancellor and two proctors, and the rest of the constitution is framed on the Oxford model, with the exception of certain reservations in favour of the archbishop. It is provided 'quod Cancellarius, de consilio magistrorum regentium, et non regentium, si necesse fuerit, statuta condere possit ad honorem et pacem Universitatis, et ad scandala dirimenda, que contingere poterint in eventu, et illa statuta debent nobis et successoribus nostris presentari, et per nos et eosdem successores confirmari'. The chancellor has jurisdiction over masters and scholars and their servants, where 'actor et reus sunt de Universitate predicta', except where a canon or a member of his household or of the archbishop's household is involved. From the chancellor there is an appeal to the regents, but the further appeal is to the archbishop, to whom also is reserved the right of appointing a regent to lecture on theology in S. Patrick's Cathedral. The chancellor is to take an oath of obedience to the archbishop.

William de Rodyard, Dean of S. Patrick's, was appointed chancellor and took the degree of doctor in canon law, while three friars were made D.D. (*Annales Hiberniae*, 1162–1370, in J. T. Gilbert, *Chartularies of St. Mary's Abbey, Dublin*, ii, 1884, 361.) The foundation had no success. John Clyn, a contemporary Franciscan, describes it as 'universitas quoad nomen, sed utinam quoad factum et rem' (Annals, *a.* 1320, in Richard Butler, *Annals of Ireland*, Irish Archaeological Society, Dublin, 1849, p. 14). In 1358 King Edward III promised special protection to scholars travelling to Dublin (*Rotulorum Patentium et Clausorum Canc. Hiberniae Calendarium*, 1828, p. 73); but in 1363 the clerks of Ireland complained that 'in all Ireland there is no university or place of study' (*Calendar of Papal Petitions*, i. 467). In 1364, Lionel, Duke of Clarence, founded a divinity lectureship to be held by an Augustinian; while in 1496 a provincial synod imposed an annual contribution upon the clergy of the province for seven years to provide salaries for other lecturers (Mason, p. 101). These are all the facts that are known as to the existence of a university: the reader must be left to judge for himself as to whether the University of Dublin has been rightly included among the stillborn universities. Clearly there were some schools in Dublin, but in the absence of any evidence of graduation (after the first formal graduations of persons educated elsewhere) the *differentia* of a *de facto* university seems to be wanting.

Cardinal Newman has a short chapter on 'the Ancient University of Dublin' in the *Office and Works of Universities*, London, 1856, reprinted in *Historical Sketches*, London, 1872. The fullest account is in E. B. Fitzmaurice and A. G. Little, *Materials for the History of the Franciscan Province of Ireland, 1230–1450* (British Soc. of Franciscan Studies, ix, Manchester 1920), pp. xxviii, 107–9).

The following account of an attempt to found a university at Drogheda in 1465[1] may be appended as evidence that no university existed at Dublin at that date (John D'Alton, *History of Drogheda*, Dublin, 1844, ii. 149). 'On the accession of Edward the Fourth the Earl of Desmond was exalted to the honour of Lord Justice of Ireland, immediately after which he convened his parliament to assemble in this town (i.e. Drogheda). The corporation and townsmen of Drogheda happily directing his attention to the fact that during the government of Sir Edmund Butler, at the instance of the Archbishop of Dublin, a bull of the Pope was procured for the establishment of a University in Dublin, which however had declined for want of funds, besought him to effect a similar distinction for their town (i.e. Drogheda), the immemorial residence of the Primate of Ireland, and an act was accordingly passed (5 Edw. IV, c. 46) of which the following is a translation:—"Also at the request of the commons, because the land of Ireland has no university nor place of general study within it, a work of which sort would cause a great increase of knowledge, riches, and good government, and would prevent riot (!), evil government and extortion within the same land, it is therefore ordained, established and granted by authority of parliament that there be a university in the town of Drogheda, in which may be made bachelors, masters and doctors in all sciences and faculties as they are made in the university of Oxford, and that they may also have, occupy and enjoy all manner of privileges, laws and laudable customs which the said university of Oxford hath occupied and enjoyed, so that it be not prejudicial to the mayor, sheriffs nor commonalty of the said town of Drogheda." The political events of the period, however, prevented the consummation of this desirable object. Ireland as well as England was in a state of complete exhaustion during the reign of Edw. IV, and in that of Henry VII was much distracted by the attempts of his enemies to make it the scene of contests and rebellions, that they hoped would overturn his government, while the more immediate circumstance of the execution of the Earl of Desmond as a traitor naturally attached

---

[1] The attempt seems to be wrongly dated 1368 by Ware, p. 82, and Ware-Harris, p. 245.

an odium to all his measures, and particularly to that which
contemplated the elevation of a secondary locality to a literary
pre-eminence above the metropolis. Dublin continuing afterwards the fixed seat of the Parliament, and the ultimate establishment of a University there in 1591, seem to have extinguished the
expectation and almost the wish for realizing this honourable
distinction.'

VERONA (1339). The *studium* may have been started by Martino
della Scala, *c.* 1270. (Cf. Bolognini, 'L'Università di Verona e gli
statuti del sec. XIII e XIV', in the *Miscellanea nuziale Biadego-
Bernardinelli*, Verona, 1896.) A Bull was granted by Benedict XII
in 1339 for all faculties except theology. (*Bull. Rom.*, Turin edition, iv. 459.) The town-statutes of 1458 provide for a doctor of
grammar and rhetoric, of civil law, of canon law, of arts and medicine, and of arithmetic (*Statuta communitatis Veronae*, Vicenza,
1475, lib. i, Nos. 111–18), and then might presumably have claimed
the privileges of a *studium generale*, but there is no evidence of
graduation. The university, if such it was, had declined in the
early fifteenth century. The bishop, the later Pope Eugenius IV,
established or reconstituted schools on more ecclesiastical lines,
and these, after the exclusion of the laity, became the type of the
later seminaries which in Italy carried on the theological traditions
of the medieval universities. (Cf. Manacorda, i. 259–61.)

CIVIDALE in Friuli (1353). On several occasions in the first half
of the fourteenth century the commune of Cividale agitated for a
studium. The earliest instance is said, though not conclusively, to
have been in 1303. On 1 August 1353 the Emperor Charles IV, at
the request of his brother, Nicholas, the patriarch of Aquileia,
established a *studium generale* at Cividale. He gave as his reason
that Cividale was more conveniently placed than the universities
of Lombardy for his subjects within or on the confines of the
patriarchate. This was the first of the numerous constitutions
issued by Charles IV authorizing *studia generalia*. It was first
printed in B. Zancarolus, *Antiquitates civitatis Fori Iulii* (Venice,
1669), p. 46, but its significance was brought to light by P. S. Leicht,
'Il primo tentativo de costituire un' Università nella Venezia
orientale' (*Memorie storiche forogiulesi*, vi (1911), 1–14. Leicht
gives the history of the various attempts to establish a *studium*
before 1353, and edits the documents. The Bull of Charles IV
was edited independently by R. Saloman, with a note, in *Neues
Archiv*, xxxvii (1912), 810–17; corrections on p. 879.

GENEVA (1365). On the petition of Amadeo VI, Count of Savoy, a *studium generale* in all faculties was founded at Geneva in 1365 by a Bull of the Emperor Charles IV for all faculties (published by J. Vuy in *Mémoires de l'Institut genevois*, xii, 1869, p. 43). Denifle (i. 649) cites an interesting document which shows that the Bull was an expedient to revive a very decaying school. The bishop had in the preceding year complained to the Pope that the chancellor of his cathedral was in the habit of selling 'regimen scolarum civitatis et dioc. Gebennen. plus offerenti', his demands being so extortionate 'quod scole ipse quasi ad nichilum sunt redacte'. This behaviour of the chancellor explains the fact that he is altogether ignored in the constitution of the university, and the unusual provision in the foundation-bull which entrusts the right of promotion to the doctors or masters themselves. For later attempts to create a *studium* before the foundation of the University by Calvin in 1559, and for the College of Versonnex (1429–1536), see C. Borgeaud, *Histoire de l'Université de Genève*, Geneva, 1900.

KULM (1366). A Bull of Urban V was granted on petition of the Teutonic Order, 'instar studii Bononiensis', which is printed in Arnoldt, *Historie der Königsbergischen Universität*, Königsberg, 1746, i, Beil. 3, and hence, apparently, by Wölky in the *Urkundenbuch des Bistums Kulm*, Dantzig, 1885, No. 369, p. 289. In both places the Bull is wrongly dated. (See Kaufmann, *Geschichte der deutschen Universitäten*, ii, p. xv.)

LUCCA (1369). Flourishing communal schools had existed in Lucca since 1322, and the time seemed to have come for the establishment of a university (Manacorda, ii. 304), when in 1369 a *studium generale* was erected by Charles IV. It is remarkable for including astrology among the 'sciences and approved faculties' to be taught there. (Baluze, *Miscellanea*, ed. Mansi, Lucca, 1764, iv. 184.) In 1387 another Bull (for all faculties except theology) was procured from Urban VI (*ibid.*, p. 185). But no *studium* except in arts appears to have really come into existence, and this is not organized as a *studium generale*. For information as to the schools of Lucca, both before and after the Bulls, see the documents published by Lucchesini, 'Della historia letteraria del ducato Lucchese', in *Memorie e documenti per servire all' istoria del ducato di Lucca*, Lucca, 1825, ix. 18 *sq.*

ORVIETO (1378). The town-statutes (Fumi, 'Codice diplomatico della città d' Orvieto' in *Documenti di storia italiana per le provincie di Toscana, dell' Umbria e delle Marche*, vol. viii, Florence, 1884, p. 780 *sq*.) testify to the existence of a considerable *studium* from 1280. It obtained the grant of a *studium generale* from Gregory XI in 1377 (*ibid.*, p. 567), while the actual Bull was issued in the following year by his successor, Urban VI; but it appears that even the *studium* which had previously existed in the place was now extinct, since after this we hear nothing even of salaries so far as the higher faculties are concerned.

FERMO (1398). Denifle has shown (i. 631) that the Bull for this university was granted, not by Boniface VIII, but by Boniface IX. It was confirmed by Calixtus III in 1455, but was only brought into actual existence by a Bull of Sixtus V in 1585. Denifle speaks of a monograph by Curi, *L'Università degli studi di Fermo* (Ancona, 1880), which attributes its origin to Lothair! Manacorda (ii. 297) gives a bibliography.

CALATAYDD (1415). A Bull was granted for a university at Calataydd, on the western borders of Aragon, by Benedict XIII in 1415 (Vincent de la Fuente, *Hist. d. las Univ. en España*, i. 321). But nothing appears to be known as to the actual existence of a university in this place.

MANTUA (1433). The success of Vittorino da Feltre at Mantua prompted Gianfrancesco Gonzaga to secure a *privilegium* from the Emperor Sigismund (27 September 1433), which was confirmed by Frederick III. See J. C. Lünig, *Codex Italiae diplomaticus*, Frankfurt, 1732, p. 1781. Cf. W. H. Woodward, *Vittorino da Feltre*, Cambridge, 1897.

GERONA (1446). On 9 May 1446 Alfonso V allowed the *jurats* of Gerona to establish a *studium generale* in all sciences, with power to confer degrees. Nothing appears to have been done in the matter, and Gerona is not even the subject of an allusion when the same monarch granted the same rights to Barcelona four years later. The university came into effective being in virtue of a Bull of Paul V in 1605. See La Fuente, *Universidades*, i. 240; Rubió y Lluch, *Documents*; Torroella, *El estudi general o universitat literari de Girona* (Gerona, 1906).

LÜNEBURG (1471). A Bull was granted by the Emperor Frederick III on 8 August 1471, and is printed by Kaufmann (ii. 564–5), after

collation with the original, from Caspar Sagittarius and Henricus
Gause in *Memorabilia Historiae Luneburgicae* (1688).

FRANKFURT-ON-ODER (1500). A Bull was obtained by the
Margrave John Cicero from Alexander VI and the Emperor
Maximilian. The actual erection of the university was suspended
by the death of the Margrave, in the same year, till 1506, when a
fresh Bull was obtained from Julius II (J. C. Beckmann, *Notitia
Universitatis Francofurtanae*, Frankfurt-am-Oder, 1707, p. 14).
The statutes were based on those of Leipzig. See P. Reh, *Die
allgemeine Statuten der Univ. Frankfurt-a.-Oder, 1510–1610*,
Breslau, 1898; also above, p. 288.

II. ALLEGED UNIVERSITIES AT LYONS,
REIMS, ALAIS, PARMA, &c.

LYONS

KAUFMANN (*Gesch. d. deutsch. Univ.* i. 379) wishes to make
Lyons a *studium generale* in the thirteenth century, on the
strength of an allusion in a royal decree of 1302 to the city's
right 'habendi insuper in dicta civitate utpote egregia studium
scolarium et regentium in iure civili et canonico ad...docendum...
artes alias liberales' (*Cartulaire municipal de Lyon*, ed. Guigue,
Lyons, 1876, p. 29; Fournier, *Statuts et Priv. des Univ. franç.* ii,
No. 1562). In a document of 1328 (*Cartulaire*, p. 82; Fournier,
ii, No. 1563) Philip VI declares that 'archiepiscopus et capitulum Lugdunense, doctoribus et bacalariis decretorum et legum in
dicta civitate huiusmodi scientias volentes publice legere et docere,
circa eorum lecturas novitates indebite inibi facere nituntur,
dictos doctores et bacalarios compellendo iurare quod, lectura sua
durante, contra eos non consulent'. This is evidence of the existence of an important school, but if a city is to be added to the list
of *studia generalia* on such evidence, where are we to stop?
Innocent IV's foundation of the *Studium Curiae Romanae*, issued
at Lyons in 1245, has sometimes been mistaken for a foundation of
a university at Lyons. All the documents are printed in Fournier,
ii, No. 1559 *sq*. A document of 1291–2 (*ibid.*, No. 1560) shows that
one doctor was licensed by the archbishop, and the other by the
chapter, no additional doctors being permitted without the consent of both.

The history of the school is dealt with by Bronchoud, *Recherches
sur l'enseignement du droit à Lyon*, Lyons, 1875, and Rougier,
Aperçu historique sur l'enseignement du droit à Lyon, Lyons, 1874.

REIMS

In the twelfth and thirteenth centuries the cathedral school of Reims occupied much the same kind of position as that of Lyons, except that Lyons was famous for the study of law, Reims for theology. When Alexander III wrote to the archbishop of Reims directing him to condemn the nihilianism of Peter the Lombard (see above, vol. i, p. 56), he directs him to summon as his assessors the masters of the school at Reims and other places ('convocatis magistris scolarum Parisiensium et Remensium et aliarum circumpositarum civitatum' (Denifle, *Chartularium*, i, Introd. No. 9; Fournier, ii, No. 1555). We have already noticed the existence of a 'Collége des Bons-enfans' here (above, vol. i, p. 503, n. 3; Fournier, ii, No. 1557). In 1258 we find a Bull of Alexander IV, in which a careless reader might detect a recognition of Reims as a *studium generale*. It is directed against the chanter of Reims, who was guilty of the common practice of getting dispensed from residence for study at a *studium generale* and then going to live on other benefices or in his native country, 'ad excusandas excursationes in peccatis scolas Predicatorum vel Minorum ordinis vel alterius docentis ibidem perfunctorie adeundo'. The chanter had adopted this subterfuge, 'licet Remis adeo utiliter sicut et alibi in dicta pagina studere, si velit, valeat'. The dean and chapter of Reims are forbidden to let him enjoy his 'fruits', 'nisi Remis in predicta pagina studenti vel alibi ubi generalis in ea viget scolastici studii disciplina' (Fournier, ii, No. 1558). This may no doubt be read as if implying that Reims was a *studium generale*; but it need not be so. The principle clearly was that he must either study at Reims, or, if elsewhere, then in a *studium generale*. It is possible that Reims *may* have been described as a *studium generale* in the vague thirteenth-century sense; it was just one of those schools that might well have developed into a *studium generale ex consuetudine*; but it did not do so. The university dates from 1547.

There is a full history of the school and university by Dom Marlot, *Histoire de la ville, cité et université de Reims* (Reims, 1846), and a *Histoire du collége des Bons-enfants de l'Université de Reims* by Cauly (Reims, 1885).

ALAIS

In the *Bibliothèque de l'École des Chartes*, xxxi (1871), 51 *sq.*, M. Eugène de Rozière published some interesting documents relating to the opening of a *studium* at Alais in 1290. There are two contracts, one with Armandus de Jeco, 'canonicus Vasionensis, doctor decretorum', the other with 'dominus Raymundus Soquerii, regens in legibus in civitate Avenionensi', to lecture on their respective subjects, as well as (in the case of the civilian) to give legal assistance to the magistrates. Professor Kaufmann remarks triumphantly that they do not seem alive to the necessity of a papal or imperial Bull—as if Denifle or any one else had maintained that such a Bull was necessary to a *studium* which had no pretensions to being *generale*. It is noteworthy that the first contract contains a clause that no other shall lecture at Alais (unless the doctor's salary is raised)—which does not accord with even Kaufmann's somewhat indefinite ideas as to the nature of a *studium generale*. Denifle has pointed out over and over again that such a *studium* of law existed in most Italian towns and in many other parts of Europe, but no one ever dreamed of considering them *studia generalia*. The documents were again printed in Fournier, *Stat. et Priv. des Un. franç.* ii, No. 1569 *sq.*

Parma

From the documents published in the anonymous *Memorie e documenti per la storia della Università di Parma ned Medievo*, vol. i (Parma, 1888), it appears that an institution claiming to be a *studium generale* was established at Parma in 1412, with a rector, university of students, and college of doctors, at which degrees were actually given and diplomas issued with the accustomed formula 'catedram magistralem ascendendi et in ea legendi, docendi, disputandi, questiones terminandi, et ceteros actus doctoreos exercendi . . . et doctorum insignia deferendi hic et ubique locorum auctoritatem et licentiam', &c. (p. 111). Statutes were drawn up on the Bologna model in 1414 (p. iii *sq.*); and the *matricula* of 1413 shows an entry of seventy-seven names. But no papal or imperial Bull of foundation was granted, though it appears that efforts were made to obtain the former, *circa* 1328 (*ibid.*, p. 74), and again in the fifteenth century (Denifle, i. 230). The evidence goes to show that such a *studium* would not have been considered 'general' or its *licentia ubique docendi* accounted valid at the time. Hence I have excluded Parma from the list of medieval universities. The documents before 1412 only show the existence of an isolated 'medicus', and a single 'eius scolaris' (p. 103), and schools of grammar, arts, and law (p. 104 *sq.*), such as existed in most considerable Italian towns without any pretensions to the appellation of *studium generale*. At one time—in the twelfth century—the town seems to have possessed considerable fame as a school of grammar and arts (*ibid.*, p. 22 *sq.*); but there is no evidence to show that it was ever recognized as a *studium generale ex consuetudine*.

There seems to have been a college of doctors with regular statutes as early as 1294 (Doc. in Affò, *Memorie degli Scrittori*, &c., p. xxiv). It is observable that Gian Galeazzo Visconti of Milan, in an edict of 1387, forbids inhabitants of the Parmese territories to resort to other *civitates Italiae in quibus studia generalia vigeant*, and requires them to attend the *studium* of Parma, but the edict studiously refrains from calling the latter a *studium generale*. In assuming that title in 1412, they were simply, as was sometimes done in other cases (e.g. Pisa, see above, p. 45, presuming upon the issue of a papal Bull, in anticipation of which the *studium* had been organized; but, as the event proved, the Parmese were counting their chickens before they were hatched. To include Parma among universities (as is apparently done by Kaufmann, i. 232) is simply to abandon all constitutional accuracy in the use of the terms. It was not till 1512 that Parma succeeded in obtaining a Bull from Julius II (Affò, *loc. cit.*, p. cii). The history of the *studium* is dealt with by Affò, *Memorie degli Scrittori e Letterati Parmigiani*, i, Parma, 1789 (Discorso Preliminare); Tiraboschi, *Ist. d. Lett. Ital.* vi. i. 149; Pezzana, *Storia della Città di Parma*, Parma, 1842, ii. 145 *sq.* The city was famous for *artes liberales* from the eleventh century, but the allusions do not prove a *studium generale*. See Muratori, *Rer. Ital. SS.* iii. 912; v. 534. Cf. Dümmler, *Anselmus der Peripatetiker* (1872), p. 21.

NÎMES

The accounts of the consuls of the city of Nîmes for 1373 contain a number of interesting details relating to an attempt to set up a *studium generale* at Nîmes. There are the expenses of journeys to Avignon and Montpellier to bribe away doctors and students and to procure a papal Bull, and for a copy of the privileges of Montpellier, which it was proposed to imitate, for presents to a cardinal ('pro decem vasis vini cum fusta . . . presentatis . . . domino cardinali Mimatensi . . . cxvii florenos, medium'), for adapting a building for schools, for going to meet a doctor from Avignon, feasting him upon his arrival, &c. The schools were evidently opened and lectures given, but it is clear that the Bull was not granted. The failure of the attempt to found a *studium generale* shows (in opposition to the views of Kaufmann and others) how indispensable the papal Bull had by this time become. The document is printed by Fournier (*Stat. et Priv. d. Un. franç.* ii, No. 1576) from Ménard, *Histoire de Nîmes*, 1874, p. 323, and Preuves. No Bull for Nîmes appears in the register of Gregory XI (Denifle, *Archiv f. Literatur- und Kirchengeschichte*, iv. 262).

GAILLAC AND ALBI

A *studium* of arts was founded at Gaillac by Bull of John XXII
in 1329, but it is styled simply 'studium in quo magistri libere
doceant, ac scolares studeant et audiant', not *studium generale*.
The object of the Bull is contained in the clause 'rectoris et
magistrorum Universitatis studii Albiensis, qui sunt et erunt
pro tempore, et cujuscumque alterius licentia minime requisita'
(Fournier, ii, No. 1573). In spite of this privilege, the bishop
of Albi excommunicates the whole town on account of these
academical pretensions—a sentence reversed on appeal to the
court of the archbishop of Bourges (*ibid.*, No. 1574).

The two cases of Gaillac and Albi are instructive, the first as
showing that a *studium privilegiatum* need not be general, the
second as illustrating the possibility of a rector and university of
masters in a *studium particulare*.

BILLOM

Denifle has printed several documents (*Les Univ. françaises*,
pp. 94, 95) from which it appears that at Billom in Auvergne there
was a *studium* of law of a kind which could be plausibly represented as a *studium generale*. The most important of these is a
document of 1345, in which a canon asks for dispensation from
residence while studying at Billom or 'in any other *studium
generale*'. This implies that students at Billom claimed that it
was a *studium generale*, but not of course that the claim was
admitted. Indeed, as dispensation was usually only granted for
residence at *studia generalia*, the canon had an adequate reason
for misrepresentation. In 1349 a cardinal petitions the Pope on
behalf of a canon of Billom who wanted to be absent from the
services of his church while teaching in the *studium*. The
'instruentium nimis raritas' is alleged as a ground for the petition.

MILAN

The following statement occurs in Baldus, *Consilia*, v, Cons.
77, fol. 21 *a* (Frankfurt, 1589): 'Ciuitas Mediolanensis ex consuetudine, cuius contrarii memoria non existit, intelligitur apud
se habere studium generale; presertim quia est ciuitas regia (cf.
above, vol. i, p. 11, n. 1) et Metropolitana.' Had this testimony
occurred somewhat earlier (Baldus died at Pavia in 1400) it might
have been natural to accept it as decisive. But it is so entirely
unsupported by what we know of the *studium* at Milan in the
fourteenth century that it must be received with very great

suspicion. We are told, indeed, that in 1288 there were in Milan 15 doctors of grammar and logic, 70 'magistri puerorum ad initiales literas', and '180 medici dicti philosophi computatis Cymicis. Inter quos plures salariati per Communitatem' (Giulini, *Memorie spettanti alla storia della Città di Milano*, pt. viii, p. 395). The same writer cites a MS. Chronicle by Flamma, for the statement that 'Iurisperiti habent publicas scholas', but from the context it would seem doubtful whether these were anything but schools for notaries. And there is no mention of teaching in medicine or philosophy. Nor is there any reason to believe that the *studium* was really looked upon as general during the fourteenth century, while there is every reason to believe that, if there were such a *studium*, we should have heard of it. Moreover, in 1387 Gian Galeazzo Visconti forbade his subjects to study except at Parma (see above, p. 334). Hence the attempt to make out that Milan was a *studium generale* must probably be looked upon as a mere counsel's opinion obtained by a client with whom the wish was father to the thought. The circumstances are partially set forth in the *casus* on which the opinion was taken:

'In Christi nomine. Casus talis est. Quidam impetrauit gratiam a summo Pontifice, in qua narrauit se studere in iure ciuili non exprimendo locum, ubi studeret, prout studebat in Mediolano; ubi licet non sit studium ordinatum, seu generale, per sapientes doctores legitur, ut lectum fuit, et hodie legitur, et per tanti temporis spacium, quod in contrarium memoria hominis non existit. Modo quaeritur, utrum gratia praedicta sit supreptitia pro eo, quod non studebat in iure ciuili in studio ordinato et deputato, vel non' (*ibid.*, fol. 20 *b*).

It is obvious that Baldus's client had obtained some 'grace', e.g. a dispensation from residence, on the ground that he was studying in a *studium generale* when he was studying or pretending to study at Milan. For the ease of his conscience, or some more material purpose, he now wanted a legal opinion that Milan was a *studium generale*. The opinion was of course forthcoming, though the grounds on which it was based could have convinced no one.

For the schools of Milan see Maiocchi, *Le Scuole in Milano dalla decadenza dell'impero romano alla fine del sec. xv*, Florence, 1881; and Manacorda, ii. 306–7.

AVILA

No authority has accepted the assertion of Gil y Zárate, *De la instrucción pública en España*, p. 208, that a university was founded at Avila in 1482 by Ferdinand and Isabella for theology, law and philosophy, and was endowed with the confiscated property of the Jews. Like the university of Luchente (1423) it is probably apocryphal.

III. THE VERCELLI CONTRACT

(Additional note to vol. i, p. 156, and vol. ii, pp. 12, 26)

[From Balliano, *Della Università degli Studi di Vercelli*, 1868, p. 38.]

Carta studii et Scolarium Commorantium in Studio Vercellarum.

Anno dominice incarnationis 1228 indicione prima die Martis quarto Mensis Aprilis. Iste sunt conditiones apposite, et confirmate, et promisse ad invicem inter Dominum Albertum de Bondonno et Dominum Guillelmum de Ferrario, Nuncios et Procuratores communis Vercellarum constitutos per Dominum Rainaldum Trotum Potestatem Vercellarum nomine ipsius Communis super statuendis et firmandis infrascriptis conditionibus, ut in instrumento facto per Petrum de Englesco Notarium apparebat ex una parte et ex alia Dominum *Adam de Canocho Rectorem Francigenarum, Anglicorum, Normanorum*, et Magistrum Raginaldum de Boxevilla, et Magistrum Enricum de Stancio eorum nomine, et nomine Universitatis Scolarium ipsius rectorie et Dominum *Iacobum de Yporegia Procuratorem Scolarium Ytalicorum*, ut dixit, et Dominum Guillelmum de Hostialio Vicarium Domini Curradi Nepotis Domini Archiepiscopi, prout ibi dictum fuit, alterius Procuratoris et Italicorum, ut dixit, eorum nomine, et Universitatis Scolarium Italicorum, et Dominum *Gaufredum Provincialem rectorem Provincialium, et Spanorum et Catellanorum* et Dominum Raimundum Guillelmum, et Dominum Pelegrinum de Marsilia eorum nomine et nomine Universitatis Scolarium ipsius rectorie ex alia, videlicet, quod Potestas Vercellarum nomine ipsius communis et ipsum commune dabit Scolaribus et universitati scolarium quingenta hospicia de melioribus que erunt in civitate, et si plura erunt necessaria, plura, ita videlicet quod pensio melioris hospicii non excedat summam librarum decem et novem papiensium, et exinde infra fiat taxatio aliorum hospitiorum arbitrio duorum scolarium et duorum civium, et si discordes fuerint, addatur eis Dominus Episcopus vel alius discretus clericus de capitulo Vercellarum ad electionem communis, ut si tamen canonicum elegerit rectores eligant quem velint, et debeat solvi pensio hospiciorum ad carnem privium.[1] Si autem

---

[1] [i.e. at Carniprivium, the beginning of Lent.]

essent plura hospicia in uno contestu apta scolaribus, licet eiusdem hominis essent, vel unum haberent introitum, non debeant
reputari pro uno hospicio, sed pro pluribus arbitrio predictorum.
Ita quod de istis quingentis hospiciis excipiantur domus que sunt
in strata, in quibus consueverunt recipi et recipiuntur hospites in
nundinis Vercellarum, et albergantur per totum annum continue.
Item Magistri et scolares hospicia que haberent conducta pro
tempore teneantur reddere potestati qui pro tempore fuerit vel
eius nuncio, et si propter rixam vel discordiam vel aliam neces-
sariam vel iustam causam ab eis peterentur a Potestate vel eius
nuntio ad voluntatem Potestatis, eis servatis indampnis antequam
exeant illa hospicia; ita quod illa hospicia debeant evacuari, postquam petita fuerint a scolaribus arbitrio praedictorum vel iudicio
Potestatis, et aptari ad opus studii infra octo dies, et si non facerent
infra octo dies, ut supra dictum est, scolares, si voluerint, possint
facere necessarias expensas de pensione domus. Item promiserunt predicti Procuratores nomine communis Vercellarum, quod
Commune mutuabit scolaribus et universitati scolarium usque ad
summam decem millium librarum p. p. pro duobus denariis ad
duos annos, postea pro tribus usque ad sex annos, et portabit
vel portari faciet commune Vercellarum praedictam pecuniam
usque ad quantitatem sufficientem scolaribus ad locum aptum, et
totum (tutum?) scilicet Venecias, et ipsam eis dabit commune
receptis pignoribus, et receptis instrumentis a scolaribus manu
pubblica confectis, quae pignora reddet commune Vercellarum
scolaribus precaria cum fuerint Vercellis in hospiciis collocati,
recepta idonea fideiussione scolarium et prestitis sacramentis
a principalibus personis de reddenda ipsa pecunia, et quod cum
ea non recedent in fraudem. Item quod cum scolaris solverit
pecuniam sibi mutuatam, quod commune Vercellarum ipsum
reservabit in erario communis, scilicet sortem tantum et de ea
providebit commune alii scolari indigenti sub eodem pacto et
simili conditioni, et quod ussure commune Vercellarum non com-
putabit in sortem, et recipietur particularis solutio a scolaribus,
scilicet tertie partis, vel dimidie, et fiet novatio predictorum
debitorum, vel fideiussorum, vel precariorum. Item quod commune Vercellarum non dimitet victualia iurisdictionis Vercellarum extrahi de comitatu eorum, sed eas asportari faciet in civitate
bona fide, et bis in septimana faciet fieri mercatum, et prohibebit
quod dicta victualia non vendantur ante tertiam aliquibus qui
debeant revendere, exceptis quadrupedibus et blavis et vino, et
hoc salvis sacramentis et promissionibus Potestatis et communis
Vercellarum de dando mercato specialibus personis, videlicet

comiti Petro de Maxino et comiti Ottoni de Blandrate et comiti
Gocio de Blandrate et comiti Guidoni de Blandrate. Item quod
commune Vercellarum ponet in Caneva Communis modios quingentos frumenti, et modios quingentos siccalis ad mensuram
Vercellarum, et illam dabit scolaribus tantum et non aliis pro
eo pretio quo emta fuerit; ita tamen quod scolares ipsam blavam
teneantur emere pro pretio quo empta fuerit, quo usque duraverit,
et hoc faciet commune Vercellarum tempore necessitatis ad peti-
tionem scolarium. Item quod commune Vercellarum constituet
salarium competens arbitrio duorum scolarium et duorum civium,
et si discordes fuerint, stetur arbitrio episcopi, et salaria debeant
taxari ante festum omnium Sanctorum, et solvi ante festum Sancti
Thome Apostoli, videlicet uni theologo, tribus dominis Legum,
duobus decretistis, duobus decretalistis, duobus physicis, duobus
dialecticis, duobus grammaticis. Ita tamen quod scolares Vercellarum et eius districtus non teneantur aliqua dona Magistris vel
Dominis dare. Ita quod dicti Domini et Magistri, qui debent
salarium percipere a Communi Vercellarum, eligantur *a quatuor
Rectoribus, scilicet a Rectore Francigenarum, a Rectore Ytalicorum
et Rectore Teotonicorum, et Rectore Provincialium* iuratis, quod
bona fide eligent meliores Dominos et Magistros in civitate, vel
extra, et substituent eis alios meliores usque ad certum gradum,
quod crediderint posse haberi ad salarium, et stabitur electioni
trium, si autem tres non fuerint concordes addatur eis qui pro
tempore reget in Theologia, promittens in verbo veritatis, quod
bona fide eliget meliorem de illis de quibus inter Rectores erit
controversia, et electioni eius stetur, et omnes praedicte electiones
fiant infra quindecim dies intrante mense Aprilis. Item qui pro
tempore erit Potestas Vercellarum mitet infra quindecim dies
post electiones factas de Dominis et Magistris propriis expensis
communis Vercellarum fideles Ambaxatores iuratos, qui bona
fide ad utilitatem studii Vercellarum querent Dominos, et Magistros electos et eos pro posse suo obligare procurabunt ad legendum
in civitate Vercellarum. Item quod commune Vercellarum servabit pacem in civitate, et districtu Vercellarum, et ad hoc dabit
operam Potestas et commune Vercellarum. Item quod nullum
scolarem pignorabit pro alio scolari nisi pro eo specialiter fuerit
obbligatus communi Vercellarum. Item quod si aliquis scolaris,
vel eius nuncius robatus fuerit in civitate Vercellarum vel eius districtu sive in alio districtu, quod commune Vercellarum faciet idem
pro eo, et (ut?) faceret pro alio cive Vercellarum, dando operam
bona fide et fideliter cum litteris et Ambaxatoribus ut suum recipiet.
Item non offendent scolares, vel eorum nuncios ad eos venientes,

nec capient propter aliquam guerram, vel discordiam, vel rixam, quam commune Vercellarum haberet cum aliqua civitate, vel cum aliquo Principe seu castro, sed vel licentiabit commune Vercellarum ipsos, vel affidabit. Item quod commune Vercellarum eos tractabit in civitate, et in eius districtu sicut cives. Item quod iusticie exhibitione serventur scolaribus eorum privillegia, nisi eis specialiter renunciaverint, et exceptis maleficiis in quibus commune Vercellarum plenam habeat iurisdictionem. Item quod commune Vercellarum habebit Universitati scolarium duos bidellos, qui eodem gaudeant privillegio quo scolares. Item habebit commune Vercellarum duos exemplatores, quibus taliter providebit, quod eos scolares habere possint, qui habeant exemplantia [exemplaria ?] in utroque iure et in Theologia competentia, et correcta tam in textu quam in gloxa, ita quod solutio fiat a scolaribus pro exemplis secundum quod convenit ad taxationem Rectorum. Item si aliqua discordia oriretur inter scolares, commune Vercellarum non favebit aliquam partem, sed ad pacem et concordiam commune dabit operam. Item quod predictas conditiones servabit commune Vercellarum usque ad octo annos. Item quod scolares vel eorum nuncii non solvant pedagia in districtu Vercellarum que sint et perveniant in commune Vercellarum. Item Massarios communis dantes pecuniam scolaribus non habebit commune Vercellarum, nisi duos, et illos non mutabit nisi semel in anno. Item Potestas Vercellarum, et ipsum commune teneantur mittere per civitates Italiae, et alibi, secundum quod videbitur expedire Potestati vel communi ad significandum studium esse firmatum Vercellis, et ad scolares Vercellarum ad studium immutandos [invitandos ?]. Item predictas conditiones commune Vercellarum ponet in statuto civitatis Vercellarum, et Potestas, qui pro tempore fuerit, iurabit eas servare in sui principio, sicut certa statuta civitatis, et faciet iurare suum successorem, et ita successive usque ad octo annos, et nullo modo de statuto Vercellarum usque dictum terminum sive octo annorum ante extrahantur, et super iis omnibus duo instrumenta uno tenore confecta fiant. Item promiserunt predicti Rectores et scolares eorum nomine et nomine aliorum omnium scolarium de eorum rectoria predictis procuratoribus nomine communis Vercellarum, quod bona fide sine fraude dabunt operam, quod tot scolares venient Vercellis, et morentur ibi in studio quot sint sufficientes ad predicta quingenta hospicia conducenda, et quod universum studium Paduae veniet Vercellis et moretur ibi usque ad octo annos; si tamen facere non poterint, non teneantur. Item quod fuit de eorum concordia quod Domini vel Magistri vel scolares non debeant advocari in aliqua causa in civitate vel districtu nisi pro scolaribus vel pro suis factis, vel coram delegatis ab utroque Principe vel in foro ecclesiastico coram ecclesiasticis personis. Item quod Domini vel Magistri vel scolares vel Rectores non erunt in aliquo facto vel consilio in detrimento civitatis Vercellarum, et si sciverint aliquem vel aliquos facere vel tractare aliquid contra honorem et statum communis Vercellarum bona fide prohibebunt ne recedant et Potestati Vercellarum quam citius poterint manifestabunt.

Item promiserunt, quod non capient partem aliquo modo inter cives Vercellarum vel eius districtus. Item fuerunt in concordia, quod quilibet rector tantam habeat potestatem in omnibus negociis scolarium quantum alius, nec aliquis ipsorum habeat maiorem potestatem propter maiorem numerum scolarium. Unde plures carte uno tenore scripte sunt. Actum in Padua in hospicio Magistri Razinaldi, et Petri de Boxevilla, presentibus Domino Philippo de Carixio Canonico Taurinensi et Bono Ioanne de Bondonno, et Martino advocato Vercellensi.

Ego Bonus Ioannes Notarius civis Vercellensis filius quondam Manfredi nequx [*sic*] hiis omnibus interfui, et hanc cartam tradidi, et iussu ambarum partium scripsi, et scribi feci.

G. Cogo (*Intorno al transferimento d. Univ. d. Padova*, Padua, 1892) has questioned the genuineness of this document, but his reasons seem to me quite inadequate.

IV. A DAY'S WORK AT LOUVAIN IN 1476

[Additional note to vol. ii, pp. 264–8.]

The following is from a ducal ordinance for Louvain in 1476:

Curabunt tutores, ut scholares de mane surgant hora quinta, et tunc ante lectionem quilibet per se legat et studeat leges in ordinaria lectione legendas, una cum glossis. . . . Post lectionem vero ordinariam missa, si voluerint, celeriter audita, venient scholares ad cameras suas et revidebunt lectiones lectas, commemorando et memoriae imprimendo ea quae tam verbo quam scripto a lectionibus reportarunt. Et inde ad prandium venient. . . . Prandio finito, libris ad mensam unicuique delatis, repetent omnes scholares unius Facultatis simul, tutore praesente, lectionem illam ordinariam, in qua repetitione servabit tutor illum modum, ut per discretas cuiuscumque interrogationes concipere possit, an quilibet ipsorum lectionem bene audiverit et memoriae commendaverit, et ut tota lectio per partes a singulis recitandas reportetur; in quo si diligens cura adhibebitur, sufficiet tempus unius horae. (J. Molanus, *Historia Lovaniensium libri xiv*, edited

by P. F. X. de Ram, for the Commission royale d'histoire de
Belgique, 1861, ii. 940.)

Then follows preparation for the evening lecture, and the lecture
itself, while the two hours before supper are devoted, the first to
a private study of the lecture, the second to a *repetitio* with the
tutor. After supper 'interponet tutor iocum honestum per mediam
horam et disputationem levem et iocundam per alteram mediam
horam et inde mittet ad dormiendum. Et diebus non legibilibus,
exceptis dominicis, fiet post prandium circularis disputatio in
qualibet tutela et alia exercitia pro providentia et discretione
tutorum' (*ibid.*, p. 941).

Tutors have power to withhold wine or flesh.[1]

[1] The appendixes to this volume correspond to Appendixes I, II, XVI,
XXIX in the first edition (vol. ii, pp. 719, 723, 746, 766).